Foundations of Social Understanding

◊

A Theory and Institutions Based Introduction to Sociology

Thomas J. Burns
University of Oklahoma
and
Edward L. Kick
North Carolina State University
with
Dallos Paz

Published by:

Line-in ™ Publishing
Norman, OK
Copyright © 2015 Line-in ™ Publishing, Norman, Oklahoma

No part of this publication may be reproduced, stored in a retrieval system, or transmitted in any form or by any means, electronic, mechanical, photocopying, recording, scanning, or otherwise, except as permitted under Section 107 or 108 of the 1976 United States Copyright Act, without prior written permission of the Publisher.

Parts of this work are in the public domain. No copyright to that work is claimed.

Line-in ™ Publishing issues a number of textbooks in print, ebook and audio format.

Visit us at our websites: lineinpub.com and audiobook101.com

Editorial Staff:
Terry Best
Joey Paz

Book Design and Graphic Design:
David Fetter

Cover:
iStock Photos

ISBN: **978-1-62667-015-0**

To Jerry Hage: Gifted teacher, innovative thinker, mentor with vision and grace

THOMAS J. BURNS (PhD, 1990, University of Maryland) is Professor of Sociology at the University of Oklahoma, and is active in the Religious Studies and Environmental Studies programs and the Center for Social Justice. He serves as Book Review Editor of *Human Ecology Review*, and as a member of the Editorial Board of *The Journal of World-Systems Research*. He has served on the Board of the Society for Human Ecology. Professor Burns was formerly at the University of Utah, where he was a member of the Sociology Faculty and also taught in, and served as Chair of, the interdisciplinary Master of Statistics (MStat) Program. He is a winner of the University of Utah's College of Social and Behavioral Science Superior Teaching Award, has been nominated for numerous other teaching honors, and is recipient of the Society for Human Ecology's Distinguished Leadership Award.

EDWARD L. KICK (PhD Indiana University, Bloomington) is a Professor of Agricultural and Resource Economics, and Professor of Sociology, at North Carolina State University. Dr. Kick publishes articles and books on the world system, environment, community building, and sustainability.

Up until recently he served as the co-Editor of the *Journal of World-Systems Research,* and he has served for seventeen years as university administrator. His research and mentoring of students is primarily quantitative and cross-national in nature, although he also has conducted more intensive studies of countries, such as his case study of peanut farmers in Ghana, Africa. In recent years he has published on a variety of subjects that he ties together as part of writing and teaching. This work includes: decision making by disaster victims in the wake of catastrophic events, such as hurricanes and flooding; what is called "the ecological footprint" or the environmental well-being of the world and nations; the military and its influences on world and national hunger; the linkages between open markets, national sound money policies and "comparative advantage" on national modernization; community building in the US and abroad with its attendant displacement of populations, and the impact of human and infrastructural waste on the well-being of those who live close to dumping sites.

DALLOS PAZ is a graduate of the University of Oklahoma where he received a sociology degree in 2010. During his time at the University of Oklahoma, his area of emphasis was social stratification, particularly the effects of social stratification on health and social mobility. Today, he resides in Norman, Oklahoma where he enjoys a career in sociological writing and research.

Contents

Preface   xii;
Acknowledgements   xiii;

1 | SOCIOLOGY: AN INTRODUCTION   1

The Discipline of Sociology 1 ◦ The Sociological Imagination 2 ◦ Social Organizations 3 ◦ Regularity and Chaos 5 ◦ Social Theory as a Way of Understanding an Otherwise Chaotic World 6 ◦ Some Major Theoretical Approaches in Sociology 7 ◦ Social Function 7 ◦ Social Conflict 9 ◦ Social Construction 11 ◦ Social Exchange 12 ◦ Freedom and Constraint 13 ◦ The Plan for the Book and Conclusion 14

2 | METHODS IN SOCIOLOGY   17

The Reasons for Research 17 ◦ Elements of Sociological Research 18 ◦ Hypothesis Testing 19 ◦ Research Methodology 24 ◦ Conclusions 26

3 | INDIVIDUAL DEVELOPMENT IN A SOCIAL WORLD: SOCIALIZATION AND SOCIAL INTERACTION   28

Socialization 28 ◦ Social Roles 30 ◦ Individual Development and the Socialization Process 31 ◦ Stage Theories of Individual Development 32 ◦ Sigmund Freud's Theory of Psychosexual Development 32 ◦ Jean Piaget's Theory of Cognitive Development 36 ◦ Social Cognition 38 Sociology of Emotions, Stress and Coping 40 ◦ Conclusion 42

4 | SOCIAL INTERACTION AT THE MICRO LEVEL: THE SOCIOLOGY OF SUBJECTIVE EXPERIENCE   44

Symbolic Interactionism 46 ◦ Research in Social Interaction and the Socialization

Process: Developing Our Self-Concept 51 ◦ Phenomenology 52 ◦ Ethnomethodology 54

5 | SOCIAL DEFINITION AND THE SOCIAL CONSTRUCTION OF REALITY   59

The Social Construction of Reality 59 ◦ The Social World as a Stage: Dramatism and Dramaturgy 65 ◦ Kenneth Burke's Dramatism 65 ◦ Erving Goffman's Dramaturgy 67

6 | HUMAN BEHAVIOR AND SOCIAL EXCHANGE   72

Basic Assumptions of Behavior and Exchange Perspectives 72 ◦ Early Work by Behavioral Researchers 73 ◦ Social Learning and Social Exchange 74 ◦ Behavioral Exchange 76 ◦ Interpersonal Relations, Interdependence and Social Exchange 78 ◦ Peter Blau's Exchange Structuralism 80 ◦ Network Exchange Theories 82 ◦ Rational Choice Theory 83

7 | CLASSICAL SOCIOLOGY AND BASIC CONCEPTS IN THE STUDY OF SOCIAL ORGANIZATION   89

Classical Theorists on Social Organization 89 ◦ Karl Marx on the Importance of Class Interests 90 ◦ Max Weber on Rationality, Stratification, Power and Authority 93 ◦ The Sociology of Georg Simmel 100 ◦ Émile Durkheim on the Division of Labor in Society 102 ◦ Focusing on Elites 105 ◦ Conclusion 109

8 | BUILDING ON THE CLASSICS: STUDYING STRATIFICATION IN MODERN SOCIETY   111

Stratification as an Organizing Principle of Society 111 ◦ Davis and Moore's Functional Theory of Stratification 113 ◦ Conflict Theorists on the Importance of Class 114 ◦ Empirical Studies of Stratification, Mobility and Status Attainment 120 ◦ The Emergence of the Precariat Class 123 ◦ Linkages between Socialization and Social Stratification 126 ◦ Toward a Synthesizing View of Stratification 127 ◦ Conclusion 128

9 | RACE AND ETHNICITY   130

Racial and Ethnic Discrimination as Status Group Stratification and Social Closure 131 ◦ Effects of Racial Stratification 134 ◦ Racial and Ethnic Assimilation 137 ◦ A Declining Significance of Race in the United States 137 ◦ Conclusion 139

10 | GENDER AND SOCIETY   141

Construction of Gender 141 ◦ Do Women and Men Have Different Ways of Perceiving the Social World? 144 ◦ Gender in the Workplace 144 ◦ Gender and Family 146 ◦ Gender and Crime 147 ◦ Gender and Sexuality 149

11 | HISTORICAL AND COMPARATIVE DEVELOPMENT AND GLOBAL INEQUALITY   152

Lenski's Eco-Technological Theory of Societal Evolution 152 ◦ Rostow's Theory of Economic Growth 157 ◦ Talcott Parsons and Social Change 159 ◦ Dependency in the Modern World-System 160 ◦ Conclusion 164

12 | FAMILY AND KINSHIP INSTITUTIONS   166

Family Functions and Structure 169 ◦ Marriage and Family in the Modern Era 170 ◦ Social Functions and Social Conflicts 173 ◦ Division of Labor and Social Exchanges 175 ◦ Functions and Conflicts: Parents and Children 177 ◦ The World System and Family Structure 177 ◦ Same-Sex Marriage and Families 179

13 | EDUCATION AND SOCIETY   182

Culture and Education 182 ◦ Education Systems and the Economy 184 ◦ Economic Functions and Expansion in Education Systems 185 ◦ Conflict Theories and Education 187 ◦ Toward a Unifying Model of Educational Growth 191 ◦ Some Causes for School Success or Failure 192 ◦ Education in a Comparative Perspective 193 ◦ Education and Third World Development 196 ◦ Current Trends in Education 197 ◦ Conclusion 198

14 | RELIGION AND SOCIETY 200

Religion as a Social Institution 200 ◦ Émile Durkheim on the Central Role of Religion 202 ◦ Religion as a Source of Social Change: Max Weber's Protestant Ethic and the Spirit of Capitalism 203 ◦ Theorizing about Social Stratification and Religion 205 ◦ Trajectories of Religious Institutionalization 205 ◦ Religious Trends and Trajectories of Social Change 206 ◦ Current Trends in Religiosity 207

15 | POLITICS AND SOCIETY 210

Types of Political Systems 212 ◦ The Distribution of Power 215 ◦ Types and Causes of Collective Behavior 217 ◦ Social Movements and Their Causes 218 ◦ Social Conflicts and Social Movements 220 ◦ Attempting a Theoretical Synthesis 221 ◦ World Market Forces 221 ◦ A Global Approach to Social Movements 222 ◦ World System Position, Political Economy, Mobilization for Collective Action 223 ◦ Current Trends in American Politics 225

16 | POPULATION AND MODERNITY 228

Demographic Transition Theory 228 ◦ Population and Environmental Impact 229 ◦ Population Pyramids 229 ◦ Issues in Current Population Trends 230 ◦ Sex Ratios 231 ◦ Life Expectancy 232 ◦ Population and Resources 233 ◦ Urbanization and Population Density 234 ◦ The Functionalist Perspective on Urbanization 236 ◦ Population Density – Attitudes and Culture in the United States 236 ◦ Rural and Urban Poverty 237

17 | ENVIRONMENTAL SOCIOLOGY 240

Level of Development, Population, Technology and Carrying Capacity 240 ◦ International Development, Inequality, and Resource Depletion 242 ◦ Individual and Group Priorities and Their Implications for the Environment 244 ◦ Environmental Factors and Public Health 244 ◦ Why We Get Sick: A Darwinian Approach to Health 245 ◦ Sickness as a Function of an Environment Out of Balance 246 ◦ Culture and the Sociology of Knowledge 249 ◦ Addressing Problems: Moving Toward Solutions 250 ◦ Conclusions: Toward a Comprehensive Model of Humankind's Interaction with the Natural Environment 251

18 | CRIME AND DEVIANCE 255

Non-Sociological Causes 255 ◦ Social Functions 257 ◦ Parsons's Functionalism 259 ◦ Social Disorganization 261 ◦ Anomie 264 ◦ Social Interactions 266 ◦ Labeling History 267 ◦ Social Conflicts 270 ◦ Social Control, Self-Control, and General Strain Theories 271 ◦ The World System and Crime 272 ◦ Current Trends in Crime in the United States 274

19 | THE SOCIOLOGICAL IMAGINATION IN LATE MODERN SOCIETY: POSTMODERNITY, CHAOS AND COMPLEXITY 277

Understanding Modernity and Its Problems 277 ◦ The Maturing of Modern Society and the Rise of the Postmodern Condition 278 ◦ Characteristics of the Premodern, Modern and Postmodern 279 ◦ Postmodern Social Theory 282 ◦ Postmodern Social Theorists 282 ◦ Theoretical Voices of Late Modernity 284 ◦ Chaos and Complexity Theories 287 ◦ Lawful Unpredictability 287 ◦ Fractals 288 ◦ Entropy 290 ◦ Non-linearities 290 ◦ Equilibria and Feedback Loops 291 ◦ Sensitive Dependence ("Butterfly Effect") 292 ◦ Self-Organizing Systems 293

THE LAST WORD   296

GLOSSARY   A1

REFERENCES   A35

ILLUSTRATIONS   A71

Preface

Our goal was to write a book that conveys the essential aspects of sociology, keeping the focus on the theoretical ideas that form the backbone of the discipline. We envision this book filling a niche for instructors and students who wish to have a rigorously presented, yet low-cost text that covers essential aspects of the field.

We have attempted to make the book concise and to the point, thereby rendering the book distinctive in the density of material it covers. Unlike many of the introductory sociology textbooks available, there is no "padding" with boxes, sidebars, and the like. The book was born of a combination of frustration with the books currently available, along with a desire to produce a text that we ourselves would have been delighted to have had as students, and can be pleased to offer now as professors.

We have attempted to move beyond the tiresome debates about which theoretical position is "really" correct and which is wrong. Our philosophy is that the discipline of sociology has a strong and integrated core. While no theory explains everything, each of those presented does well at shedding light on something. Part of what needs to be considered in conjunction with the study of theory is the question of what domain of social reality it is most useful at explaining.

In each chapter, there are references to further material, should students desire to gain an in-depth knowledge about any of the ideas covered. It presents each topic in some depth, and is amenable to the instructor assigning a number of ancillary readings in conjunction with any of the chapters.

In generating the book, we necessarily made a number of decisions about what it would not be. Instructors and students wanting a text that focuses mainly on social work and/or direct interventions into social problems will not find that here. Likewise, those hoping for a book that furthers a political agenda will no doubt be disappointed. People wishing for an elaborately produced textbook with multi-colored boxes and other filler, will be better served by one of the dozens of such books currently on the market.

The very core of a discipline is the theories it has developed. For better or worse, the discipline of sociology has spawned a sometimes dizzying array of studies, empirical and otherwise. These are necessary, but not sufficient, to have a rich and worthwhile discipline, and one that offers insight into the human condition. Theories—the worthwhile ones—come about more slowly. Theory is not about what happened in the latest studies. It is born of hard-won insight, sometimes over the course of years or decades, or even lifetimes.

We have attempted to produce a book that appeals to the intelligence and sociological imagination of serious students and their teachers. Our approach is to offer students a "cognitive map" of the field in a scholarly, yet straightforward, way. We believe that Sociology, particularly when considering it through the framework of the theory that underpins it, is not only a worthwhile avenue of inquiry; it is endlessly fascinating in its own right.

Acknowledgements

We owe a tremendous intellectual debt to the sociologists who have gone before us, both those we feature in this book, and our own teachers.

We also are in debt to our many students. What started as a series of class handouts have over the years, developed into what you now hold in your hands, and years of student feedback have helped us tremendously as we have honed and modified over the years.

Working with the folks at the Line-In Publishing has been delightful. John Cox's charisma and vision to establish a College Textbook Division that is of the highest caliber, and to reach out to connect with us to be an integral part of that, is an inspiration.

David Fetter is a Developmental Editor par excellence. He was able to keep us on track with grace, a work ethic that would give pause to Calvin himself, and no small dose of good humor.

The editorial and support staff, including Terry Best, Joey Paz, April Jones, and Angela Gray have been uniformly helpful and professional throughout the process of completing this book. Thank you all for your hard work and good cheer. The arduous process of developing a book has been, with you folks, a great experience. Thank you all.

1 Sociology: An Introduction

The Discipline of Sociology

Welcome to the exciting discipline of **sociology**. **Sociology** is the study of **social collectives**, such as small groups, the family, the bureaucracies for which we work, our nation itself, and the world as a whole.

Is the scientific study of society challenging? Yes, it is, in part because science itself is very systematic and must be exact. Sociologists consider significant and far-reaching social issues that impact everyone, sometimes in ways that are not readily apparent. The study of the social can broaden your horizons greatly, and you will join a huge number of other students in over three thousand colleges and universities in the United States who will study sociology this year.

With such a broad range of topics and methods it is fair to ask, is sociology a practical course of study? Surely, it is. You will learn, among other things, a great deal about the factors that shape your relationships to virtually everyone else in your culture. You will place yourself in the context of all others you know, and a host of others whom you may not even know, but who are influenced by you and who you, in turn, impact.

Let us be even more practical—will sociology help you find a job? Here too, the answer is yes. Sociology offers valuable preparation for careers that involve investigative skills, research, analysis, critical thinking, and cross-cultural understanding. A student of sociology will also be prepared for fields that require working with a wide range of people.

In fact, sociology offers ways of thinking that can be used concretely in many different jobs in business, politics, health, criminal justice, and the social services, such as caring for the elderly. Sociology prepares people for literally hundreds of careers. It is not uncommon for sociologists to become directors of research, policy analysts, consultants, and human resource managers.

Even more profoundly, a serious student of sociology sees the world open as she or he learns the intellectual tools of the discipline. These tools help us to make sense of the world in which we live. The backbone of sociology, the very fabric that holds it together and makes it so valuable, is the wide array of theories it brings to bear on the social world.

In our discipline, a theory is an intellectual tool for analyzing some aspect of the social world. Much as you would use a wrench to help loosen a bolt, or a hammer to drive in a nail, you can use social theory to help pry open meaning in an otherwise senseless situation.

While there are just a few families of theories, there are dozens, if not hundreds of variants, each of which is useful at times and not useful at others. Just as a hammer is less useful than a wrench in tightening a bolt, but more useful in driving a nail, so theories are used best when we apply them to the situation at hand. Part of learning a theory comes in gaining a sense of where it applies. One of the "rookie" mistakes of would be social theorists is misapplying theory. And part of the power of the discipline, as well as the fun of learning it, is in seeing where theories best apply, and then using them to gain clarity and focus on an often bewildering world.

In this book, we take those theories seriously, considering how they apply from the individual life, through interpersonal interactions between people, to the largest of social collectives, such as the nation state or even the world as a system of interrelated institutions. What connects each of the theories is a common thread known as the Sociological Imagination.

The Sociological Imagination

What is so special about sociology? One of the most valuable things you will gain as you study sociology is a way of seeing the world—a paradigm known as the **"sociological imagination."** A **paradigm** is a model or way of looking at the world. It is so encompassing that it even determines what kinds of scientific problems are appropriate topics of study, how to study these problems, and the types of perspectives that are generally accepted as explanations of such problems. Students of physics will recognize the works of Sir Isaac Newton, Albert Einstein, and the quantum mechanics theorists as paradigms of matter and energy.

The sociological imagination, as articulated by C. Wright Mills (1959) will help you develop a new way of thinking and a new way of analyzing the world. With it, you will think critically about things that others take for granted. You will see general patterns in life where others just see the coincidence. You will see a commonality with all others, instead of considering only the differences between you and them.

The sociological imagination also involves the ability to see the social on a number of levels: the **"micro"** (small scale, such as the relationship you have with a friend), the **"meso"** (mid-size collectives, such as a business), and the **"macro"** (large scale, such as relations between nations). As you learn to think about each level of analysis, you will come to see **emergent properties**, or aspects of the social that are not necessarily reducible by their individual parts. In fact, **sociology** can formally be defined as *the study of the emergent properties of human collectives*.

There are aspects of social collectives that are not reducible to its individual members. This underlying principle of sociological analysis is the **principle of emergence**. Let us consider the following statement to illustrate the principle of emergence: *With increasing size and interaction, an organization tends to become more differentiated, both vertically (in terms of levels of hierarchy), and horizontally (in terms of types of specialization).* Notice that this statement applies to many organizations, independent of the particular individuals who happen to be in any one of those organizations. Applying this principle to an organization such as a university or business, we can make an educated guess that the larger the organization, the more levels of supervisors and bosses we would expect to see, and the more types of specialties we would expect to see. For instance, we would expect there to be more departments (and specialties within those departments) at a large university than we would at a small college. The important point here is that while individuals tend to operate within social organizations, many of the properties of the organization are independent of the individuals in them.

Much of this book will be about such emergent properties of social collectives. As another example of how the principle of emergence operates, think of a couple in a dating relationship. In such a situation, we may observe that there are a number of aspects of the "couple" that we could not necessarily predict just from knowing the particular individuals involved. There are certain qualities that come out in the interaction between the individuals that may not be characteristic of either individual (for instance, think of two individuals who "come out of their shells" when in each other's company). As we will see, every individual develops in a larger social context. It is important to understand the dynamics of that context, relating the individual to society and its institutions.

As you progress in the study of sociology, you will become conscious of yourself as well as others, and how you and all the others in your life fit together. You will link what is going on in the modern world to the world that once was, and the world that will be.

All this may seem easier said than done at the moment. Nevertheless, it is the sort of thinking and analyzing that sociologists do. That is the model, or paradigm, that we hope you will enjoy adopting as you learn more about sociology. It is a paradigm that increases in importance with each passing day, as we become part of an increasingly interdependent world made up of vastly different peoples.

Social Organizations

Sociologists study a broad range of what we call social organizations. Examples of organizations include families, groups, bureaucratic organizations, communities, classes, societies, confederations, and the world system. Each of these types of social organization is embedded in the next greater domain. Consider that you and your family are part of a community, which is part of a society called the United States, which is part of a larger system of nations. Let us briefly describe each of these types of social organizations before considering the synergy between them.

Groups. A group is a social organization whose members personally know and identify with each other. Within groups there are primary groups and secondary groups. **Primary groups** are groups where individuals are very close to one another and share emotional bonds, such as the family. Groups such as workers on an assembly line in a factory, or even the students in your introduction to sociology class make up *secondary groups*. People in secondary groups come together more to achieve a collective goal than for socio-emotional reasons.

Families. A family is a social group that is characterized by ties of kinship among all of its members. In other words, a family is united by biology, or by marriage among its members, and by identification with one another as well.

Bureaucratic organizations. These are social organizations that are created for obtaining relatively specific, yet limited goals. The university you are attending is a bureaucratic organization. The place where you work is more than likely a bureaucratic organization as well.

Communities. A community is a social organization that is territorially localized. In

Social Organizations - Families
Families are social organizations that are characterized by ties of **kinship** among all of its members.

Social Organizations - Bureaucratic Organizations
Bureaucracies are social organizations that are created for obtaining relatively specific, yet limited goals.

communities, members satisfy most of their daily needs and deal with most of their common problems within the context of that territory. Your hometown is a good example of a community.

Classes. A class is a loosely ordered and unified social organization that is based on similarities in the **power,** the **privileges,** or the **prestige** of its members. Power is the ability to gain what is desired despite resistance from others. Privilege can be defined as access to desired goods and services. Prestige refers to favorable evaluations received from others. As you can see there are a lot of different bases to a class. Some individuals associate with one another because together they can maintain social control over others, or because together they have access to certain privileges that others do not, or because other members of society look up to them or defer to their recognized status.

Societies. A society is a broad and inclusive form of social organization. For the most part, it is both functionally and culturally autonomous, which means it is relatively independent of all other societies. In today's world we must think in relative terms, however, because all nations do impact one another in some way. To be sure, other types of social organizations that we have discussed so far are embedded in society.

Confederations. Sometimes societies are linked together on a larger, more global scale. A confederation is a loosely organized combination of societies. These societies often cooperate in a mutual activity, but generally retain their independent power. An example of a confederation is the United Nations. When a confederation such as the United Nations uses military force to intervene in a society experiencing civil unrest, for example, it acts as a social organization, even though the combat troops may come from many nations (which themselves are also social collectives, organized at a different level).

World System. Finally, the most macroscopic or large-scale form of social organization is the world system. The world system includes all the interdependent societies on the globe. In today's world, every society is interdependent. That is, each society depends on other societies for fulfillment of a range of social goals. Taken as a whole, we can think of the world as a giant social web. All other forms of social organizations are embedded in it. This is not to say that only the most encompassing forms of social organization (the world system) impact the ones embedded in them (societies or communities). Rather, there is a synergy—each social organization influences all others, as will be seen in the sociological perspectives presented subsequently.

Regularity and Chaos

An important part of any social science is the assumption that there is significant **regularity** in social life. Science assumes that the world is characterized by regularity, and that worldly events are not randomly ordered or chaotic in their character. So also do sociologists believe there is a high degree of regularity in the social actions that are part of social organizations. This permits sociologists to discover those regularities or patterns, instead of operating as if the social world is characterized by chaos. You may wonder whether or not this is really true. As an illustration though, conduct some experiments yourself. Sit a safe distance away from a stoplight, but close enough to observe drivers. When the light turns green, drivers could, in principle, slow down, stop or weave from side-to-side in the roadway, but they usually "go." When the light turns red, they usually stop. This might be less true, and dangerously so, late on a Friday night when some drivers have had too much to drink. Most of the time, however, people's stoplight behaviors are regular, highly patterned, and predictable. Even the variations that occur on Friday nights have a pattern to them!

This is just one example of social regularities. If you think for a moment, you will probably be able to recall many social regularities in your own life. You probably go through just about the same practices or "habits" every morning when you wake up. Habits are patterned. Certainly, you engage in the same set of routines just about every day.

You probably also go to about the same classes each week, at least in any given quarter or semester. You take particular courses—the ones you think are the most helpful in obtaining a degree. We would even be surprised if you picked a different chair to sit in today when you go to class! Most of the time, students sit in about the same place every time they go to class. You will probably notice this if you take a look around during your next class meeting. This is called **territoriality**—a social regularity in which most of us engage all day long.

These tendencies occur not only in classrooms, but in many other places as well. Observe the way people behave even in an elevator, for example, and notice that their actions are far from chaotic. Remember the social rules of the elevator that govern or determine our behaviors: look at the numbers, the door, or the floor; do not stare directly at others in the elevator or they will surely be uncomfortable; do not stand extremely close to someone in an otherwise empty elevator, or the person may hit the call button or scream for the police.

These regularities of social life are the very things that sociologists observe and investigate. Sociologists develop very different perspectives on why these regularities occur as they do. This is the corpus of sociology, the sociological imagination. The sociological imagination, you will recall, is the ability to see the world in many different ways. It is the paradigm that all sociologists share and cherish.

Social Theory as a Way of Understanding an Otherwise Chaotic World

You might have noticed the subtitle of your textbook— *A **Theory** and Institutions Based Introduction to Sociology*— and wondered what use theory could possibly have. Isn't that for the more arcane aspects of a discipline? Do we need theory once we have learned the important basics of a subject? More to the point, why not learn about society as it "really is" instead of worrying about theories of society? For that matter, why learn about theory at all?

Social theories provide a framework for perceiving the world that helps us make order out of the chaos. But why is that important? As an analogy, consider the case of one of the authors' (Burns) former jiu-jitsu instructor, Walt. One day I was doing what I do best in Jiu Jitsu, which was flailing around, wondering why none of the moves I was trying seemed to work. My opponent at the time, a fellow named Dale and I, were fairly evenly matched, and neither of us could "finish" the other. Neither could either of us seem to get any of our moves to work the way we wanted. Walt just watched us go at it for what seemed like an interminably long time, while holding a conversation with someone. Both Dale and I were completely exhausted. Each of us had the other in an ankle lock, but could not seem to apply it well enough to make the other give up. My arms were so tired I could hardly move them, yet I held onto Dale's ankle with all I had, while Dale clung just as doggedly to mine. Finally, Walt stopped the conversation he was having long enough to say nonchalantly, "Tom, slide your right hand down about an inch and pull up." As soon as I did, Dale cried out in pain and gave up. The jiu-jitsu match had been chaotic up until the very last moment, when Walt, from across the room was able to see something very clearly that Dale and I could not see. The adjustment in my arm position was a matter of inches or even less, but in that case, it meant the difference between flailing and thriving.

I learned a very valuable lesson about life in general, at least as much as about jiu-jitsu, that day. As a trained observer, Walt was able to see something that neither Dale nor I (as not very well-trained and relatively undisciplined observers) were able to see. And that difference in perception had consequences.

The ability to see order where others see chaos is true of disciplines in general, and it is certainly true of sociology. This is, perhaps, what one keen observer of human beings, Kurt Lewin, had in mind when he quipped, "there is nothing more practical than a good theory." A concerted study of sociology and the theories that comprise it, when combined with a developing sociological imagination, will allow you to "make sense" of social things you see, experience, and hear about in the news. The social theories you will be learning in this book and this course are applicable to a wide array of human circumstances. As you apply them in the ways you think about the world and the people in it, they will serve as tremendous tools of understanding.

Some Major Theoretical Approaches in Sociology

The sociological imagination is a paradigm that takes its powers of explanation and analyses from several different interpretations of the social. While it would be comforting to have just one interpretation that is the master key for all social doorways, that simply does not square with social reality. Sociologists choose to explain very different forms of social organizations, thus their perspectives must be selected accordingly. The sociological imagination does not lead us to reject all other perspectives in favor of only one. Instead, it forces us to consider the nature of the social organizations under study, alongside the pertinent understandings given by a range of interpretations. We briefly introduce the four major such theoretical approaches below. They are: social function, social conflict, social construction, and social exchange.

Social Function

Under the **social function** perspective, society is explained in the same terms that a biological organism might be. That is, it consists of a number of different parts that are gathered together in a system of total interdependence. The interdependent parts function to maintain the entire social body, or the social organization. One of the first social scientists to think of the social in these terms was Auguste Comte, who coined the term *sociology*. Interestingly, Comte referred to the discipline as "social physics" before calling it sociology. Comte's very use of the term social physics makes it clear that he was trying to pattern his new science of the social after the hard sciences. Ultimately, he felt sociology would become the dominant science. We've still got a long way to go on that!

Sociology, Comte believed, should be concerned with existing patterns, which he called **social statics,** and the change in those patterns, which he called **social dynamics.** Statics and dynamics occurred for him in a holistic social environment.

For Comte, harmonious societies were large moral units that were based on consensus and agreement. It is not surprising that he emphasized the family, the church, and the community as the core of society. It is in these forms of social organization that people's selfishness is kept under control through bonds of service, love, and loyalty.

Though Comte wrote well before the famous biologist Charles Darwin, he had a number of ideas that we would treat as evolutionary, in theme, today. He argued that in societies around the world, we can see the various elements of the social change together. That is, the evolution of one society can show us how the rest of the world will evolve in the future. Comte was able to place all societies known at the time on a continuum of development. This continuum ranged from the "primitive" tribes described by the early explorers of America, to the empires of history, and to the highest stage of civilization, nineteenth century France (Comte was a Frenchman)!

Émile Durkeim (1858 - 1917)
Durkheim spent most of his career looking for a scientific basis for the social order.

Another sociologist who made significant contributions to the study of social functions was Émile Durkheim. Durkheim spent most of his career looking for a scientific basis for the social order, and he took his main thesis from Auguste Comte. Durkheim maintained that the basis of society is, in fact, a **moral order**. What Durkheim emphasized is that when there is a fundamental solidarity in society, it brings people together so that they can share and exchange with one another and improve one another's well being. This is not an intellectual agreement, according to Durkheim, but instead it is an emotional feeling. Durkheim said that society develops a **collective consciousness**, which is a feeling of belonging to a community with others. This sentiment of belonging to community is coupled with the stiff obligation to live up to other's expectations. One way in which both of these are upheld is through **rituals**. In more traditional societies, religion and daily rituals become an important way for people to develop a shared or collective conscious. Durkheim's term for this is called **mechanical solidarity**. Under conditions of mechanical solidarity, people are held together, since they resemble one another, especially in beliefs.

Durkheim said that mechanical solidarity eventually gives way to what he called **organic solidarity**. Organic solidarity is reflected in specialized production and exchange or a **high division of labor**. This means that people and groups come to depend on one another more and more for what they produce and exchange. Rather than grouping together on the basis of shared moral sentiment alone, people group together on the basis of mutual need. This is not to say that the collective conscious that brought them together in the first place has vanished completely. It still remains, as it does in your life today.

Do you doubt that there is much daily ritual in your own life? Some of you attend church regularly and are quite familiar with what ritual is. But even if you do not attend church, more than likely you have gone to an athletic event and experienced ritual. What is the first activity undertaken at most sporting events in the United States? The National Anthem is sung, and it is sung by most everyone. Ritual is far more pervasive than this. In all likelihood, the majority of you recited the Pledge of Allegiance to the flag every morning in elementary school. That was certainly a ritual, and one, undoubtedly, you now know by heart. Almost everyone in the United States knows these rituals, and they continue to bring a moral consciousness to our society even though we also are bound together tightly in organic solidarity.

Durkheim believed that mechanical solidarity and organic solidarity both served important social functions in holding society together. Some of Durkheim's other ideas about social functions may seem controversial. For example, Durkheim also felt that crime could be functional for society. One might ask, what possible social function could crime serve? Durkheim maintained that crime helps solidify the group in a feeling of moral indignation and anger, or **moral outrage** against an enemy. Think about how you and your family react as you watch the nightly news report and hear that a vicious crime was committed in your community. The crime has served a social function, binding your family and other people together in your feelings.

These are just a few of Émile Durkheim's seminal thoughts. He also addressed the macroscopic causes of suicide, as well as the feeling of "disconnectedness" or **anomie** people experience due to the nature of rapidly advancing social organization, among many other themes, which we will examine more closely later. For now, we emphasize that these two early sociologists, Auguste Comte and Émile Durkheim, are often considered as representatives of the social function's perspective in sociology. Because their work has become very important in modern day sociology, they are called **classical theorists**. After all, many of their ideas still are current today, even though they wrote well over a century ago. Later on, we discuss a number of other theorists who have written about social functions, including the evolutionary theorist, Herbert Spencer, and the social institutions theorist, Talcott Parsons, among many others. Now, we will turn our attention to another of the four major perspectives in the paradigm of sociology, the social conflict perspective.

Social Conflict

Just as the social functions perspective does, social conflict theory attempts to explain the structure of society as well as changes in that structure adopting a macroscopic approach. Proponents of social conflict explain that as people pursue their interests, those interests conflict with others, as all other individuals compete to gain resources from their environment. Conflict theory builds on an important theorist named Karl Marx, but it also builds on the works of an eminent sociologist named Max Weber. Karl Marx witnessed the pernicious impacts of industrialization and the factory on workers, especially in England, and was the principal author of the work we call the *Communist Manifesto* in 1848.

Karl Marx believed that even though economics causes the social dynamics people can see, such as politics and culture, it also has a hidden quality that most people cannot see. For him, what the masses see is merely a deception covering over an economic reality that is based, as it historically has been, on the exploitation of one group by another. This age-old exploitation is significant. Marx felt that by our very nature, we are basically good as human be-

Karl Marx (1818 - 1883)
Karl Marx believed that even though economics causes the social dynamics people can see, such as politics and culture, it also has a hidden quality that most people cannot see. The key, for Marx, was whether or not one owns the *"Means of Production."*

ings. However, as a result of these exploitative social relationships throughout history, we have been turned against our nature, or **species being**, and made into selfish beings.

According to Marx, in the modern capitalist and industrial period, this class struggle places the **bourgeoisie**, the owners of production, against the workers or **proletariat**, who toil for them. We will provide more detail on this later, but for right now it is important to know that for Marx, much of the essence of what we may think of as **profit**, derives from the exploitation of labor. In other words, the price that is paid for any commodity comes from the extra hours of work over and above what the worker is actually paid for; it has a **surplus value**.

Marx's work is filled with the sociological imagination, although he may seem to be primarily an economist. He argued that people are initially unable to see the reality of their lives, at least until they come to a higher awareness through a combination of hard experience and by association with enlightened coworkers. This awareness he referred to as **class-consciousness**. But for Marx, the reality that most of the masses see is only one that presses them to work very hard for relatively little money and to buy commodities to help their resulting feelings of alienation. They come to accept this and the misery that accompanies it as a natural condition, though it is not natural at all, according to Marx. Marx thought that someday, under capitalism, people would become conscious of the truth of their existence and become conscious of their **class**, or economic position. This class-consciousness, he thought, would make it more likely that the people will revolt and establish a new social order.

Another classical sociologist who has had an enormous impact on modern sociology, Max Weber, wrote, at least in part, as a reaction to Marx's work. While he readily acknowledged that people had economic conflicts, he also added that people have political and cultural conflicts as well. In fact, people are likely to act and associate together based on their economic status, their political status, and their cultural status, and to try to exclude all others from their company. This is known as **social closure**. It is easy to see what Weber had to say at work in our society today. Consider what happens when people marry, or even date one another. Most of them choose other people from the same economic circumstance, people with about the same social status, and people who typically have the same political views. In other words, people who are just like them.

Weber was also one of the first social scientists to extensively address different types of organizational leadership as well as **bureaucracy**, which is an organizational form based, among other things, on relatively clear lines of authority, careful record keeping, work specializations, and rules and regulations. He was particularly interested in the increasing pace of **rationalization**, the use of machines **(mechanization)** and science to improve upon efficiency and the quality of work output.

His contributions were far greater than just this. Weber (1904 - 05) offered yet another important contribution in his treatment of ***The Protestant Ethic and the Spirit of Capitalism***. Weber, unlike Marx, argued that culture fashioned economics. Specifically, he felt that certain characteristics of Protestantism allowed capitalism to flourish in Western Europe. Put simply, he argued that Calvinists, early Protestants, believed that if they accumulated wealth, it would be evidence of their predestination for an afterlife in heaven instead of hell. Thus for Weber, a religious or cultural desire to obtain heaven motivated hard work, hence the Protestant ethic toward work gave rise to the spirit of accumulation that is capitalism.

Social Construction

Thus far, we have discussed classical sociological writings that deal with large-scale, or macroscopic, sociology. We turn now to two other sorts of perspectives on the social. The first of these, social interaction, is a great deal more concerned with small-scale or microsociology.

A significant contributor to microsociology was University of Chicago professor William I. Thomas, better known as W.I. Thomas. Thomas made the critical observation that *"if [people] define situations as real, they are real in their consequences."* With this statement, Thomas was suggesting that it is not necessarily the objective conditions of life that matter; instead it is our subjective perceptions of those conditions. This observation is an example of the sociological imagination. It clearly is another view of the way our world operates. Surely you will appreciate this sort of perspective if, as a child, you were accused of doing something wrong when you really did not do it at all. The accusation itself became a label that was objectively untrue. Although it was untrue, in other words, it was still likely that people subsequently responded more to the label rather than to the truth itself.

Erving Goffman is another very important sociologist of the social interaction perspective. Goffman is a contemporary writer who addresses difficult situations like the feelings of uneasiness, self-consciousness or awkwardness that sometimes overcome us. What is most important for our present purposes is that he views society as a big theater in which we all play a part. The theater of the social world has a **front stage** and a **back stage**. Our back stage is the reality of our life; while by contrast, our front stage is what we allow other people to see. When we are on front stage, we are performers. When we are back stage, we can let down our hair a little bit, relax, and gain some privacy.

Goffman maintains that the interactions or communications between people who share a common back stage often are a great deal more intimate that the interactions that take place on the front stage. This is because people may trust one another a great deal more on the back stage. Consider the drama of a married couple as they try to purchase a new family car, for example. They adopt a front stage to the car salesman by showing interest, but not too much, lest the salesman notice their eagerness and establish a higher price for the car. When the salesman is gone, the couple communicates or interacts with one another in a much truer fashion. In their back stage, they admit how much they like the vehicle (or not) and privately plan out the delivery they will make to the salesman and the dealership. At the same time, the salesman is back stage, too, perhaps hard at work with his colleagues planning the best pitch with which to bait the prospective buyers. To be sure, the salesman's front stage posture will be aggressive or docile, depending on his take on the couple's front stage and what he feels will result in a successful deal.

Thomas and Goffman's observations are important to our everyday life. Their interactionist perspectives emphasize the fact that our dealings with other people may in some real sense be false, even if others accept them as true. In our current era of "political spin," these observations resonate, as government officeholders often appear to say one thing but mean something entirely different. It may hit home to you, too, when you consider the drama of your everyday life as you present your role in life's play to others, including your loved ones.

Social Exchange

The last perspective we will cover in this chapter is the social exchange perspective. This is a more recent theoretical perspective, but we think you will agree that it is a very important one as well. Just as is true for the other perspectives, the social exchange perspective is filled with the sociological imagination.

Exchange theorists argue that in your dealings with others, the history of **rewards** and **costs** that are established leads you to select a posture of **exchange** with them in the future. Some of the exchanges that you have with other people are highly rewarding. Other exchanges are very punishing, indeed. Exchange theorists believe that you will repeat your rewarding exchanges, but you will try to avoid your punishing exchanges as best as you can.

Apply these principles to the next item that you buy in the store. It is likely that you tried to find the item that gave you the most of what you wanted for the least cost, or amount of money. Now, apply these same principles to your relationship with others. Do you associate with others who "cost" you less, but give you more?

Think now about the resources that you personally have to offer. Are some of your resources in high demand? These factors will make an important difference to all who will exchange with you, establishing how much they will give you for the resources that you personally have. Of course, exchange theorists also talk about **alternatives**. They maintain that because we sometimes simply have no reasonable alternative, we stay in a particular exchange relationship. We may do so, even when we find that our trading partner is a **free rider** who pays essentially nothing in trade for the resources we have to offer. They add that when we find that alternative, if it appears to be a more highly rewarding one, we will move to that alternative and leave our current exchange partner behind.

When applied to human relations, this may be uncomfortable, because we like to think of others and ourselves as being unselfish or **altruistic** most of the time. The exchange theorists, however, argue that the opposite is probably true. Once again, in looking at the social from a perspective so different from our "common sense," they are exercising their fertile sociological imagination.

Social exchanges characterize human social organization at more macroscopic levels as well. In the Middle Ages, people would graze their sheep and cows on their own property but also on a common area for all. This use of the common area reduced the costs to individuals in business of raising livestock while raising the costs to the collective as a whole. This dynamic is known as the **tragedy of the commons**, and is a larger-scale illustration of our willingness to use others for our benefit.

Try exercising your own sociological imagination here. Could the same principles that exchange theorists offer be applied not just to your personal relationships, but also to the whole world? Countries trade commodities with one another, just like individual people do. Just as they apply to people, these same principles of exchange undoubtedly apply to the world as well. Scarce resources in the world economy, such as gold and jewels, are worth more, just as are high-demand commodities such as the latest technological innovations. Corporations also seek (new) global trading partners, which are cheaper and bring more "bang for the buck."

We urge you to do an experiment in your home to note your exchange relationships with others outside your society. Take a look at the underside of new commodities in your home to see where they were made. Were they made in the United States, where labor rates are relatively high? We bet that most of the items in your home were made instead in Asia, particularly China. In all likelihood, your tennis shoes were made in a faraway country, by very low-paid laborers, who are most likely children. To borrow from our drama theorists, while we may abhor such practices in our front stage conversations, some of our back stage behavior may be based on them.

Freedom and Constraint

Sociologists have long struggled with the question of how much a person has freedom to act (this freedom is sometimes referred to as "agency"), and how much of a person's behavior is constrained by one's culture and the institutions within it (see Archer 1988; Dietz and Burns 1992). Most of us take for granted a perspective of free will in human behavior. We assume, in other words, that what we do in life is something that we determine for ourselves, and others do not determine it.

Is your behavior the product of your own willpower, or is it perhaps instead the result of outside forces beyond your recognition and control? A sociological approach to this question was articulated by Karl Marx over a century ago, when he observed that "[People] make history, but not in circumstances of their own choosing." The sociological approach is to examine those "circumstances." As we will see, sociology has a well-developed set of theories for making sense of these circumstances and their influences on our behavior.

The issue of freedom and constraint is a complex one, but consider an example that shows a sociological approach. Remember as you do, that the paradigm of the sociological imagination encourages us to see the world from different perspectives than those we usually take for granted. Consider the possibility that you just tripped on the sidewalk as you were walking to class. In tripping, were you exercising your freedom? Or were there other factors that somehow constrained your actions, such as a break in the pavement? We often seek external causes for our unwanted outcomes, and we sometimes say it simply was somebody else's fault. Then, when we experience favorable results, of course, we say the accomplishment was due to our own initiative. Sometimes we are hard on other people, attributing to them full responsibility for the bad things that happen in their lives. Yet, we often say that they were just plain lucky when something good happens to them.

As a science, sociology requires a more systematic approach than this. The fact is that our freedom is limited by certain social and cultural constraints. We are part of the series of embedded social organizations described above, which influence or cause us to act in particular ways. We are not all affected by the same sets of causal forces, nor are these causative patterns simple ones. But we are affected indeed, and it is precisely the nexus of these causal forces that is the subject matter of sociology.

The Plan for the Book and Conclusion

The sociological approach is to recognize that our freedom is often constrained by a number of social factors. Those factors range from the most micro-level (e.g., individual attitudes, which in turn stem in no small degree from social arrangements, such as those associated with your upbringing), through the most macro-level (e.g., whether you live in a poor nation or a wealthy and powerful one). Somewhere in between the micro and the macro, is the meso-level (examples of important sociological questions at this level would be what institutions you are a part of, and what influences those institutions have on your behavior).

Which of these levels is the most important? The answer is that they all are important. You, like everyone else, have ways of interacting with the world around you as well as ambitions in life. Those ambitions and interactions are very much tempered by the social collectives of which you are part, from the most micro to the most macro, and include the meso-level as well.

The sociological perspectives we will examine in the book and throughout the course address each of these levels. After a brief introduction in Chapter 2 to some of the methods sociologists utilize, we'll give a systematic overview of theoretical perspectives in sociology. The book is organized so that we cover a range of theories, first examining micro-level interactions (such as how we develop as individuals), and gradually moving to the macro-level (such as how it affects people's lives to live in a rich and powerful country in the "world system," as opposed to a poor and relatively powerless one—and how it got to be that way in the first place). That takes us through the first half of the book (or more precisely, through Chapter 9). We'll then examine four of the most important social institutions—family, education, religion, and the political system— in which we spend large portions of our lives, and which are a vital part of virtually every society. In our analysis of those institutions, we build on the theoretical knowledge gained through the earlier part of the book. In the last two chapters, we look at two topics of much social discussion and debate in our society—population dynamics, particularly as they affect the environment; and crime and deviance. We examine these from a sociological viewpoint, and once again draw on our knowledge from earlier chapters.

Good theory is made of hard won insights and tends to change slowly. Particularly in the first half of the book, we focus on time tested theoretical ideas. In the second half of the book, we do introduce later and more current work, but the text itself is grounded in these older theories with deep roots in the discipline of sociology.

In this chapter, we have introduced the discipline of sociology, the paradigm in which it operates, and the levels of analysis, or domains of social collectives, that sociologists study. The formulation of approaches to examining social collectives is an important part of doing sociology, and we discussed four such approaches: social function, social conflict, social construction and social exchange. More generally, as human beings we are constrained by social arrangements on a number of levels of analysis, from the micro to the macro. The book is organized to examine those social arrangements across a wide arrangement of viewpoints, and to integrate those insights through the sociological imagination, which involves the ability to see where these constraints are present, and how they relate back to us as individuals and as members of social collectives.

CHAPTER SUMMARY

- Sociology is the scientific study of the social. More precisely, it is the study of the emergent properties of social collectives.
- Social organizations, or domains, such as the family, the community, or the society comprise the particular subject matter of sociology.
- We build our analysis of society and our roles in it upon the foundational concept of the sociological imagination.
- We examined four very common theoretical approaches in sociology—social function, social conflict, social construction, and social exchange.
- Sociologists emphasize that, while humans have freedom and creative potential, we also are constrained by the social arrangements in which we participate throughout our lives.
- Sociology has a number of theoretical perspectives, because the array of social arrangements goes from the micro to the macro levels of social organization. Each of those theoretical perspectives help to make sense of the social world that correspond to those levels of social organization .
- Sociologists tend to view the world as regular in pattern, rather than chaotic. By learning social theory and applying it through our sociological imagination, we can more easily make sense of what otherwise seems like a chaotic world.

2 Methods In Sociology

Just as the sociological imagination encourages multiple perspectives on social dynamics, it also encourages the use of multiple methodologies in examining social issues. These examinations are, however, conducted with value-free sociology and objectivity in mind. It is one thing to say that the science of the social should be conducted fairly, objectively, and free of values. But, is that even possible? This is a fair question.

There are certain difficulties related to objectivity in all branches of science. For example, imagine that you and your friends were asked to rate the best musical groups in the United States. It is likely that you would encounter drastic differences in preferences and personal values. There is the possibility that these differences are just as sharp among scientists and that they impact the conduct of scientific research. Yet, sociology is a science that seeks to be neutral in the conduct of research. What this amounts to is our effort to adhere carefully to specific scientific procedures so that we do not bias the results we gain from the application of methodologies in data analyses. You might think that it is never possible to be completely objective, but our position must be that we have to try as best we can to be objective. This objectivity is made possible by widespread agreement among scientists about the use of scientific methods. The scientific method, fortunately, allows for an agreement or consensus that may not be possible with other preferences in life, such as our favorite musical groups.

The great sociologist Max Weber, whom we met in Chapter 1, spent a significant amount of time dealing with the issue of personal values and scientific study. Weber believed that our personal beliefs must inevitably play some part in our selection of topics for sociological research. After all, why are some people interested in studying world hunger rather than race relations, or issues of community development or crime? But Weber made it clear that we must be certain to be as value-free as possible in reaching conclusions from our scientific studies, even though our research may be value-relevant. In other words, we must make every effort to be completely aware of our own biases and to take them into account as we conduct our research.

Replication is one important criterion that enables us to be objective and value-free in the conduct of our sociological investigation. Replication is the ability for other researchers to conduct our research again, precisely, in order to check our results. Other social scientists, in this way, may assess the accuracy of our results. If they arrive at the same results and conclusions by repeating our study using the same procedures, then the scientific community becomes more confident that the original research that we conducted was done objectively. Scientists conduct their research knowing the importance of replication. The ability of others to check our work, so to speak, ensures that our research is as value-free and as objective as it should be.

The Reasons for Research

Theoretical refinements require ongoing conduct of research—that is to say, improvements in explanations such as the key perspectives of sociology. What this means is that for us to gain greater and greater truth, we need better and better theories that are motivated by research. Our theoretical perspectives provide explanations of a given phenomenon to be analyzed, in turn setting up analytical problems for our subsequent research. This provides the course for what is called our **empirical inquiry**. Of course, our empirical inquiry suggests new problems for theory, inviting new theoretical formulations in turn. This occurs because our research findings often reveal some aspects of our theoretical perspectives as inaccurate. Theoretical refinements are therefore necessary, and, of course, those refinements then need to be tested in new research applications. When all this is taken together, it is clear that theory and research are interwoven. The explanations that we give in our perspectives guide later research, which, in turn, guides subsequent theories. Thus, theory and research cooperate to help us gain sociological truths.

Elements of Sociological Research

Conceptualization is the most fundamental element of sociological research. Conceptualization is the mental process whereby we take imprecise understandings and make them far more exact and specific. More concretely, conceptualization is the process of giving names to the phenomena that we are most interested in, and these names are given with precision in mind. When we try to describe and explain poverty, for instance, we must define exactly what we mean by poverty. A reasonably precise conceptualization of poverty could be "a living circumstance in which even the basic necessities of life are uncertain in their availability on a daily basis."

This brings us to the term **measurement**. Measurement is most visible when we construct variables from concepts, while seeking the goals of **reliability** and **validity**. Let us now examine each of these terms in turn. A variable is a concept that is measured, meaning that it varies across a certain range of values. Age, when it is measured, is a variable. We usually measure age in terms of years, except, of course, when we are speaking of infants, when we might alternately use months, days, or even hours as measurements. A valid measurement truly reflects the concept that we intended to measure. Because infants are not yet a year old, we would not consider years to be a valid measure of age for infants. Months and/or days, however, would be a valid measure of infant age, although months would not be for infants under thirty days old.

Reliability is a quality of measurement, which means that if different observers were to measure the same variable, they would derive exactly or close to the same results. In other words, results should not vary if different researchers use the same measures, on the same subjects, but at different times.

Once we have constructed variables, we may link them in a causal ordering, specifying a **cause-and-effect** relationship. In a cause-and-effect relationship, a given **independent** or causal variable influences or determines a caused or **dependent** variable. For instance, we might follow substantial sociological evidence and state that an individual's income is a result of his or her education. In this case, income is treated as a dependent variable, and education is treated as an independent variable.

Of course, explanations of any given phenomenon, or independent variable, are usually far more complex than this. There are numerous causes of income in addition to education. An individual's income depends on the nature of his or her job, for instance, not to mention the number of years of seniority. Each time we specify that one variable determines another we are specifying a cause-and-effect relationship between an independent variable and dependent variable. The expected outcome of each of these measured cause-and-effect relationships is referred to as a **hypothesis**.

A theoretical concept becomes a hypothesis as it is cast in measurable terms. Because a hypothesis is tested with observation or measurement, it is verifiable or falsifiable. In other words, a hypothesis can either be *supported* by evidence in its favor, or *refuted* by counter-evidence.

A hypothesis states an expectation of the nature of a relationship between two variables, placing them into a causal ordering. Hypotheses are derived from a much larger theoretical perspective. Using the social conflict theoretical perspective discussed earlier, for example, we might suggest the hypothesis that the wealth of one's family of origin is vitally important in determining one's education and later income. If we were instead to use the social functions perspective, we might pose another hypothesis—that one's individual ability is a vitally important factor in one's subsequent income, for example. The exchange approach would lead us to hypothesize that what one has to market in the real world is crucial in determining one's income. A social interaction approach might emphasize that it is a favorable presentation of self that is responsible for the success suggested by greater income. In each of these cases a hypothesis is drawn from a larger theory. The hypotheses together specify that income, a dependent variable, is the product of different independent variables.

The strategy that we have just adopted involves what is termed a **deductive** approach. In a deductive model, specific expectations or hypotheses are developed from a general theory. **Induction** is an alternative approach, in which we examine events in the world and make generalizations on the basis of individual events to hypothesize about them. We do not need to have a theory, per se, to do induction.

Both deduction and induction are utilized in almost all theory construction exercises. Our observations about the world are truly guided by the explanations that we already hold. Conversely, our explanations also lead us to specific observations. The constant weaving of induction and deduction leads us to conclusions about the social processes involved. This weaving process, which scientists use to bridge induction and deduction while at the same time deriving hypotheses, is sometimes referred to as **retroduction**.

Hypothesis Testing

The process of hypothesis building is intended to function as a vehicle for testing overall perspectives, such as those outlined in the previous chapter. What we want to know is whether the expectations provided by a particular hypothesis, which is part of a larger explanation, exists in the real world. Is it true, for example, that education leads us to greater income?

To test a hypothesis, data are collected to support or **confirm** it or, alternatively, to disconfirm or **refute** it. Confirmation (support) or disconfirmation (refutation) of a given hypothesis depends on the collection of data, usually for a particular **sample** or representative portion of the population. It is impossible, in most cases, to gain data or information from all of the respondents in a population. Hence, we must resort to sampling techniques.

When we sample, our goal is to choose a **representative sample** so that we can **generalize** to a larger population. A truly representative sample, by definition, has the same distribution of important characteristics as the population from which it was drawn. If our population is racially diverse, for example, then our sample should be as well. If we have chosen our sample well, and if it does reflect the characteristics of the population, then any analysis of the data that we do based on that sample can be generalized to the population. What this means is that our results, rather than representing simply the dynamics of the sample, also accurately represent what is occurring in the larger population.

All of this implies, of course, that some form of **analysis** will be conducted on the gathered data. Sociologists often use **quantitative analysis** of data for the purposes of judging hypotheses and theory. Quantitative analysis depends on numerical representation and manipulation of observations. Basically, researchers assign numbers to variables, and then test the relationship among these variables using these numbers.

Quantitative analysis often relies upon **descriptive statistics**, such as the **mean**, the **median**, and the **mode**. You have used the mean before, although you may know it better as the arithmetic average. Summing the values of the observations for a variable and dividing that figure by the number of total observations yields the mean. When you calculate your average test score in a class, or your grade point average, you are using this figure. On the other hand, if you were to list all of your scores from the lowest to the highest and take the one in the very middle of the distribution, you would have chosen the median. Sometimes, the median and the mean are close to the same number, but they also can be very different and then your choice of one or the other is critical to the conclusions that you reach in your quantitative analysis. This applies, too, to the use of the mode, which is another type of average. You would be choosing the modal score if you were to array all of your scores and choose the one that occurred most frequently.

Since these descriptive statistics are so commonly used in the media as well as sociology, an illustrative example would be useful. Imagine that you have just gained from a sample of adult respondents their scores on the total years of education they have completed. For this scenario, imagine that there are only 5 respondents in the sample. Normally, the sample would be much larger. Suppose, in addition, two of the respondents said that they had completed 12 years of education, one respondent completed 13 years, another 15 years, and still another, 23 years of education. The modal (most frequently occurring) number of years for this sample is 12, the median (middle) years for their sample is 13, and the mean of the sample is 15.

Which of these figures offers the best reflection of the average of the sample, the mode, the mean, or the median? The median is probably the best representation in this case. Your choice of a mode, median, or mean depends on the nature of the distribution you are examining. Keep this information in mind when you read newspapers or view statistical presentations in the media. These presentations often depend on choice of a mean, median, or mode descriptive statistic, and the choice that is made may be defensible or it may be frail.

Standard deviation is another measure sociologists use. This gives an estimate of dispersion around the mean. A large standard deviation indicates that the observations are scattered widely around the mean, while a small standard deviation indicates the observations are fairly tightly clustered around the mean. For example, suppose we had two groups, both with a mean height of 5'8". Suppose further that in the first group everyone is clustered between 5'7" and 5'9", while a second group has a wide array of heights from 3-foot dwarves to 7-foot giants. The first group would have a small standard deviation while the second would have a large one.

Using the standard deviation allows us to estimate how much confidence we would have in generalizing a finding from a group, or in making an educated guess about how likely something is to occur in that group. Following the given example, we would tend to have more confidence that a person from the first group would be within an inch or so of 5'8", than we would in making such a guess about the second group.

This brings us to the related concept of **reliability**. When social scientists speak of reliability, they refer to the idea that separate measures of a similar phenomenon will indeed be close to identical. To say a measure has low reliability implies that two or more measures of the same thing (say the length of your back yard where you and a friend count your steps) come out differently. Conversely, when two or more measures tend to come out close to identical, there is a high reliability (when you and your friend both measure your backyard, but this time using a standardized measuring tape, for example).

Yet another related idea is that of **validity**. When we speak of validity, we are referring to how close a measure comes to tapping what the scientist

Validity vs. Reliability

Reliable, not Valid: Measurements are consistent (clustered), but they don't hit the target. In this case, they are reliable but not valid. Usually indicates that the concepts require substantial rethinking.

Reliable/Not Valid

Valid/Low Reliability: Measurements are scattered all around the target but they are not tightly clustered. This indicates that the measurements are valid, but not reliable. The indicators are not focused on the core concepts.

Valid/Low Reliability

Not Valid/Not Reliable: Measurements are scattered but not focused around a core concept. The measures are neither valid nor reliable. This suggests a complete rethinking of the study.

Not Valid/ Not Reliable

Valid and Reliable: The measurements are consistent and tightly focused around the core concept. This indicates that the tool is a solid measure of the concept.

Valid and Reliable

actually hopes to measure. For instance, a measure would have very low validity if someone were trying to measure height and yet measured weight instead. For a measure to be valid, it is important for it also to be reliable. Keep in mind that high reliability does not ensure high validity, however.

Sometimes more sophisticated techniques of analysis than descriptive statistics are required, for example when sociologists use quantitative methods to test hypotheses. We will not discuss these techniques in detail now, but we will emphasize that in most cases, they are utilized to determine the degree of relationship between the independent variable and the dependent variable. Statistically, this boils down to the question of whether variables **co-vary**, that is, vary together. They can co-vary *positively*, meaning that as one increases, so does the other—education and income are an example of this. They can co-vary, *negatively*, meaning increases in one accompany decreases in the other. Or, they can fail to co-vary, being unrelated to each other.

One measure of covariation that is used across a wide array of disciplines, including sociology, is called **correlation**. By definition, the correlation between any two variables will always fall between 1.0 and –1.0. While the details of how to calculate the correlation are usually covered in just about any elementary statistics course (and we do not go into those details here), the correlation is so useful because it has *intuitive* meaning. A correlation of 0 means there is no relationship whatsoever between the variables. For example, the relationship between the IQ and height of adults is virtually zero—short people exhibit the entire range of IQs, as do tall people. On the other hand, the correlation between height and weight is about .4—there are certainly underweight and overweight people at all heights, but as a person increases in height that person also tends to increase in weight as well (if for no other reason than the extra bone and muscle involved has some weight to it). The correlation between height measured in inches and height measured in centimeters is 1.0—since every inch has a precise metric equivalent, it is irrelevant whether height is measured in inches or centimeters; if you are taller than someone else using one measure, you will also be taller than that person when using the other.

Sociologists often use correlation as a shorthand way of communicating and thinking about relationships between social variables. In some studies in the sociology of education for example, researchers find that the correlation between the amount spent in schools and performance on standardized tests of the students in those schools is about .3. One way to interpret this is to say the correlation between spending and performance (as measured, or "operationalized" in the studies in question) is in the "moderate" range—it is certainly higher than zero, but it is way lower than one. Notice that a correlation here of zero would indicate no relationship between spending and performance whatsoever. A correlation of one would indicate a perfect one-to-one relationship, in which the higher the per capita spending in the school, the higher the performance of the students there. Just to complete the possible scenarios, a correlation of –1.0 would mean the higher the spending, the lower the performance (that is not the case here, but we bring it up only to work through the range of possibilities).

We find many cases of correlations in the moderate range when we move from textbooks to the real world. So what are we to make of this correlation of .3? Our sociological imagination and reasoning capacities come into play here. One possible scenario is that with more spending, the school can hire good teachers and have more resources, which over time would likely result in better learning opportunities and ultimately higher test scores for the students. And that is probably at least part of the story. But why is the correlation then not higher? There are probably other attributable factors at play here as well. As it turns out, there is some pretty good evidence that the influence of family on a child's learning are often at least as great in academic performance, as are the quality of the schools. So the spending in the schools leads to greater performance, but that effect is largely mitigated by family influences.

The technique of **regression analysis** builds on correlation analysis. In regression, the researcher also looks for relationships between variables, but the analytical framework is one in which there is an expectation of causality. Let's use the previous example of the relationship between education and income once more. While in correlation analysis we only test the strength and direction of the relationship, we set up regression analysis so that one of the variables is the outcome, or **dependent variable**. The other is set up as a predictor of that outcome, or **independent variable**. Since we would expect higher levels of income to result from a person having gotten higher levels of education in our example, the regression model would have the result (income) as a dependent variable, and the cause (education) as an independent variable.

Bivariate regression is when we do regression with two variables in which one is a dependent variable and the other is independent. Yet in practice, researchers almost always seek to predict an outcome using a number of predictor variables. This is referred to as **multivariate regression** (or **multiple regression**). Returning to our income example, if we were to predict income with a number of variables such as education, years of experience, aptitude of the job, and situation of the labor market, this would involve a multiple regression model. In fact, what we have just described is a common model used by **human capital** theorists, which we will cover later in the text.

There are many reasons why multiple regression is a common and useful technique. By using multiple variables, often drawn from an array of theoretical positions, the analyst is able

Interpreting Regression Lines

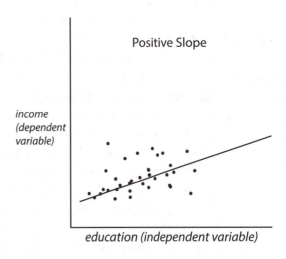

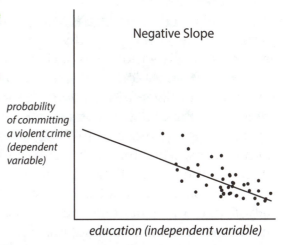

to compare the relative strength of each independent variable with the others, while simultaneously controlling for the relationships among the independent variables themselves. Multiple regression models can also have the virtue of **parsimony**, in that they contain a lot of information in a relatively small space.

Further complicating the picture is the question of **spuriousness**. Spuriousness is a situation in which two things are correlated, but that correlation stems from their *both* being correlated with some other social factor. In the case of school spending and performance, it may be that families with more material resources tend to spend more time helping their children with homework and other school assignments. Furthermore, those families tend to live in areas with higher property values, and therefore a higher tax base, which in turn goes to the schools (there is strong evidence that this is also the case).

We could continue inquiring into correlation and regression, but for now we will finish by simply pointing out that there are several important lessons contained in this one scenario—one of which is that the first and easy explanation may not necessarily be the most correct one. Correlations here are an *analytical tool*, as is regression analysis, and as such, they should never be confused with the analytical process itself. More broadly, though, you can now see how the sociological imagination works, with each bit of information leading to another question, which over time allows us to delve deeper into a problem. This sort of "puzzle-solving" process is a major reason why sociology is such a rich and fascinating discipline.

Much of sociology relies on quantitative analysis, which, as we have seen, tends to operationalize and measure relationships (in ways such as finding correlations) and to use these mathematical relationships as tools to help us clarify the way we see the social world. Sociologists also use **qualitative analysis**, however. Sociologists report on events, rather than offer enumerations, when they conduct historical research. When sociologists participate in groups to conduct their study, they sometimes rely on the group's report and conversations overheard instead of using any quantitative measures of what was said. When a sociologist conducts an analysis of the content of the media, it is more likely that he/she will interpret what is said and what is meant rather than assigning a number to it. Some of the most fruitful sociological investigations use both qualitative analysis and quantitative analysis as a check on the strength of the results obtained from each technique.

Research Methodology

Our discussion of qualitative analysis and quantitative analysis leads us to describe the various research methodologies that are most commonly employed by sociologists at work. One of the most important techniques that sociologists use is **survey analysis**. Surveys are polls taken by researchers to gather facts, and then determine the relationship between variables based on those facts. You have probably taken surveys yourself and have likely also administered them as well. Some methods of collecting survey data include **personal interviews**, **telephone interviews**, or **mailing questionnaires** to respondents, some of whom return them.

In an interview, the sociologist asks a series of questions, recording the respondents' answers. **Structured interviews** are often used, in which the same questionnaire is given to all respondents. It is preferable to adopt either a telephone survey or questionnaire, because such interviews are often expensive. In telephone surveys, respondents are called and their responses are coded over the phone. Respondents, as you might expect, may give different answers over the phone than they would give in a personal interview. Computer and Internet surveys are becoming increasingly popular because of the ease of use and sometimes wide access to potential respondents. They too, of course, are subject to concerns about sampling. The investigator must determine whether any particular sample results would be different using one method instead of the other. In these cases, the cost of using a particular technique must be weighed against the probable validity and reliability of the results obtained.

Field research is another important method. With this technique, sociologists study social life in its natural setting, observing and interviewing people where they play, work, or live. Sometimes sociologists become **participant observers** to gain the confidence of groups. As a participant observer, the researcher actually becomes part of the activity of the group they are studying. There are disadvantages to this sort of strategy, in that respondents may act differently when a researcher is among them. A major advantage, by contrast, is people in the longer run may become more comfortable when an observer is one of their group and may feel freer to provide important information to the researcher.

Yet another methodology used by sociologists and psychologists alike is the **experiment**. You may also be familiar with the experiment from your natural science classes. Here the researcher commonly identifies what is called an **experimental group** and a **control group**. The experimental group contains subjects who are exposed to a given experimental condition, and the goal of the research is to discover whether that experimental condition has an impact on the subjects. It is necessary to also have a control group in order to determine this. The control group contains subjects who are not exposed to the experimental condition. The experiment compares the results of the two groups to see whether the experimental condition actually made a difference or not. The particular advantage of an experiment comes when the groups are perfectly **matched**. When the groups are perfectly matched, it is possible to say, with a great deal of certainty, that the experimental condition either did, or did not make a difference. This technique, however, has a drawback in that it is often difficult to carefully match groups. Also, people sometimes behave differently in experimental circumstances. Thus, conclusions reached through an experiment may be erroneous when participants behave unnaturally.

Secondary data analysis is another common methodology used by sociologists. When researchers conduct secondary analysis of data, they use already existing data originally collected by others. Sometimes these are official reports of public records conducted by government agencies, or reports contained in newspapers or other media presentations. In still other cases, they are primary or original data collected by researchers in other settings. Secondary data analysis is less costly than some other methodological alternatives, giving it an important advantage—namely, that more data may be collected and analyzed, in order to better verify or refute the hypotheses that stem from the sociological perspectives. A possible disadvantage of secondary data analysis is that sometimes researchers cannot be sure precisely how the original data were collected, and if liberties were taken in original data collection that limit the data. Problems with the original method of collection, in other words, may render conclusions drawn from it unreliable or invalid.

There are important tradeoffs in selection of a sociological methodology, as you can see. Each technique has its advantages and disadvantages and the choice of methodology is tailored to the research needs of the investigator. It is essential to **triangulate methods** whenever possible, since each methodology has its shortcomings. The triangulation of methods means the use of multiple methodologies in any given research project in order to determine whether each methodology provides the same or different results.

If comparable results and conclusions emerge when different methodologies are employed, then the researcher can feel a great deal more confident that the research has been conducted appropriately. If different results or conclusions emerge from each different methodology, on the other hand, questions concerning the appropriateness of the employed methodology arise. When such questions are raised, it is important to conduct additional inquiry to determine the source of the methodological difficulties.

Conclusions

It is essential that social researchers use caution in their choices of methodologies. Erroneous results and conclusions can adversely affect pure sociology, as well as obstruct the application of basic, or applied sociology, ultimately impeding the advancement of sociological knowledge.

Applied sociology is geared toward public decision makers and public programs; thus accountability with respect to decisions and implementations is crucial. **Evaluation research** in sociology evaluates the impact of social interventions, as recommended by research. If the methodologies upon which the interventions are based are inappropriate, and the findings and conclusions are inaccurate, public time and money may be wasted, and the public can hold the investigator accountable.

With these issues in mind, let's turn our attention now to foundational studies in the social sciences. These form the backdrop for the sociological perspectives that comprise the paradigm of the sociological imagination.

CHAPTER SUMMARY

- The use of many different methodologies to verify or refute theoretical perspectives is supported by the sociological imagination.
- Sociologists must try hard to be objective and value-free, and others who may replicate or build on their research check their work.
- The basic elements of sociological research are conceptualization, measurement, independent and dependent variables, and hypotheses.
- Correlation and regression analysis are common and useful shorthand ways of thinking about relationships between social variables.
- There are many statistical techniques and methodologies used by sociologists, each with advantages and disadvantages.
- Using both quantitative and qualitative methods together can help ensure more trustworthy conclusions.

3. Individual Development in a Social World: Socialization and Social Interaction

The process through which people learn about society, its social institutions and their respective places in them, is known as **socialization**. Because this process occurs within a larger social context, people are socialized to be members of some particular larger collective such as a family, a society, or a religion, for example. In the socialization process, people learn the roles that they will play and the expectations governing them. In addition to developing physically, they develop mentally and emotionally. Let's examine more closely these processes of socialization.

Socialization

Socialization typically involves learning the "right" way of doing things relative to the collective. From where does the knowledge of what is "right" come? Every society has a manner of teaching its new members how to be members of the society. As we've mentioned, the process through which this occurs is commonly referred to as socialization, and can be further broken down into **primary socialization** and **secondary socialization**. The first socialization an individual encounters as a child is called primary socialization, while secondary socialization takes place at later points in life, in which an already (primarily) socialized person learns new aspects of something about the world in which he or she is living.

There are a number of ways in which secondary socialization (also referred to as "adult socialization," although it could also be said to apply to teenagers as well) essentially differs from primary socialization, as outlined by Brim (1966):

- Primary socialization involves the internalization of core values, upon which later socialization experiences can be constructed; while in secondary socialization, the changes that do occur tend to be in objective behavior, rather than in subjective values.
- In primary socialization, children learn "absolute" norms. In secondary socialization, however, individuals are able to make finer distinctions among positions, and to see exceptions to the rules—to take the rules with a "grain of salt."
- Children learn a general direction in life through primary socialization, while in secondary socialization, people tend to gain a specific, more narrowly focused skill; or they learn the norms of a new situation in which they find themselves—those norms typically are not seen in absolute terms, but rather are seen as one way of doing things, applicable primarily in a more narrowly circumscribed situation, such as one's workplace.

The way in which people are socialized largely determines how they construct their respective social realities. An in-depth view of the socialization process was developed by Berger and Luckmann (1967), whose work we will discuss at length in Chapter 5. Primary socialization, according to Berger and Luckmann, is the principal vehicle through which a person becomes integrated into society. It is then that the person first encounters the significant others who will be so crucial to the socialization process. In fact, a vital component of primary socialization is forming emotional attachments to these significant others. These are ideally, though by no means necessarily, loving attachments.

As children become emotionally attached to significant others, they **identify** with those others, meaning that he or she tries to imitate them. Berger and Luckmann wrote that "The child takes on the significant others' roles and attitudes, that is, internalizes them and makes them his own" (1967:131-132). This process of **internalization** is a necessary step in child development. As implied by the term, the important point is that the child regulates his or her own behaviors, based on the attitudes communicated by others.

> In primary socialization, there is no *problem* of identification. There is no choice of significant others...although the child is not simply passive in the process of his socialization, it is the adults who set the rules of the game...The child does not internalize the world of his significant others as one of many possible worlds. He internalizes it as the world...It is for this reason that the world internalized in primary socialization is so much more firmly entrenched in consciousness than worlds internalized in secondary socializations. (Berger and Luckmann 1967:134-135)

Language, and the constructions of reality it implies, is among the most important things for a child to learn and internalize. For example, by learning meanings for words like father, mother, sister, brother, cousin, uncle, aunt, grandmother, etc., the child is learning a kin network structure upon which other more complex ideas later can be added (e.g., caring for one's kin, or taboos against incestuous relations). No matter how far someone travels in life, the "home environment" is still the environment against which all others are measured, because it is the world of primary socialization.

During primary socialization, the child comes to see the roles and attitudes of significant others in progressively more abstract terms. Over time, these are seen as roles and attitudes in general. This abstraction process is quite similar to what George Herbert Mead termed the *generalized other*. A child comes to develop a sense of what *society* is like, and his or her place in it, by formulating this concept of the generalized other. An individual tends to take into account what "other people" will think about their behavior, signifying that he or she has, to a large degree, been socialized.

Of this stage, Berger and Luckmann (1967:137) write, "Primary socialization ends when the concept of the generalized other (and all that goes with it) has been established in the consciousness of the individual. At this point he is an effective member of society and in subjective possession of self and a world." The internal world of the child now conforms in many ways to the external objective world. While there are degrees, however, there is never total congruity between the objective and subjective worlds of the individual. For this reason, *all socialization is partially incomplete by its nature.*

In secondary socialization, a person learns sets of specialized terms associated with distinct areas of the social world which themselves are embedded in some institutional arrangements, such as school or the workplace. We acquire specialized languages (as well as the roles and perceptions of the world attendant to them) during secondary socialization. Anytime someone begins a new job, for example, the person typically is socialized into the new job. This would include learning the "way things are" in that particular place of work, as well as in the role one takes in that workplace.

Social Roles

As we develop a symbol system, we develop with it a set of shared behavioral expectations that stem from interaction with others. An important class of these expectations involves **roles**, which are the social behaviors that are relatively stable over time and place. In turn, these roles inform many of the shared behavioral expectations that people have. The professor and students in a class play certain roles in each other's lives. Each has certain expectations of the others *before even meeting* that are then enacted throughout the time of the class. As an illustration, students expect their professors to be knowledgeable and articulate about the topic being taught. At the same time, the role of the student involves an expectation of the professor to spend time and energy learning about the topic, under the guidance of the professor, and to be graded on that learning.

By nature, institutions involve many people, all behaving in some kind of coordinated manner. This does not imply that everyone in an institution is doing the same thing. On the contrary, people in institutions typically are each doing something different from one another, even though those different activities are coordinated with one another. Individuals experience these institutions through the roles they play within them. No one, for example, experiences "the family" as such. Your experience of a family comes to you as a daughter or a son in your family of origin. It comes to you through a different role (mom, dad) in your family of procreation. The experience of someone else's family comes to you in your role as a neighbor, friend, or casual observer. Thus, a person's subjective experience of an institution is profoundly influenced by his or her role relative to that institution.

While primary socialization teaches us our basic roles in being members of a society, secondary socialization is the process through which we learn to function in other social roles, which can be learned at any time of life. For example, the transitions from grade school to high school, and then from high school to college, necessarily involve secondary socialization, in which new types of behavior are learned. That learning does not take place in a vacuum—it is grounded in what a person already "knows" about society and the institutions and people in it.

Learning includes the internalizing of norms, or rules, governing behavior. Norms are typically acquired through interaction with others, but are effective only to the extent that they have become part of the individual's subjective experience of the world, or internalized. An example might be the "Golden Rule" to do unto others, as you would have them do unto you. The rule is only effective to the extent individuals make it part of their life experiences.

A role, when considered in this way, is a relational position in society, which typically is governed by norms. For instance, father, husband, student, wife, or daughter all are roles—they are relational positions in that they imply a relation with other people in the society, and they are governed by norms of behavior.

Robert Merton (1957, 1968) provides a useful vocabulary for discussing social roles. The various roles a person plays (e.g., student, employee, team member, etc.) constitute the person's

role set. Participation in role sets may cause an individual to experience **role conflict** when a person must choose *between* the competing demands of two or more roles within their role set. For example, role conflict may occur in the life of a parent who is also a student. In that case, time studying may infringe on family time, even while time spent with the family may take away from study time. Often, there are even competing expectations *within* a given role; this is known as **role strain**. For example, a professor is expected to teach and nurture students, and also to assign grades. Sometimes the very act of grading detracts from the teaching. A specific type of role strain is **role overload**; this is a situation in which a person cannot meet the expectations of a role due to not having enough time or energy (Goode 1960).

Individual Development and the Socialization Process

In times past, theories of socialization tended to be categorized as "nature" (or heredity) vs. "nurture" (or environment). The theory of nature was genetically based, in which *who* a person became was primarily, or even solely, a function of his/her genetic make-up. Theories of nurture, on the other hand, emphasized interaction with one's natural environment. Today, most serious theories acknowledge that some combination of heredity and environment interact to make the individual what he or she is.

Because sociology is the study of the emergent properties of human interaction, an exclusively genetic approach is widely rejected for a number of reasons—mainly, since the emphasis on genetics largely precludes such an approach, sociologists tend to underemphasize genetics as something out of the purview of human interaction.

Sociologists tend to approach *primary socialization* with an emphasis on interactions between heredity and the environment in the form of stages through which a child progresses. However, in *secondary socialization*, the emphasis shifts to focus almost exclusively on the interaction between an individual and his or her environment, with virtually no emphasis on the genetic make-up of the individual.

There are several approaches to socialization, which broadly speaking can be divided into two groups of theories. The first group can be said to follow a **structural** or **stage** approach, and emphasizes the *stages* of development through which a child passes on the way to adulthood. The second approach places the emphasis more on **social interaction**. Stage theories tend to focus on "nature" while social interaction theories tend to emphasize "nurture." As we will see, however,

Secondary Socialization

Secondary socialization occurs when an adult learns the rules and procedures of a new job.

the structural or developmental approach and the interactive approaches are far from mutually exclusive. In fact, most theories or models of socialization involve both stages and interaction, but tend to place the *emphasis* on one or the other.

Let's now examine some stage theories, including Sigmund Freud's psychodynamic theory and Jean Piaget's theory of cognitive development. Then we will discuss more interactive approaches, which include Melvin Kohn's theory of socialization and social class and Morris Rosenberg's theory of self-concept formation.

Stage Theories of Individual Development

Sigmund Freud's Theory of Psychosexual Development

Sigmund Freud was a psychologist who was famous for working with patients exhibiting physical symptoms for which there did not appear to be any physical cause, which he referred to **psychosomatic** symptoms. In examining people with psychosomatic symptoms, Freud found some interesting commonalities. Namely, serious **traumatic experiences** (bad or painful events, leaving an emotional scar) occurring in childhood. This caused Freud to study physical and emotional development in a great deal of depth. It is largely from this work that Freud built the foundation of his theory.

Freud (1923, 1952, 1959) believed that important motivators for individuals' behavior come from drives of which they may not be fully aware. Freud termed this aspect of the human being the **unconscious**. One aspect of the unconscious, which he termed the **libido**, described the unconscious sexual energy. Much of what happens in a person's life, according to Freud, is motivated by these unconscious sexual drives.

There are three major aspects to the personality, according to Freud (1923): the id, ego, and superego. The **id** is that part of the personality that serves the "pleasure principle." Its interest lies in gratifying basic instincts, especially desires of the libido. The id is not particularly concerned with consequences, and is intolerant of any delay in gratification. The **superego** acts as a restraint to the id. It can be thought of as serving a function of an individual's conscience. It is formed over time as a child internalizes the discipline of his/her parents and, because the values of the parents typically are part of a larger culture, superego development thus facilitates binding the child to the larger culture. The **ego** serves the "reality principle." It serves as a mediator between the id's unbridled desires and the superego's cautiousness and guilt. In so doing, the ego is that part of the personality that deals with the outside world.

Freud believed that children went through a number of stages in which gratification was derived primarily through different parts of the physical body, which he termed **psychosexual stages**. For Freud, the stages through which a child passes on the way to adulthood (and the approximate ages during which they occur) includes: the oral stage (birth to one year of age), the anal stage (one to three years), the phallic stage (ages three to six), the latency stage (six until puberty), and the genital stage (puberty and beyond).

Freud saw an important interaction between the external environment and the psychosexual processes during each of these stages, especially in terms of the channeling of psychosexual energy. If a given stage is not resolved properly, it results in an energy blockage, which causes a number of problems of which the person typically is not consciously aware. If the problem is not resolved satisfactorily, the person has an unconscious need for stimulation in that particular area which could last throughout the person's life. In each stage, the child craves stimulation in a given place in the body.

During the first stage of life, the **oral stage**, the child seeks stimulation through the mouth. This occurs approximately throughout the first year after birth, and explains why infants tend to put objects into their mouths. If a child is deprived of oral stimulation during this critical period (e.g., because of frustration from not being able to put things in one's mouth, or from not being breast-fed), he or she may develop an **oral fixation**, which is characterized by a deep craving for oral stimulation of some sort throughout his or her life. This may take the form of smoking, constant snacking, or being overly talkative.

The next stage, typically in ages one to three in the child's life, is the **anal stage**. During this time, the child derives pleasure from anal functions, such as the holding in or expulsion of feces. It is typical that the child undergoes toilet training during this time. If toilet training is successful and untraumatic, the child tends to pass through this stage successfully, developing a sense of autonomy and self-control in the process. However, an anal fixation may develop if toilet training is traumatic in some way. There are two types of anal fixations. If toilet training is too harsh or takes place too early, the child tends to want to retain his or her feces inside their body, which may lead to the child becoming compulsive in a quest for neatness and order. Freud characterized this as an **anal retentive** tendency. On the other hand, if toilet training is overly lax, the child may develop habits of sloppiness; this is known as an **anal expulsive** tendency.

During the next stage, the **phallic stage** (sometimes referred to as the **Oedipal stage**), the child develops a sexual attachment to the opposite-sex parent. There are some crucial differences between how boys and girls are likely to experience this stage. Boys develop sexual feelings for their mothers, and see their fathers as competing for the mother's emotions. This concept includes a key paradox: while the boy sees himself as competing with his father, he also comes to admire his father for his superior physical attributes and seeming mastery of the external world. Ideally, the boy comes to **identify** with his father, perceiving desirable traits that he himself wants to emulate.

If this stage is unresolved and the boy does not adequately identify with his father, he does not internalize the norms of society represented and conveyed by the father, and is therefore likely to develop contempt for authority and, in extreme cases, an an-

Freud's Theory of Psychosexual Development - Oedipal Stage
If the Oedipal stage is properly resolved, the boy comes to identify with his father and develop a healthy relationship with him.

tisocial personality. Freud referred to this as an **Oedipus complex**, named after the tragic figure in Greek mythology who killed his father and married his mother.

It is also during this stage that a girl develops her superego. Yet the mechanism is a bit different than for boys. A girl may feel inadequate for not having a penis. While in the normal course of development, a girl is likely to come through this stage with normal heterosexual tendencies. However, if she does not properly learn to identify with her parents (especially her father, if he is overly domineering, for example), she may develop an **Electra complex**, in which she herself becomes domineering, often with a particular desire to dominate men.

A crucial aspect of what the child internalizes during this time, for both sexes, is the sense of norms, rules and limits to behavior that are imposed by the father. In this way, the superego is incorporated into the personality. If this occurs successfully, the child is likely to develop into a law-abiding citizen, and one who is able to participate in the normal give and take of life without becoming overly offended by perceived slights of others.

Following the sometimes-stormy emotional period of the phallic stage, the child enters a somewhat calmer **latency stage**. Here, the child focuses on the development of social and intellectual skills as the id becomes less strident in its demands for gratification. During this period, the superego and the ego become more developed. In some cases, there is unease with members of the opposite sex, and so much of the social activity is with members of one's own sex. The identification process with adults is crucial in this stage. Ideally, the child develops self-assurance without becoming arrogant. If the child does not have adequate opportunity to engage in a range of social activities, and to receive adequate exposure to adults with whom to identify, he or she may become withdrawn or overly detached from the rest of society.

In the final psychosexual stage, the genital stage, come the beginnings of what will develop into adult sexual desires. The adolescent takes pleasure in sexuality. The tendencies toward exhibitionism and aggressiveness in the genital stage tend to overshadow the modesty of the latency stage. Satisfying the id again becomes of paramount importance, as does impressing members of the opposite sex. If the adolescent experiences success during this time, he or she is likely to be able to enter into mature heterosexual relationships without major difficulties such as being overly "needy" in placing demands on his or her partner. If, however, the individual experiences repeated frustrations during this stage, he or she may have trouble in forming and maintaining sexual relationships, and thus may have sexual or marital problems. Fixations from any of the prior stages, if unresolved, carry into the **genital stage**. When this happens, the adolescent is less than fully equipped to deal with the challenges of the genital stage.

Freud argued that we play tricks on ourselves in order to keep unpleasant emotions or threatening thoughts out of our consciousness. Because anxiety is so closely associated with danger, it serves a survival function by warning the person, who then strives to avoid the anxiety-provoking situation. However, people often attempt to escape the unpleasant feelings by avoiding anxiety itself, rather than properly confronting the situation causing the anxiety in order to understand it. Freud described several **defense mechanisms** by which people do this, or techniques used by the ego to avoid negative emotions. While Freud discusses a number of such mechanisms, we'll look at the four most common here: repression, projection, rationalization, and sublimation:

- **Repression** is the defense mechanism in which thoughts and emotions are pushed out of conscious awareness. This is particularly true of highly traumatic events. For instance, it often occurs that when a person experiences a severe accident, that person cannot remember the details of what happened during the time surrounding the accident.
- **Projection** is a defense mechanism in which a person who fears or loathes some aspect of him-or-herself tends to "see" that trait in others, or project it onto them. People who fear latent homosexuality within them tending to see and to be overly critical of homosexual traits in others would be an example of projection.

Defense Mechanisms - Sublimation

When people channel frustrations into creative outlets, such as playing music with friends, sublimation occurs.

- **Rationalization** occurs when a person adduces a very "reasonable" explanation for otherwise irrational behavior. According to Freud, most of why people do what they do is for irrational reasons. However, a cogent and logical explanation for one's behavior helps it to be seen as acceptable to oneself and to others in polite society. When we are frustrated and rage at innocent others, for example, and then justify our behavior inventing an excuse for verbally assaulting them, we are engaging in rationalization.
- **Sublimation** occurs when we channel energy from unacceptable impulses into socially acceptable behavior. For example, a person who is continually frustrated sexually may channel energy into other outlets, such as his or her career.

Thus, in the Freudian perspective people are largely motivated by unconscious impulses. How we feel and manifest those impulses are greatly shaped by how we go through the various psychosexual stages in life. Much of what people actually do in civilized society is involved with channeling psychosexual energy into socially acceptable behavior, and defense mechanisms play a key role in shaping how that energy is channeled.

While most of Freud's work is directed at individual development, he explicitly places individual psychodynamic processes into a larger sociological context in one of his later works entitled *Civilization and Its Discontents*. For Freud, civilization itself is made possible through harnessing the instinctual drives of individuals:

> [M]ost important of all, it is impossible to ignore the extent to which civilization is built up on renunciation of instinctual gratifications...This **cultural privation** dominates the whole field of social relations between human beings...(Freud 1952 [1929]:781).

Another of Freud's insights about the interface between the individual and society looms large here as well. Drawing on another ancient legend, that of Narcissus who fell in love with his own image, Freud developed the idea of **narcissism**, in which a person is so self-absorbed, they cannot put themselves in the place of another person, and so lack much of the social empathy on which a functional society is based.

In infancy, *all* children see the world as revolving around them. This, what he termed **primary narcissism**, Freud saw as normal. Ideally, as a child develops through the stages, the narcissism of childhood gives way to normal adult attachments. However, if the stages (particularly the Oedipal stage) are not resolved properly, the child may never fully develop a sense of empathy for others.

When this happens, and the inability to empathize and see the world through another's eyes is brought through to adulthood, Freud thought this condition (what he called **secondary narcissism**) served as the touchstone for many of society's problems. We can see this manifested in countless instances, from the road rage of someone maiming or even killing another after a perceived slight of being cut off in traffic, to a serial killer who has no real sense of, or care for, the suffering they cause.

While Freud has been criticized on a number of fronts, his theory was momentous for a number of reasons. Many of the details of his theory may at best be unverifiable, and at worst, simply wrong. Yet it is important to see Freud in a broader context. By developing a theory that put an emphasis on hidden and irrational motives, rather than straightforward and rational ones, he helped to revolutionize how people thought of socialization processes. Also, by pointing to the crucial importance of early childhood experiences in laying the foundation for adult socialization, he was a pioneer for a great deal of later work by social scientists.

Jean Piaget's Theory of Cognitive Development

While Freud's work was largely focused on the unconscious and emotional development, Jean Piaget's work focused on the development of cognition, or the ability to think, reason, learn and remember. Piaget spent much of his career studying children during their developmental years. In doing so, he developed a theory that certain cognitive "structures" existed, which limited learning and socialization. His theory, which is known as structural theory of cognitive development, has become a basis for understanding many of the processes involved in socialization.

Like Freud, Piaget found evidence for the existence of *critical periods* of development. Piaget believed that if a child did not develop key skills during each of the respective periods, then the child would have serious problems in *ever* acquiring that skill, and those problems would manifest themselves throughout one's life. He found evidence for four developmental stages. He identified the following stages that we list here with the times in life in which they are encountered:

1. **The sensorimotor stage** (birth to age two). This is the stage in which the infant develops senses and motor skills, and begins rudimentary language acquisition. The

child also develops a sense of "object permanence," or a sense that objects are still in existence, even when out of sight, in this stage.

2. **The preoperational stage** (ages two through seven). Language acquisition continues during this stage, but symbolic representation also begins—meaning that the child learns not only what is in the language but also what is not in the language. Work subsequent to Piaget's (e.g., Flavell 1985), has indicated that the babbling sounds of an infant contain every sound of every language. The child has yet to learn how to communicate in what will become its native tongue. Much of this language acquisition involves learning what not to say, including which sounds to drop. During this stage, in other words, the infant learns to match the sounds he/she makes with the language that will become its native tongue.

Jean Piaget (1896 - 1980)
Piaget's study of children during their developmental years inspired his theory of cognitive development.

A critical aspect of primary socialization is, of course, language acquisition. The farther one gets from this stage, the more difficult it is to acquire (really to re-acquire) an accent appropriate to what is not one's native tongue. In addition, the child learns another absolutely crucial aspect of being human during this pre-operational stage. In "taking the role of the other" (Mead 1934), a child, for the first time during this pre-operational stage, begins to have glimpses of what the world must look like through another's eyes. As the child comes to take the role of the other, she comes to see *herself* as others see her. Thus, the sense of self that one acquires is one of the key outcomes of primary socialization.

3. **The concrete operational stage** (ages seven through twelve). During this stage the child learns "conservation rules." Before the concrete operational stage, for example, Piaget points out that a child believes there to be more water in a tall and skinny glass than a short fat glass, even if the child sees the water being poured back and forth between the two glasses so that no water is lost and no water is gained. Once in the concrete operational stage, the child recognizes that the *amount* of water is constant, regardless of whether it is in a tall skinny glass or short fat glass. This then serves as the basis to address complex problems, but only with *physical* manipulation. We might mention here that even some normal adults never go beyond this stage.

4. **The formal operational stage** (ages twelve and above). The child learns full symbolic manipulation of mind and abstract theoretical thought during this stage. Knowl-

edge of this stage gives us a way of making sense of the social awkwardness often found among adolescents. For Piaget, it is no accident that adolescents beginning at about age twelve frequently tend to get into arguments with adults, especially adult authority figures such as their parents and teachers. The child first begins to test her reasoning capacities during this time. An important way in which this testing takes place is in debating abstract ideas with others capable of carrying on a discussion at this level.

The existence of cognitive structures limits what can be learned at a given time and suggests certain "critical periods" for learning. According to Piaget's theory, in other words, children tend not to learn things ahead of the appropriate critical period, and in fact can be traumatized by being forced to learn under such circumstances. For example, it does no good to insist that a child who has not passed into the formal operational stage, and who therefore does not yet have the intellectual capability, should learn analytic geometry.

We can witness the dramatic effects of these processes in the case of so-called **feral children**—that is, children who have grown up and passed through several of these critical periods without learning a language and the norms and beliefs attendant to a society. Research indicates these people may in fact never be able to learn a language. The "Wild Boy of Aveyron" is an example of this. Discovered in 1800 running around on all fours with a pack of wolves in woods around Aveyron, France, he was captured and brought into civilization. However, he was unable to acquire even basic language skills and was viewed for the rest of his life as severely retarded.

Thus, a number of key processes occur during primary socialization. One of the very most important of these is the acquisition of symbols we use to communicate and through which we perceive the world. It is upon these symbols and the relationships among them that our subsequent learning and knowledge are built. We now turn our attention to **social cognition**, the study of how people come to acquire knowledge in a social context.

Social Cognition

The acquisition and use of knowledge are most often understood as psychological processes, yet they have profound social implications. Work by the philosopher Immanuel Kant (1783/1950; 1781/1958) led to the development of an idea of **schemata** (plural form of **schema**), in which an individual develops abstract representational models for how the physical and social worlds are organized. A roadmap provides a useful analogy. The roadmap is not the same as the road itself, yet it gives its reader a sense of what to expect—what lies ahead on the road and how far to go before the destination. In this same way, a schema provides an overall framework for what the person is likely to expect in a given situation.

Re-introduced to the social sciences in the twentieth century by Jean Piaget (1951, 1952, 1954), and by Frederick Bartlett (1932), schemata can be seen as interrelated sets of rules for prioritizing new information (for an in-depth discussion of schemata, see Fiske and Taylor 1991:96–179). At any given moment, we are taking in so much sensory information that that the sheer volume of it is potentially overwhelming. The prioritizing rules allow people to attend to the most pragmatically useful information by essentially ignoring other information.

Put another way, a schema also allows us to "fill in the blanks" in an ambiguous situation, starting from a few symbolic anchor points. (This "filling in the blank" process is quite similar to what ethnomethodologists call the et cetera principle," which we will discuss further in Chapter 4). Because of this process, it is not surprising there is a good deal of empirical evidence that people tend to "remember" things that are *consistent* with their overall schemata (e.g., Bransford and Johnson 1972; Brewer and Nakamura 1984).

Piaget goes on to articulate how a schema helps to organize new information, and to modify itself if sufficient evidence comes in that is contradictory to it. A person adds new information onto her or his store of knowledge through the process of **assimilation**; that information is categorized in ways consistent with the person's schemata. Having a schema that incorrectly models reality exacts a cost in rendering the individual ineffective or even self-destructive, albeit unintentionally, when relating to the outside world (Crocker et al. 1984; Taylor et al. 1978).

If incoming information is consistent with the schema, it tends to reinforce the schematic structure, and the details of the specific consistent piece of information tend to be forgotten. However, **cognitive dissonance** occurs when new information does not fit well into existing conceptual categories (Festinger 1957). This dissonant information accumulates until the person reorganizes the schema to make the conflicting information compatible in a cognitive process known as **accommodation**. (Weber and Crocker 1983). The new schema, ideally, accounts for both the old and the new information.

While the term **"schema"** is itself a somewhat abstract concept, some researchers have attempted to focus on those aspects of information processing that are empirically verifiable. One such empirical approach has been to attempt to describe **semantic networks**, or associations that people make among bits of information that are organized into a coherent knowledge base (Smith et al. 1974; Anderson 1983). In the semantic networks people segue between, or connect, different bits of information. For example, in the semantic network of someone accustomed to perceiving cats and dogs as common house pets, the concepts of "cat" and "dog" may be closely associated, while such an association is less likely in the semantic network of one for whom said perception is not the case. Semantic networks develop out of the commonalities found among "chunks" of perceived information. These commonalities can be found spontaneously, but almost invariably are found in social and cultural contexts.

How do people construct schemata, or semantic networks, in the first place and, once constructed, how are they changed? To address this, the theory draws a distinction between **episodic memory**, or the memory for specific experiences (or "episodes") that happen and can be remembered as such; and **semantic memory**, a sense of "the way things are generally" (Tulving 1972).

Through learning related facts in specific "episodic" moments, a person comes to develop a "semantic" network of how those facts and episodes are related to one another (Tulving 1972; Neely 1989). In a process of **induction**, the semantic network is no longer grounded in specifics, but becomes a model for how phenomena cohere *in general*. Members of a culture tend to formulate schemata, or semantic networks, for how the world works in general, and more specifically for their respective places in it. These collective considerations feed back to the individual.

In other words, cultural categories include schemata for what one's own place is in a society in addition to how society is structured in general. These self-schemata are subject to similar principles as schemata in general (e.g., Markus 1977). In this way, schemata serve as an important way of organizing communication between the individual and the society (Kunda and Nisbett 1988).

An even more inertial model of a "perceptual cycle" was developed by Ulric Neisser (1976), in which information that is too foreign relative to the schema is simply not perceived at all. This idea tends to receive at least qualified support from recent research into the human "orienting response" (Maltzman 1990; Sokolov 1990), which indicates that a person will selectively attend to some stimuli while disregarding others. A stimulus's practical implication for the person's survival is the best predictor of attention given to it. Put another way, we attend carefully to stimuli that matter to our life or death, but we can safely ignore others that are of little consequence to our survival. This is a key starting point of symbolic interactionism that we consider in the next chapter.

There appears to be support for the idea that schemata learned in the early years tend to endure although there is some disagreement among cognitive psychologists themselves about the precise details of how the process takes place. Certainly, they are modified as a result of personal crises, and crisis becomes a way, and perhaps the most effective way, to break into the perceptual cycle and significantly alter schemata once those schemata are firmly in place.

Yet schemata develop a type of counter-revolutionary inertia. As a person gets older, Piaget points out, schematic accommodations are less likely to occur. Each individual is born into a world in some specific place and time, and that specific circumstance tends to come with its own set of institutions and roles that have already been largely defined long before we arrived. We then learn of those institutions and roles through socialization processes.

In summary, people use schemata as follows:

- Because the volume of incoming information is too much to process all at once, we utilize prioritization rules to selectively process some aspects of available information and to ignore others.
- While prioritizing has pragmatic value by allowing us to process *some* information, prioritization rules necessarily *distort* information by focusing on some aspects at the expense of others. Thus, memory by its very nature necessarily involves some distortion.
- Semantic memory develops out of the commonalities found among chunks of perceived information. These commonalities are almost invariably encountered in a social context.
- Cultural similarities can be understood as similarities in ways of prioritizing and making sense of information.

Sociology of Emotions, Stress and Coping

Over a century ago, Charles Darwin ([1872] 1965) described how emotions carry survival benefits for human beings. Since then, a great deal of evidence has arisen indicating that the feeling and expression of emotions have been instrumental in the survival of the human species. Fear and anger, for example, are useful in energizing a person for a "fight or flight" response to some dangerous situation; satisfaction orients someone to get needed rest, and in itself serves as a reward for successfully obtaining some goal (Kemper 1987; Plutchik 1980).

While virtually no one would deny the existence of human emotions, there is a certain element of controversy surrounding exactly what emotions are and how they come to be felt the way they do. Because they have such profound implications for society in general, as well as the individuals experiencing them, the study of emotions has assumed a prominent place among sociological researchers.

Recent work in the sociology of emotions indicates that even in something as personal as emotions, what a person feels is often influenced by a complex set of interactions among heredity and environmental components. While some researchers propose that emotions are strictly physiological in nature, others, known as social constructionists, argue that emotions are also profoundly influenced by social factors.

Traditionally, social scientists had thought that emotion was solely a physiological process centered in parts of the brain, such as the thalamus or cortex (e.g., Cannon 1929). In a landmark study in 1962, Stanley Schacter and Jerome Singer demonstrated that a person's emotional response to a given situation is a result of both physiological responses as well as the individual's interpretation of the situation.

The details of their study are interesting. Schacter and Singer (1962) gave epinephrine (adrenaline) to people in the study. The physiological responses to adrenaline include shakiness and an increased heart rate. The experimenters then suggested various reasons for *why* the participants were experiencing shakiness and an increased heart rate, in other words, offering different **contextual cues**. These cues included such things as verbal explanations for the physiological responses; further, different co-participants in the study demonstrated different kinds of behavior to different groups. The different contextual cues produced different emotional responses. The presence of the epinephrine led to a heightening of the emotion, but the emotion itself (e.g., happiness or anger) was largely a function of the contextual cues.

Considering that both cognition and physiology are involved in emotion, we may ask ourselves, which one precedes the other—physiological arousal or a cognitive interpretation of the situation? Richard Lazarus (1991; Lazarus et al. 1980) proposes that the first reaction to a situation is a cognitive appraisal of it. Only if and when a person perceives the event as having pragmatic consequences (either positive or negative), does he or she respond physiologically. The resulting emotion, then, is a function of a cognitive response, followed by a physiological one.

The implication of Schacter and Singer's work, and the research stemming from it, is that emotion is not just a physiological process. A crucial component of emotion is cognitive and, as we have seen, cognition occurs in a social context.

Building on earlier research, such as that of Schacter and Singer, Theodore Kemper (1978, 1981, 1987) develops a sociological theory of emotions. Kemper (1987) finds evidence for four physiologically grounded **primary emotions**. Namely, he describes four distinct physiological processes, or actual bodily reactions, with associated emotional concomitants (e.g., fear and the release of adrenaline). The emotions most closely associated with these are *fear, anger, depression,* and *satisfaction*. Other researchers have reached similar conclusions (e.g., Epstein 1984; Fehr and Russell 1984; Shaver and Schwartz 1984; Trevarthen 1984), finding evidence for four or five primary emotions: fear, anger, sadness, joy (or happiness), and love.

In each case, the primary emotion is correspondent to some particular physiological response, in addition to some social construction of the situation. The emotion of depression serves as an example in this regard. It tends to inhibit activity, may be instrumental in the person, and serves as a mechanism of adapting to some loss of social status or power (Kemper 1987; Price 1967; Henry and Stephens 1977). This serves the function of allowing the person to do the internal work in which one's thinking accommodates the new status. Such a loss of status takes some time to work through all its implications, and the "down time" of depression allows for such processing to occur. Additionally, by keeping activity to a minimum, the person may be able to avoid other problems, such as the provocation of anger in some other higher status person.

Kemper (1987) summarizes how emotions are based in physiological responses and are also a function of the larger society:

> An emotion-poor culture differentiates fewer emotions because its social life is less differentiated...Where social patterns are more complex, social construction differentiates emotional life more finely in order to accommodate the greater variety of socially differentiated conditions. But even these new emotions, if they are experienced as emotions, must contain their connections with the autonomic substrate that is available through linkages with the primary emotions. (P. 284)

It follows, then, that emotional development is an integral part of human development. It is intimately linked to other processes attendant to the social system, such as social differentiation.

Conclusion

Individual development occurs in a social context. Even experiences of human life that are seen as highly individual, such as emotions, cognition, and self-concept, are strongly informed by the society in which they occur and in which the individual develops. In this chapter, we have discussed several ways in which an individual's society exerts a profound effect on the ways in which that individual experiences the world, not only objectively, but subjectively as well.

CHAPTER SUMMARY

- The learning of language, norms, values, beliefs and roles, and the development of relationships with significant others are aspects of socialization.
- Primary socialization happens in our lives first by the most important people to us, and therefore it is foundational to the way we see reality from that point forward.
- Secondary socialization happens at later times in our lives, any time one enters a new group. It emphasizes fitting into the new group, such as the acquisition of a new skill. What we learn here is filtered through the grids of reality established in primary socialization.
- Stage theories focus on internal processes or "nature," emphasizing that one stage typically is worked through before another can begin in earnest.
- Even individual cognition is influenced by social factors. This is because people learn to process information in a social context.
- How a person prioritizes information is a vital aspect of culture that is manifested on the individual level.
- Interaction theories emphasize how the external environment influences, or "nurtures" the individual.
- Social and cultural factors profoundly affect the way an individual experiences emotions.

4 Social Interaction at the Micro Level: The Sociology of Subjective Experience

How do we come to see and to talk about the world in the ways we do, and how does that influence how we act? These questions have been engaged by many sociologists in great detail. W.I. Thomas, an early sociologist, in his 1928 work The Child in America: Behavior Problems and Programs, expressed a central tenet of the **social definition** approach when he said: "If men define situations as real, they are real in their consequences." This often quoted expression, (or a variant, such as one substituting the word "people" for "men") has come to be known as **Thomas's dictum**. It will be helpful to keep this dictum in mind as we discuss the social definition approach.

Thomas's dictum helps to make sense of what happened to one of the authors of this book (Burns) who once rode a bicycle from Maryland to Florida in college. On the way, he had a memorable experience, recalled in the following way:

> Riding on a nearly deserted road in rural North Carolina, I heard a car coming up from behind, quickly approaching my friend and me on our bikes. We got as far to the side of the road as we could, but the narrow and shoulderless road didn't afford us much space. Every time we looked back, it came closer and closer. It just kept bearing down. It whistled by at what had to have been over one hundred miles per hour, passing so close that our bicycles were caught in the wind of the displaced air. In my mind, I was certain that I had literally come within inches of being killed or seriously injured. Afterwards, I could think of little else than my near-death experience and the driver's disregard for other human beings.
>
> I continued stewing about this (aided by the blistering North Carolina sun). When we arrived to a town a few miles later (one with a hospital—no doubt the one I would have been relying upon to save my life had I been hit), I noticed the same car and several people nearby. My heart was pounding in my chest and every muscle was ready for a confrontation with the driver. Normally a non-violent sort of a fellow, I was ready to knock his block off (even if mine were to be knocked off in the process)!
>
> "Whose car is this?" I fumed.
>
> "It's my car."
>
> "You very nearly killed us."
>
> "You're the guys on the bicycles. I tried to honk the horn to warn you." His eyes cast down. "I had to rush my mother to the hospital. She's in the emergency room right now. They don't know whether she's going to make it or not. We're here praying for her."

Immediately, my hostility towards the man subsided. If anything, I even felt a bit guilty for having become so angry with someone who merely had been doing his best to help a loved one in an emergency.

What was defined as real? The near-death experience was at first attributed to the driver's recklessness, for which there was no excuse. Yet, once the driver had explained the situation, there was suddenly a convincing excuse that "chilled out" the irate bicyclist and even filling him with sympathy and perhaps even a twinge of guilt for being angry at someone whose overriding concern was his ailing mother.

The objective reality remained that the driver had come dangerously near the cyclists, but the relevant lesson was that, after learning the facts, the *subjective* reality drastically shifted. The social construction went from one of recklessness and perhaps criminal negligence, to an emergency that called for immediate dramatic action. Upon receiving an explanation from the driver of the car, the bicyclist's anger was immediately defused, and the probability of a confrontation was nullified.

Sociologists working from a social definition perspective emphasize the **subjective meaning a person places on a situation.** How do people make sense out of their experiences? Why do some people see the world as threatening while others see it as nurturing? While subjects like these may present more difficulties in their study than more objective situations, such as mapping income distribution or birthrate of a population, for example, it does not mean they are less important.

What allows us to understand another person's subjective reality? From a social definition perspective, a person's use of symbols, especially the highly elaborate symbolic system of *language*, is of central importance. For this reason, a common thread among sociologists working from a social definition perspective is the focus on use and exchange of symbols.

A related question is how people focus their attention. All around us, there is a constant multitude of sense experiences, and we tend to focus our attention on some particular aspect of those experiences, as we saw in our discussion of cognition in the previous chapter. Thus, the same "objective" reality is likely to be experienced quite differently by different people, depending upon what aspects of that objective reality they focus upon as it is happening, and also later when reflecting upon and discussing it.

Thus, which perceptions of experience are defined as real depends largely on: **1)** what aspects of the overall experience a person focuses on at the time it happens; **2)** the language the person uses to label the experience at the time it happens; **3)** how the person organizes it in memory; and **4)** how the person thinks about and discusses the experience later. We can see all four of these coalescing in the previous anecdote about the bicycles and the motorist, including how the experience itself is remembered and discussed in this very chapter.

Human behavior is motivated by subjective experience. From this perspective, it is the **definition** of a social situation that makes, literally, all the difference in the world. How do people arrive at their subjective definitions of the world? And what do sociologists know about the process of doing so, for that matter? Several analytically distinct—yet by no means mutually exclusive—intellectual traditions shed light on the question. These include symbolic interactionism, phenomenology, ethnomethodology, dramatism and dramaturgy, and the sociology of knowledge. We will direct our attention to each of these in turn, concluding the chapter with an in-depth discussion of a sociology of knowledge approach, which builds on and synthesizes many of the other ideas.

In each of the approaches, a common theme is the paramount importance of how a situation is socially constructed. The use of symbols, namely language, acts as a major vehicle for this construction. Those symbol systems are external to social actors, but they are internal to individuals as well. An integrated view of the particulars of this process can be found in symbolic interactionism, to which we now turn.

Symbolic Interactionism

Symbols are of primary importance in this approach. A symbol is a noticeable sign that stands for something, and can be used to represent that thing in thought and language, in order for an individual or group to plan or coordinate activity. The relationship between a symbol and what it represents is generally arbitrary. Consider the relationship between the word "car" and the automobile it represents, for example—there is nothing inherent in the word "car" itself that would necessarily tie it to the object it represents. Rather, the object and the symbol for it are connected by social convention.

When a given symbol means the same thing to both the person communicating it and to the person it is communicated to, it is said to be a **significant symbol**. When using significant symbols, the people communicating are engaging in symbolic interaction, and the focus in symbolic interactionism is on the use and exchange of these significant symbols. However, symbols have other uses besides merely representing objects. Because thought generally precedes any sort of meaningful action by an individual, and thought itself involves the use of symbols, symbols often are used to *transform* the natural and social environments of human beings (Hewitt 1997:34).

Thus, because thought is always about something, and whatever it is about can be represented symbolically, even human thought itself, in its most fundamental sense, is dependent upon the use of symbols. Thus, for symbolic interactionists, in order to communicate, to think, and also to have a sense of who we are as individuals, requires that we use a set of symbols. Those symbols in turn derive largely from the culture of which we are part, and in which we act. A large part of a culture, in fact, is the set of symbols that the people in it share.

Many of the important points of symbolic interactionism can be organized around the key feature of **symbolic classifications** that people make (e.g., Blumer 1969; Stryker 1981; Fine 1990; Charon 1992; Hewitt 1997). Symbolic classifications are the words that a person uses to categorize and characterize their experiences. When a person observes some behavior by another, to the extent it has any meaning at all, the person tends to attach a label to the other's behavior.

Consider, for example, a group of students hearing a professor making a remark. The first student immediately either finds it informative, funny, offensive, or perhaps none of these things at all. In other words, the student categorizes the remark in a number of ways, and may do so *even without consciously thinking about it*. More than one student may observe the same thing, yet may categorize it quite differently. In this case, the heard remark was *objectively* the same to two different observers, yet one of them may classify the professor as funny, while the other may classify the professor as obnoxious.

These perceptions have tremendous social consequences. People's behaviors are largely dependent upon the subjective *meanings* they attribute to their perceptions of the world around them. Those meanings are a function of the *subjective* ways in which we interpret our experiences, which in turn are largely the result of how we symbolically classify the world. What this means is that how we see the world is chiefly a function of the symbols with which we perceive it.

Symbols, such as the words we use to describe things and the relationships among those words, are learned as part of the socialization process. The most important aspect of socialization takes place early in life in what Charles Horton Cooley (1916) termed **primary groups**, which are groups "characterized by intimate face-to-face associations and co-operation" such as the family. We first learn to make sense of our world as a social place in these primary groups.

One of the most important things we must do in a social world is to understand our own place in it, and it is largely in the primary group that we come to develop a sense of who we are. Cooley characterized this self-definition process as the **looking-glass self** to emphasize his observation that we come to perceive ourselves as we believe significant others perceive us.

Charles Horton Cooley (1864 - 1929)

Cooley's **looking-glass self** emphasized his observation that we come to perceive ourselves as we believe significant others perceive us.

As we develop a symbol system, we develop with it a set of shared behavioral expectations that stem from interaction with others. Based largely on these expectations, people tend to define situations as they enter them. This social definition process involves defining the situation (e.g., classroom, wedding, bar room, fist fight, walk in the park, etc.), identifying the other people involved (e.g., salesperson, bride, groom, friend, jerk, etc.), and naming one's own role in the situation.

These early definitions constrain us to some degree, as we tend to gear our behavior relative to them. Definitions that are different from those of others in the same situation often tend to be "negotiated" through symbolic exchange with others, and thereby a situation can come to be re-defined. Thus, as symbolic interactionists understand it, social situations are not at all set in stone, but rather, quite fluid and open to change.

In order to fully understand the symbolic interactionist perspective, a brief summary of its historical origins is in order. Although Herbert Blumer first coined the term "symbolic interactionism" in the 1930s, it was three early twentieth century academics, George Herbert Mead, Charles Horton Cooley and W.I. Thomas who were most instrumental in the development of symbolic interactionism. The contributions of all three emphasize the *subjective* nature of human existence. In this approach, even macro-level societal institutions are seen as inter-subjective constructions, or the products of a *shared symbol system*.

A compilation of George Herbert Mead's (1934) lectures, in a book entitled *Mind, Self and Society: From the Standpoint of a Social Behaviorist*, was the first systematic statement of principles that would come to be known as symbolic interactionism. Three major schools of thought in particular influenced Mead in the construction of his manifesto—Darwinism, Pragmatism, and Behaviorism.

Darwinism. As it stands, human beings cannot compete with animals such as tigers or oxen in terms of physical prowess. However, our ability to use **symbols** gives us a *competitive advantage*, in that it allows us to: **1)** plan and coordinate activity; and **2)** mentally rehearse before acting. In this sense, the most important use of symbols is language.

Pragmatism. Rather than knowledge being based on objective reality, it has meaning only insofar as its potential in serving some specific purpose. This is sometimes referred to as **instrumentality**. The meaning something has is specifically the response it precipitates in the individual, but the meaning *itself* is mediated by symbols. Put another way, in pragmatism, there is no such thing as "pure" perception of something "as is."

In other words, not only is it the thing being perceived, but also the *categories* we use to perceive it, as well as the use we see for it, that determine the way we perceive something.

Behaviorism. Human behavior can be seen as driven by the desire to *maximize rewards* and *minimize punishments*. However, consistent with his pragmatic leanings, Mead believed that the stimulus *itself* was of far less importance than its *subjective* meaning (based on the way a person categorized the stimulus, and how useful to the person it was likely to be).

Rather than focusing on material rewards such as food and water, and material punishments such as electric shock, symbolic interactionists preferred to emphasize rewards (or punishments) resulting from interaction with others as the primary motivators of human behavior. W.I. Thomas (1951/1961) described four "forces which impel action": **1)** the desire for *new experience*; **2)** the desire for *security*; **3)** the desire for *response*; and **4)** the desire for *recognition*. These social desires often override even physical desires. Because they are met primarily in a social context, in seeking these four desires, human beings tend to monitor how others are likely to perceive their actions. This, in turn, is what primes people for socialization. It is thus not surprising, in the an-

George Herbert Mead (1863 - 1931)

George Herbert Mead's book, *Mind, Self and Society: From the Standpoint of a Social Behaviorist*, was the first systemic statement of principles that would become known as symbolic interactionism.

alytical framework of symbolic interaction, that people will sometimes engage in behavior that puts their own material being and safety at great risk in order to help others. Because we are social beings, it is not the material nearly so much as the social that motivates our actions.

Thus, for symbolic interactionists, the *social* nature of the self cannot be emphasized enough. In this sense, Mead articulated Cooley's concept of the looking-glass self to assert that the basic human need to feel esteemed in the eyes of others is of critical importance, because it is precisely this need for esteem that makes human beings willing to internalize the norms that make it possible for society to function.

The pronouns **I** and **me** have distinctive meanings to the symbolic interactionist—people are not only *subjective* perceivers (what Mead referred to as the I), but can also be the *objects* of their own perceptions (the **me** part of the self). Even a person's own *individual thoughts* are largely comprised of mental rehearsal of social activity, according to Mead. This is commonly referred to as **taking the role of the other**, and requires using a system of symbols to represent one's own behavior and the behavior of others. You have been in countless situations yourself in which you were both a subjective perceiver of the situation, and an object of perception to others but also to yourself. Anytime you have a quick thought like "How am I doing in this situation?" or "What does she think of me now that I have just insulted her?" you are doing what Mead meant by taking the role of the other.

The ability to take the role of the other, or to see things from the perspective of another person, is an essential social skill that most people develop in varying degrees as part of growing up. Success in many of the activities we do in life depends upon this ability. Take the game of baseball, for instance. In order to be an effective batter, one should be able to anticipate what kind of pitch is likely to be thrown, where the fielders are likely to be standing, and so on. The pitcher and the fielders, for their part, are also trying to put themselves in the place of the batter in order to figure out how to throw the ball and play the field. Ted Williams, the last major league player to hit over .400 in a season, was able to do so in large part because of his well-developed ability to anticipate precisely where in the strike zone a pitch was likely to be thrown. After that season, although he remained a splendid hitter, Williams was never again to hit over .400, largely because fielders figured out where Williams was most likely to hit the ball (a disproportionate number of hits had been in the "alley" in right-center field), and to shift into position in anticipation of that.

This ability to take the role of the other has several important consequences for the individual and for the society that go far beyond the world of sports. In symbolic interactionist terms, the ability to take the role of the other is essential in a mature, fully functional human being; conversely, some types of adult mental illness stem from the *inability* to take the role of the other.

Once someone learns to take the role of the other, that person is able to develop a sense of how "other people" in society are likely to behave in a given set of circumstances. Mead refers to this sense as the **generalized other**. The internalization of norms and other rules of behavior stems from this view of what "society" is like, so also does the ability to engage in abstract thought. As Mead (1934/1962) expresses it:

The very universality and impersonality of thought and reason is from the behavioristic standpoint the result of the given individual taking the attitudes of others toward himself, and of his finally crystallizing all these particular attitudes into a single attitude or standpoint which may be called that of the 'generalized other.' (P. 90)

Once a person has developed a sense of the generalized other to complement the sense of one's self, the person has been sufficiently socialized to be a "member of society" in the full sense. In fact, there is now such a strong bond between the self and society that, in the words of Charles Horton Cooley (1902):

'Society' and 'individuals' do not denote separable phenomena, but are simply collective and distributive aspects of the same thing. (P. 1-2)

A socialized person has such an elaborate set of symbols for oneself, significant others, and the generalized other, that the person is part of society, *even when alone*. In these terms, what we normally think of as "conscience" is a person regulating one's own behavior relative to the symbols for self and others—*whether or not those others are physically present*. Further, a person's significant others could physically be long dead and buried, but "alive" in the sense of the mental images of them the person continues to carry. Thus, it is in the milieu of these symbols that an individual's view of the world, and therefore much of his or her behavior, takes place.

Building on the work of Mead, Cooley and Thomas, Herbert Blumer argued that the essence of society is found in "actors and action," and that people largely create their own social reality. To address the question of society's relevance to the individual, Blumer developed the concept of **joint acts**, which arise through repetitive or habitual behavior patterns. The meaning of these joint acts is established inter-subjectively through culturally embedded symbols. While these joint acts are the framework giving meaning to individual behavior, this framework does not determine one's behavior.

Manford Kuhn was the first in the symbolic interactionist tradition to develop empirical measures of subjective phenomena such as one's self-perceptions. The best known of his instruments is the **Who Am I Test**—a twenty-question battery designed to measure empirically how a person views oneself. During the evaluation, participants are instructed to describe themselves in terms of social constructions such as roles (e.g., sister, student), and expressive adjectives (e.g., kind, timid).

From this theoretical base arose subsequent symbolic interactionist work. Some of the other people who made important theoretical breakthroughs were Sheldon Stryker, a theorist attempting to integrate symbolic interactionism with approaches which focus more on social structure; Morris Rosenberg, who used a symbolic interactionist perspective to develop an elaborate theory of self-concept and mental health; and Tamotsu Shibutani, a researcher investigating the importance of *reference groups*, or groups of significant others and their importance in contributing to how an individual comes to see and behave in the world.

Many insights into how humans think and communicate can be found in symbolic interactionism. Its strength lies in using the sociological imagination in the interpretation of subjective processes. It has been criticized for largely ignoring the macro-structural aspects of society, such as social class. *Those* parts of the sociological imagination are better addressed in later chapters, such as those on stratification.

Research in Social Interaction and the Socialization Process: Developing Our Self-Concept

Our self-concept— the way we see ourselves, is a key social psychological and social variable. A number of sociologists, especially those in the symbolic interaction tradition, see the formation of the self-concept as the *central* process of socialization (Stryker 1980; Gecas 1981; Rosenberg 1979, 1981). How does our self-concept form? That is, how do we come to believe we know who we are? After spending much of his career posing these sorts of questions, Morris Rosenberg (1979, 1981) identified **four principles of self-concept formation**: reflected appraisals; social comparisons; self attributions; and psychological centrality.

1. **Reflected appraisals.** We come to see ourselves, as we believe others see us, as the intellectual progenitors of symbolic interaction theory pointed out. Charles Horton Cooley makes this point in articulating his ideas of a "looking-glass self," and George Herbert Mead theorized that we come to see ourselves as we believe significant others see us. If during our socialization process, people view us as smart, strong or tall, and they give us repeated messages to that effect, we tend to internalize those messages—over time, to make them part of the way we think about ourselves. We come to see ourselves in those terms.

Rosenberg (1973) posed the question of *which* significant others' reflected appraisals are most influential on our self-concept. He found that, over time, people giving us positive messages about ourselves tend to become more significant, while those giving us negative messages become less so. However, there is a major exception to this—during primary socialization, we tend to internalize appraisals of significant others, even if they are quite negative. We then gradually render them less significant, beginning *only after having gone through* primary socialization. The reflected appraisals of significant others, in sum, are a major component of the socialization process.

2. **Social comparisons.** No matter what social system we're born into or how primitive or modern the society, a universal aspect of human nature is to compare ourselves with other people. In a society of very short people, such as Pygmies, persons who are five feet tall would see themselves as tall, while in a society of very tall people, a person five feet tall would tend to see herself as short. In this way, how we formulate our self-concepts stems largely from how we compare to other people in our social experience.

3. **Self-attributions.** In addition to being subject to reflected appraisals and social comparisons, we also tend to see outcomes as a result of some cause. The attributed cause may be internal (seeing ourselves, or some trait internal to us, as the cause of our actions); or that cause may be external (as in another person, or external circumstances, such as the weather or some social institution).

   In this scenario, an interesting defense mechanism of the ego comes into play. When something positive happens to us, such as getting a raise for example, we tend to attribute that outcome to some inherent trait such as strength of character. However, when something negative happens to us, such as being fired from a job, we tend to attribute the negative occurrence to external circumstances. This is sometimes referred to as the **fundamental attribution bias**—we tend to make attributions that are positive to ourselves or people with whom we are closely linked, while making negative attributions to others, especially those with whom we have little in common. Considering the number of situations in life that are potentially gray areas—that is to say areas in which all the information is not available to make an objective decision—the implications of this fundamental attribution bias are profound.

4. **Psychological centrality.** If something occurs that we do not perceive as central to our being, it tends to have little effect on our self-concept. When a competitive cyclist loses a race, for example, does this have a negative effect on his self-concept? Simply having the objective information that a person loses a race will not tell us that. What we need to know is how *central* it is to a person's subjective being. For someone who defines his entire self around being a cyclist, losing a race may be a devastating experience. Such a case indeed is likely to have a negative effect on one's self-concept. For someone who is cycling in the race but for whom that particular race is not important, losing it or winning it has little effect on one's self concept.

   In turn, an astonishing number of social outcomes are significantly impacted by our self-esteem. For example, a large body of empirical research indicates that self-esteem has a *positive* effect on a number of desirable social outcomes, such as academic performance (Brookover et al. 1964), occupational attainment (Wang et al. 1999), and participation in public affairs (e.g., Rosenberg 1954-55, 1981; Carmines 1978). Self-esteem also has a *negative* effect on a number of undesirable social outcomes, such as the likelihood of engaging in deviant behavior (Kaplan 1976 1980), and social distress (Pearlin and Lieberman 1979).

Phenomenology

While many social theories take "social facts" such as class, structure, status, norms, roles, etc. as a given, social construction of reality theorists focus on human construction of what is real. Their approach is based on phenomenology, which questions how these come to be viewed as real in the first place. The philosophers Edmund Husserl and Martin Heidegger initiated early questions in phenomenology. The starting point for their philosophy was the crucial distinction Immanuel Kant drew between **noumenon** (plural form: noumena) and **phenomenon** (plural form: phenomena). According to Kant, the **noumenon** is what actually exists—it is the same regardless of how it is perceived. The **phenomenon**, on the other hand, is the human representation of the noumenon, which is obscured by our incomplete and faulty sense perception and limitations in our capacity to reason. Noumena, in other words, can be thought of as objective, while phenomena are subjective.

According to phenomenologists, noumena are unknowable through the normal human capacities of sense and reason. Because of this, phenomena, or imperfect representations of reality, are all that we know. A succinct metaphor for virtually all human perception can be summed up in the *Parable of the Blind Men and the Elephant*: the blind man who holds the tusk believes an elephant is like a sword, the blind man who holds the leg believes the elephant is like a tree, etc. The important point is not so much that each is wrong, but that each has only a part of the larger truth.

Phenomenologists distinguish between the **"natural attitude"** on one hand and the **"phenomenological attitude"** on the other. Ordinary people under ordinary circumstances hold the natural attitude (or **life world**, as is referred to alternately. It has several component processes:

- People act as though an objective world exists as they perceive it.
- People assume that other people think and perceive things in the same way as they themselves do.
- Over time, these perceptions and behavior become routinized, which in turn gives the impression of stability of an objective world.
- In order to maintain that stability, as new and unfamiliar information is perceived, a person attempts to fit the new information into existing categories to "make sense" of it.

These components of the natural attitude (especially the last) imply an underlying assumption that things that are truly new and unknown cause anxiety; thus, new perceptions only become comfortable when "sense" can be made of them by assigning them to familiar categories.

The phenomenological attitude, in contrast to the natural attitude, questions how we tend to make sense of the world around us. This is done by the technique of **bracketing** (which Husserl alternatively refers to as **epoche** in other writings). In bracketing a perception, an attempt is made by the perceiver to isolate a phenomenon from the perceptions of it. In so doing, the perceiver attempts to suspend judgment about what is being perceived. Through this process, **reduction** occurs in which insight is gained into the nature of subjective experience itself. For example, recall the story about the blind men and the elephant; reduction is the realization by each blind man that his perceptions are limited.

Since knowledge of the external world is mediated by the subjective experience of consciousness, only by first understanding consciousness itself (or "pure mind"), can we then hope to separate those aspects of perception produced by the object being perceived from the perceiver. Phenomenologists have tended to focus on how incomplete and inaccurate perceptions tend

Recipes
People generally follow typical procedures for dealing with experiences in everyday life, such as facing forward in a crowded elevator.

to limit people, and the adoption of the phenomenological attitude thus becomes an avenue toward liberation. Thus, the perceiver attempts to move from a *particular* way of perceiving to a more *universal* way of perceiving by adopting the phenomenological attitude.

While Husserl never really solved the problem of consciousness per se, the sociological implications of his project were recognized and developed by Alfred Schütz. Much of human thought and action, Schütz argued, takes place in less than a fully conscious state, which has a tremendous significance for the society at large.

Schütz maintained that most human interaction follows set ways of perceiving (which he termed **typifications**), and set procedures for acting (which he termed **recipes**). Recipes, for example, extend into many human relationships, but also include such mundane things as showering and getting dressed in the morning. There is a natural human tendency to follow habits and to expect others to do so as well. This gives the world the appearance of consistency and gives people a certain level of comfort. These recipes and typifications, which are learned in a social context, however, often replace more objective perceptions and spontaneous ways of acting, thereby tending to limit people from reaching their full potential as human beings.

Phenomenology has been criticized for placing an over-emphasis on human perception as the root of virtually all social problems, ignoring larger social structures by doing so. Furthermore, it has been criticized for failing to inspire a rigorous program of empirical research, although ethnomethodology, which owes a good deal of its intellectual inspiration to phenomenology, tends to foster some empirical investigation.

Ethnomethodology

Harold Garfinkel was interested in ways in which people make sense of the everyday, mundane world around them. Building on the insights of phenomenologists and other theorists, Garfinkel coined the term **ethnomethodology** to refer to the everyday methods used by people "in the street" to do this. The goal of ethnomethodology can be understood as providing insight into "the body of knowledge and the range of procedures and considerations by means of which the ordinary members of society make sense of, find their way about in, and act on circumstances in which they find themselves...[it is an] open-ended reference to any kind of sense-making procedure" (Heritage 1984:4-5).

Ethnomethodology, as in symbolic interactionism and phenomenology, emphasizes the use of language as a medium of constructing the social world. Because of this emphasis on language, a major activity of ethnomethodologists is conversation analysis (e.g., Sacks 1984; Schegloff 1968; Zimmerman 1988; Boden 1990). This method contains some distinctive aspects of ethnomethodology. In understanding its distinctiveness, a good place to begin is with the key concepts of "*indexicality*" and "*reflexivity*."

Indexicality (Garfinkel 1967:4 ff.) refers to the fact that social interactions and the language we use to talk about them, depending upon their *contexts*, take on different meanings. Even a sentence as simple as "It's raining" can have several different meanings, depending upon whether it has been raining for many days already, for example, or whether there has been a drought of late (Handel 1982). Further, to say "It's raining" to a loved one who is going outside may imply the meaning "Perhaps you should consider taking your raincoat or an umbrella." The same sentence to a child may, depending upon habitual practices (or "rules") of the household, be a negative response to the question "May I go out and play?"

Taken to its extreme, we could spend all day constructing different possible meanings from even the simple two-word sentence "It's raining." Just as a dictionary defines words in relation to other words, things have meaning only in relationship to other things, and those relationships are virtually limitless. Try reading a foreign dictionary (e.g., a Chinese dictionary for a person who does not know Chinese—not a Chinese-English dictionary, but one written entirely in Chinese), for example. The knowledge contained within the dictionary holds no meaning for us without some critical mass of prior knowledge to use as an "index" against which to compare it.

Broadly speaking, in addition to people having knowledge *about* things, we have knowledge *of* that knowledge. For instance, not only do you know *how* to ride a bicycle, you know that you *know*, and could probably discuss the "rules" of how to ride a bicycle. Garfinkel refers to this human tendency to reflect on and to talk about our practices as **reflexivity**. We reflect on our own behavior, and reflect the behavior of others. Similarly, we reflect not only on ourselves and other individuals, but also on the larger collectives of which we are part. This is quite similar to what symbolic interactionists refer to as "taking the role of the other," and the related process of seeing ourselves through the eyes of others via "reflected appraisals."

One of the key things we do in the process of reflexivity is to give **accounts** of our behavior. That is, we tend to discuss the reasons for our actions—not only with others, but with ourselves. Every reference to anything is indexical to something else, as we've seen, and any concept can be put in terms of other concepts. In giving accounts (or "accounting"), we discuss *which* context (of an otherwise potentially infinite number) to put something in. In this way, through accounting, it is often the case that we offer others a way to "make sense" of our behavior.

We generally use accounting with other people in order to establish a context upon which a common definition for the social situation at hand can be built. A significant part of establishing a common definition of a social situation is often directed to the **repair** of a situation in which a *breakdown* of common definition has taken place. In so doing, a person is likely to give accounts for behavior that otherwise threatens the comity of a situation, such as arriving late to a date. As an attempt at repair, in this context, the person might say something to the effect of "I came here as quickly as I could, my car got a flat tire on the interstate!" By attributing the cause to some external circumstance, the hope is to give repair to what might otherwise be construed as "He is late, he doesn't care about me. What an insensitive jerk. We should break up."

Thus, we tend to construct a social reality through the use of indexicality, reflexivity and accounting. From an ethnomethodological perspective, social reality is, specifically, a body of knowledge that *coheres* in some way (Mehan and Wood 1975). What makes knowledge coherent for a person is that it can be "indexed" by the person, and there are others with whom that person shares the same general understanding of its coherence.

When there is a coherent body of knowledge, people tend to have expectations that whatever happens will be consistent with that body of knowledge. People tend to "know" things that may not have explicitly occurred, but would be *likely* to have occurred, given the way they have socially constructed reality. As such, we tend to "fill in the blanks" accordingly, in a process referred to by ethnomethodologists as the **et cetera principle**.

To illustrate this principle, imagine that you've met someone who is a baseball fan from Baltimore. You may not know for *certain* that he would know the best way to get to the stadium at Camden Yards during rush hour. According to the et cetera principle, however, you would likely *assume* that the person does have such knowledge, because it would be consistent with other information you possess (viz. baseball fans tend to go to baseball games in their home town, many of the games probably start shortly after rush hour, going to such a game in Baltimore likely requires negotiating rush hour traffic, etc.). Whether or not true, the specific assumptions we make through the et cetera principle tend to serve as part of our overall sense of the way the world hangs together. It is on this overall sense that we are likely to base our behavior.

Thus, we tend to base our interpretations of reality on what we view as a coherent body of knowledge. What happens when some fundamental aspect of the way we construct the social world is challenged? Garfinkel (1967) refers to such challenges as a **breach**. In **breaching experiments**, Garfinkel had his students deliberately violate some social convention (and therefore, presumably, the underlying social reality of which it was a reflection). By this, he hoped to gain insight into the ways in which people go about constructing social reality in the first place, and in repairing it when it is challenged.

One of these breaching experiments, for example, required students to treat their family members or friends as though they had just met them for the first time and knew nothing about the person they were meeting. At first, the reaction on the part of others tended to involve an attempt to repair the situation by giving an account such as "He's just in one of his moods again."

Typically, when a minor breach occurs, attempts at repairs may be made by the parties involved, either by ignoring the breach if possible, or by giving some account that upholds the overall way in which social reality is constructed. In the case of more serious or longer-lasting breaches, however, there is an implied threat to the entire way in which people construct their social reality—at least relative to the person initiating the breach. When this occurs, people tend to shun the individual or individuals causing that breach.

We can outline important aspects of the ethnomethodological perspective in the following way, drawing on work by Mehan and Wood (1975):

- **Social reality is constructed through social interaction.** Social reality is dependent on continuing interaction among people, rather than being objective, or something simply "out there."
- **Social reality is a coherent body of knowledge.** People tend to construct and maintain a sense that there is a coherent social reality through the indexicality of putting things in social context, and also through the process of "filling in the blanks" by way of the et cetera principle.
- **Social reality is reflexive.** We tend to have expectations of others and ourselves. These expectations include such everyday activities as saying hello to others in the hallway, and expecting the same from them. In this way, we reaffirm our social reality.
- **Social reality is fragile.** Because social reality is continually constructed and reconstructed through social interaction, it is subject to being "breached." When those breaches are minor, repairs are usually attempted; however, breaches are sometimes more serious and difficult to repair.
- **People often take part in several social worlds, and those worlds are "permeable."** A student may live in a "university world" part of the day, and a "working world" another part of the day, going back and forth between the two, for example. Each of these social worlds involves a distinct way of constructing social reality.

CHAPTER SUMMARY

- The social definition perspective emphasizes how people think about and communicate their social reality.
- Social definitions generally use symbols, which in turn are embedded in language.
- Symbols are such a fundamental aspect of the human experience that not only communication, but even thought itself, is dependent upon the acquisition and use of symbols.
- A primary way in which a person uses social definitions is in terms of how that person comes to acquire a sense of *self*. Thus, even the formation of something as personal as the self-concept is deeply affected by the social context in which a person develops.

5 Social Definition and the Social Construction of Reality

In this chapter, we build on our knowledge of socialization and symbol exchange, and broaden the inquiry to some of the larger social implications of those processes. To begin with, Peter Berger and Thomas Luckmann's work in the sociology of knowledge provides us with a systematic example of how the social definition perspective can be applied to the understanding of the larger social world. With a firm foundation in the framework of phenomenology, it brings together many of the elements we have discussed thus far, and extends our analysis well beyond individual symbol usage into the larger social world. Let us then begin the chapter with an extended discussion of this landmark work in sociological analysis. Afterwards, we'll turn our focus towards the more philosophical foundation for Berger and Luckmann's work, found in the writings of phenomenologists Husserl and Schütz, and reflected in modern studies of ethnomethodologists.

The Social Construction of Reality

Peter Berger and Thomas Luckmann (1967) begin their classic work *The Social Construction of Reality: A Treatise in the Sociology of Knowledge* with a deceptively simple question: How do subjective experiences and the meanings associated with them become "objective?" They point out that social institutions often seem to take on a life of their own despite the fact that they are created from human interaction. Like Durkheim's social facts, those institutions become external to, and coercive of, the people coming into contact with them. Berger and Luckmann define social "reality" as something independent of people's volition—something that cannot be wished away. Similarly, they define *knowledge* as "the certainty that phenomena are real and that they possess specific characteristics."

The construction of the social order stems from human interaction, which Berger and Luckmann describe as an "ongoing human production." To make sense of this process, they build upon the work of phenomenologists, especially that of Alfred Schütz. Like Schütz, they make a distinction between the natural attitude and the phenomenological attitude (or "the theoretical attitude of the philosopher"). Those aspects of everyday life that people perceive as "real" are those which they take for granted, according to Berger and Luckmann.

Much of this quality of being taken for granted is reflected in the *language* we use to describe and even to think about things. Thus, groups tend to evolve their own languages with which to talk about things that are very real to them. As a matter of fact, as a student of sociology, one of the most important things you are doing right now by reading this is learning the language of sociologists. The implications of this extend far beyond accumulating a collection of "buzz words." Rather, use of a language implies a way of perceiving the world, as we've seen. This does not mean that people speaking the same language don't disagree, for indeed they often do. Instead, the important point is that these people tend to take for granted certain first principles, which sometimes are referred to as *prolegomena*.

Prolegomena are the underpinnings of discussion and of thought (the word, taken from Greek, literally means "before saying," such as is expressed in the common phrase "it goes without saying"). These are the "givens" in a person's or a group's perception of reality. Our language and even our thoughts arise from these prolegomena, which we typically take for granted. Individual or group disagreements often stem from conflicting prolegomena, or from conflicting views of what is just "common sense."

Consider, for instance, the protracted debate surrounding abortion in the United States and around the world, at least since the *Roe v. Wade* decision by the US Supreme Court in 1972. These debates often are characterized by bitterness and the perception of the other side as just not being "reasonable."

Even beyond the *overt* disagreement or conflict, each side *perceives* the world in radically different terms, and has different vocabularies with which to describe it. For one side, life is sacred, it begins at conception, and there is nothing that can be said or done to change that. For the other side, the right to determine one's own destiny, including the right to choose the destiny over one's own body, is paramount. No amount of discussion or debate is likely to change anyone's mind about the matter because these assumptions are basic to the people themselves.

How do these unshakable ways of knowing what is "right" come about? Every society has a way of teaching its new members about how to be a part of the society. As we saw earlier in this book, socialization plays a central role here. Berger and Luckmann build on this knowledge of socialization.

Advanced industrial societies such as ours tend to have a highly elaborate division of labor. The greater the division of labor, according to Berger and Luckmann, the more we see relatively exclusive **sub-universes of meaning** (or bodies of knowledge that are distinct from, yet are embedded in, the overall culture). People acquire these sub-universes of meaning as part of the socialization process, particularly in *secondary* socialization.

For example, take a plumber and a lawyer. While both are part of the same overall culture, each of them would nonetheless be required to engage in their own distinct processes of secondary socialization. The plumber would probably have gone through an apprenticeship and journeyman process as part of secondary socialization, while the lawyer would have attended law school and various clerkships. Both individuals would then have a body of knowledge and vocabulary that was *exclusive of the other*—the lawyer would have a "legalese" sub-universe of meaning, in which phrases like *pendente lite* or *voir dire* would be part of the language he or she would share with other lawyers. Those other lawyers would understand what such phrases meant, and would have sufficiently integrated those meanings into their own thinking to be able to use them in the way they relate to the world.

These sub-universes of meaning can coexist without being integrated with one another, according to Berger and Luckmann (1967:83). The important point, however, is that for each division, there is a language and a package of knowledge to go with it. Berger and Luckmann found the phenomena Alfred Schütz referred to as **"the social distribution of knowledge"** far more profound than the material social fact of a society's division of labor. A social distribution of knowledge occurs when different people and groups in a society use different symbols and have different types of knowledge from one another. People with different knowledge bases from one another (e.g., physicians and plumbers) tend to have different vocabularies that the other would have a difficult time fully understanding. It is in this differential allocation of knowledge that social differences in general are embedded.

If they are **legitimated**, these sub-universes (and sometimes the overall universe of meaning of which they are part) tend to survive indefinitely. "Legitimation 'explains' [and]...justifies the institutional order by giving a normative dignity to its practical imperatives...[it] has a cognitive as well as a normative element" (Berger and Luckmann 1967:93).

Max Weber spent a great deal of time pondering the problem of legitimation, coming to the conclusion that for social systems to be stable, they must have legitimacy. An institutional system is legitimated through a number of processes, as described by Berger and Luckmann (pp. 92 ff.). The most important of these processes is when a person learns and internalizes the *vocabulary* of the institution being legitimated. Put another way, if individuals learn to use and *think* in the vocabulary attendant to the institution, they also are likely to see it as legitimate. The second important aspect of legitimation is the learning of **"rudimentary theoretical propositions"** from the perspective of the legitimate institution. These are statements about how the world works, and that often offer prescriptions for action, which often take the form of proverbs or wise sayings, such as, in the case of an extended family system, "My brother and I against my cousin, my cousin and I against the world."

The third level of legitimation occurs when people learn the more *formal theories and practices* associated with specific sub-universes of meaning within the institution. Someone learning what is expected of him or her at work can exemplify this. For instance, consider when a cashier learns the standard procedure for taking money and giving change, such as leaving the tendered bill on top of the cash drawer until change has been given, and only then putting the bill away in the cash drawer (the recipe for what to do is the **"formal practice"**). This procedure is necessary because it is too easy to forget which bill was used on any given transaction, particularly on a busy day. Failing to adhere to the formal practice would increase the risk of giving incorrect change, which in turn would either alienate the customer or lose revenue for the store (this logic is an example of the kind of **"formal theory"** Berger and Luckmann are referring to that people do in this stage).

The fourth level of legitimation occurs when people internalize and work with relatively **universal symbol systems**. These are symbol systems that integrate the respective sub-universes of meaning within the overall institutional order. As sub-universes become increasingly autonomous, they increasingly encounter difficulties legitimating themselves unless there is some effort on the part of some people to engage in this process of integration using a universal symbol system. In other words, the job a person is engaging in needs to be tied back to something that will, at least potentially, benefit the larger collective. For instance, it is not enough for physicians to learn the practices and vocabularies relative to their role. If the status of the physician is to be seen as legitimate, by the society and by the people who themselves are physicians, there must be some general sense that physicians contribute to the overall health of the society, and they do so, in part, because of their specialized knowledge, vocabulary, and way of seeing the world.

Ultimately, the legitimation process is largely dependent on people generally *taking their perceptions and behaviors for granted*. The surest sign that a behavior enjoys social legitimacy, in other words, is when society engages in that behavior without questioning whether they should be doing it in the first place. For instance, the status of physicians is reinforced every time people assume that the proper thing to do when they are seriously ill is to go to a physician—they may question whether they are sick enough to go, but generally will not question whether someone, no matter how sick, should see a physician. When certain perceptions and behaviors (e.g., having a temperature of 106° is a sign of being ill, and being ill implies the need to see a physician) are taken for granted by a wide portion of society, people tend to talk about them in a language that is mutually intelligible. Social constructions are maintained through everyday conversation (e.g., "You have a high fever, so let's get you to a doctor.").

Berger and Luckmann, building on Schütz's ideas about "recipes," find it particularly informative that human activity tends to be repeated in set ways, which they refer to as **habitualization**. This allows for an economy of effort in action and, more importantly, in thought—people don't have to "reinvent the wheel" every time they do something.

In habitualization, choices are narrowed. This is not necessarily a negative thing—for example; think of all the possible choices there are in driving a car on the interstate. A few of the nearly unlimited choices available to you are that you could continue to go in a straight line, or you could swerve into the next lane causing the other drivers to either slam on their brakes or crash, or you could drive down the left side of the interstate, or you could, while cruising at sixty-five miles per hour, put the car in reverse. The point is, that under the "everyday" circumstance of driving on the freeway, most people would not consider most of those "options" seriously, for the objective is to get from one place to another safely. In other words, a person does the expected, routinized thing, in most cases.

In fact, a major part of learning a new skill involves a process of elimination—learning what *not* to do. In our previous example, a person learns a multitude of options to forego, such as the choice of turning into ongoing traffic, or the choice of skipping from first to fourth gear. The choices a person makes as a learner become habitualized, and this habitualization in turn allows the person, on subsequent uses of those skills, to preclude making avoidable mistakes. This is an example of something that we as socialized people do on a daily basis, generally without reflecting much on the fact that we do it. Yet it serves an essential function: "the background of habitualized activity opens up a foreground for deliberation and innovation" (Berger and Luckmann 1967:53). When you are learning how to drive, for example, you spend a great deal of attention on the process. Once the process becomes habitualized, however, you can do it more easily, so you can and do think about other things (e.g., the song on the radio, social theory, the fight you just had with your significant other, or some combination thereof).

Once these actions become habitualized, we rarely give much thought specifically to what we are doing when we perform them, because we take the fact that we can perform them for granted. When you drive to school or work, you typically no longer worry about whether or not you know how to drive—you just drive because you "know" how to. Yet consider for a moment everything you do in a habitualized manner, and how much time you spend in habitualized activity; and then think about virtually every human being spending as much time in habitualized activity of their own (albeit on skills somewhat different from your own). The *sociological* implications of this are indeed far-reaching explain Berger and Luckmann.

As we come to take for granted that we—as well as other people—know certain things, we tend to make **typifications** about what we and others are expected to do in certain situations. Consider, for instance, that although you've most likely never met the driver going the other way on a busy street in the United States, and that person knows next to nothing about you, you can nonetheless pass each other at a rapid speed, often coming within inches of one another, without getting into an accident. This is because you engage in what Berger and Luckmann call a **reciprocal typification**, or a social convention, in which both parties expect the other person will drive on their right side of the road and not swerve into the other lane. People in England would engage in the same kind of social process; but because the social convention there calls for driving on the left side, their reciprocal typification would call for passing on the left, and expecting the other person to do likewise.

Social **institutions** are built upon the habitualized activity that becomes *coordinated* among people. Berger and Luckmann declare that "Institutionalization occurs whenever there is reciprocal typification of habitualized actions by types of actors...any such typification is an institution" (p. 54). Put another way, institutions such as family, religious, economic or political systems, are able to function as they do because of a few basic ingredients, which go back to ways in which people think and communicate. For the aforementioned reasons, people both habitualize their actions, and come to "know" what they and others are likely to habitualize. This process allows us to make educated guesses about what others and we are going to do in certain situations. Thus, it is the complex habits of us and others that we collectively act upon and come to expect, that form the basis of institutions.

Yet Berger and Luckmann (1967) were interested in the human tendency to see subjective experience as objective reality. People tend to see their world as having some order, rather than as random, chaotic events. Two people, however, tend to see different "objective" orders of the same reality, especially those from very different cultures.

Thus, the "objective" nature of an institution's reality is more accurately described as what Alfred Schütz termed **intersubjective** reality among many individuals across time and space. By intersubjective, Schütz meant that by aggregates of individ-

Reciprocal Typification

Drivers on a busy highway generally drive on the correct side of the road and expect other drivers to do the same in order to avoid accidents. Berger and Luckmann called this **reciprocal typification**.

uals, each having similar (though by no means precisely the same) subjective constructions of their social worlds, those constructions seem to take on a life of their own. These are in turn seen as "objective" because, like Durkheim's social facts, they seem to have a reality "external to, and coercive of" the social actor.

Here Berger and Luckmann introduce an idea borrowed from a Hungarian scholar by the name of György Lukács (1922/1968): the problem of **reification**. Reification is the perception that humanly created social arrangements are naturally occurring. The word comes from the Latin *res*, which means "thing," and is also the Latin root of the word "real." Reification can thus be understood as treating an inter-subjective social construct as if it were a "real [objective] thing" where the natural and social worlds appear to merge.

To illustrate the difference between a reified reality as opposed to an objective reality, compare the economic "law of supply and demand" on the one hand, with the physical "law of gravity" on the other. Regardless of whether most people (or, for that matter, any people) in a society agree to it, objects fall with a given degree of acceleration—in other words the law of gravity applies no matter what people think or do about it. Regardless of how the situation is "constructed" a person walking off the edge of a cliff will fall. The "law" of supply and demand, on the other hand, in which a market price is established at the intersection of the two curves describing the supply of a good or service and the demand for that same good or service, only applies in very specialized, constructed circumstances. Yet many people still talk about the law of supply and demand as if it were naturally occurring and universal. Thus, from a social constructionist's perspective, an example of reification has occurred.

According to Berger and Luckmann, "Reification implies that man is capable of forgetting his own authorship of the human world...as soon as the objective social world is established, the possibility of reification is never far away." In this view, when people engage in reification, they tend to rob themselves and others of their human agency, thinking in the process that "that's just the way things are." They fail to remember, in other words, that we "create" our world first, only afterwards to give it some type of objective status.

An element of reification can be said to occur when a person says something like "I didn't do this because it was me. Rather, I did it because of my role as (e.g., teacher, parent, etc.)." In Berger and Luckmann's view, this is an abdication of the responsibility we have to be true to our own individual nature, rather than to some social organization that we have wittingly or unwittingly cooperated in making. When we reify, we relinquish our own power and hand it over to the social constructions of the society, thereby giving them more momentum than they had before, and making them even more "objective" than they were before. That is, we fail to remember that we as humans "create" our world, but then give it some type of objective status.

The important emphasis in the social construction of reality approach, as in each of the approaches discussed in this chapter, is on how people go about defining the reality of their social worlds. Those definitions are generally created through the use of thinking about things in symbolic terms. The symbols used are acquired in a social context and in turn can be used as tools for changing the social context of which a person is part.

The strength of the social definition perspectives lies in their explanations of how subjective meanings are constructed and communicated in a social environment. Their theoretical ideas provide us with several helpful tools in making sense of an otherwise bewildering array of social circumstances. They have been criticized for their tendency to reduce larger social institutions to inter-subjective social constructions. Thus, their usefulness is primarily in analyzing micro-level processes involving thought and communication, rather than in more macro-level phenomena, such as conflicts between and among nation-states. That said, it is important to remember the power of the subjective, as well as objective, nature of phenomena, regardless of the level of analysis.

The Social World as a Stage: Dramatism and Dramaturgy

When attempting to explain the social world, some social theorists use metaphors. One somewhat common metaphorical strategy for social theorists is to analyze the world as if it were a stage, and the people in it players. The most notable social theorists of the twentieth century to use the stage metaphor were Kenneth Burke and Erving Goffman. Both men constructed several helpful insights into the human condition, especially in terms of face-to-face interactions, using this general framework (which Burke called **dramatism**, and Goffman called **dramaturgy**).

Kenneth Burke's Dramatism

Even more than in the experience itself, Kenneth Burke was interested in how people describe experience. Burke distinguishes **dramatism** ("language as act") from **scientism** ("language as definition"). For Burke, the study of "dramatism" implies that language and thought are more than simply means of conveying information; they are "modes of action" in and of themselves, at least as important as, for example, labor or other types of physical activity.

His framework is instrumental in helping us understand how people come to think and communicate about the experiences they have. In his work *A Grammar of Motives*, Burke (1945/1969) identifies five key elements present in virtually every social interaction, regardless of the time, place, or culture. These are termed Burke's dramatistic pentad. These five elements are:

Act, which describes *what* took place in the social interaction.

Scene, which describes the background of the act—the time, place, and situation *where* and *when* it occurred.

Agent, which describes *who* (what person or kind of person) performed the act.

Agency, which describes *how* the act was performed. Important here is the question of what means or instruments were used (including other people) by an agent to perform the act.

Purpose, which addresses the issue of *why* the act was performed.

While virtually every social situation is characterized by all five of these elements, a specific social situation can be characterized by the **ratios** among them, which are variable from society to society, and from one social situation to another within a society. Identifying the ratio in a given situation relative to others forms a framework of analysis. One social situation might be dominated by scene, for example, while another might allow for a great deal of agency. In an agency-dominated situation, the emphasis is on human free will. In a scene-dominated situation, the emphasis is on how that free will is constrained by external circumstances.

The **scene-act ratio** and the **scene-agent ratio** are the two ratios upon which Burke focuses the most. In both ratios, the scene *contains* both the act and the actor (or "agent"). "It is a principle of drama that the nature of acts and agents should be consistent with the nature of the scene" (Burke 1945/1969). Thus, the scene in some sense *always* constrains what action is likely to take place. That notwithstanding, some situations are more constrained than others, and that constraint (or lack thereof) is a crucial *variable* of human activity.

Burke was primarily interested in how people use rhetoric in everyday life, or, in other words, in how we utilize language to get people to "see things our way." In *A Rhetoric of Motives*, Burke (1950/1969), develops the central use of the process of **identification**. When we **identify** with someone, we conceive of ourselves as united with that person, because we see something of ourselves in the other. To induce someone to identify with oneself, is to produce a reaction favorable to one's position. The chief way this is done is to put one's own position in symbolic terms that are part of the listener's vocabulary, and to draw connections between those symbols in ways similar to the listener's.

What is the vehicle through which this process is accomplished? In *Language as Symbolic Action*, Burke (1966) writes that "[R]eality could not exist for us were it not for our profound and inveterate involvement in symbol systems." In other words, *every* perception is mediated by the symbols we use to describe it, according to Burke. To illustrate this, he developed the concept of the **terministic screen**, by which he meant a symbolic filter, which skews and largely determines our perceptions of the world. Quite literally, the "terms" we use to label things we perceive become the "screens" of our perceptions. Those terms have meanings in and of themselves, and create a rich sense of possibility in each situation when they interact with other symbols with which they are associated.

Yet our use of terministic screens implies much more than that. Once we have symbolically labeled a situation and our role in it, much of our subsequent thinking about it fulfills the *ramifications* of those labels. Consider the case of a new father, to illustrate. By labeling himself a father, a man is likely to be struck by the implications of all the other symbols he associates with the symbols for fatherhood, such as love, joy, and responsibility. This labeling process involves symbolic experiences going back to his early childhood and his sense of what his own and other fathers were like, and its associations are multitudinous.

Burke was an analyst of language and, ultimately, of ways in which systems of knowledge are organized. All human activity flows from these systems of knowledge. To understand how knowledge systems are organized and how the language attendant to them is used is, for Burke, the basis of understanding the most fundamental aspects of humanity itself.

Erving Goffman's Dramaturgy

Like Burke, Erving Goffman was centrally interested in details about how people use symbols to communicate. Also like Burke, he utilized a theater metaphor in his analysis, which he termed **dramaturgy**. Despite his interest in social definition and the use of symbols, there are some marked distinctions between his dramaturgical analyses on the one hand, and other social definition approaches to understanding human relations, such as symbolic interactionism, phenomenology and ethnomethodology on the other.

Dramaturgy
According to Goffman, when interacting with others, individuals attempt to manage the impression they have on others.

Goffman's early work, for example, was profoundly influenced by Émile Durkheim, especially Durkheim's (1912/1965) study of ceremonial activity such as religious ritual, as detailed in *The Elementary Forms of Religious Life*. Goffman (1956) uses the term **ritual** to describe social behavior such as "ceremonial activity...perhaps seen most clearly in little salutations, compliments, and apologies which punctuate social intercourse." In identifying ritual behavior all throughout society, Goffman secularizes an analytic strategy that for Durkheim was primarily religious.

The two major aspects of this ceremonial activity or ritual, according to Goffman, are **deference**, "which functions as a symbolic means by which appreciation is regularly conveyed [to someone];" and **demeanor**, which is part of a person's "ceremonial behavior typically conveyed through deportment, dress, and bearing, which serves to express to those in his immediate presence that he is a person of certain desirable or undesirable qualities" (Goffman 1956).

Throughout their lives, people engage in ritual on a daily basis. Even an action as simple as making brief eye contact while nodding to a stranger when passing on the street constitutes ceremonial activity in Goffman's analysis. This ritual activity in a sense signals the acceptance of an underlying code of conduct and symbolizes that the person would be likely to engage in acts guided by this code should the need arise. As such, it serves a crucial function in the society, and thus "[t]he gestures which we sometimes call empty are perhaps in fact the fullest things of all."

When a person interacts with others, according to Goffman (1959), "he knowingly and unwittingly projects a definition of the situation, of which a conception of himself is an important part." Goffman here describes two fundamental elements of the social individual: the **performer**, who engages in **information control or impression management**, and the **character**, who has characteristics the person is trying to represent through the performance, either real or imagined. The character chosen is "typically a fine one, whose spirit, strength, and other sterling qualities the performance was designed to invoke."

A successful performance leads the people who are witnessing the performance (which Goffman, in keeping with his dramaturgical metaphor, refers to as the **audience**) to see the character being played as indicative of the true self of the performer. When this occurs, the performance can be said to be **credited**. Conversely, the performance is **discredited** when it does not achieve this effect.

An important variable is how closely a performer identifies with the character or the role being played. It is sometimes the case that a performer will distance herself from the role she is playing by conveying the message that the role being played is not really commensurate with the true self. Goffman calls this process **role distance**. For example, a person may distance herself from a low status role such as that of a cleaning person by acting lackadaisically; in so doing, she conveys in her performance that being in this role is not very important. The message to the audience is that this is a task beneath her. In this regard, role distance may function as a face-saving device.

Goffman (1963) extends these themes in his work on *Stigma: Notes on the Management of Spoiled Identity*. He differentiates between who the person would be under ideal circumstances (a person's "virtual social identity"), and who the person really is (the "actual social identity"). Under ideal conditions, these two would be identical. Yet it is often the case that there is some disparity between a person's virtual and actual social identities. When this occurs, there is disgrace, or the presence of social **stigma** for the person.

Stigmatization is one of the central things that people do to each another, and this constitutes one of the primary characteristics of social life, according to Goffman. This can be seen in the obvious delight many people take in the embarrassment of others, such as the reaction to the news that President Bill Clinton had been caught in compromising circumstances with White House intern Monica Lewinski. Comedians such as Jay Leno geared their monologues around the stigmatization, and entire web sites were devoted to Clinton-Lewinski jokes.

There are two states of stigma between which Goffman distinguishes: **1) discredited stigma**, in which the disparity between virtual and actual social identity are obvious to others (e.g., in the case of someone with a prominent physical deformity) and **2) discreditable stigma**, in which the disparity is not known publicly (e.g., in the case of someone with a sexual preference who is not "out of the closet"), but which has the *potential* of becoming known at some point. Before the Lewinski affair was common knowledge in every home in the country, Clinton had a discreditable stigma. Once it hit the media and the world found out, Clinton had come to have a discredited stigma.

Having a discreditable stigma is a source of anxiety for the individual. In this case, impression management (which involves devising ways to continue to promulgate a virtual social identity at odds with one's true self, because one is "living a lie") takes up a considerable amount of time and attention. A discredited individual may try to "live it down" by employing role distancing strategies such as emphasizing other characteristics.

According to this view, social life is sufficiently balkanized that every human being is "out of place" *somewhere* or sometime. As a result, *everyone* potentially has a stigma, thus giving every individual in a society the potential to become a scapegoat for some other social group at some time. This could stem from something as profound as standing for Christian beliefs in a totalitarian and largely atheist society, or it could be as simple as rooting for the team "other" than the one favored by most of the people in a partisan crowd.

For this reason, a person needs to be vigilant to avoid being stigmatized, often engaging in impression management to do so, which necessitates performance. While there are numerous occasions for solo performances, it is quite common for performances to take place in "teams," which are groups of performers engaged in putting up a common front. This is exemplified when parents create the impression of a "united front" of authority when disciplining their children. In so doing, both parents play authority characters and support such characterization in the other, for example, by referring to each other as "Mom" and "Dad," rather than by first names.

There is a distinction between **front stage** and **back stage** demeanor to be noted, says Goffman. When a performer or team of performers is front stage, they realize an audience is present and are actively engaged in giving a performance. When back stage, performers are not attempting to make an impression and can "let down their hair."

As a result, the most common back stage time is when someone is alone. Certain aspects of a person's behavior can be back stage when in the company of trusted team members, although if anyone else is present, an individual is rarely if ever *fully* back stage. This is because even the most intimate relationships involve some impression management.

Power struggles play themselves out in terms of people managing impressions while trying not to be discredited in so doing. A way to achieve power over another is to discredit that person. Even back stage, a person must be somewhat vigilant, for an important way in which a person can be discredited is to be "caught" back stage.

Goffman was further interested in society's division of labor. Yet unlike Durkheim's division of labor based on societal functions, Goffman's conceptualization of this division is between those engaged in front stage labor and back stage labor. Those in

Backstage

When an employee is away from bosses and coworkers they are said to be **backstage** where they are not concerned with the impression they have on others.

back stage are behind the scenes, whereas in the front stage, the important thing is image, or impression management. An example can be found in modern political operations, in which a back stage group of operatives concentrates on formulating social policy, and a front stage politician concentrates on giving those policies the best face, thereby "selling" them to the audience—which in this case is the public polity.

The strength of Goffman's work thus far is found in his analysis of face-to-face interactions. In his book *Frame Analysis: An Essay on the Organization of Experience*, Goffman (1974/1986) provides a model for linking the microsociology of face-to-face interaction with the macrosociology of the larger society (Berger 1986). To begin with, he addresses the question of how people come to find *meaning* in a social situation. The **frame**, or framework of a situation arises from the social *context* in which it is perceived. "[s]ocial frameworks...provide background understanding for events that incorporate the will, aim, and controlling effort of intelligence, [with] a live agency, the chief one being the human being," writes Goffman (1974/1986:22). Similarly to the ratios among the elements of Burke's dramatistic pentad, Goffman's frames provide a way of generating expectations about a social situation.

A number of frames may be operating in any given situation. According to Goffman, even the declaration "We waited till the rain stopped and then started the game again," could at least potentially involve numerous frames including, for example, those of: **1)** games, **2)** a particular kind of game (e.g., baseball), and **3)** weather, and particularly what a likely response would be to rain. In each of these, the action at hand is provided with some context.

A social situation provides context clues, or **keys**, about which frame(s) are applicable to the situation at hand. For instance, the phrase "The batter walked on four straight pitches, and then stole second," is likely to key a baseball (or softball) frame.

Yet how a person relates a key to a frame is likely to vary by social group or by culture. The primary frameworks of a social group "constitute a central element of its culture" in Goffman's words (1974/1986:27). In other words, an individual is likely to be part of many social groups. Thus, it is not unusual for a given situation to key a number of possible frames, which may compete with one another for being chosen by the individual as the most appropriate.

In Goffman's dramaturgical approach (1974/1986:569), "[o]rdinary behavior, then, is taken as a direct instance of, or a symptom of, underlying qualities..." Yet, it is important to understand here that behavior does not occur in a vacuum. Rather, it is always experienced in some context, and that context to a large extent depends on which frames of reference are chosen. The frames chosen, in turn, are generally a product of the larger social milieu of which the individual is a part.

There are certain limitations to the metaphor of the world as a stage. For example, in reading Goffman, one could get the impression that virtually every social situation is yet another instance of people doing "impression management," and attempting to keep from being discredited, while simultaneously seeking to find information to discredit others. While much social theorizing involves some level of cynicism, this seems to extend it to even the most personal levels.

CHAPTER SUMMARY

- All experiences are interpreted in some context, and the experience itself is fundamentally affected by this context.
- Because language and symbols are learned in a social context, humans are largely a product of the cultures in which they were socialized. Cultural similarities are thus attributable in no small part to similarities of language and symbols.
- Social reality, as we know it, is primarily constructed through human interaction.
- Much of what people experience as objective in the social world is attributable to a social definition that is mutually agreed upon by oneself and others in the society.
- *Impression management* characterizes much of human interaction in which people act out roles, and try to avoid being discredited.
- Situations or *scenes* vary in how much or how little they restrain individual behavior.
- A large part of how people define a situation is attributable to how it is *framed*, or the social context into which it is cast.

6 Human Behavior and Social Exchange

Over a hundred years ago, the social theorist Georg Simmel observed that countless interactions between and among people in many different times, places, and circumstances, tend to take the form of exchange, in which we give something and receive something in return. In one exchange, we may give more than get, and in another we may get more than we give. Virtually on a daily basis, we enter into exchanges of one sort or another. Throughout our lives, we will likely participate in exchanges with many different people over time. In fact, exchange is such a common form of social interaction that a number of social theories have arisen to explore the nature of exchanges. Many of these theories are powerful predictors of human behavior, as we will see in this chapter.

In this chapter, we examine human interaction from the standpoint of exchanges between and among individuals. Based on this emphasis, this group of theories can be primarily understood as operating from a micro perspective, although they also can be very useful in explaining larger macro social processes, such as exchanges between organizations or even nation-states.

Basic Assumptions of Behavior and Exchange Perspectives

Exchange perspectives begin with the assumption that people will typically attempt to maximize their benefits while minimizing their costs, and to do so on the individual level. The assumption here is that when individual and group interests are in conflict, people will tend to pursue their own individual interests—even if they are not necessarily part of the group interest.

In this paradigm, the terms "benefits" and "costs" are meant in a social sense, rather than in a strictly economic one—that is to say, a "benefit" is anything the individual desires, and a "cost" is anything the individual would rather avoid. For example, a benefit could be something as simple as hearing a kind word, while a cost could be something as simple as having to walk across the kitchen to take the teakettle off the stove when one would rather not.

When a person's actions are successful, the person is more likely to perform those actions in the future. On the same note, actions that are punished tend to be less frequently performed in the future. In this sense, a punishment is any situation in which the costs outweigh the benefits.

A number of important theoretical predictions can be made from this basic set of assumptions. In many cases, those predictions have been supported by findings from empirical research.

In keeping with its focus on micro level interactions, particularly those taking place between individuals, psychologists conducted much of the early research in exchange theory. However, as sociologists came to recognize the profound *social* implications of this work in the latter half of the twentieth century, it was not only incorporated into sociology, but was extended far beyond its psychological roots in many important ways.

Thus we'll begin our discussion with this early psychological work in order to best understand these perspectives. We then will turn attention to how that work helped to inform sociological theorizing, and how those sociological theories eventually made major advances beyond the original psychological ideas, in terms of explaining and predicting human behavior.

Early Work by Behavioral Researchers

Around the dawn of the twentieth century, a psychologist in the United States and a physiologist in Russia made independent discoveries regarding the roles of rewards and punishments in learning and in influencing behavior. The first of these was E.L. Thorndike (1898, 1913) who observed that a behavior that is consistently rewarded tends to become a habit. Based on this observation, he postulated three laws of human behavior:

- **The Law of Effect.** Often, a person makes a connection between a situation (sometimes referred to as a "stimulus") and a response to that situation. This connection becomes stronger when it is followed by a "satisfying state of affairs" (Thorndike 1913). Conversely, this connection is weakened when that person experiences punishment in the form of an "annoying state of affairs." This is important because in subsequent situations, the greater the strength of a connection, the more likely it is to be acted upon.
- **The Law of Exercise.** The more a connection is made between a situation and a response to that situation, the stronger and more habitual that connection becomes. On the other hand, each time a connection is *not* made, the weaker that connection becomes. This law explains how some things we do become habits while others do not.
- **The Law of Readiness.** If a person is in a state of physiological and psychological readiness before performing an action, the results are more satisfying than if the person were not in a state of readiness. On the same note, if a person is stimulated to perform an action for which he/she is not ready, a state of annoyance will ensue. Here, the important point is that even if the laws of effect and exercise would seem to predict a positive response to a stimulus, the response could still be negative, if the law of readiness is not met.

Meanwhile in Russia, the second of these important breakthroughs occurred, for which Ivan Pavlov received the Nobel Prize in 1904 for his physiological research. Through this research, he discovered almost by accident what would soon become a fundamental tenet of later behavioral research. In a series of experiments, primarily with dogs, Pavlov recorded responses to various stimuli (a stimulus is something to which one or more of the senses reacts).

To begin his experiments, Pavlov elicited a reaction from the dogs by giving them meat powder (which he termed an **unconditioned stimulus**), afterwards recording the dogs' response in terms of increased salivary activity (what he called an **unconditioned reflex**). Next, Pavlov introduced the variable of an otherwise neutral stimulus (such as a bell ringing), pairing it with the giving of meat powder. Over time, the animals "learned" to salivate each time they heard the bell, regardless of whether or not the meat powder was present as well. The response to the bell had become a **conditioned reflex** (we should note here that sometimes the term "response" is used in place of "reflex"). The bell had become a **conditioned stimulus**, so named because

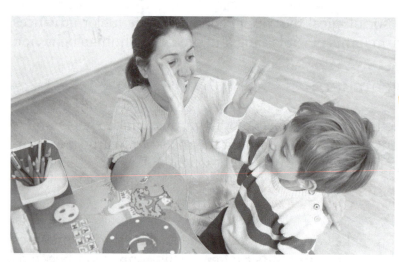

Positive Reinforcement
When a child's behavior is met with encouragement, he or she is more likely to repeat that behavior in the future. Skinner called this **reinforcement**.

the dog had become "conditioned," through repeated pairings of the bell and meat powder, to associate the bell with meat powder, and thus to associate the bell with the reflexive response of salivation.

A conditioned stimulus, then, is one that provokes a response to something it is **associated** with. In the case of Pavlov's dogs, the bell had come to be associated with meat powder, the proper reaction to which, for a dog, would be salivation. Thus, Pavlov set the stage for decades of subsequent behavioral research by proposing that the very act of **learning** is merely the making of associations between various stimuli.

In this sense, the important lesson for human beings is that we often respond to things we associate with something else. In fact, the pattern of associations an individual has is crucial in understanding how that individual is likely to react to a given social stimulus. It is on this understanding of the concept of learning that much of exchange theory is built. This is especially true in the early work on social exchange which views exchange as a function of social learning.

Expanding upon the research of Thorndike and Pavlov, John Watson made a very important modification that was to shape the direction of behavioral psychology for decades after that. Watson felt it was crucial to develop psychology as an *objective* science that could be used to predict behavior with unfailing accuracy. Watson thus dismissed any references to subjective states (such as those we discussed in the last chapter) as being too immaterial and difficult to verify in measurable terms, and thus unsuitable for true scientific research.

Watson hypothesized that Pavlov's breakthroughs concerning the conditioned reflex could be expanded to construct an entire predictive science of human behavior. The work of Thorndike and Watson, in turn, was formative in the highly influential work of B.F. Skinner, who also sought to establish a science of **behaviorism**, in which a given response could be predicted with accuracy from a given set of stimuli. That prediction, he and the other behaviorists argued, is to be based only on objective observation, without recourse to conjecture about subjective states of consciousness.

Social Learning and Social Exchange

A fundamental aspect of human interaction, according to B.F. Skinner, was how people influence their own and others' behaviors through rewards and punishments. Skinner developed his theory of social learning around the process of **operant conditioning**.

Using Thorndike's Law of Effect as a foundation, Skinner argued that a behavior (or "operant") that met with positive **reinforcement** (some reward or benefit, such as a desired food) would be more likely to be performed in the future. On the other hand, a behavior that resulted in a "punishment" (something that would preferably be avoided, such as electric shock) would likely be performed less frequently in the future. Both reinforcement and punishment are more effective if delivered very close in time to the behavior—the longer the lag between the time of the behavior and the reinforcement of it, the less effect that reinforcement has.

In fact, Ferster and Skinner (1957) delineate several ways in which reinforcement can be administered, and the effects they have in influencing or **shaping** someone's behavior, either by making a response more likely, or by eliminating a response entirely (response **extinction**). While each of these reinforcement patterns lead to different outcomes, a few of the patterns are particularly worth noting.

Total (or continuous) reinforcement occurs when someone is given benefits or rewarded each time he or she performs a behavior; while **partial reinforcement** happens when a person is rewarded for a behavior only some of the time (e.g., precisely every fifth time, or at imprecise increments which *average* every fifth time). Almost counterintuitively, research has found that behaviors that were partially reinforced take *longer* to reach response extinction than do behaviors that were continuously reinforced (Jenkins and Stanley 1950). This pattern is particularly pronounced when the rewards were "intermittent" or variable (viz. occurred every once-in-a-while at times that were hard or impossible to predict). On the same note, behavior that had been *both* rewarded *and* punished tends to persist much *longer* than behavior that had been only rewarded, once rewards are discontinued altogether.

This phenomenon, referred to as the **partial reinforcement extinction effect** has profound implications for a number of human conditions, such as addictions. Consider a scenario in which a person is addicted to gambling on slot machines. Most of the experiences could be considered punishment (losing money), with only an occasional reward (winning money). Despite the fact that losses generally far outnumber wins, the behavior (playing the slot machine) persists, often becoming stronger over time. Later behavioral researchers theorized that this occurs because a person learns to persist longer by virtue of adapting to a pattern of being reinforced only occasionally. The discontinuation of reinforcement represents a dramatic difference for the person who had been reinforced continuously; whereas for the person who had been only occasionally reinforced, discontinuation is not such a drastic change, because many of the responses had not been reinforced anyway (Jenkins and Stanley 1950; Amsel 1958).

So what happens if punishment, rather than positive reinforcement, is administered in a random fashion? In a situation in which an individual receives an "aversive stimuli" (punishments, or things the person would rather avoid, such as loud or unpleasant noises) at odd intervals and no behavior seems to stop the punishment, a strange phenomenon tends to occur. In this scenario, the individual begins to perceive the punishments as being beyond his or her control, tends to quit trying different behaviors, becomes less active, and then simply accepts it. This condition is referred to as **learned helplessness** (Seligman and Maier 1967; Overmier and

Seligman 1967).

The lesson learned during situations of learned helplessness is that avoidance of punishment is impossible, the possibility of escape seems remote and unlikely, and the learning process itself becomes less active (Maier and Seligman 1976). Research has shown learned helplessness to be associated with depression, health problems, and impaired intellectual achievement (e.g., Garber and Seligman 1980).

It is worth noting here that many of the behaviorists discussed thus far, most notably Pavlov, Seligman, and Skinner, conducted most of their experiments on animals in controlled laboratory settings. This leads to the question of what aspects, if any, of behaviorists' work apply to human beings in diverse social settings, which sometimes bear little similarity to a controlled laboratory situation. In response to this question, Skinner and the behaviorists argued that because the crucial element is objective behavior, rather than subjective states, virtually all of their work was applicable to human beings as well.

However, as Skinner's critics have pointed out, the operant conditioning framework fails to address several uniquely human activities, such as the acquisition and use of complex language patterns, for instance. This is underscored, for example, by the fact that people often use sentences that have never been used before, and thus could not have been the subject of previous reinforcement. Operant theory, for this reason, is insufficient at explaining why people do things in the first place, *before* being reinforced.

From a sociological perspective, it is important to focus on which aspects of this work apply most directly to human collectives. The theories we'll examine throughout this chapter expand upon the insights of the early behaviorists in explaining human behavior. Let's begin with the most micro-level of those theories, and then move to theories with more macro-level implications.

Behavioral Exchange

George Caspar Homans, extrapolating the principles of Watson, Thorndike, and Skinner, developed a theory known as **behavioral exchange**, or **exchange behaviorism**. In bridging the tenets of behavioral psychology from the individual into the social realm, Homans developed several **"principles"** to explain human behavior. The most important of these are:

- **Success.** A rewarded action or behavior is more likely to be performed in the future (comparable to Thorndike's *law of effect* and Skinner's *positive reinforcement*).
- **Stimulus.** The more similar a stimulus is to previous stimuli that have resulted in *success*, the more likely the person is to respond to it (comparable to the behavioral psychology idea of *stimulus generalization*).
- **Value.** The more valuable the *result* of an action is to an individual, the more likely that individual is to perform that action.
- **Deprivation/Satiation.** Having received many rewards in the recent past tends to decrease the desirability of that reward in a process referred to as **satiation**, or "too much of a good

thing," while conversely, not having received many such rewards in the recent past tends to increase the desirability of those rewards (**deprivation**).

- **Aggression.** If a person expects a reward as a result of **approval** of an action, but then does not receive that reward, the person is likely to become aggressive. On the other hand, if a reward *is* received, that person is likely to give approval to the person providing the reward.
- **Rationality.** When selecting from among a set of different actions, the individual tends to select the one with the highest *utility* (the benefits must outweigh the costs). The utility is calculated by multiplying the value of the desired outcome by the perceived probability of achieving that result. This is derived by taking the success and value propositions together.

Homans also formulated concepts to explain power and status differences in social situations:

- **Power.** The person with the least to lose in terminating a relationship has the most power in that relationship. This is referred to as the **"principle of least interest."**
- **Status.** The person providing scarce resources or benefits to a relationship has high status in that relationship (known as the **"principle of scarcity"**). In exchange for providing scarce goods, a high status person often receives many goods that are in abundance.

Think of a dating relationship between two people as an example of how these principles apply to actual human exchanges— let's call them Alice (who loves skateboarding and dancing) and Fred (whose idea of a good time is going to backgammon tournaments and watching re-runs of *The Simpsons*). For Fred, Alice is the woman of his dreams, the only one for him. For her part, Alice thinks Fred is a nice enough person, yet Fred is only one of a number of possible suitors—Ed, Ted, or Fritz would do at least as well. Considering the *alternatives* available to her, Alice is likely to have less interest in pursuing a relationship with Fred than Fred is with Alice. What's more is that because in Fred's mind, she is the only one for him, Alice's company is a relatively scarce resource. This confers Alice with a degree of power in the relationship, and the related warrant of being entitled to more advantageous resources. For Homans, this dynamic between them might play out in the form of a much greater likelihood that, if they go out at all, the date would more likely be centered around Alice's preference of dancing than around Fred's heartfelt need to watch *Simpsons* re-runs.

In exchange relationships, individuals tend to have a sense of the expected rewards in proportion to one's costs, which is referred to as a sense of **distributive justice**. A person's sense of justice, according to Homans, involves the expectation that "the greater the investment the greater the profit" (Homans 1961:75). When that expectation is unfulfilled, the person tends to become *angry*. Conversely, a person for whom perceived rewards are greater than the perceived costs tends to feel *guilty*. Those respective feelings of anger and guilt tend to influence behaviors and expectations in *future* exchanges. When a person's sense of distributive justice is violated, he or she is more likely to avoid future exchanges with the aggrieving parties, or even to engage in violent behavior.

Interpersonal Relations, Interdependence and Social Exchange

Thibaut and Kelley (1959) attempted to explain the social outcomes of how people in small groups become interdependent upon one another. For Thibaut and Kelley, a fundamental question was why people choose to interact with some people and not with others. In essence, when the rewards outweigh the costs of an interaction, people will choose to enter into it. Thibaut and Kelley conceptualized rewards and costs in social terms (e.g., bonding with another or receiving a compliment in public), as opposed to strictly physical terms (e.g., food).

Developing this theory, Thibaut and Kelley describe several factors external to an exchange that make interaction more likely. These factors include:

- **Desirable Attributes or Abilities.** People often choose to interact with others who possess some desirable ability or social characteristic, because the interaction is more likely to be rewarding to the person choosing. Because it is generally a reciprocal choice, rather than a one-way interaction, people tend to choose one another for abilities they find rewarding, while at the same time being chosen based on what they have to offer to an exchange.
- **Complementarity**. Particularly in a two-person relationship (or a **dyad**), people prefer to interact with someone who possesses abilities or attributes that the person does *not* her- or himself possess. The ideal exchange relationship according to Thibaut and Kelley is one in which the parties can provide each other benefits, while the interaction itself is not costly to them. A business partnership in which one person specializes in the back-office matters such as accounting and finance, while the other handles the marketing and public relations could be used as an illustration of this concept. In this example, the ideal such partnership would be one in which the two parties involved truly like what they themselves are doing, but would prefer to have someone else handle what the other is doing.
- **Similarity of Outlook and Preferences**. We often choose to interact with people who share similar attitudes and values, and tend to avoid those whose values, tastes, etc., are dissimilar to our own. This is true, theorize Thibaut and Kelley (1959:43), because "two people with similar values [reward] each other simply by expressing their values." Conversely, consider the example of two people who like very different kinds of music, such as new age and hip-hop. Simply listening to the other person's music amounts to a punishment, and thus something to be avoided.
- **Physical or Geographic Proximity.** Obviously, it is easier to interact with people who are in close physical proximity than with people who are far away. Put in exchange terms, there is a greater cost to interacting with someone who is not easily accessible than there is with someone more readily available. For this reason, we are more likely to interact with those in close proximity than with those far away, all other factors being equal.

Thibaut and Kelley (1959) cite empirical work for each of these factors, supporting their theoretical propositions finding that physical proximity is a very strong predictor of interaction patterns (e.g., Newcomb 1956; Gullahorn 1952). These patterns are manifest in terms of interpersonal attraction between members of the opposite sex, for instance. College dormitories can be thought of as another example of the predictive application of this theory—people are most likely to develop friendships with people whose doors open into a common area, and rather unlikely to interact with people living on the other side of, or away from, the campus.

The attraction or repulsion to another is seen in *relative*, rather than absolute terms, in almost all social situations. A person tends to weigh the costs and benefits of interacting with another against the costs and benefits of possible *alternative* interactions, or interactions with other people. In other words, although a specific interaction may not be optimal in terms of one (or any) of the determinants of rewards and costs, an individual may still choose to enter into that interaction if the alternatives are not seen as beneficial or are seen as more costly.

Thibaut and Kelley, in agreement with other exchange theorists, point out that in any given interaction, an unequal distribution of power between the individuals involved is likely. Power is a function of how much control one individual has over the rewards and costs affecting the other person. The precise opposite of power is dependence—the more power one person has over another, the more dependent the second person is on the first.

Since being in a dependent relationship is in itself costly, there is incentive for a person to avoid it. You may ask, then, why so many people seem to be in relationships of dependence, in which someone holds power over them? Thibaut and Kelley also address this in terms of alternatives. It is a strong possibility that a person is in a dependent, negative relationship, because his or her perception of the *alternatives* is such that leaving the relationship may be seen as having a greater cost than staying in it. As a matter of fact, a great indicator of whether or not a spouse will seek to escape an abusive relationship, for instance, is whether there is an available alternative living arrangement that does not itself impose some greater cost, such as a battered women's shelter that is not a violent place.

In an exchange relationship, there are several strategies a person can utilize to increase his or her power. These include such things as decreasing the other person's alternative exchanges, increasing the rewards or incentives the other person has for entering into exchanges with oneself, devaluing the other person's contribution (even while enjoying the benefits of it), or displaying a willingness to defer the gratification of some desire that the other person meets.

The question arises of how some relationships come to achieve a large degree of stability. The key to such stability, according to Thibaut and Kelley, is reciprocity of power and dependence, or **interdependence**. Two people are interdependent if both simultaneously: **1)** are dependent on the other to obtain some benefit; and **2)** hold some power over the other by virtue of being able to confer some benefit to the other.

In this regard, the most stable relationships are those in which people meet each other's needs in a way that is beneficial to both parties, and not very costly to either. This is most likely to occur when people bring different strengths and weaknesses that are complementary to each other into a relationship, so that interactions take the form of *cooperation* and mutual benefit rather than destructive competition. While most of their early work focused on dyads, in later work, Kelley and Thibaut (1978), expanded their efforts to explain behavior beyond that context. Even then, however, they tended to turn their focus only as far as triads. Thus, while the Thibaut and Kelley model is quite helpful in making sense out of micro-level interactions, it is less helpful than exchange structuralism, network exchange, and rational choice theories, for example, when attempting to explain behavior in larger collectives. It is to each of those, respectively, that we now turn our attention.

Peter Blau's Exchange Structuralism

Peter Blau (1964), who extrapolates on the earlier work of George C. Homans, among others, proposed a more nuanced version of exchange theory. Blau begins with the same assumption as Homans—that in any social situation, people will attempt to maximize their benefits and minimize their costs. Money to a hungry person could be a benefit, as could companionship to someone who is lonely. Doing a task that someone does not want to perform could be a cost, as could be the paying of money.

Although we typically think of the words "benefit" and "cost" in economic terms, it is important to understand that exchange theorists are generally referring to a wide range of concepts far beyond the economic sphere. It is also important to realize that, because of the diversity of preferences of individual human beings, one person's benefit may be another's cost (think of two people on a long-distance run, in which one enjoys running and the other is a couch potato who would rather be doing anything else—the relative merits of this activity are going to be quite different for each person).

Blau criticized Homans' theory for reducing all social interaction to micro-level exchanges, charging that Homans tended to ignore social institutions. It is the process through which such social structures "emerge" that much of Blau's theory emphasized.

The **principle of emergence** operates in the following way, according to Blau:

- The satisfying of the others' needs predicates any elementary exchange relationship.
- In these elementary exchanges, individuals endeavor to maximize their own benefits while minimizing their costs.
- Individuals often attempt to present their contribution in as favorable a light as possible while making exchanges, often tending to exaggerate the contributions they are making.
- A person who is perceived as bringing a scarce resource to an exchange holds relatively more power in that exchange, and tends to receive deference from those receiving that scarce resource.
- Over time, patterns of exchanges tend to become repeated or **routinized**.
- Status differences become rigid as these exchange patterns become routinized. This is the foundation of the **stratification system**, a system where individuals are sorted hier-

archically. In other words, the systematic status differences between people become **institutionalized**.

- As the stratification system becomes structured, those who provide a scarce resource for which demand is high come to occupy a relatively higher position, *and do so on a regular basis.*
- As the stratification system itself becomes routinized, it takes on **legitimacy**, meaning that people take its routines for granted and tend to follow those routines, rather than challenging them. Blau borrows the term **"authority"** from Max Weber to characterize this process. To say someone has authority is a simplified way of saying that person holds power in some sort of routinized relationship, and that the patterns of that relationship tend not to be challenged by the people affected by them.
- The legitimacy of authority is accepted not only by the members of a society, but is passed on to new members of the society (e.g., children) through **socialization**. When a little boy perceives his father showing deference to a physician, for example, the little boy is socialized to perceive the occupation of physician as having a legitimate claim on authority.

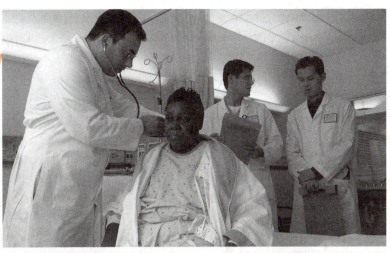

Principle of Emergence

According to the **principle of emergence**, those who provide services which are in high demand, such as doctors, occupy a high position in the stratification system.

Through each stage of the above process of emergence, the stratification system goes beyond individual exchanges and comes to take on the character of a social structure. That structure is then inherited by subsequent generations. The authority of those whose power has been routinized via the stratification system is known as **legitimate authority**.

If the ratio of costs and benefits comes to the point of no longer being reflected in the stratification system, however, that system comes to lose its legitimacy. When an occupation or status group high in the stratification system is no longer perceived as providing a scarce resource, for instance, it tends to lose its legitimacy *over time.*

For a time, such an actor or group may attempt retain the old power and reward structure, in a situation referred to as **coercive** authority. The presence of **coercive** authority, however, tends to breed conflict in the society. The more profound the mismatch between people's respective positions in the stratification system and the reward structure of that system, the more likely that serious social conflict, including revolution, will occur.

However, there is a contradiction to this inherent in most societies. While the needs of people are somewhat fluid and can change rather quickly, the stratification system has more momentum and changes rather slowly. For this reason, there is bound to be some mixture of legitimacy and coerciveness in its institutions, especially in a rapidly changing modern society.

Network Exchange Theories

Network exchange theories begin with the same assumption as other exchange theories—that actors seek to maximize their benefits and to minimize their costs. However, there is an important difference in network theories in that they describe the ability of actors as being either constrained or facilitated by their social connections with other actors. It is also important to note here that an "actor" in a network may be an individual or a collective, such as a formal organization or even a nation-state.

In fact, the emphasis in network theorizing is on this facilitation or constraint of the actor, which stems from that actor's position in a network. A key concept in network theory that addresses this is **centrality** (e.g., Freeman 1979; Sabidussi 1966). This can be seen graphically in the following figures:

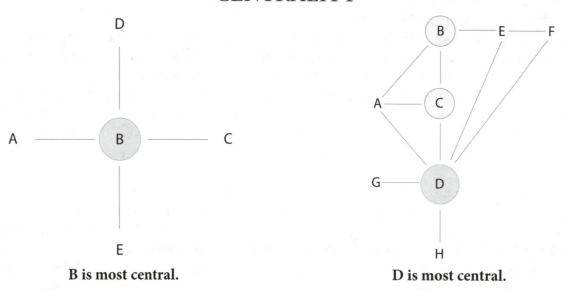

A number of interrelated propositions arise from this idea of centrality:

- The more central an actor, the more the other actors are **dependent** on that actor to complete exchanges (in order for A and B to enter into an exchange, for example, they must go through C—in this way, they are dependent on C, even if C is not particularly interested in A or B (Emerson 1962).
- The more one actor (e.g., A) is dependent on a second actor (e.g., C), the more **power** the

second actor (in this case, C) holds over the first. Thus, in network theory, there is a *reciprocal relationship between power and dependency.*

- The *more alternative* linkages that exist between actors, the *less dependent* they are on any single or particular linkage. (In the example given, a direct link between A and B gives them an alternative to going through C, thereby giving A and B the power to enter into an unmediated exchange).

Thus, actors in relatively central positions often have the power to influence the behavior of those in dependent positions. However, it should be emphasized here that actors in networks, as elsewhere, make their own decisions. Network position does not *determine* behavior, but only *constrains* or *facilitates* it.

Multiple centers of power often develop in large networks. These can be understood as regional centers, resembling "petty kingdoms in an encompassing empire" (Cook et al. 1983:302). Although a given actor may have a high degree of overall centrality, that actor's position still could be threatened by its *lack* of centrality relative to some regional center; this is known as **vulnerability** (Cook et al. 1983). Consider an agent of the federal government, for example, whose influence stems from a close connection to the central power source in Washington, D.C. When that agent is "in the field" he or she is vulnerable to harm from *locally* centralized power sources, such as an organized crime syndicate.

Understanding this emphasis on relationships among actors is key to understanding network exchange theories. In other words, rather than focusing on social actors, the focus is on the connections (or lack of connections) among actors (Wasserman and Faust 1994).

Thus, an individual's relative position in a network functions to either facilitate or constrain his or her actions. Even social norms, or prescriptions for behavior, can be seen in network terms, because of the constraints and expectations promulgated by the ties inherent in it (Burt 1976).

While the original concept of network analysis was conceived in terms of links among individual persons, it is important to note that it has subsequently been used to offer insights into linkages among social actors at virtually any level of analysis, such as organizations (e.g., Mizruchi and Galaskiewicz 1994). Many researchers (e.g., Snyder and Kick 1979; Smith and White 1992; Kick et al. 1995), for example, have used insights from network theory to analyze relationships among nation-states.

Rational Choice Theory

Similarly to exchange-based theories, an assumption of rational choice theory is that the primary motive governing interaction among individuals is maximization of individual "utility." This assumption states that individuals act rationally (albeit selfishly) in an attempt to attain the greatest possible benefits while incurring the least possible costs for themselves. As understood by rational choice theorists, even seemingly altruistic behavior is an attempt on the part of the altruist to achieve some benefit for themselves. A corollary is that, in the absence of some mechanism discouraging such behavior, people will continue to take what benefit they can in any given situation, without paying anything in terms of cost if it is possible to do so. This situation is referred to as the **free rider problem**, and its implications are fundamental to the perspective of rational choice theory. In other words, the free rider problem describes a situation in which an individual receives the benefit of an exchange, without paying the fair cost associated with it (consider the example of a free-rider on a bus — one who rides without paying the fare).

Rational choice theorists such as James Coleman (1986) and Mancur Olson (1965) extrapolate upon the connections between the micro and macro levels of social reality when they describe "emergent" (macro level) social phenomena in terms of individual (micro level) rational choices. Their major theoretical contributions can be found in their explanations of three related phenomena: 1) how **irrational, or perverse, social consequences** occur in situations in which people make choices that are rational for them as individuals, 2) how **collective decisions**, often different from what is optimal from any individual perspective, arise from individuals acting rationally in their own behalf, and 3) ways in which individuals and collectives discourage the **free rider problem**.

Theorists indicate two major causes in attempting to explain why there are often "perverse" (undesired, unplanned, and often irrational) social consequences of individual rational Theorists indicate two major causes in attempting to explain why there are often "perverse" (undesired, unplanned, and often irrational) social consequences of individual rational choice: 1) Because of inadequate information and incomplete communication about the options and likely alternatives of other people, individuals rarely coordinate behavior between themselves and others (*uncoordinated social action*). 2) For many actions, the benefit is conferred to the individual, while the cost is conferred to the larger collective (e.g., society as a whole). The social actor makes calculations based on his/her own *individual* utility. Thus, as a result of uncoordinated social action, the individual social actor tends not to take the larger cost into consideration, because he experiences it personally only in a very indirect manner, while he experiences the benefit personally and directly.

This scenario is illustrated by the concepts of the **prisoner's dilemma** and the **tragedy of the commons**. The *prisoner's dilemma* best exemplifies the proposition that uncoordinated social action often results in less than optimal consequences for those involved. The *tragedy of the commons* focuses on the idea that a social actor makes decisions based on individual utility, while a larger collective shares the costs. These two illustrations are relevant in that they function as metaphors for a wide range of human behavior—virtually any case in which benefits accrue to individuals more than costs (but in which costs are shared by others in the society), and/or situations in which individuals make decisions that are not coordinated with others.

The prisoner's dilemma, originally developed by social scientists during World War II, is a way to optimize strategic outcomes such as the interrogation of enemy prisoners, and is now used regularly in a variety of legal contexts. It is one popular variant of a broader class of methods (these methods and the predictions attendant to their outcomes are sometimes referred to as "game theory"). The following scenario illustrates the prisoner's dilemma: Two "prisoners" are suspected of having conspired to commit a major crime, but the authorities have insufficient evidence to convict either without a confession. The prisoners are taken into separate rooms and not allowed to communicate with one another (thus ensuring *uncoordinated* social action between them). They are then given the following information:

> If one prisoner confesses and the other does not, the one confessing gets a light sentence (e.g., one year) and the other gets a heavy sentence (e.g., ten years). If both prisoners confess, both get moderate sentences (e.g., five years). If neither person confesses, both will go free.

Whether or not to confess, of course, is the dilemma for both prisoners. The most rational choice would be for both to agree to remain silent, thereby ensuring freedom for both. However, because neither one can discuss it with the other prisoner, neither can be sure the other will not confess. Thus, each entertains the possibility that the other *will* confess—which, of course, would doom the non-confessing prisoner to a heavy sentence. Furthermore, the prisoner cannot be sure that not confessing will get him off (because the other would also have to *not* confess), while not confessing could potentially lead to a much heavier sentence for him than would confessing. The individual is likely to confess in order to minimize the heavy sentence. Thus, rational choice theorists maintain that, in such a situation, *both* prisoners are likely to confess. The implication here is that without the option to coordinate action by way of communication, the collective outcome of individual rational action is often far worse than would have been the case if the parties involved had been able to plan and coordinate their actions.

The "tragedy of the commons" (Hardin 1968, 1993), also referred to as the "public goods dilemma," is illustrated by the following scenario: Shepherds can allow their sheep to graze on their own private land or on public "common" land. No matter where his sheep graze, the shepherd gets the benefit (fat, healthy sheep). However, if his sheep graze on his own private land, the cost to him will be greater than it will be if they graze on the public land (where the cost, in terms of eaten hay, would be shared by all). In this scenario, then, the rational thing for any individual shepherd to do would be to have his sheep graze on the common land, rather than on his own private land. What is rational for a given shepherd is rational for each of the shepherds, especially when considering that there is a tendency for each *not* to coordinate his actions with others. The *perverse* consequences (the "tragedy") come into play when the common area becomes unusable as a result of over-grazing. Many environmental and other social problems are illustrated in this metaphor.

Rational choice theory is also instrumental in understanding how collective decisions are made. The political process provides a prime example of collective decisions. Rational choice theorists argue that throughout this process, there are several important implications that largely determine the result: **1)** While an individual has opinions on many different issues, only a very few (generally no more than three, and sometimes as few as one) of those issues are *vitally* important to that individual. **2)** In *exchange* for support (or a vote, in a political situation) on an issue that is vitally important to one individual, that individual will support some other issue that is less vital to him, but which *is* vital to another person or group of people. **3)** The greater the number of issues to be addressed by the collective, the greater the chances to get a given issue resolved in the direction desired by the individual, even if opinion of that individual is in the minority.

This theory of collective decisions has important implications for several reasons. It highlights the fact that a sheer majority of opinion—even a very large majority—does not ensure passage. While numbers are not unimportant, the critical consideration is *how many* hold the issue as vitally important. In this way, it wonderfully explains how single-issue voters and special interest groups can be so effective. It emphasizes the fact that many positions held by many people are "negotiable," and implies that news of public opinion (e.g., public opinion polls, etc.) has a major element missing if it does not provide insight into *priorities* of positions, as well as the positions themselves. It also emphasizes how collective decisions sometimes differ from a simple aggregate of individual preferences, although these collective decisions are the outcome of a process in which individuals each are attempting to maximize their own benefits and minimize their own costs.

The previously mentioned free rider problem is frequently encountered. While this involves an individual profiting from a situation or exchange without paying the true costs associated with the benefit gained, this problem has several manifestations. An example of a free rider in the collective decision process is someone who leads someone else to believe he/she will vote a certain way on a given issue in exchange for some other benefit (such as a vote on an issue important to the free rider), but then does not keep his/her part of the bargain. For instance, a free rider in the "public goods" dilemma could be someone who enjoys the comforts of living in clean shared housing, but who leaves his dirty laundry, dishes, and garbage lying around for others to clean up.

Rational choice theorists argue that an individual or a group can impose **sanctions** (penalties) on a free rider, as a way of discouraging free riding behavior. While a sanction can be either a reward or a punishment, rational choice theorists tend to focus on the latter in discussing the free rider problem. Depending upon the size and strength of ties among the members of the social group in which the free riding occurs, the type of sanctions that are most effective can vary. For small, close-knit, *Gemeinschaft* type groups (**obligatory groups**), the type of sanctions typically invoked is informal but often highly effective. This can include, for example, withholding friendship or, in extreme cases, shunning or expelling the free rider from the group. For large, *Gesellschaft* type collectives (**compensatory groups**), sanctions tend to be rational-legal, such as lawsuits or other formal procedures.

The costs associated with formal sanctions tend to be much higher than that attendant to informal sanctions. Thus, it is more efficient for individuals to conduct exchanges within a small group of well-known and trusted people whenever possible. Further, such groups tend to screen potential members, tending to select people for what appear to be altruistic tendencies for the mutual benefit of its members. Groups also tend to screen for values held in common with group members; thus, both tendencies are likely to minimize the chances of free-riding in the first place.

Rational choice theory continues to grow in popularity despite its weaknesses, not the least of which is the somewhat implausible assumption of an emotionless, "utility maximizing" actor. This popularity largely stems from the fact that, with a relatively small number of assumptions and propositions, rational choice theory informs the discussion of a wide array of pressing social problems (e.g., Friedman and Hechter 1990), and addresses the age-old question of how macro level social phenomena emerge from individual action.

CHAPTER SUMMARY

- Exchange theories focus on micro-level interactions, emphasizing that people attempt to maximize their benefits and to minimize their costs.
- A wide range of predictions about human behavior can be made from an analysis of costs and benefits, including when addictive behavior will persist, with whom people are likely to develop relationships, and how power is obtained and used in human collectives.
- Power is a fundamental concept. An individual's power is largely a reflection of how much others need that person for scarce and desired resources, or for how central that person is in mediating exchanges through which others are able to obtain those resources.
- Power and dependence are inversely related. The more power someone holds in an exchange relationship, the more dependent on that person someone else is.
- The modern world is replete with examples of the "tragedy of the commons." This is due to the human tendency to maximize benefits and minimize costs on the *individual* level; which often results in perverse consequences for the *collective*.

7 Classical Sociology and Basic Concepts in the Study of Social Organization

The major classical social theorists whose work laid the foundation for the discipline of sociology each had an elaborate sense of how societies were organized. The classical theorists we will consider here are Karl Marx, Max Weber, Gaetano Mosca, Vilfredo Pareto, Georg Simmel, and Émile Durkheim.

Classical Theorists on Social Organization

Karl Marx believed that while stratification was a critical aspect of social relations in both ancient times and in contemporary society, it was by no means equitable or inevitable. Marx organized his theory of stratification around the concept of **relations of production**, which explains how those with economic ownership of businesses were able to parlay this ownership into more general forms of domination of the non-owning working classes.

Max Weber viewed stratification as reflecting power or authority differentials. Those differentials occurred in political and social arenas as well as in economic arenas. While for Marx, relations of production in the economic arena influenced activity in all other arenas, Weber's theory of stratification was a multi-dimensional one, in which domination in one arena, while potentially influencing the others, was by no means reducible to any of those others.

Émile Durkheim developed the idea that societies developed stratification systems as a means not only of producing goods and services more efficiently, but also as a means of optimizing the interdependence among the various members of society. This, he proposed, promoted **solidarity**, or feelings of cohesiveness among the members of the society. In sum, he placed great emphasis on the interdependence of the respective parts of society.

While Marx and Weber's theories have been most influential in the development of **conflict** oriented theories of stratification, or theories that emphasize the oppressive nature of inequality and the conflicting interests between different groups in the society, Durkheim's theories have lent themselves more towards the development of theories with a **functional** orientation, which stress the consensus members of the society have over the values and norms of the society.

In this more theory-based chapter, the themes we will discuss lean slightly more toward conflict theories, while the chapter discussing empirical work will touch more upon functional themes. The elite approach has resulted in very little empirical work, or even follow-up theorizing, and as such we spend less time discussing it here than we do the functional or conflict approaches, with one important exception—elite themes help us see the holistic nature of stratification processes, a benefit which is sometimes lost when viewing them from only the functional or conflict view. While elite views have something in common with both of the other views, it still is beneficial to keep them analytically distinct. That said, we will attempt to synthesize each of these views on a theoretical level later in this chapter, and then again on an empirical level in a later chapter.

As we shall see, the dichotomy between functional and conflict theories stems largely from the relative degree of primacy given to one aspect or another of the stratification system.

Durkheim and the functional theorists that follow him, such as Talcott Parsons, tend to focus on the overall, holistic or organic nature of society. Marx and the conflict theorists that follow him on the other hand, focus more on the incompatibility of interests among the various elements of society. While Max Weber's theories have been most influential on the subsequent work of conflict theorists, certain aspects of his work have also informed later functional- and elite-oriented theorizing. With these very broad outlines in mind, let us now turn to a more detailed examination of the work of the classical theorists and to those who have followed in their traditions.

Karl Marx on the Importance of Class Interests

In the *Manifesto of the Communist Party*, Karl Marx and his co-author, Friedrich Engels, argue that "The history of all hitherto existing society is the history of class struggles" (1848/1948). The overall essence of Marx's theory is expressed in that one sentence. According to Karl Marx, **class** is the single most important dimension of stratification.

For Marx, class is determined by one's position within the "relations of production," which highlights whether one owns a business and hence is able to act as an employer, or alternatively, whether one does not own a business and hence must labor for subsistence, typically in the form of wages. In modern industrial society, as Marx describes it, the **bourgeoisie** class owns the means of production, while the **proletariat** class owns no means of production, but rather is forced to subsist by selling its labor to the bourgeois for wages.

While Marx did acknowledge other classes such as the self-employed **petite bourgeoisie**, and the **lumpenproletariat**—the "reserve armies of the unemployed," the two major classes in industrial capitalism are the bourgeoisie and the proletariat. These two major classes are unique to industrial capitalism.

Every historical epoch, according to Marx, is characterized by a class struggle between the two major classes of that time—freemen vs. slaves in the relatively primitive slave states, lords vs. serfs in feudal times, etc. In *all* epochs, the key to whether one is on the top or the bottom is determined by one's position vis-à-vis the relations of production. In the capitalist system, this dynamic is exemplified by the proletariat being forced to sell its labor for subsistence wages, the surplus value of which is taken by the bourgeoisie.

It is through labor that a person expresses his or her humanity, Marx believed. Further, the value of something is directly related to the human labor that went into it. These ideas, sometimes referred to the **labor theory of value**, inform a great deal of Marx's theory, serving as a base for other central tenets of his theory such as *surplus value, alienation,* and *fetishism of commodities.*

Surplus value is the difference between the actual value of the product and what the worker is paid for the labor that went into making it. According to Marx, the principle of surplus value works the same in any type of society (except the prehistoric "primitive communal" societies, and the heretofore unknown truly communist societies) in that the owners of the means of production (such as businesses or land) are able to extract the excess product of labor from the non-owning workers by virtue of their ownership and control of the means of production. For example, in the feudal system, because the lords controlled the land, they were able to extract the excess from the product of serfs' labor—mostly agricultural products, in this case. In industrial capitalism, it is the bourgeoisie who own the businesses and factories, and thereby benefit from the surplus value of the labor of the proletariat.

Thus, the key to class is *ownership*—or lack thereof—according to Marx. Following this theory, in any historical epoch, the two major classes would develop **class interests**. These interests were inherently oppositional, and therefore served to separate the two classes. In essence, the interest of the bourgeois class was to maximize production and to minimize wages, which was accomplished through keeping the bulk of the surplus value of the productive labor of the proletariat for itself, severing the natural relationship between workers and their labor. The bourgeoisie would thereby use its wealth to become even wealthier.

In Marx's analysis, historical *progress can only occur through conflict*. Namely, conflict between classes with material interests. The idea that conflicting class interests are the primary source of social progress is referred to as *"dialectical materialism."* Out of the ruins of class conflict (which at that stage, was primarily between the lords and serfs) of feudalism, comes the "bourgeois" (or capitalist) era. This bourgeois era spawned its own class conflict, primarily between the bourgeoisie (business ownership class) and the proletariat (working class).

In the era of bourgeois capitalism, the interests of the proletariat are to share in the benefits of what it creates through its own labor, and to live in relationship to its labor and to others in the society. However, through a number of mechanisms of the stratification system itself, the class interests of the proletariat are concealed from it. Primary among these mechanisms was what Marx identified as **ideology**, which was an interrelated system of beliefs that served to encourage the proletariat masses to see their plight from a perspective advantageous to the bourgeoisie. The proletariat, for example, would see its misery as part of a religious plan or as a function of its own ineptitude, rather than as a function of bourgeois domination. This was made possible because, as Marx and Engels (1845-46/1970) express in the *German Ideology*:

> The ideas of the ruling class are in every epoch the ruling ideas, i.e., the class which is the ruling material force, is at the same time, its ruling intellectual force. The class which has the means of material production at its disposal, has control at the same time over the means of mental production, so that thereby, generally speaking, the ideas of those who lack the means of mental production are subject to it. The ruling ideas are nothing more than the ideal expression of the dominant material relationships...grasped as ideas. (P. 64)

This ideology could lead people in the proletariat, for example, to see the materially less successful among its members as, perhaps, not working as hard or lacking in natural ability, rather than as exploited and having a commonality of interests in conflict with those of the bourgeoisie. In other words, the working class is deceived by ideology to view their struggles as resulting from something other than the fact that a dominant class is exploiting them.

Marx elaborates on this by introducing the concept of "consciousness." Namely, he articulates a situation known as **class consciousness**, in which a class (e.g., the proletariat) becomes aware of its class position and class interests. The opposite of class consciousness, he terms **false**

consciousness. More specifically, class consciousness has several distinct but related components, which are: **1)** recognizing the class divisions that exist in society; **2)** recognizing that these class divisions are more profound and important than any other social divisions, such as race, nationality, or religion; **3)** recognizing one's own place in the overall class structure; **4)** recognizing the commonality with others in a similar class position; **5)** arousing the intent to change the class-based system through collective action. This last aspect Marx referred to as **praxis**, or the tendency to put consciousness into action.

The ideological apparatus of the bourgeois system was a powerful force inhibiting the formation of class consciousness. All five of the aforementioned elements of class consciousness are necessary for it to occur. A deficiency of any of the five elements was a sufficient cause of false consciousness. For example, dwelling upon national differences through jingoism, or on racial differences through racism, would constitute a false consciousness through a breakdown of the second component. A breakdown of the fourth element could come in the form of an overemphasis on individual achievement. Each of these would be an example of false consciousness.

Marx argued forcefully that a rise in class consciousness among the masses is the only way for a society to move beyond capitalism and establish communism in its place. Yet how can there ever be an ascendance of class consciousness in bourgeois society with such powerfully entrenched ideological apparatus creating so many opportunities for false consciousness? Marx addresses this riddle by pointing out several "contradictions" of capitalism, which become increasingly severe as capitalism matures. These contradictions would help to undermine capitalism on a material level, but also on the human level by facilitating a rise in class consciousness. Thus, for Marx and Engels (1848/1948): "What the bourgeoisie, therefore, produces above all, is its own grave-diggers. Its fall and the victory of the proletariat are equally inevitable."

Marx enumerates several of these contradictions of capitalism. Each epoch, Marx believed, but especially in a maturing capitalist system, would be characterized by an increasing polarization of the classes, centered on conflicting class interests, which in turn would serve as a means of ushering in the demise of capitalism. A rise in class consciousness would be the catalyst for this to occur. In capitalism, the residual middle classes (e.g., petite bourgeoisie, etc.) would increasingly be pushed to the side of the proletariat because they would find it increasingly difficult to maintain their way of life and work outside of the mainstream capitalist system. Hence, they would eventually come to an existence closer to the kind led by the proletariat, so would come to identify themselves as such.

Marx went on to propose that the triumph of the proletariat would eventually come, most likely (although not *necessarily*), by way of a revolution. This triumph will be led by a "vanguard of intellectuals," which will find their support from the increasingly class-conscious masses. With popular support, this vanguard of intellectuals will help to usher in the next epoch through the "expropriation" (or taking, probably by force) of private, productive property.

Once the transitional stage (of expropriating private productive property) has begun, this vanguard of intellectuals will form into a "dictatorship of the proletariat," which will function as stewards for the temporary stage of socialism. Ultimately, this new state apparatus will provide the foundation upon which a classless, egalitarian communist society can be established.

In this type of society, Marx envisioned, humanity will no longer have a life characterized by **alienation**, or an estrangement from the product and process of one's labor. Further, individuals will not be estranged from others in the society and from the human potential within oneself. Rather, it will be the antithetically opposite situation of **species-being**—an ideal state in which people are connected to the product and process of their labor, to others in the society and to the human potential within.

Capitalism contains the "seeds of its own destruction" for several reasons, according to Marx. It sets the necessary preconditions by production of the basic necessities. When what Marx calls the "idiocy of rural life" characteristic of agrarian systems is ended, a corresponding massive rise in urbanization will occur. Urban factories become a vehicle for proletarian discourse, and the hardships suffered in capitalism help to galvanize the proletariat, thereby making them strong through adversity. Meanwhile, the capitalist system ultimately weakens and fractionates the bourgeoisie through increasingly stiffer competition and collapsing profits.

Further, as capitalism matures, it tends to become more globalized, incorporating even the most primitive of peoples into its grasp. Also, as capitalism matures, it produces a surplus of goods at a rate heretofore unseen in society. Yet its *distribution* of these resources becomes increasingly one-sided as the classes continue to polarize. All of this together increases the likelihood of rising class consciousness, thus precipitating the arrival of the communist revolution.

Several criticisms have been leveled at Marx's theory. Many have pointed out the poor likelihood of there ever being an egalitarian society, such as the one envisioned by Marx. Rather, they see the "dictatorship of the proletariat" as merely another elite group—while they replace the bourgeoisie as the dominant elites, the plight of the masses is destined to be much the same as before, according to elite theorists.

Even followers of Marx have been forced to criticize his theory, as they have been forced to adapt his theory to account for a dramatic rise in the size of the middle classes (e.g., managers, professionals, small business owners and artisans) rather than a decline as Marx predicted. Another serious criticism is that Marx was overly focused on economic materialism. This caused him to have a tendency to reduce such important forces as the military, the polity, and the socio-cultural apparatus of society, to functions of the economic order. Despite criticisms, however, Marxism has many adherents; it serves as a major influence in the work of modern day theorists working in the *conflict* approach.

Max Weber on Rationality, Stratification, Power and Authority

The work of Max Weber was at least as influential in conflict approaches to sociology as Karl Marx, and probably more so overall. While there are some parallels between Marx and Weber's theories, there is a multitude of contrasts between them as well, as we shall see. While Karl Marx's theory resonates with many people, the weaknesses pointed out by his critics limit the usefulness in explaining certain aspects of social reality. Because of this, many social theorists see Max Weber's work as more useful than, or at least a necessary complement to, Marx's. As Hans Gerth and C. Wright Mills (1946:47) point out: "Part of Weber's own work may thus

Formal Rationality

Weber explained that formal rationality was primarily concerned with utilizing the most efficient means possible to achieve an end. George Ritzer expanded on Weber's thesis by theorizing about the formal rationality in fast-food establishments like McDonalds.

be seen as an attempt to "round out" Marx's economic materialism by a political and military materialism." But Weber does much more than round out Marx—in general, his theories are a good deal more nuanced and applicable to a relatively wider array of circumstances than Marx's.

Central to Max Weber's (1921/1978) theory is his emphasis on **rationality**, and Weberian scholars (e.g., Kalberg 1980; Ritzer and LeMoyne 1991; LeMoyne et al. 1994; Ritzer 1993) tend to agree on four major types of rationality for Weber. They are:

- **Practical rationality**. This is the type of rationality we use to carry out individual pragmatic needs. With practical rationality, we tend to accept the situation as it is, and attempt to discern the most expedient means of achieving a goal under the circumstances.
- **Theoretical rationality**. This is the type of rationality used when attempting to understand reality through general principles of abstraction or deduction, with mathematics, for example. This type of rationality is involved with attempts at understanding general principles—not necessarily bounded by place and time.
- **Substantive rationality**. This is the type of rationality involved with choosing the means of achieving an end within an internally consistent set of values. There is a striving for value compatibility and revulsion toward hypocrisy. Substantive rationality sometimes is simply called "reason." When we use it, we often assess the means of achieving an end in terms of abstract or metaphysical human values such as "justice," "peace," or "happiness."
- **Formal rationality**. Formal rationality is concerned with utilizing the most efficient means possible to achieve an end. This type of rationality, it is important to note, has an emergent property, meaning it can be practiced on an institutional level as well as on an individual level. The prototypical or ideal type of formal rationality is found in social institutions such as bureaucracies. Formal rationality is characterized by:
    - o quantifiability and calculability
    - o efficiency
    - o predictability
    - o increasing tendencies for gaining control over uncertainties
    - o replacement of humans with non-human technology

Weber predicted an increasing strength of formal rationality as society "progresses," at the expense of substantive rationality. This has **irrational consequences**, however. This ultimately tends to be dehumanizing, as people begin to be viewed as interchangeable, and efficiency becomes more important than human values.

Although we, as human beings, create formally rational structures such as bureaucracies, they eventually come to dominate us. This is what Weber meant by the **"iron cage of rationality."** Weber believed that due to an increasing dependence on, and a predilection for, efficiency, there was no real long range solution to this iron cage problem.

Weber did, however, see temporary solutions to this iron cage dilemma. Conditions would eventually become so bad, he argued, that people would feel generally disgusted with the situation. Occasionally, a **charismatic** person who leads by the strength of his or her personality and appeal would come along and help galvanize the people to challenge rules and create a situation in which the iron cage becomes a little less restrictive for a brief time.

However, Weber argued that when the charismatic leader dies, the leader's movement would evolve into either a **traditional** authority structure based on past practices or a **rational-legal** authority structure based on rules and regulations, not just past practices. The rational-legal system would tend to become the dominant one over time, because it is the most efficient. In turn, the new rational-legal structure would have restrictive rules that would tend to dominate people.

Power is another key concept in Max Weber's sociology, which he conceptualized as the probability of one actor (in the form of either an individual or, more interestingly from a sociological standpoint, a group) carrying out its will, even in the face of opposition from others. His ideas about stratification stem from his insights about the unequal distribution of power. According to Weber, there were three primary dimensions along which these power differentials were likely to occur: 1) an economic dimension of **class**, 2) a socio-cultural dimension of **status**, and 3) a political dimension of **party**.

In Weber's view, **social closure** is a common way in which power is exercised on the group level. This refers to the process of restricting membership or rights "against outsiders so far as, according to its subjective meanings and its binding rules, participation

Authority Figures

According to Weber's concept of authority, Jesus and Martin Luther King, Jr. would be considered charismatic leaders while the President of the U.S. would represent rational-legal authority. Clockwise from top - Jesus (central figure), President Barack Obama, Martin Luther King, Jr.

of certain persons is excluded, limited, or subjected to conditions" (Weber 1921/1978:43).

Weber conceptualized classes as economic categories developing from interaction in a market, in which "utilities" (goods and services) are exchanged, unlike Marx, who envisioned class as all-encompassing and oppositional in nature. Further, Weber viewed class as merely one (albeit an important one) of several dimensions of stratification. A class, for Weber, is an aggregate of individuals facing similar situations in the marketplace, and therefore is a group of people with common "life chances."

Property (or lack of it) is not the only determinant of class, although it is an important one. Here, we must make a key distinction between Weber and Marx. Specifically, Weber (1921/1978:302 ff.) defines a "class situation" as the probability of: **1)** procuring goods and services, **2)** gaining a position in life, and **3)** finding inner satisfaction. These in turn stem from the "relative control over goods and skills and from their income-producing uses within a given economic order."

Several aspects of Weber's conception of class bear mentioning here. Weber focuses not on ownership per se, but rather on control over property and expertise. Thus, (ownership and control) are not necessarily the same things, although ownership clearly implies control in many cases.

With Weber's more open-ended definition of class, it is possible to envision an almost unlimited number of classes. However, we will only examine a few types of classes, which Weber analyzes in some depth:

- **Rentiers**, or a privileged class receiving income from investments in entities such as banks, factories or land. Rentiers typically make their money by virtue of their investments, rather than working for wages. The investment money they do have is often "old money," obtained through inheritance.
- **Entrepreneurs**, or a privileged business class. This class is engaged in the actual day-to-day operation of commercial enterprises, unlike rentiers.
- **Petite Bourgeoisie** (alternatively called Petty Bourgeoisie), or a class of small business owners. A "mom and pop" store owner/operator would be an example of someone in this class. Weber thought this class would get progressively smaller over time, as more people are pulled into the next class discussed—the bureaucratic class.
- **Bureaucrats**, or salaried non-manual specialists. This class would expand over time, Weber theorized, parallel to the expansion of "rational-legal" authority. Due to modern society's increasing tendency toward highly specialized and routinized tasks, a class of people to perform these tasks would arise and become increasingly salient.
- **Craftsmen**, or highly skilled manual workers. This class would likely perform social closure through its own system of credentials, such as journeyman or master craftsman status.
- **Semi-skilled Manual Workers**. In terms of life chances, this class would have relatively less than the highly skilled craftsmen, but would perform closure through what job skills it did have, as well as through unionization.
- **Unskilled Workers**. Somewhat analogous to Marx's reserve armies of the unemployed,

this class would tend to be the "last hired and first fired," and would only be able to garner subsistence wages in dangerous and/or unpleasant work.

Entrepreneurs and rentiers together comprise something akin to Marx's bourgeoisie. Property is important in this sense—but even here, the distinction between entrepreneurs and rentiers could serve to divide what Marx saw as a more coherent bourgeois class. Rentiers and entrepreneurs are very different classes in Weber's scheme because what these two groups do and expect in life differ sharply.

These two classes (rentiers and entrepreneurs), in Weber's theory, are property-owning classes, in the sense of *investment* property, while the others, for the most part, are propertyless (an exception is the petite bourgeoisie, who do own small businesses, but whose "life chances" are significantly less than either the rentiers or entrepreneurs).

While both Marx and Weber believed that self-employment would become less feasible over time, Weber (unlike Marx) predicted a rise in the salaried non-manual class. In this, Weber accurately presaged the dramatic increase of a class of people engaged in the routinized sorts of tasks found in modern bureaucracies over the course of the twentieth century.

There were other dimensions of stratification in addition to class, according to Weber—namely status and party. The three dimensions of stratification each represent a potential basis for coalition in pursuit of personal interests. While class was of the economic realm, status was from the social realm, and party from the political realm.

The primacy of the economic realm was a given for Marx, with action in the social and political arenas stemming from it. However, Weber thought that class and status did not necessarily coincide. Religious priests and bishops, who do not necessarily own much of anything, often are of high status nonetheless, for example. This status itself becomes a way of exercising power.

Class and status could furthermore interact in ways that have important implications for society. Recall the distinction Weber made between the entrepreneurial and rentier classes, for example—while both owned the means of production, the rentiers typically came from socially prominent families such as the German *Junkers*, or descendants of the British aristocracy. One aspect of many members of high status groups, such as those of European aristocracy, was a tendency to hold the direct involvement in a money-making enterprise in low regard. Members of this class tended to be overrepresented in public offices (Armstrong 1973).

This brings us to another way in which Weber develops the concept of status, in which he describes how the vestiges of class from a former time become status in the present. More specifically, certain elements left over from the feudal class system (e.g., the aristocratic tendency to have its children receive an education in the Greek and Latin classics, as opposed to the bourgeois emphasis on more "practical" pursuits, such as engineering and business), become status characteristics in the modern era.

Weber saw that groups of people with some common social characteristic would tend to come together or coalesce and perform social closure toward those who do not possess said characteristic. These groups he termed **status groups**. Status group closure is exemplified by ethnic or racial bigotry, for example, in which members of an ethnic group treat those in the group in a privileged fashion, and those not in the group in an inferior way.

While status was said to inhere in groups that tend to have a distinct "style of life," parties were described as voluntary associations organized for the collective pursuit of political interests. Modern day examples of this are political action committees and special-interest lobbying groups such as the American Medical Association and the National Rifle Association, etc. These parties differ from classes and status groups because they have a **rational-legal**, or bureaucratic, structure. Such attributes as formal organization with an administrative staff, routinized procedures, and formally codified written rules characterize this structure.

According to Weber, class stratification was primary during times of crisis, discovery, or dislocation in the society, while status stratification became prevalent during periods of relative stability or stagnation. Weber viewed social stratification as inevitable, unlike Marx, who was more optimistic about putting an end to the inequality attendant to class. The imposition of socialism or other schemes meant to abolish inequality would not relieve people from being dominated, in Weber's view. In fact, capitalism was preferable to socialism to Weber because of its competing power structures (e.g., private industries, cultural institutions and political parties, etc. in addition to the state). Weber felt that the imposition of socialism would lead to one huge, seamless state bureaucracy that would usher in an "icy winter of rationality" and its attendant domination over its subjects.

While class, status groups, or political parties are likely to provide the conditions for social closure to occur, certain features of social interaction would make the exercise of closure more or less likely. For Weber (1921/1978:46), there are three "principal motives" that increase the likelihood of social closure: 1) a group relatively high in material advantage or prestige attempting to maintain their quality of life (e.g., a group of physicians seeking to maintain their relative advantage by limiting the number of places in medical schools), 2) the contraction of advantages relative to consumption needs (e.g., factory layoffs during low sales periods in order to maintain profit margins for elites), and 3) an increasing scarcity of opportunities for acquisition of needed goods or services (e.g., in a time of famine, rationing food based on social position). When skilled laborers exclude unskilled laborers through such mechanisms as journeyman credentials, for example, (e.g., see Gray 1974), we also see closure in action.

A society generally has some governance mechanisms, which are manifest in terms of standardized procedures, regardless of its class, status and party structure. When power relations becomes **routinized**, or replicated over time, geographic space, and with large numbers of people, Weber acknowledges the emergence of a special type of power, which is quite useful in the study of stratification—**domination**.

Regular structured patterns of inequality are established through domination, whereby subordinate groups become routinized in a subordinate position. When domination becomes **legitimated**, usually because it corresponds in important ways with societal beliefs, values or conventional patterns of behavior, it becomes **authority**. While power tends to be exercised on a face-to-face human level, domination and authority tend to be more structural. Yet, here it is important to note, that what makes authority legitimate is when a critical mass of the society treats it as if it is legitimate. There were three ideal types of authority in Weber's theory:

- **Rational authority** (*or* **rational-legal authority**), which is legitimized through "belief in the 'legality' of patterns of normative rules and the right of those elevated to authority under such rules to issue commands."
- **Traditional authority**, which is legitimized through "an established belief in the sanctity of immemorial traditions and...the status of those exercising authority under them."
- **Charismatic authority**, which is legitimized through "devotion to the specific and exceptional sanctity, heroism or exemplary character of an individual person, and of the normative patterns of order revealed or ordained by him."

In following his concept of the **ideal type**, an analytical construct or schema which accentuates key characteristics of structures or actions which are found repeatedly in society, Weber adduces these three types of authority for analytical purposes, pointing out that they are not likely to ever be encountered in their "pure" form in actual history. We witness innumerable instances of cases having some or nearly all of the elements of these types of authority, however.

Rational authority, Weber argued, was the most efficient of these forms, due to its institution of rules applicable to everyone, as well as the meritocracy those generally held rules would engender. Thus, as society continued to modernize, rational authority would out-compete other types of authority (most notably traditional authority).

Consider the prevalence of rational-legal systems replete with elected officials in virtually every developed country, for example, and juxtapose this with the traditional authority of kings, princes and tribal chieftains of prior times (or contemporary times in many Third World countries); then compare the efficiency with which the institutions function in the different locations.

However, along with the efficiency of rational-legal systems came also the **iron cage of rationality**, in which the rules and procedures would seem to take on a life of their own, dominating people in the process and taking the fun out of life for them, as it were. With an increasingly constricted ability to act independently, people would thus be more likely to reach out and follow a charismatic leader who was able to articulate common concerns. This charismatic movement would result in a loosening of the strictures of the old rule system (which could be either traditional or rational-legal), and a decline in legitimacy of that old system.

As the charismatic leader gained momentum by accumulating followers and legitimacy, eventually it would come to eclipse the old way. However, in order for the movement to survive the death of the charismatic leader, there must be a "routinization of charisma," in which the main tenets of the charismatic leader's philosophy would become the basis for either a traditional or (increasingly more likely in modern society because of its relative efficiency) rational-legal authority.

With its tendency to create its own rules and procedures that newly routinized authority eventually picks up the negatives of the old way and becomes an "iron cage" in itself. When this happens, society is ripe for the rise of yet another charismatic leader. Thus, the course of history is a continuous process of stable authority which becomes too constrictive, becoming challenged by a charismatic authority which itself eventually becomes routinized into yet another type of relatively stable authority.

Thus, Weber did not envision a "utopian end of history" that would usher in the end of conflict and suffering in this world, as Marx did. Recall the major critiques of Marx are that he predicted a revolution that never came, missed the fact that the state is very unlikely to ever "wither away" and failed to account adequately for the rise of the middle classes. None of those criticisms could reasonably be leveled at Weber. However, Weber's critics (primarily Marxists) charge that he is a "bourgeois" sociologist who examines the system but offers no particular policy prescriptions. Thus, he could be criticized for maintaining a putatively unjust status quo. Nonetheless, Max Weber is probably the single most influential figure in modern sociology.

The Sociology of Georg Simmel

Trained as a philosopher, Georg Simmel was especially influenced by several philosophers writing in the German tradition, including: **1)** Immanuel Kant, who made a distinction between "form" and "content," and who had a special interest in identifying the relatively timeless forms of thought that were imposed on the content of everyday life, **2)** G.W.F. Hegel, who was particularly interested in dialectical thinking, especially as it indicated many of the conflicts and contradictions inherent in ideas and in life, and **3)** Wilhelm Dilthey, whose work illuminated the connections between the subjective consciousness of individuals and the objective outer world.

Primarily considered as a social philosopher, Simmel's subject matter ranged from highly metaphysical ideas to the more mundane, everyday lives of people living in society. In terms of the latter, Simmel (1908/1959) made a distinction among several levels of analysis. For him, there were three such levels: **1)** the individual subjective level, **2)** the interpersonal, or small-group level, and **3)** the level of the larger society and culture.

Simmel is known for his work in articulating distinctions among these levels, and also ways in which the social process on the respective levels interact with one another. In conceptualizing these, Simmel constructed his **principle of emergence**, which contains two major elements: **1)** each level of analysis is a thing unto itself (*sui generis*), not reducible to other levels and **2)** there are contradictions and conflicts among and between those levels. The first aspect is exemplified in the fact that a family, for instance, has characteristics that are not reducible to the individuals within the family. The second aspect, which reflects the profound importance Simmel ascribed to dialectical thinking, is exemplified when an individual in a group, acting in his or her own behalf, does something detrimental to the interests of the overall group.

Simmel was also interested in identifying common social forms—modes of interaction that were commonly found in so many times and places, that they seemed to transcend the individual instances of them. Simmel discussed several examples of common social forms:

- **Superordination/subordination.** According to Simmel (1908/1971a), most if not all human relationships involve power differentials. However, there is an ironic aspect to this, in that virtually no power differential is absolute. Furthermore, it is sometimes the case that a superordinate person can become subordinate and vice-versa. This phenomenon has come to be known as "role reversal." Pointing out these ironies is typical of much of Simmel's work.

- **Strangeness**. There are certain elements of strangeness in every relationship, even the most intimate (Simmel 1908/1971b). There are always parts of individuals that are unknown and secret from others, in other words. In social situations, strangers to a group have an ironic place, in that they are part in and part out. In some situations, because of this, group members will trust a stranger with secrets even their intimate partners do not know about (priests, rabbis, bartenders, and psychotherapists are all examples of such strangers). Thus, a stranger, because of their unique position, is often able to offer insights that group members themselves ironically may not have because they are so deeply enmeshed in the group.

In his work on The Philosophy of Money, Simmel (1907/1978) articulates his vision of the central contradiction inherent in modern life, which he refers to as the "tragedy of culture." Individuals are inherently creative, in Simmel's view. However, as part of living, people create objects and institutions that seem to take on a life of their own. As this occurs, the "objective culture" of these objects and institutions creates an obstacle for the creative process of the individuals.

A further contradiction is posed by the use of money. It serves as a general medium of exchange, and bolsters a free market economy that has a tremendous potential for growth. At the same time, money serves as a yardstick against which virtually everything can be measured. This leads to a sense that "everything and everybody have their price" and the profound cynicism about human nature that accompany it.

Simmel's work is reminiscent of Durkheim's in certain ways, particularly in his emphasis on social forms, and on emergent properties of social institutions and the society of which they are part. As you will recall, Durkheim emphasized social facts, which have an existence beyond the people living in them.

In terms of the dialectics and contradictions of life, his theory resonates with Marx's. Simmel's theory has some parallels with Max Weber's ideas about the "iron cage" of rationality, in which the institutions created by people come to dominate them.

However, Simmel's theory lacks an overarching theme, unlike the work of these other three theorists. Rather, his theory is more remarkable primarily for hav-

Georg Simmel (1858 - 1918)

Georg Simmel, developed several important sociological concepts, including the "Principle of Emergence" and the "Tragedy of Culture."

ing a series of brilliant insights about a number of disparate social phenomena.

Émile Durkheim on the Division of Labor in Society

Stratification systems were bound to arise as societies modernized, according to Émile Durkheim. This is because societies tended to develop an increasingly elaborate division of labor. Durkheim viewed the division of labor in the society, and the social solidarity and stratification systems that accompany it, as social facts of the society. As such, the stratification system was a property of the society to which the individuals in it were subject. In other words, stratification systems are seen as a product of the society itself, which Durkheim saw as an organic whole. The overall structure of the stratification system was not subject to the wishes of the individuals in it.

Durkheim's ideas about stratification were closely intertwined with his sense of how societies functioned, and in so doing how they kept from dissolving into chaos. In examining these themes, he focuses on the relationship between the individual and society. Under optimal circumstances, that relationship leads to **social solidarity**, or a cohesiveness in which the welfare of the group is more important than that of any of its individual members.

In *The Division of Labor in Society*, Durkheim (1893/1964; for a good scholarly interpretation see Aron 1965) discusses two major types of social solidarity—**mechanical solidarity**, characteristic of primitive societies, and **organic solidarity**, characteristic of modern societies. These two types are found in different types of societies, and therefore take different forms. However, both types of solidarity share the same *goal* of allowing for the smooth functioning of society. Mechanical and organic solidarity can be summarized as follows:

- **Mechanical solidarity.** Individual differences are small. Members of the society feel similar emotions and hold similar values to one another, leading to a strong sense of social cohesiveness. There is little or no **division of labor** (i.e., most people perform similar type labor, such as agriculture or hunting). The legal system is repressive. In the mechanical solidarity characteristic of primitive societies, there is very little stratification, because there is such a minimal division of labor.
- **Organic solidarity.** There is a differentiation of labor, in which specialization occurs. It is only in this kind of society that there is a rise of individualism. Accompanying an expanding domain of science and rationality, there tends to be a decline in tradition and traditional authority structures. The legal system is more restitutive than repressive, which leads to a rise of civil proceedings based on a philosophy of individual rights, such as lawsuits. In the modern societies characterized by organic solidarity, we see the rise of an elaborate division of labor, and thus the inevitable rise of specialized labor and stratification systems.

One thematic commonality of both mechanical and organic systems is that society ultimately functions by placing the interests of society *above* those of the individual. In primitive societies, this is accomplished through a strict enforcement of rules *external* to the individual—

hence the repressive legal system. Modern societies, on the other hand, function best when the **norms** (principles of the group which guide the behavior of its members) of a society are **internalized** (become part of a person's thought process) by the people in it. A person's place in the stratification system helps to bind the person back to the overall collective. Put another way, the division of labor and the stratification system that comes along with it serve to promote the organic solidarity of modern society.

How do we determine where a society falls on the primitive to modern spectrum, and hence whether it is more likely characterized by mechanical or organic solidarity? There are three factors involved: **1) volume**, or numbers of people, **2) material density**, or number of people per unit of space, and **3) moral density**, or frequency of interaction among people in the society.

In Durkheim's conceptualization of **organic solidarity**, the interdependence of the different parts of the society was analogous to the human body. The functional society was one that operates effectively. Durkheim's famous quote: **"The individual is born of society, not society of individuals,"** illustrates his belief that *there is no such thing as individuality outside of modern society*, with its attendant division of labor.

With the rise of the individual, however, also come individual desires that can sometimes be at odds with society's needs. When there is an insufficient internalization of norms, such that individual desires are out of synchronization with the goals of society, a state of **anomie** (a breakdown or **absence of norms**) can be said to occur. In the Durkheimian view, this condition of anomie in modern society is the primary cause of social pathology such as crime and suicide.

In modern society, there are two primary causes of social pathology, according to Durkheim—one is anomie, and the other is **egoism**, or a lack of attachment of the individual to the larger collective. In fact, Durkheim (1897/1951) saw these as the two leading social factors contributing to suicide, particularly in modern society. These would be particularly prevalent in situations where the society was very "loose-knit"—a condition generally found in industrial society. A third cause of suicide Durkheim identified as **altruism** (a situation in which the individual is so tightly integrated into the collective that there is little or no sense of the individual outside of that collective). This was much more typical of either primitive societies or of tight-knit collectives in modern society.

Durkheim's first major work was *The Division of Labor in Society*, which laid the foundation for a great deal of his subsequent work. It is also notable for several reasons:

- In focusing on the interests of society as opposed to those of the individual, Durkheim's was the initial work in what was to become the social functions school. Functionalists attempt to explain how the various components of society act ("function") or fail to act as agents in a society's progress, as you'll recall from Chapter 1.
- Durkheim was critical of Marxists and other conflict theorists who construed modern society's division of labor, and particularly its stratification system, as something necessarily evil.

To extend the organic analogy of the human body—each part of the body serves an essential function, in which all can take pride in the overall whole and in the part they play in it. "If the brain is of importance, the stomach is likewise an essential organ," in Durkheim's (1893/1964:42) words.

While the stratification attendant to the division of labor was an inevitable feature of modern society for Durkheim, he did not view it as necessarily a bad thing. Rather, the challenge of modern society was to have a "normal" division of labor, in which those in a position to set the standards for the society as a whole were those who were most attuned to the needs of the whole.

Many "functional" theories of stratification can claim Durkheim's theory as a prototype in that it viewed the positions most crucial to the society as those deserving to be the most highly rewarded. But how are we to determine which social positions are the most crucial? Later functional theorists answered this question in a number of ways. For Durkheim, however, the most crucial, and therefore the most highly rewarded, positions in the society were those articulating the spirit and will of the people:

> Why is this privileged position accorded to what is occasionally called the 'brain' of society?...The problem is easily solved when we perceive that wherever an authority with power to govern is established its first and foremost function is to ensure respect for beliefs, traditions and collective practices—namely, to defend the common consciousness from all its enemies, from within as well as without. It thus becomes the symbol of that consciousness. (Durkheim 1893/1984:42)

It was not inevitable that societies would necessarily stratify along these lines, in Durkheim's view. He warns of three possible **abnormal divisions of labor**. In an **anomic division of labor**, relationships among people are not properly regulated, thus resulting in a splintering of society (1893/1984:304). This arises from a situation in which "...occupations that fill our daily lives tend to detach us from the social group to which we belong...[one's job therefore] never occupies more than a small part of our field of consciousness, [and] will never be sufficient to hold us" (Durkheim 1893/1984:298).

In a **forced division of labor**, people are compelled to perform tasks that are disagreeable to them. This tends to occur when people are not sorted into occupations based on interests and abilities. This most commonly occurs when one's position in society is determined by birth, for example. In such a case, the stratification system "...no longer corresponds, to the distribution of natural abilities" (p. 311). Such a situation, Durkheim believed, is likely to result in a class war if it gets bad enough. (p. 310). This aspect of Durkheim's theory comes quite close to Marx.

Durkheim warns of a third abnormal division of labor, which he does not specifically name, but which we may characterize as **improper levels of specialization**. Durkheim (pp. 326-327) points out that as the labor force in a society specializes, the skill level of individual workers are able to increase within their specialties, and there is not a lot of lost time, moving from one occupation to another. Societies are thus not able to develop beyond the most rudimentary stages when there is not sufficient specialization in them. There must be a balance, however, between specialization and the ability of the society to coordinate the respective specialties. It follows that the more complex the coordination process becomes, the more specialties there are.

Here we must emphasize the importance Durkheim attaches to the *solidarity* of the society in order to properly summarize his views on stratification. The most crucial positions are therefore those that promote solidarity among the people by, for example, ensuring that people understand and respect collective beliefs and practices. Members of society must also understand how each element of society cooperates, and their place in that overall whole. Because "solidarity in general depends very closely upon the functional activity of the specialized parts" (p. 324), the coordination of those parts itself becomes a crucial function of society.

Focusing on Elites

Many social thinkers have observed that there are always elites in any society. While the specific nature of who is in charge at a given time may change, what never changes is that there is always a set of elites, or people in power.

One of the most prolific and incisive theorists in this regard was **Vilfredo Pareto**. Pareto dedicated a large portion of his long and distinguished career examining the question of how elites come to be in positions of power in the first place, how those elites change over time, and how these processes are integral parts of the overall operation of the social system.

Before turning to his theory of elites per se, we need first to examine Pareto's overall idea of a social system. Pareto (1935) saw society as a system, which tended to find its state of **equilibrium**, or balance. In order to maintain this equilibrium, any change to the system led to change in other parts of that same system. A societal change in a more liberal direction, for example, would tend to be followed by a reactionary period, in which society becomes more restrictive.

Pareto was interested in society as a system and especially in the *stability* of that system. He had an engineering background, and was thus heavily influenced by concepts of physics, such as Isaac Newton's laws of mechanics. One idea he borrows from physics is that of **equilibrium**, or a relatively stable balance point in the system. He goes on to articulate two types of equilibrium—the relatively more common "stable" equilibrium, and the less common "unstable" equilibrium:

- **Stable equilibrium**—change in one part of a system stimulates a reaction that reverses or minimizes that change.

A useful analogy is of a tightrope walker who starts to fall off one way (e.g., to the left) and adapts by pulling back the other way (to the right)—the result is a **restoration of balance**.

A plethora of examples can be seen in politics. When things get far to the left, people tend to vote for the right, and vice-versa. Take the presidency of Teddy Roosevelt, for example. Roosevelt was famously called a "trust buster" because of his challenges to big businesses (some of which were operating as virtual monopolies). "Pro-business" presidents such as Coolidge and Hoover, whose policies would eventually lead to the accumulation of capital in relatively few hands, which in turn precipitated the Great Depression, later countered these challenges to big business. In turn, that resulted in the liberal "New Deal" era of Franklin D. Roosevelt and Truman, to an extent. After that, the more liberal Kennedy and Johnson era followed the conservative time of Eisenhower. After swings through Nixon and Carter, the more liberal Clinton, and then the conservative George Bush Jr. followed the conservative Reagan and Bush Sr. regimes. Pareto would not have been surprised in the least to find out the congressional elections of 2006 showed a reversal of the conservative politics that had been dominant during the early part of the Bush regime. The point here is that swings in one direction eventually tend to be counteracted by counter moves toward the other direction, with a balance or equilibrium point somewhere in between. More recently, the regimes of Bush Jr. and Obama can be seen through this spectrum.

- **Unstable equilibrium**—change in some part of the system results in even more change.

When some violence leads to even more violence, and the escalating violence leads to a riot, is a social example of this. To follow the tightrope analogy, the tightrope walker leans one way, which causes him to lean even farther, until eventually, he falls from the rope. Unstable equilibrium in one part of the system eventually results in a stable equilibrium in a broader sense (in this case, the tightrope walker's falling body eventually coming to rest on the floor).

The social system has many interdependent parts, and change in one part can influence the whole system. However, Pareto believed that societies went through cycles rather than stages, evolutionary or otherwise, unlike other theorists such as Marx and Durkheim.

A stable equilibrium tends to maintain the status quo. An unstable equilibrium, on the other hand, tends to push society into the next phase in the cycle. Ultimately, however, cycles are like changes in season, rather than linear, progressive time.

For a time, part of society (e.g., the economy) could be in a stable equilibrium, while another part (e.g., the polity) could be in an unstable equilibrium. Eventually, however, every part influences every other part, although the influences take time and some influences take longer than others.

Society never reaches fully stable equilibrium (as in rest), because it is not a totally closed system. In other words, there is practically always some new outside influence in a society (e.g., a new invention, an earthquake, a drought, etc.), which disturbs the status quo and causes the social system to seek a new equilibrium. Thus, rather than societies actually reaching equilibrium, it would be more accurate to say that social systems tend to move in the direction of equilibrium.

Gaetano Mosca, another theorist of elites, observed that people in a position to capitalize early on a new resource could sometimes garner power and privilege, achieving upward mobility in the process. With this observation, Mosca (1939) offers insight into how elites change over time. With the advent of computers, for example, people who were able to capitalize early on the invention and to position themselves to take advantage of it relative to others, often were highly successful financially. Bill Gates, founder of the Microsoft Corporation, is an example of someone who was able to do this successfully.

Pareto refers to this situation, in which new people cycle into or out of elite status, as a *circulation of elites*.

Generally, a circulation of elites occurs as part of an unstable equilibrium period (which in turn is often caused by perturbations to the system resulting from new conditions such as the advent of computers, or weakness of old elites). Specific elites come and go, but there are *always* elites, according to Pareto.

Societies in general tend to be stable systems. As such, even if there is some tremendous disturbance, which results in catastrophe such as war, revolution, etc., there is also a tendency for society to become reorganized under a new set of elites and that reorganization tends to be similar in many ways to the old organization.

Often, after a time of turmoil or excessive liberalism, there is a conservative movement to restore order. The more extremely a society has moved in one way, in the extreme liberalism of Weimar Germany, for example, the more extremely it tends to move in the other (to follow the German example, the extreme reaction of Nazism) as a result.

There are two ideal types of elites, according to Pareto, which he derived from the political philosopher, Niccolo Machiavelli:

- **Lions**—are strong and daring, but inattentive to detail and not particularly clever.
- **Foxes**—are guileful and cunning, but too rational, and clever, with too many new ideas and too attentive to detail.

After periods of chaos, people follow lions, who appeal to the masses' inherent conservatism and need for order. The lions impose a crude order, while foxes quickly figure out the system and how to work it toward their own ends. Through their cunning, foxes rise to the top, but as the number of foxes increases, their self-serving cleverness conflicts with other foxes, resulting in instability.

This instability may lead to a revolution or other type of chaos, or it may lead directly to a time of conservative reaction led by lions, and thus the cycle continues. The new lions are generally different from the old lions, but the new foxes are often similar (or the same as) the old foxes.

Oleg Gubin, in his research on the circulation of old Soviet elites, for example, finds that many elites in communism are now elites in capitalism. The common denominator is that they are clever and could figure out how to navigate both systems quickly, using resources (e.g., education and connections) from the old system to work the new. These types of people are Pareto's foxes.

Most people do not act rationally, in Pareto's view. Instead, people behave according to sentiments first, and then construct rational reasons later to *justify* (or "rationalize") their behavior. Yet sentiments cannot be directly observed—only their evidence can be seen. Of this evidence, there are two types:

- **Residues**, or the actual behaviors that people display.
- **Derivations**, or what people say about their behavior.

People oscillate between wanting change and conformity. Too much of one (after a lag time to work its way through the system) increases a desire for the other, and the call for the corresponding set of elites. A crucial skill of elites is to be able to read the masses correctly (in terms of the relative importance it places on one of these, relative to the other, at a given time, for example), which, through a correct assessment of residues and derivations, they are able to achieve.

As society is ready to move on to a new set of elites, the old elites attempt to hold on to their elite status. Some of the ways they attempt to do this are:

- **Recruiting (co-opting)** the most capable from the masses, in order to prevent them from becoming leaders of an opposition movement. Instead, they are incorporated as a partially privileged underling in the status quo (e.g., financial elites who support liberal redistribution programs, thereby averting the much more serious possibility of a revolution and its accompanying radical redistribution of resources).
- **Creating/defining problems** in such a way that old elites are in an optimal position to solve them, assuring that they remain in a leadership role by doing so (e.g., starting a war).

However, the decadence and weakness of the old elites ultimately yields to the ability and strength of the new elites. What does not change is that there are *always* elites. Hence, we consider Pareto's famous line about social change: "The more things change, the more they remain the same."

Some strengths of his theory are:

- It views society as an overall system, rather than one of its isolated parts, and thus offers a relatively broad perspective.
- It acknowledges the *irrational* elements of human motivation.
- It offers a coherent model for fluctuations in public opinion and attitudes (e.g., liberal/conservative cycles).
- Pareto attempted to develop a universal set of principles to apply to all times and places, that could make specific predictions about what elites would be in power when and for how long.

Conclusion

In this chapter, we have considered a number of classical theorists' work on social organization in some depth. The work of Karl Marx has been profoundly influential in later theorizing and research in the *conflict* tradition, and Émile Durkheim's writings have deeply informed subsequent research in the *functional* tradition. Max Weber, perhaps *the* central figure in classical sociology has inspired work in both the conflict and functional traditions. Theories of elites, such as Pareto's, have not been as influential on further work as has the work of Marx, Weber and Durkheim. They do, however, offer important insights that continue to inform later work, and to be incorporated into the conflict and functional traditions. In the next chapter, we'll discuss research that has extrapolated on the classical foundation we have just examined.

CHAPTER SUMMARY

- Functional approaches to stratification stem largely from the seminal work of Émile Durkheim. They emphasize how the division of labor contributes to the overall operation of society, and the role interdependent parts play in that overall operation.
- Simmel's insights into the workings of society, including the tragedy of culture and the principle of emergence, are both important concepts in sociology.
- Conflict approaches build largely on the work of Karl Marx and Max Weber, and focus on the conflicting interests of different social collectives (such as classes or status groups), including how those interests manifest themselves in the material world.
- Elite theorists, such as Pareto and Mosca, emphasize how in virtually every form of social organization, the masses are subject to the rule of elites, and how those elites circulate over time.

8. Building on the Classics: Studying Stratification in Modern Society

Observing modern industrial societies such as ours, we can see massive differences among people in the distribution of money, class and social status. We see these accruing differentially to people with the power to acquire and maintain them, and the increased hazards to those lacking such power. Yet our modern society is not unique in these patterns of social inequality (often referred to by sociologists as social **stratification**). Indeed, it has been a social fact of life for millennia and will likely continue to be in the future. While virtually every society has some degree of social inequality, the precise *nature* of inequality—that is, the form and degree of stratification—tends to vary from one society to another.

In all its various manifestations, social inequality itself is an integral part of virtually every modern society. As such, sociologists sometimes think of the stratification system as a central (or even *the* central) principle of social organization in any given society. In this chapter, we'll examine the nature of stratification systems, and the crucial roles they play in society.

Stratification as an Organizing Principle of Society

Robert Michels, an historian and social theorist in the early twentieth century, attempted to answer the question of why stratification is so pervasive. While Michels's work falls far short of an exhaustive or comprehensive view of stratification processes, it does serve as a rough outline for understanding their pervasiveness. It also will be useful in synthesizing some of the respective views on the stratification system that we will discuss throughout this and some of the following chapters.

Michels (1911/1949) observed that there must be some form of organization in order for collective action to take place. People supplying the organizational capability tend to be the ones who are either placed in charge, or who successfully seize control. Once there is a relatively small group in charge, the leaders tend to work not only for the interests of the collective, but for their own selfish interests, including consolidating and maintaining the power they already have. Thus, the priorities of those in power are often at odds with those of the relatively less powerful masses.

To illustrate various aspects of this phenomenon, consider the dynamics of a meeting. If everyone is trying to talk over each other, nothing gets accomplished—it is simply a waste of everyone's time and energy. In order for anything to be accomplished, someone or some small group takes charge of the proceedings. Then, once an agenda is set, something may even be accomplished, but it is not necessarily what most of the people may have had in mind when they first went to the meeting.

This process serves as a simple analogy of how stratification processes often work. Let's take a look at the process in a little more depth, and then we'll examine more specific theories of stratification.

The philosopher Rousseau once observed that "there never existed a true democracy, and none can ever exist. It is against natural order that the great number should govern and that the few should be governed." Michels extrapolated on this observation by pointing out that throughout history, the masses have always been under the rule of a small handful of relatively more powerful elites. Michels characterizes this as "oligarchy," by which he means rule by a few. Michels (1949/1961) observes that:

> Our consistent knowledge of the political life of the principal civilized nations of the world authorizes us to assert that the tendency toward oligarchy constitutes one of the historic necessities, one of the iron laws of history, from which the most democratic modern societies and, within those societies, the most advanced parties, have been unable to escape. (P. 606)

Known as Michels's **iron law of oligarchy**, this observation points out that the masses are always destined to be ruled by a handful of elites, regardless of the specific type of political regime. He sums up his central observation tersely: "Whoever says organization says oligarchy."

Elites tend to ideologically differentiate themselves from one another (referred to as a "centrifugal" tendency), Michels notes. Conversely, there is an even more powerful "centripetal" tendency, which is the tendency to consolidate everyone in its power into a common mold.

Michels ([1949/1961]:608) observes that "In truth, the *raison d'etre* of the political party is the push for power." Thus, once people achieve power, the maintenance and consolidation of that power becomes an end in itself, regardless of the original ideology.

Michels can be thought of as a theorist of elites considering his focus on the universal nature of the masses being ruled by a relatively few powerful people. In the following pages, we will examine several views of stratification processes, which can be understood analytically as functional views, conflict views, and elite views.

At the outset we will say that most analyses of stratification treat functional and conflict views as irreconcilable opposites, while either ignoring elite views or incorporating them into the conflict or functional "camps" for discussion purposes. In this book, the approach we take is to see all three as views of a larger process.

That said, depending upon what aspect of the process one is trying to understand, one or some combination of the views (or schools of thought within one of those views) may be most useful. Yet it will be useful not to lose sight of the overall picture while examining each of the parts, even those stemming back to the classical roots of the discipline. The overall picture in this case is that virtually every society and every institution within every society is stratified in some way.

Michels's fundamental observation was that there is

Iron Law of Oligarchy

Michels's Iron Law of Oligarchy states that the masses of people are destined to be ruled by a class of elites. One such example is the Fascist dictator, Benito Mussolini.

an oligarchic tendency in virtually all organizations, regardless of the ideology involved. His insight was hard won from his own experience. Michels himself participated in the activities of the "Social Democrats" in Germany, a group whose ideology was heavily influenced by Marxism. Bitterly, Michels noted that despite all the talk about equality and democracy, the small cadre of elites in the Social Democrats had the habit of enforcing discipline within the ranks by ruthlessly turning on those who challenged their own ideas of what "democracy" should look like. The stark gulf between the ideology and the action served as the catalyst for Michels's ruminations about the universal character of the process.

Pitirim Sorokin (1959), the early twentieth century Russian-American social theorist, similarly pointed out that historically, attempts to "level" a society, or to do away with the stratification system, have not lasted long. More often than not, in fact, once established in power, the "levelers" turn out more brutal than those preceding them. Sorokin himself, who was woefully aware from first-hand experience of the Russian case, could easily see the brutality of a Lenin or a Stalin, relative to the Czar who preceded them. Like Michels, Sorokin was perceptive enough to see the difference between the ideology and the social reality, and thereby to see the relatively universal character of stratification systems in general.

Each of the classical theorists we will consider here—Karl Marx, Max Weber, Gaetano Mosca, Vilfredo Pareto, and Emile Durkheim—whose work provided the foundation for the science of sociology, had a strong sense of the central role that stratification played in the society.

Because most of the stratification literature is organized around either conflict or functional themes, we spend the bulk of this and the other chapters in this section examining the research stemming from these two views. It is crucial not to lose sight of the bigger picture of the overall society, however, regardless of which of these themes is being developed. Examining these two themes together generally helps to accomplish this, especially in combination with "**elite**" themes, such as Robert Michels's theory of oligarchy, which acknowledges that there is bound to be a system of inequality in virtually any society. For it is certainly true that every society ever studied has been stratified, with the possible exception of the most primitive.

When we use the term **stratification**, we are generally referring to a relatively permanent state of social inequality in terms of several characteristics, including power, money, occupational prestige and status. For example, recalling from our discussion of Max Weber, power is the probability that a social actor (individual or collective) will achieve its goals, even in the face of opposition.

Davis and Moore's Functional Theory of Stratification

Sociologists in the **functionalist** school, following Durkheim's lead, tend to focus on the overall society, rather than on its individual members or groups within that society. From this framework, a functional theorist is likely to ask how a given institutional arrangement benefits the society at large. In other words, how is that institution functional? Operating from this theoretical perspective, Kingsley Davis and Wilbert Moore (1945) ask a specific question regarding an important characteristic of society—its **stratification** system: "**Why is there inequality?**"

Davis and Moore propose that the stratification system makes society possible because it serves as a vehicle by which individuals with **innate ability** or **talent** for performing **"functionally important"** tasks in a society, for which there is an inadequate workforce or **relative scarcity of personnel**, are sufficiently motivated to obtain the necessary training to perform those tasks.

The functional importance of a task is proportional to how critical that task is to benefiting members of the society or to keeping the society running smoothly. However, depending on the immediate needs of the society, the functional importance of a task can change. A well-trained soldier is of more functional importance during wartime than during peacetime, for example.

Societies reward those performing functionally important tasks, argue Davis and Moore. Whenever a scarcity of personnel occurs, the rewards tend to be increased in order to entice more members of society into that field. Typically, these rewards are some combination of: **1)** *material* (money and other goods); and **2)** *symbolic* (status and privilege).

In the long run, Davis and Moore point out, such a system benefits *all* members of society—not only those who receive relatively greater rewards. A differential reward system serves as an efficient means of: **1)** *recruiting* talented people into an occupation, **2)** enticing them to focus on long-term success in order to persevere in sometimes long, arduous and otherwise unrewarding *training* (the practice of medicine, for example, requires first spending years attending college and medical school—if the medical field were not so rewarding, both materially and symbolically, it is doubtful that many people with a talent for this field would enter it in the first place, Davis and Moore argue), and **3)** enticing people to perform the tasks of the occupation in an optimal manner once established in the occupation.

Melvin Tumin has criticized Davis and Moore for failing to acknowledge that there may be differential access to more highly rewarded occupations on some basis other than talent or ability. For instance, **inheritance**, or the passing of wealth across generations, seems to explain a great deal of social position and wealth—many government, corporate, and entertainment elites coming from privileged backgrounds provide examples of this. Despite criticism, however, the Davis and Moore theory continues to serve as a backdrop for sociological research.

Conflict Theorists on the Importance of Class

Conflict theorists, in direct contrast with a functional approach, blame the stratification system for many severe social problems. In fact, conflict theorists view the existence of the stratification system itself as arising from some combination of force, coercion and fraud, and the strong unjustly dominating the weak, rather than serving a positive function in society.

An absolutely central concept in the study of stratification for most conflict theorists is that of class. A **class** can be understood as a group of people with a common position in the stratification system. This implies a number of things, as we will see presently. Class is important because with it comes the ability (or lack thereof) to control resources, and because attitudes and beliefs often are related to class position. Thomas Bottomore (1966), in his work *Classes in Modern Society*, observes that:

[T]he division of society into distinct social classes is one of the most striking manifestations of inequality in the modern world...it has often been the source of other kinds of inequality, and... the economic dominance of a particular class has very often been the basis for its political rule.

There are two important questions among sociologists working from a conflict perspective: 1) what is the correlation between the distribution of resources on the one hand, and power differentials on the other? and 2) what societal factors lead to greater or lesser chances of conflict in a society, considering the unequal distributions of power and resources? Such conflict may take the form of civil unrest, revolt or, in extreme cases, revolution. From this perspective, power and resource distribution patterns predict such conflict, and thus the focus on *stratification*, or the unequal distribution of power and resources, is a crucial one. When that inequality is seen in terms of relationships between or among fairly stable groups, *class* becomes of critical importance.

Conflict sociologists often take Karl Marx's and/or Max Weber's theories about stratification as a starting point in discussing unequal distributions of power and resources. Marx viewed industrial society as being divided by class, in which there is a small but highly capitalized *bourgeoisie* (those who own the "means of production") on one hand, and an undercapitalized *proletariat* (relatively poor working class) on the other. Through private investment in productive property such as factories and businesses, the ownership class would be able to exercise a great deal of power in dictating the terms of exchange with the working class.

For Marxist theorists, then, a key arbiter of inequality is the economic *ownership* of the means of production, as articulated in Marx's ideas about class. As capitalism matured, Marx explained, there would be an increasing polarization between the two major classes of owners and workers, with a gradual decrease in residual middle classes, such as managers and professionals. However, at least in industrialized countries such as those of Western Europe and the United States, the opposite has been true. During the past century, the middle classes have actually become much larger. Many of these middle classes have greater earnings and potential for upward mobility that is not based on their owning the means of production. For instance, managers typically do not have an ownership interest per se in the businesses they manage. Thus, even sociologists of a Marxist persuasion have been forced to consider seriously other dimensions of class besides ownership, especially in the late twentieth century.

In other words, while for Marx, there are two great classes—by definition in opposition to each other (he would hold that one class cannot exist without the other), it was not such a clear dichotomy for Weber. While Weber was a theoretician, Marx held that the purpose of class analysis was "praxis." Marx wanted to cultivate the development of class-consciousness, thus precipitating the revolution.

One problem with Marx's theory is that, over one hundred years later, there has still not been a socialist revolution in an advanced capitalist nation. Many theories attempt to understand why this is the case.

In developed societies such as the United States and Western Europe, many workers do not fall neatly into Marx's primary class categories of a powerful bourgeoisie (owners) on the one hand, or of a relatively powerless proletariat (workers) on the other. The Marxian theorist Erik Olin Wright refers to these as "contradictory class locations." For example, in the case of a manager, the individual does not own the means of production, and hence is an employee of someone else. However, compared to the working class, a manager is in a position of authority. In industrial societies, managers, together with the *petite bourgeoisie* (self-employed persons, but without supervisory power over significant numbers of other people), comprise a significant portion of the workforce.

However, it is crucial to ask whether the *trend* is toward larger or smaller middle classes. While there are many people with "contradictory class locations," the income and wealth distributions between the highest echelons and the rest of the people (including many in the middle classes) are quite skewed. For instance, a recent study sponsored by the United Nations found that in a world with about five billion people, the richest five hundred people control more wealth than do the poorest two-and-one-half *billion* people. While the middle classes have gotten larger in the *industrialized* world, a large portion of the proletariat can now be found in Third World countries as a result of the increasing globalization of the economy.

Although the precise definition and boundaries of the respective classes may be a source of endless debate, the main issue for Marx was one in which the rich would get richer and the poor would get poorer, and this dynamic was such that the ensuing exchange relationships could be used to further advantage investors relative to workers.

A number of researchers, including Erik Olin Wright, have found that a good predictor of how much money someone makes is the power associated with class membership. Why is this the case? Frank Parkin, extrapolating on Weber's ideas about social closure, theorizes that those with power in the workplace are able to use that power to influence the distribution of rewards. Over time, managers can use power over the bureaucratic structure of the organization to weigh the reward system more heavily in their favor. Over the last three decades, for example, executive officers of companies have increased their relative earnings accordingly. Forty years ago, the chief executive officers of Fortune 500 firms made about forty times the wages of the average workers in those firms. Today, however, CEOs now have an average wage of well over one hundred times that of the average workers in their companies.

The organization of the society itself often parallels the distribution of money, especially for Marxian theorists. As the income and wealth of the few "haves" becomes increasingly greater relative to the many "have nots" the preponderance of people have a decreasing stake in the society at large. Yet there have been allusions about the separation of ownership and control in the literature since as early as 1932 (Berle and Means). Recently, the Ehrenreichs have written about a "professional-managerial" class that is truly a middle class, in that it is in opposition to both the owners and workers.

For instance, Barbara Ehrenreich, who in 1979 co-authored an article about the increasing presence of a new and formidable *"professional-managerial class,"* (a growing collection of highly educated experts and persons with authority in the workplace) was, in less than a decade, able to observe a rapidly *shrinking* middle class, in which "there will be no mainstream, political outlets for the declining middle class or the desperation of those at the bottom...there will be more crime, more exotic forms of political and religious sectarianism, and ultimately...not one nation, but two."

Many Marxist theorists (e.g., Nicos Poulantzas (1975; E.O. Wright 1985), have argued that any sort of revolution becomes less likely as the middle class grows. As long as some people have it better than others, they reason, they will be unlikely to revolt, because to do so would jeopardize the slight advantage they already hold. What could polarize the situation such that the middle class sides with the proletariat might be a continued deskilling, or a degrading of the skills required of middle class work, and an inevitable proletarianization of that work. This deskilling has been observed in both white-collar (e.g., Glenn and Feldberg 1977, who observed it among clerical workers), and in blue-collar work (e.g., Wallace and Kalleberg 1982, who found skill levels in the printing industry have declined, primarily as a result of a shift to more capital-intensive printing techniques).

There is empirical evidence that the *type* of work being done is changing as well, even in the United States. As early as the mid-1970s, Glenn and Feldberg found that many jobs considered as middle class, such as clerical and secretarial jobs, were becoming increasingly "degraded and de-skilled." The work in many of these jobs, they found, is becoming more routinized, automated, and boring. This dynamic can be understood in class terms. Harry Braverman (1976) argues that, in industrial capitalism, the crucial class distinction centers around the planning of the work process:

> [T]he essential element is the systematic pre-planning and pre-calculation of all elements of the labor process, which now no longer exists as a process in the imagination of the worker but only as a process in the imagination of a special management staff...to control each step of the labor process and its mode of execution.

However, one problem that is encountered in the idea that deskilling in itself will lead to a revolution through polarization of the classes, is that somebody (actually some class) must be the one to do the deskilling and rationalizing of the work process.

Poulantzas posits a *"new petty bourgeoisie,"* one of whose key functions is the planning of the work process. Thus, it could be argued that deskilling itself helps keep the capitalist system in place, because it grooms a large managerial class to do it. This managerial class becomes a stabilizing, counter-revolutionary force in capitalism, because it acts as a buffer between the owners and workers. Granted, Poulantzas proposes other class determinants besides whether one does mental or manual (planning or carrying out) work. Those dimensions are ownership (in the Marxist sense of ownership of the means of production), and authority. Poulantzas does not see the loyalty of the "new petty bourgeoisie" to the working class as automatic. Rather, if the overthrow of capitalism is to occur, this class must be won over by the proletariat.

Ralf Dahrendorf, in attempting to explain the dynamics of stratification systems in industrial societies, argues that the most important types of inequality are those based on differential authority in a system of social positions or roles. The relations of production focused on by Marxists are but one manifestation of a more universal class of relationships based on authority differences, according to Dahrendorf. In other words, while ownership of the means of production certainly puts one class (owners) in a position of authority over non-owners, there are many other types of dominant/subordinate relationships that are based on something other than economics, such as the military rank structure.

Here, Dahrendorf (1959) coins the term "**imperatively coordinated associations**" (or **ICAs**). These refer to lines of authority in the society, in relation to which conflict develops, or "**quasi groups**." In contrast to Marx, for whom class was based on economic considerations (ownership or non-ownership of private productive property), Dahrendorf observes that while much of the conflict in society is based on economic considerations, much of it is not. Race conflict is not easily reducible to economic class terms, for example. Although the distributions of given races within given economic classes are not random, to reduce race to economic class terms fails to acknowledge the major point that *within* any given race, there are both bourgeois and proletariat class members.

While class was much more immutable for Marx, a person could potentially be in a number of quasi groups simultaneously according to Dahrendorf, and these quasi groups could change over time. In Dahrendorf's words: "If, in a given society, there are fifty [imperatively coordinated] associations, we should expect to find a hundred classes, or conflict groups."

Several conditions occurring in conjunction would make mass conflict more likely, in Dahrendorf's view. The three major conditions which lead to conflict are: **1)** the vast bulk of resources going to those in positions of authority, with precious little going to those in a relatively powerless position, **2)** relatively little chance for mobility for those in powerless positions to advance to positions of authority, and **3)** the same people consistently being at the powerless end of a number of imperatively coordinated associations. When these three occur in conjunction, there is greater likelihood of a charismatic leader to galvanize those in low power positions against those in authority, especially one having the technical and material means to reach large numbers of people and to organize them.

Such organization would ultimately result in "*quasi-group awareness*" in which the authority of those in the higher authority groups would be de-legitimated. This delegitimation would likely lead to conflict culminating in a redistribution of resources, such that those on the relatively powerless end of authority relationships would receive greater resources relative to what they had been receiving. Yet this conflict has a feedback mechanism. The impetus for conflict based on those imperatively coordinated associations (and the related quasi-group awareness) becomes less intense as resources become equalized in terms of a given set of imperatively coordinated associations.

Conflict is inevitable in every society, yet considering the feedback mechanism just mentioned, as resources are redistributed relative to a given ICA, that ICA becomes less prone to conflict. As the three conditions of conflict arise around *other* ICAs, however, *those* ICAs become the focus of conflict.

In some cases the conflict becomes *institutionalized*. When this occurs, society is often able to safely manage social strife. For example, race conflict has been partially institutionalized through the advent of equal opportunity and affirmative action laws, and class conflict, to some extent, has been institutionalized through labor unions and collective bargaining agreements.

The intensity of conflict is kept in check by having crosscutting imperatively coordinated associations. An authority group from one imperatively coordinated association (such as priests and church leaders, relative to their congregations), is not necessarily in an authority position in another imperatively coordinated association (such as high elected officials from the "state" relative to the average citizen within that state). As such, the separation of powers (such as into church and state, for example) serves to at least partially subvert the potential for overt social conflict stemming from the delegitimation of authority.

When members of a society are in positions of power in some, but not all, quasi groups, the society is more likely to be stable, according to Dahrendorf. In such a case, each person would have some *vested interest* in maintaining the status quo.

Many Weberian theorists acknowledge a multidimensional "class" system, in which class can be constructed along several dimensions (as in the case of Dahrendorf). Other Weberians, while not necessarily acknowledging as many possible dimensions of power differentials as does Dahrendorf, nonetheless understand the importance of more than two classes.

In empirical work, Thomas Burns (1992) uses class-based theory to explain political behavior, such as party membership and voting. For example, he found that ownership of one's own business is strongly associated with a conservative political orientation and, in the United States, with voting Republican. Why is this the case? An important insight can be gleaned from examining this through a perspective of class interest, in which members of a collective such as a class, have an "interest" in social policy which potentially redistributes resources in the economic, social, or political realm. Business owners, who bear a relatively heavier burden with rising taxes, have an interest in voting for the party most likely to keep taxes down. On the other hand, non-business owners do not have such a strong interest in the economic conservatism often promulgated by (in the United States) Republicans.

For conflict theorists of Marxian *or* Weberian orientations, a key point is that class theory must move beyond Marx's dichotomy between the bourgeoisie and the proletariat in order to have explanatory and predictive power in advanced industrial society. In fact, in many of the class theories discussed, the greater the size of the middle classes (which include, for example, small business owners, as well as professionals and managers), the less likely there is to be dramatic social upheaval, such as revolution. This is largely because members of the middle classes have a vested interest in holding their own positions, and therefore in maintaining the status quo, despite *not* being in the top class position.

Power differentials lead to major societal divisions according to conflict-oriented sociologists. Those power differentials can occur along one or more of several dimensions—economic, political, and ideological. Whatever dimension along which there is inequality, those who have a scarce resource tend to want to hoard that resource, and in fact to garner even more. The very have/have-not relationship is often exploited such that those with the resource get more, and those without get less.

Empirical Studies of Stratification, Mobility and Status Attainment

Sociologists distinguish between "ascription" and "achievement" when examining how a person comes to inhabit a position in the stratification system. **Ascription is said to occur when people acquire occupational roles as a result of inherited characteristics.** This happens when children come to occupy the parents' occupational roles (e.g., in feudalism, in which the children of nobles became nobles themselves, and the children of serfs remained serfs throughout their lives, and passed that status down to their own children). **Achievement**, conversely, describes a situation in which people rise or fall in the stratification system, based on their own merit.

A stratification system characterized by total ascription is sometimes referred to as a "closed" system, while a system characterized by the ability to move up or down is known as an open system. However, very few stratification systems are either totally open or totally closed, and thus the openness or closedness of a system is often a matter of degree.

Structural Mobility

Structural mobility describes a scenario in which a shifting labor market causes widespread change in occupational structures. The Industrial Revolution resulted in a substantial shift from agricultural to factory work in the United States and England.

Changing occupations in the stratification system is referred to as **occupational mobility**, or sometimes just "mobility" for short. **Vertical mobility** refers to moving up ("upward mobility") or down ("downward mobility") along one or more dimensions (e.g., in terms of money or prestige), in the stratification system. **Horizontal mobility** refers to changing occupations but not moving up or down in terms of occupational prestige. When a sociologist uses the term "mobility," it is typically referring to vertical mobility.

Intragenerational mobility refers to mobility within a generation, such as when a person starts out as a garbage collector and that same individual later comes to occupy a higher status position, such as manager, for example. **Intergenerational mobility** refers to one's occupation relative to one's parents. Historically, the focus was on father-son mobility patterns. There are two major types of intergenerational mobility: **1) structural mobility** describes a scenario in which many members of society move (generally up) without any downward movement, due to a shifting occupational "structure." A society experiencing a rapid transformation in occupational structure (during times of rapid industrialization, for example) will tend to create a number of new positions, such as skilled laborers and managers, while **2) exchange mobility** (or **circulation mobility**) describes a situation in which for everyone who goes up in the stratification system, someone else must go down. This generally occurs during times characterized by little change in occupational structure.

Researchers conducting empirical research of mobility generally distinguish between different types of occupations, such as whether someone is employed in a white-collar occupation (e.g., a dentist, lawyer, or physician), a blue-collar occupation (e.g., a bricklayer, mechanic, or heavy equipment operator), or a farm occupation (e.g., a farmhand or migrant farm worker). They then compare the occupation of a parent (generally the father) with the occupation of the child (generally the son).

Reinhard Bendix and Seymour Martin Lipset, in a groundbreaking study of occupational mobility, compared father to son mobility rates in several countries, observing some very interesting patterns in the process. There appeared to be a moderated amount of upward intergenerational mobility (viz. from father to son) in most of the countries studied, regardless of the country's geographic location. The main arbiter of mobility, in fact, tended to be the level of industrialization.

This mobility was attributable to the changing composition of the occupational structure that occurred as a result of industrialization, according to Bendix and Lipset. As a country industrializes and becomes less agrarian, it tends to have relatively fewer farm jobs, but more blue-collar jobs for workers, and more white-collar jobs because of the professional and managerial occupations that are created in the process of industrialization.

Status attainment studies extrapolate upon the method of mobility studies, but with an added degree of precision. Status attainment studies tend to measure stratification using an interval scale (typically 1 to 100), using finer distinctions than traditional mobility studies did. The occupational prestige scale was generated by asking people in surveys to give a relative prestige rating or "general standing" to hundreds of occupations, and taking average rating scores for each occupation. Across a large number of studies, regardless of specific methodology, or which (national) population, the findings indicate a tremendous convergence. In other words, the prestige of occupations is remarkably similar across cultures. Some examples of occupational prestige scores from a recent scale (Nakao and Treas 1994):

(table 8.1)

Occupation	Occupational Prestige Score
Lawyer	75
Clergyman	67
Banker	63
Policeman	59
Airplane Mechanic	53
Farm Owner and Operator	53
Insurance Agent	46
Secretary	46
Bank Teller	43
Restaurant Cook	34
Bartender	25
Janitor	22

Occupational Prestige is related to income, but distinct in important ways. They are based on Weber's idea of "utilities" which have economic, social, cultural or political value—meaning that they do not hold just economic value, but "use" value as well, which is to say some jobs have certain advantages that are *not* economic. In many cultures, for instance, members of the clergy earn very little money (less than janitors in many cases); yet hold a position of higher esteem. Generally speaking, *most* occupations have non-monetary (e.g., discretionary time, fulfilling activity), as well as monetary, utilities associated with them. The concept of occupational prestige takes into account these social values, as opposed to strictly economic exchange.

Professional occupations tend to have relatively higher prestige, while manual laborers have relatively lower prestige, as we note in the table presented above. However, we also observe some considerable overlap, in which certain manual occupations (particularly highly skilled jobs) have higher prestige than certain professional jobs (particularly those not requiring as much formal education as the high end professional jobs). Thus, we note that the occupation of airplane mechanic has a higher prestige score than does that of insurance agent.

Empirical research has indicated several predictors of an individual's occupational prestige. These include the parents' education (in some cases, the mother's education is more important than the father's), occupational prestige *and* income of the head-of-household in one's family of origin, the individual's education level, and the prestige of the first job the individual held. Furthermore, several socio-psychological factors have been shown to affect where an individual eventually finds themselves in the occupational hierarchy, including the level of aspiration a person has for him or herself, as well as the aspiration the parents have for them. Also having an effect (although a relatively weak one) is the aspiration levels of one's peers growing up, as well as the socioeconomic status of those peers (Featherman and Hauser 1978).

Social scientists have pointed out that many desirable social and economic outcomes tend to be highly correlated. **Socio-Economic Status (SES)** is a theoretical concept intended to encompass this aggregation of characteristics. Specifically, a person's SES is a combination of:

- Education
- Occupational prestige
- Income
- Personal or family wealth
- Location and/or cost of one's residential neighborhood

Several researchers have observed the correlation among the aforementioned characteristics (e.g., Duncan 1965/1966). Socio-Economic Status is an important idea because it tends to be associated with many other social characteristics. Some examples of social characteristics that tend to co-vary with Socio-Economic Status (or at least many of its components) we list here:

There is an *inverse* relationship between SES and:

- social and environmental risk, such as residing near dangerous and dirty places like high

crime areas and toxic waste dumps, for example;
- being the victim of crime (violent crime especially);
- being diagnosed with certain mental conditions, such as schizophrenia and depression;
- the likelihood of being arrested for some crime or act of deviance.

There is a *positive* relationship between SES and:

- access to professionals such as lawyers and physicians;
- occupational self-direction, or the level of autonomy an individual experiences in the workplace;
- the probability that a person will participate in civic organizations;
- political participation (a greater likelihood of running for office, as well as a greater likelihood of voting).

In fact, SES is one of the single most important variables we examine in sociology. Some other characteristics that tend to co-vary with some aspect of SES, and may be less obvious:

- People generally marry someone with a similar level of education.
- Higher SES women tend to have fewer children, more widely spaced apart in years, and born later in the mother's life, compared to lower SES women.
- Higher SES is related to a greater sense of control of the circumstances of one's life.
- Lower SES is related to a shorter life span.
- Certain diseases and disabilities are more common among specific ranges of SES, sometimes in surprising ways. For instance:
    o Multiple sclerosis is more prevalent among higher SES women.
    o Traumatic brain injury is more prevalent among lower SES men.

The Emergence of the Precariat Class

As we saw earlier, much of the twentieth century, at least until the last few decades, saw a rise in the middle classes. Yet recently, there has been an erosion of many of those gains.

Life in the early twenty-first century, for increasing numbers of people, has come to be risky and full of challenges that many thought were going to fade away with advancing industrialization and development. There are increasing numbers of people who live paycheck to paycheck when they are able to find work, and do not have the luxury of non-salary benefits, such as health insurance, paid vacation, retirement, or sick leave. Sociologists (e.g., Standing 2014) have come to refer to this class of people as the **precariat** (a neologism combining the terms precarious and proletariat).

Rather than the social collective taking responsibility for vulnerable members "slipping through the cracks," there is an increasing burden on private citizens to fend for themselves in times of trouble. This can be seen as a symptom of the weakening social bonds wrought by late modern society.

Precariat

An increasing number of people live from paycheck to paycheck and lack substantial job benefits. Sociologists have begun referring to this class as the "**precariat**." The Occupy Wall Street movement was an attempt by members of the precariat to address this situation, among others.

This is not to imply that the precariat is monolithic. British sociologist Guy Standing (2014) identifies a number of "factions" within this larger collective, each with its own set of particular interests. Three of the factions are:

1. **Former members of the stably employed working class**. Much of the twentieth century saw increasing gains for the working class, particularly those who were in strong unions. Now, many of the unions have been weakened by processes such as competition from labor pools in developing countries where there is little or no regulation to promote the safety and health of employees, and where the competition for work will drive down wages and deminish benefits.

2. **Migrants and ethnic minorities**. Examples of this group include undocumented workers from other countries who may not speak the dominant language and have little to safeguard their rights. This group often times, in addition, can be the target of discriminatory practices.

3. **Overeducated and underemployed people**. At this time in history, there are large numbers of people working in jobs where their education far outstrips the demands of the job itself. While there has been an increase in overall education levels over the two and one half centuries since the advent of industrialization, now for the first time in history, advanced industrial societies have large numbers of people who are "overeducated" for the jobs they perform. Examples of over education include when a college graduate works for minimum wage at a fast food restaurant, or when someone with a law degree works in retail at a strip mall.

In addition to the jobs performed by the precariat bringing low wages, the employment they do find typically is unstable, affords little room for advancement, and comes without benefits such as sick or vacation leave, health insurance, and retirement. Particularly for people in their twenties, there is an increasing trend of moving back in with parents after college or a few attempts at independence, because of not being able to find a well-paying job.

Sociologists have pointed out parallels between the rise of the precariat on the one hand, and the increasing concentration of wealth in fewer hands among elites in business and finance. Standing sees an *oligarchy* (recall from Michels, this means rule of the many by the few) dominated by *plutocrats* (a small cadre of the super-rich, in a world where most of the power and privilege devolves back to wealth), which have allegiances to nobody but themselves. This pattern of wealth and power concentration at the top of the stratification system has led to a situation where many of the jobs that had formerly been in the stable working or middle classes, now fall into a precarious state.

It does bear noting that Karl Marx predicted a century and a half ago that something like this would come to pass. Marx theorized that as capitalism matured and globalized, there would be increasing class polarization, with the middle classes falling into increased immiseration, low wages and poor working conditions. Marx found hope for a rising class consciousness as a result, which necessarily would involve discerning and articulating class interests. According to Standing (2014), the precariat has three immediate class interests:

1. **Recognition.** As Marx and Dahrendorf saw, the beginning of social recognition is self-recognition. Members of the precariat need to see themselves as such, and to see the commonality between their own situation and that of others. Recognition then takes a collective turn, as witnessed in many of the mass protests in recent years.

2. **Representation.** As it stands now, many of the people in the precariat are under-represented, if not totally excluded, from the political process. The precariat are more like "denizens" who live in a place but do not enjoy the full rights of empowered citizens.

3. **Redistribution.** While redistribution of wealth is not an unimportant component of precariat interests, there are other dimensions as well to consider. In addition to economic security, these include control over personal time, a healthy environment, education that goes beyond mere skill training to a more personally and socially enriching consciousness.

Because of the potential for social conflict stemming from the deprivation and exclusion of the precariat, Standing sees the precariat as a "new dangerous class." If the precariat were to develop a sense of class interests and class consciousness, there would, he holds, be significant energy there to challenge much of the power and privilege currently hoarded by elites.

Migrants and Ethnic Minorities

Migrant workers and ethnic minorities are often the targets of discriminatory labor practices.

Linkages between Socialization and Social Stratification

Recognition/Representation/Redistribution
Historically, unionized workers have used strikes in order to achieve **recognition, representation** and **redistribution.**

Sociologists have observed an association between adult social class and self-esteem (e.g., Rosenberg 1979). There is also a body of work demonstrating that social class is associated with feelings of control over one's destiny (e.g., Kohn 1969; Kohn and Schooler 1983; Pearlin and Kohn 1966). For these and other reasons, one's class position has a profound influence not only material gain, but also satisfaction with life in general.

There is a great deal of research indicating an inverse relation between social class and pathology, such as schizophrenia. Faris and Dunham (1939) found schizophrenia rates higher in low socio-economic status parts of town. Hollingshead and Redlich (1958) observed that pathology was generally higher among the lower classes. They found, in addition, that the quality of treatment a person was likely to receive was primarily a function of that person's position in the stratification system. The more resource- and time-intensive treatment types, such as psychotherapy, were preponderant among the higher classes, while the less time- and resource-intensive, "cost-effective" types of treatment, such as shock treatment, were more common among the lower classes.

Melvin Kohn investigated the question of how social class could be inversely related to schizophrenia. The potential for schizophrenia, he found, was maximized when a specific combination of three conditions occurred: **1)** genetic predisposition; **2)** stress; and **3)** low social class. Even taking into consideration the fact that those with genetic predisposition may tend to "drift" into the lower classes over several generations, there was still a general belief that something about lower class life was simply less happy or less satisfying than upper class life.

What factors could account for higher rates of dissatisfaction and schizophrenia among lower class positions? Kohn (1969) observed that, compared to white-collar families, blue-collar families tended to raise their children in a more rigid fashion. Kohn theorized that white-collar work tended to demand more self-direction for its successful discharge, while blue-collar work tended to demand more conformity from those performing it. Another way of viewing this is to say that blue-collar work required conformity to external demands, whereas white-collar work was more tolerant (and in fact rewarding of) internal self-direction. Further, Kohn argued that these material conditions of the workplace were not confined to the workplace, but were brought home and became integral to the socialization of the children (Kohn and Schooler 1983).

Clearly, however, there are blue-collar family members who are no more conforming than certain white-collar family members, thus suggesting the conclusion that there is something at work besides the color of one's collar. Kohn and Schooler (*Work and Personality*) addressed this fundamental defect of the earlier Kohn work. Rather than simply focusing on the color of one's collar in a job, Kohn and Schooler examined occupational self-direction itself—and in the process observed an even more dramatic effect than Kohn did in his class and conformity study.

The implication of the work of Kohn and his associates is that the lower class position tends towards the psychological phenomenon that one is at the mercy of external forces in a hostile external world; whereas upper class psychology reflects the belief that one is largely in control of one's own destiny, and that the world is an essentially benign place.

If this is true, then the locus of life satisfaction (at least as far as it is related to feelings of internal locus of control) is internal rather than external. Thus, while it is true that life satisfaction is inversely related to one's position in the social order, it need not necessarily be. The crucial factor is for one to have upper class psychology, much more so than it is to have upper class material reality. In any case, the psychological aspects of one's position in the stratification system are intimately connected with satisfaction, happiness, and quality of life.

Toward a Synthesizing View of Stratification

We have discussed several issues regarding the causes and consequences of stratification in society. Many positions tend to support one view while excluding others, seeming to find support for their positions regardless of the specific circumstances. In our view, a more nuanced understanding of stratification processes would be one in which a synthesis of these perspectives is utilized. Such a synthesis should pay close attention to the scope of conditions addressed by the respective theoretical positions. In other words, what are the circumstances under which a given perspective is the most illuminating?

Each of the three major intellectual traditions discussed in this chapter—elite, functional, and conflict models—best explain a *certain* aspect of stratification systems. Each is analytically distinct, although not mutually exclusive. For a universal view of the origin, development and effects of stratification systems, we must carefully consider all three in conjunction with one another (You may wish to read Gerhard Lenski's 1966/1984 work, *Power and Privilege* for a look at an in-depth attempt to synthesize parts of the functional and conflict traditions).

We propose the following general outline for the comparative strengths (and weaknesses) of each position. The strength of elite models is in their ability to explain why stratification systems are so ubiquitous and why any attempts (utopian or otherwise) to "abolish" stratification systems invariably lead only to another stratification system. Functional models best capture how stratification systems arise in the first place, and what they do for their society. Conflict models best outline how distortions occur within stratification systems, along with the likely consequences of those distortions.

Research in the Marxian tradition has generally adhered to a more radical class model. Research in the Weberian tradition has followed more of a status model, and is generally more conservative and specific in its analysis. Thus, Marxian research has looked more at intergenerational patterns in an aggregate (e.g., mobility), while Weberian research has operated more along the lines of status attainment, in which the focus is more on individual or "human capital" type attributes. Examples of research in the Marxian tradition are Vanneman (1977) who examined intergenerational mobility and neighborhood residential patterns to locate class boundaries. Blau and Duncan (1967) examined the issue in a status attainment framework, using data similar to that of Vanneman.

The majority of stratification work, as well as in a number of other subfields of sociology, is informed either by a conflict or a functional perspective. The view we take here is that these perspectives are far from mutually exclusive, although, with some exceptions, little work has been done to attempt synthesis.

Conclusion

Social stratification can be understood as an organizing principle of society. Throughout much of the rest of the book, we will extrapolate on the ideas presented in this chapter, giving nuance to the idea of inequality. Stratification is an important aspect of the way social institutions are organized as well. For these reasons, some sociologists believe, with sufficient justification, that "stratification is the backbone of sociology."

CHAPTER SUMMARY

- Virtually every society ever studied has been stratified, with very few exceptions.
- Many of the discussions of stratification are centered on either "conflict" or "functional" themes.
- Sociologists have conducted many empirical studies of stratification systems. These studies indicate that stratification is linked to numerous other aspects of social organization, including individual development and health.

9 Race and Ethnicity

It is a central sociological process that social action affects ways in which resources are allocated by defining group boundaries and the hierarchies relative to them through "social closure" (Weber [1978]; Parkin 1971, 1974, 1979). Elaborating on Max Weber's [1978] description of social closure, or "the process by which social collectives seek to maximize rewards by restricting access to rewards and opportunities to a limited circle of eligibles," Frank Parkin (1974:3 ff.; also 1979:44-116) identifies three specific closure strategies: **1)** "exclusion," **2)** "usurpation" (or "solidarism"), and **3)** "dual closure." While Parkin (1974:5) points out that "the language of closure can be translated into the language of power," such a translation has yet to occur in any systematic manner in the existing sociological literature. Parkin's work represents a step in that direction.

When one social group attempts to "maintain or enhance its privileges through the process of subordination—i.e., the creation of another group or stratum of ineligibles beneath it," it is defined as exclusion. In turn, an excluded group, or part of it, may then attempt "closing off access to remaining rewards" for others whom they are excluding, thereby "multiplying the number of sub-strata" (Parkin 1974:4-5). This is a strategy whereby "insiders" keep "outsiders" out. Examples of this type of closure can be seen in a caste system, in which members of lower status castes are excluded from some of the rewards and resources available to higher status castes, as well as the system of industrial capitalism when ownership and management attempt to maintain possession of the highest percentage of the profits generated by the business as is possible. Another example can be found where credentials (e.g., academic degrees), provide differential access to certain kinds of jobs and the resources associated with them (see Collins 1979).

Recognition/Representation/Redistribution
In the U.S., exclusion occurred up until the 1960s through Jim Crow laws, which established separate facilities for blacks and whites.

One defined response to exclusion, known as usurpation, is a strategy practiced by excluded groups hoping to gain "resources and benefits accruing to dominant groups in society—a range of possibilities extending from marginal redistribution to complete expropriation" (Parkin 1979:74). This is a strategy practiced by "outsiders" in attempting to gain access to the resources available to "insiders." An example of a usurpationary strategy is a labor union attempting to gain wage concessions from ownership and management.

A combination of the first two kinds of

closure, known as dual closure, is when a group engages in usurpationary activities against a group with greater power and/or resources, while practicing exclusion against less powerful or organized groups (Parkin 1979:91). An example of this is the "aristocracy" of skilled labor (Gray 1974), in which an occupational group maximizes its own access to resources by attempting to usurp resources from ownership and management in the form of wages and benefits on the one hand, while simultaneously excluding less skilled members from its ranks on the other hand.

Parkin points out that when labor unions have succeeded in procuring extra rights or other concessions, they have done so primarily through "moral appeals to certain principles of justice rather than from the ability to back up demands by the threat of negative sanctions" (Parkin 1979:101). These moral appeals involve rhetoric, regarding both the way the appeals are made, and in terms of how those principles of justice are established in the first place. Broadly speaking, social closure is a common feature in the exercise of power among and within social collectives.

Racial and Ethnic Discrimination as Status Group Stratification and Social Closure

As articulated by Max Weber, racial, ethnic and other cultural groups can be considered as status groups. Racism and ethnic discrimination are cases of *social closure*. In such cases, economic, social or political resources are allocated differentially on the basis of group membership.

As sociologists, it is important to note the difference between prejudice and discrimination. **Prejudice** is an *attitude* or perception about a person, based on group membership. On the other hand, **discrimination** involves an actual *behavior* toward someone based on group membership. The behavior may involve differentially withholding benefits, or actually harming a member of another group. Discrimination is often motivated by prejudice. However, while the two often go hand in hand, there are many cases where they are mutually exclusive. In a classic study of differences between attitudes and behavior, for example, LaPiere (1934) found that people who expressed prejudicial attitudes did not necessarily behave in a way that could be considered discriminatory.

Simpson and Yinger (1985) articulate an array of types of interactions between and among cultural, racial and ethnic groups. Of the *six types of ethnic group interaction* that they delineate, the first three are relatively benign, while the second three are characterized by violence and are sometimes deadly:

1. **Assimilation.** When a minority group is absorbed into the larger culture, assimilation occurs. Over time, this leads to a situation in which the minority group is no longer discriminated against, due to the dissolution of the previous boundary distinguishing minority from majority. For instance, consider the case of Irish-Americans. A century ago, particularly in the Northeastern United States, Irish immigrants often faced serious discrimination. Over time, that discrimination has subsided as Irish-Americans have become *assimilated*.

Pluralism

Pluralism, which can be seen on many college campuses across the U.S., describes a scenario in which people of different racial and ethnic backgrounds coexist relatively peacefully.

2. **Pluralism.** Different ethnic or racial groups are able to maintain their group identity with relatively little tension between groups while cohabitating within the same society. In other words, distinctions are maintained among groups, but there is not a great deal of hostility between them. An example can be found in Canada, where native French and English speakers keep their respective group identities and, although there are some exceptions, tend to live together rather peacefully.

3. **Protectionism.** This is a situation in which the government may enact legislation intended to safeguard the rights of minority groups. An example of this would be in the "hate crimes" legislation recently passed in the United States, in which an act motivated by prejudice against a minority group member carries a special penalty.

4. **Population Transfer.** In this situation, a minority group migrates, or is forced to move. A historical example of this can be seen in the "Trail of Tears," during which the United States government forced the migration of Cherokee people from their homelands in the Carolinas and Georgia to reservations in Oklahoma in the 1830s, causing the deaths of thousands of people.

5. **Subjugation.** A situation in which a dominant group keeps a minority group in a subordinate position is subjugation. While slavery is an obvious example, the ongoing legal marginalization that occurred after the abolition of slavery would fall into this category as well. Thus, the "Jim Crow" laws in the Southern United States that consistently upheld an atmosphere of inequality between blacks and whites would also be an example of this.

6. **Extermination.** The most extreme form of interaction between groups, in which members of one group kill another. Examples include major atrocities, such as the Nazi holocaust against the Jews. More recent instances of such "ethnic cleansing" can be seen in Bosnia, and also the systematic slaughter of Hutus by Tutsis in Burundi.

However, although these different sets of behavior can be clearly distinguished, the distinct forms of interaction they take are not necessarily mutually exclusive, as Simpson and Yinger point out. It is important to note here as well that, in general, the more hostile the *attitudes* toward other groups, the more hostile the *behavior* that follows from those attitudes.

In some cases, significant upward mobility among a large number of members of a minority group can be observed. This is particularly true in cases where there is some sort of pluralistic living pattern in the society. Sociologists who study race and ethnic relations (e.g., Hirschman and Wong 1984 &1986; Hirschman and Falcon 1985; Light 1984; Portes and Manning

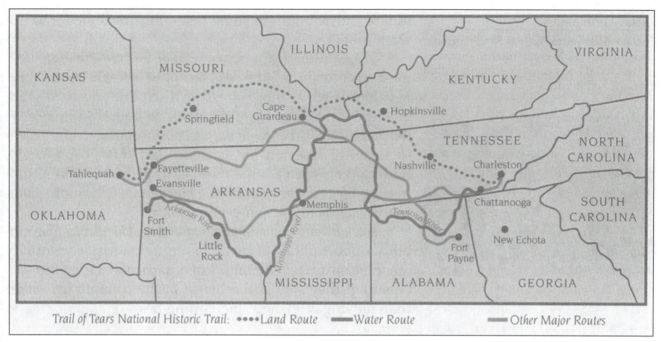

Population Transfer

The United States enacted the Indian Removal Act of 1830 that forcibly removed the Cherokee, Muscogee, Seminole, Chickasaw, and Choctaw nations from their ancestral homes in the southeastern United States to Indian Territory in what is now the present-day state of Oklahoma. Known as the "Trail of Tears," thousands of Native Americans died during the exodus.

1986), have found a number of characteristics in minority groups where this has been the case. While these characteristics can be observed individually throughout many groups, there is also an important synergy effect. In other words, when all of these characteristics are found together, they tend to reinforce one another. From this often follows a large degree of upward mobility among group members, which sometimes serves to facilitate the mobility of the community as a whole. The characteristics are:

- *Geographic concentration in urban areas*. Many of the Cuban exiles in South Florida, for example, have been quite successful. This is partially attributable to the phenomenon Durkheim referred to as "moral density"—the concentration and physical proximity of one group within a geographic location allows for a great deal of interaction to occur, in which members of the group offer social support for one another.
- *Internal economic development and "enclave" economies*. The geographic concentration mentioned previously makes it possible for members of an ethnic group to support each other economically either by patronizing each other's businesses or, in some cases, with an informal barter system.
- *Occupational specialization*. It is sometimes the case that a proportionally large number of members of a given ethnic group will tend to go into certain fields of occupation. For example, during the early to mid-twentieth century, a high percentage of Irish-Americans pursued careers

Enclave Economies

Enclave economies, such as San Francisco's Chinatown, enable group interaction as well as social and economic support within minority communities.

in law and politics. In some cases, this translated into upward mobility.

- *A high value is placed on education and self-discipline.* Almost a century ago, Max Weber found broadly held cultural values (such as those stressing discipline and hard work among its members) could have a profound influence on the economic fortunes of entire communities. More recent sociological research has corroborated this phenomenon, finding that when a large number of people within a community place a high priority on such values, the entire community tends to prosper economically.
- *A tendency to stay in the community and reinvest.* The mobility opportunities of members in a minority community are increased when members of a particular group are successful, if they stay and reinvest in the community, rather than moving elsewhere and cutting ties.

Effects of Racial Stratification

In racially diverse societies, stratification surfaces in a number of ways, not the least of which occurs in the workplace. It is well known that minorities earn less, on average, than whites across almost all occupation types. In one recent study, it was revealed that racial disparities increase as one moves up the occupational earnings hierarchy, particularly in the private sector (Grodsky and Pager 2001). These findings are important because income disparities are sometimes attributed to differences in types of employment. Minorities, for example, are less likely than whites to be employed in high-level professional and managerial positions. To a certain degree, this would explain differences in average income levels between whites and minorities. Research indicates, though, that racial disparity in income still exists higher up in the occupational hierarchy. In fact, it increases. So even when minorities occupy higher-level positions, they earn less than their white counterparts, on average.

The result of income disparity is observed when comparing poverty levels of different races in the United States. According to the U.S. Census Bureau, about 14 percent of the population had income below poverty level between 2007 and 2011. During that time, the poverty rate was 27 percent for Native Americans, 25.8 percent for African Americans, and 23 percent for Hispanics and Latinos. Compare those rates to that of white poverty, which was about 11 percent (U.S. Bureau of the Census 2013). Why is poverty so much higher for minorities than it is for whites? This is an important question that has been up for considerable debate in government and academia. Some point to the so-called "culture of poverty" to explain racial disparity. This refers to the idea that there are aspects of the culture in which minorities live that perpetuate poverty and inequality. In other words, racial stratification has to do with the habits and behavior of those at the bottom of the social hierarchy. This view stands in opposition to other views that look to structural causes of poverty, such as wage discrepancy between whites and minorities. The dissolution of the nuclear family in poor, minority communities, for example, is an aspect of the "culture of poverty" that some believe to be the driving force behind racial stratification. Single parent homes are more common in communities where poverty is prevalent, and it is well documented that children who grow up in single-family homes are more likely to be incarcerated and to experience poverty later in life. From this perspective, the prevalence of childbirth outside of wedlock among the poor can be viewed as a driver of stratification.

The concept of the culture of poverty was particularly prevalent during the Reagan/Bush Era (Steinberg 2011). As many sociologists have pointed out, though, it does not sufficiently explain the extent of racial stratification. The main criticism is that it removes the emphasis from the social, structural, and historical factors that must be considered when examining stratification. The flaw of such a premise is well summarized by the following statement: "[Culture of poverty theorists] confuse cause and effect, arguing that lack of social mobility among black youth is a product of their culture rather than the other way around" (Steinberg 2011).

Wilson (2010) posits that one of the effects of living in racially segregated neighborhoods is exposure to habits and worldviews that are not conducive to upward social mobility. These traits, however, are not simply inherent in those minorities living in poverty. Rather, they are a result of historical patterns of racial exclusion. In this way, Wilson explains that the cultural factors that perpetuate poverty among minorities are a result of historical, structural patterns.

In addition to income and wealth disparities, residential racial segregation remains across the United States, despite the fact that Jim Crow laws have been abolished for decades. It has been argued that such segregation exists because of discrimination in the real estate market, reflecting whites' desire to be isolated from minorities (Krysan and Farley 2002). Whites tend to view neighborhoods as less attractive as the proportion of blacks and Hispanics increases, though the proportion of Asians has no impact (Lewis, Emerson, and Klineberg 2011). In 2002, researchers used data from a multi-city survey to determine whether or not this preference for racial segregation also exists among blacks. That is, do blacks, like whites, prefer to reside in areas that consist primarily of members of their own race? The survey revealed that the majority of blacks preferred to live in areas with an even split of blacks and whites. The preference for racial neutrality among blacks has more to do with fear of white hostility than solidarity or neutral ethnocentrism (Krysan and Farley 2002).

In *American Apartheid: Segregation and the Making of the Underclass*, sociologists Douglas Massey and Nancy Denton describe how black ghettos were created in the early 1900s to isolate growing black populations in urban areas. They go on to explain how residential segregation is perpetuated today through individual actions and institutional practices. One such practice is called gentrification. This is a process wherein real estate developers purchase properties in deteriorated, poverty-ridden areas, which are typically inhabited by minorities, and renovate them as investments. After the properties in an area are renovated, the cost of living in them goes up, thus driving out minorities who have lived in the area for generations. The upgraded properties are then inhabited by whites that are generally better able to afford the higher cost of living. In recent years, this process has been particularly prevalent in Brooklyn and San Francisco.

As the geographic concentration increases among minorities, often so too does poverty. In many high-poverty areas occupied by minorities, crime and unemployment are higher than average. As residents adapt to this increasingly harsh environment, they develop attitudes and behaviors that further marginalize their neighborhoods and undermine their chances of success (Massey and Denton 1998). This relationship between economic restructuring, long-term joblessness, and cultural behavior is one of particular importance in the examination of stratification (Wilson 1987).

The aforementioned inhabitants of poverty-ridden areas are commonly referred to in sociology as the *underclass*. This concept is used to describe those who are **1)** outside the mainstream of the American occupational system—including those who lack training and skills and either experience long-term unemployment, individuals who are engaged in street crime and other forms of aberrant behavior, and families that experience long-term spells of poverty and/or welfare dependency—and **2)** share the same social milieu (Wilson 1987). In an analysis not unlike that of Massey and Denton, sociologist William Julius Wilson posits that "this underclass exists mainly because of the large scale and harmful changes in the labor market, and its resulting spatial concentration as well as the isolation of such areas from the more affluent parts of the black community." Unemployment, particularly the lack of low-skilled manual labor in inner cities, is inextricably linked to poverty, crime and the social life of neighborhoods (Wilson 1996).

W.E.B. Du Bois (1863 - 1963)

Du Bois developed the concept known as **double conciousness**. Du Bois was among the first to study the sociology of race, and was one of the founders of the NAACP.

Among the most important sociologists to study racial stratification was **W.E.B. Du Bois** (1863-1963). Before becoming the first African American to earn a Ph.D. from Harvard University, Du Bois attended Fisk University in Tennessee. It was there he first encountered Jim Crow Laws, which would be influential in his sociological focus on race. Du Bois developed a concept known as *double consciousness*, which refers to the psychological challenge faced by African Americans to consider their African heritage in the context of a European upbringing. The concept is best summarized in the following excerpt from Du Bois' seminal work *The Souls of Black Folk*:

> It is a peculiar sensation, this double-consciousness, this sense of always looking at one's self through the eyes of others, of measuring one's soul by the tape of a world that looks on in amused contempt and pity. One ever feels his two-ness,—an American, a Negro; two souls, two thoughts, two unreconciled strivings; two warring ideals in one dark body, whose dogged strength alone keeps it from being torn asunder. (Du Bois 1903)

Racial and Ethnic Assimilation

The rich racial and ethnic diversity that characterizes the United States is a result of a long history of immigration. Early in U.S. history, the majority of immigrants came from Europe. Today, however, the majority comes from Latin America and Asia. Through the process of assimilation, immigrants become absorbed into the mainstream as they internalize and adapt to the ways of the culture. The concept of assimilation is important in a discussion of racial and ethnic stratification because it involves the degree to which minority groups become integrated into society rather than remaining marginalized.

Immigration has undoubtedly been an important political issue in recent years, particularly as it pertains to those arriving in the United States from Mexico and their impact in the social and economic arena. In one recent study, sociologists compared the assimilation process of modern immigrants to that of immigrants in early America. The study found that "the distinctions between contemporary and past immigrations have been overplayed (Alba and Nee 2003). More specifically, the authors stated that, in terms of acculturation, language, and educational attainment, modern immigrants are assimilating into the mainstream and converging with the characteristics of whites in the same way as immigrants in the early twentieth century (Alba and Nee 2003). There are distinctions between immigrant groups, however, as some move more readily into the middle class, while others start at the bottom of the socioeconomic ladder and tend to stay there.

A Declining Significance of Race in the United States

When one looks at figures over the last several decades of the twentieth century, the gap between the income of blacks and whites did decrease, yet substantial differences still remain (e.g., U.S. Bureau of the Census 1970, 1992, 1998; c.f. Farley 1984). William Julius Wilson (1980 & 1996), after devoting a large part of his career to studying race and class stratification in the United States has concluded that simply to look at the overall figures on average differences between racial groups can be misleading, because of huge differences *within* racial groups.

According to Wilson (1980), unlike in industrial and pre-industrial periods, economic class is now more important than race in determining job placement for blacks. Because of decentralization of American business and a shift from a goods-producing economy to a service-producing economy, a segmented labor market has developed in which different subgroups of blacks have very different mobility opportunities.

Wilson argues that there are now two basic groups of blacks, vis-à-vis the class structure:

1. Young, unskilled, inner city blacks, often from ghetto schools. Members of this group are often locked into a low-wage sector, with a high rate of turnover and few opportunities for advancement.

2. Skilled and highly educated blacks who, due to the structural expansion of white-col-

New Black Midde-Class
The legal and social shifts of the 1960s enabled blacks to enter and successfully compete in fields that had previously been inaccessible to them.

lar jobs and affirmative action, now have opportunities to work in corporations and government sectors.

Utilizing a Weberian class model based on life chances and the social relations of exchange, Wilson also argues that racial strife has largely shifted from the economic to political and social sectors. The civil rights movement of the 1960s, he contends, reflected the needs and interests of the black middle class, but did not adequately address the issues of class subordination and de facto segregation experienced by the black underclass.

In the 1960s, children of better-educated and wealthier black parents accounted for the black upswing in college enrollment—there was little effect from the ghetto on this pattern. Employment problems of blacks in the ghetto are not only due to racial discrimination, Wilson further argues; but also increasing labor market segmentation, relocation of industry, and growing use of technology.

This problem is compounded by the fact that in many cases, when industry relocates out of major U.S. cities, it does not return. Increasingly, businesses are moving to less developed countries, where the wages are a fraction of what they are in the United States.

While historically, Wilson continues, blacks have made the greatest gains in times of economic expansion, and suffered the greatest losses in times of decline, the economic recession of the 1970s proved to be an exception: career trajectories of trained and educated blacks improved compared with whites, while the circumstances of inner-city blacks—especially at the lower end of the age range—became even worse.

Wilson holds that in the middle class, age is a primary factor to which black/white wage disparities can be attributed. Younger, educated and talented blacks have reached virtual parity with their white counterparts—here Wilson compares black men with white men, and black women with white women. He does not do a cross-gender comparison, or look at any sort of interaction effect between gender and race.

Wilson's policy prescription stems from the preceding arguments: full employment will help ghetto blacks far more than will affirmative action. As the system of production and policies of the State change, the racial norms and structural relations between races follow.

In *The New Black Middle Class* (1987), Bart Landry provides a critique of Wilson's underestimation of the effects of racism. In doing so, Landry investigates the advent of the "new black middle class," which he describes as different from the old black middle class in several important ways. In the 1960s, a congeries of prosperity and legal incentives for employers to treat blacks more equally with whites, led to a climate in which blacks were able to enter and successfully compete in fields that had previously been inaccessible to them. As such, the new black middle class was characterized by professionals serving the society at large (e.g., engineers, architects, etc.), whereas the old black middle class was comprised mostly of professionals serving primarily the black community itself. The key difference between the old and new black middle class is that there is now *one* standard of success for blacks and whites, whereas before there were separate standards. While this is the case, however, Landry also points out how many middle class blacks, while working during the day with whites, prefer to socialize with other blacks during their off-hours. The subtle (and sometimes not so subtle) patterns of discrimination can still be observed, with many blacks preferring not to subject themselves to that possibility.

Unlike Wilson, Landry holds that racism remains a salient characteristic of the economic sphere as well—even within the middle class. Landry cites the "economic price of being black": for men, salary is lower for blacks than for whites, even when taking a number of other factors into consideration. For Landry, these factors include occupation, age, supervisory status, seniority on the job, economic sector, and geographical area. For women, the situation is similar—although more black women than black men have made it into the middle class, many of those jobs are low-end clerical—black women still suffer the double discrimination of race and gender.

Furthermore, federal education cuts have especially hurt blacks. This is because college education is an especially important prerequisite for mobility into the middle class. Also, when considering education vis-à-vis the standard status attainment model, parental encouragement is a more strongly motivating factor for educational achievement among blacks than it is among whites (where family SES is a better predictor).

Bonacich (1980) holds that the salience of race correspondingly decreases as blacks become less identified with a class position. Farley and Bianchi (1985) specifically investigated the question of social class "polarization" (as of the type articulated by Wilson) among blacks. Using census data from 1960 to 1980, they found mixed evidence for such polarization. Educational attainment and family income showed no polarization; non-participation in the labor force, occupational prestige, and family type (they found a disparity between the incomes of husband-wife vs. female-headed households).

Conclusion

Is there a declining significance of race? Clearly, its significance has declined somewhat from the demeaning days of Jim Crow laws and the legal exclusion of blacks from certain occupations. However, as demonstrated by Landry, the economic price of being black still exists. Although on the other hand, non-participation in the labor force appears to be more class-based than race-based.

CHAPTER SUMMARY

- Social closure is defined as the process by which social collectives seek to maximize rewards by restricting access to rewards and opportunities to a limited circle of eligibles.
- Inequality based on status group can be viewed in terms of Max Weber's ideas about social closure. Social action affects ways in which resources are allocated by defining group boundaries and the hierarchies relative to them through social closure.
- Prejudice is an attitude or perception about a person, based on group membership. On the other hand, discrimination involves an actual behavior toward someone based on group membership.
- A number of patterns surrounding issues of race and ethnic inequality can be identified. Over the course of history, these have included things such as discrimination, genocide, and assimilation.
- While a number of cogent arguments have been put forward about the declining significance of race, there are still a number of issues in this regard.

10 | Gender and Society

Construction of Gender

As we saw earlier in our discussion of personality development and socialization, the cultures and social structures of which we are a part play a significant role in influencing our self-identity. In most societies throughout history, cultural expectations have played a significant part in the formulation of self-expectation as well as expectation of others. These cultural expectations, and the behaviors with which they are associated, are often formulated in relation to gender roles. Here, sociologists make a distinction between sex and gender. We are born with a **sex**—male or female. **Gender** refers to how we develop ideas, roles and norms, behaviors, and expectations relative to our sex in a social and cultural context. Thus, when sociologists speak of gender roles, they are typically referring to the significant cultural context of such roles rather than biological sex.

The role of social and cultural influence is paramount in a discussion of gender. Outside of a sociological context, we see variation in ideas and perceptions when it comes to the concept of gender. The differences in ideas and perceptions regard the degree to which gender is shaped by social factors, rather than biological factors. The term **biological determinism** describes the argument that social behavior can be attributed to biological characteristics. The idea that men are typically more aggressive than women due to higher testosterone levels is an argument made by biological determinists, for example. Research has shown, however that considerable differences exist in levels of aggression between young boys and girls despite very little difference in the levels of testosterone and other sex hormones during early childhood. Such research illustrates the social construction of gender, which begins at an early age. **Gender socialization** can be described as the process by which individuals learn about the norms, behaviors, and expectations

Gender Socialization

Through **gender socialization**, young boys and girls learn what types of behavior are expected of them. This is often seen in the types of toys that boys and girls play with.

associated with each gender. Through this process, individuals learn to conform to such norms and expectations.

In her influential 1935 book *Sex and Temperament in Three Primitive Societies*, cultural anthropologist Margaret Mead laid the groundwork for much of the current sociological discourse on sex and gender. Her observations of gender roles in three New Guinea tribes, the Arapesh, Mundugamor, and Tchambuli, launched a discussion that led many to reconsider the established assumptions of gender roles in society. During her studies, Mead discovered varying gender roles amongst the societies she observed. Among the Arapesh, for example, both males and females equally displayed what we often define as feminine traits: sensitivity, cooperation, and low levels of aggression. Within the Mundugamor tribe, both men and women alike displayed similar attributes of aggressive behavior and insensitivity. In the Tchambuli tribe, Mead observed that women tended towards aggression, but were also rational and socially dominant, while the males of the tribe were more passive and assumed roles of art and leisure.

Of her research, Mead writes: "The material suggests that we may say that many, if not all, of the personality traits which we have called masculine or feminine are as lightly linked to sex as are the clothing, the manners, and the forms of head-dress that a society at a given period assigns to either sex" (Mead 1935).

Observing these varied and unique manifestations of gender during her research, Mead began to question whether it could be that culture was just as powerful as biology in determining gender roles. Mead's groundbreaking work helped establish the belief that biology is only part of the equation in determining cultural definitions of gender.

In her article "Gender as Social Institution," sociologist Patricia Yancey Martin (2004) states "gender is a product of people who occupy different positions and have conflicting identities and interests." From this perspective, we begin to view gender as a sort of social role, which, like other roles, comes with certain cultural expectations. Of course that is not to say that biological differences between men and women don't exist. Men generally have a higher ratio of muscle density, which creates the tendency for men to be physically stronger than women. But, although this is the biological norm, it is not as static as may sometimes think. Women are capable of developing strength and endurance beyond that of many males. The tendency for men to be physically stronger than

Gendered Division of Labor

Historically, differences in types of labor between men and women, called **gendered division of labor**, are demonstrated by the fact that the majority of secretarial and administrative type positions are held by women. Such occupations generally pay less than many occupations that are typically held by men.

women is just that—a tendency, not an absolute.

Theorizing about gender differences, Chafetz (2001) articulates a number of salient issues drawing on aspects of theories from the macro, meso and micro levels. First, Chafetz stresses the importance of questions about "agency" versus "structure." How are actions constrained by the social structure, and how "free" are men or women to act?

According to a number of feminist theorists, much of both women's and men's behavior is informed by the structures of society. Differences between men and women in this context are sometimes referred to as a **gendered division of labor**. While this division of labor is often reflected in the workplace as we saw in the last chapter, it is more ubiquitous, even going so far as to profoundly influence personal and familial relationships.

Women in Positions of Power
Although a **gendered division of labor** still exists, it is becoming more common for women to hold positions of power. For example, Condoleezza Rice (left) became the first female, African American Secretary of State and Meg Whitman (right) is the current CEO of Hewlett Packard and a successful business woman who has served as an executive at several large corporations.

While we will take up some of these issues in the family context in the chapter on family, a number of issues are worth mentioning here. Even within families, this gendered division of labor can be observed. As an example, Chafetz (2001:617), in examining this phenomenon, adduces two propositions linking domestic family considerations and the workplace. These are:

- The greater the share of domestic labor women are responsible for (such as, but not limited to, child-rearing), the lower level of rewards they are likely to receive from their economic roles.
- The more control women have over income and other means of exchange, the less salient gender inequality becomes (also see Blumberg 1984).

For instance, in the context of marriage, divorce is commonly seen as an *alternative* to being in an unsatisfactory relationship. In a study of this, Greenstein and Davis (2006:268) conclude that "women's economic activity does seem to be related to divorce as it provides opportunity for autonomy."

There also is evidence that at least some of these differences are attributable to the sex ratio (proportion of women relative to men) in a society (Guttentag and Secord 1983). For example, after a war in which a significant number of one sex (typically men) has been killed, there will be a far greater number of women than men in a society. This tends to influence the manner with which gender is approached, compared to a more even ratio.

Guttentag and Secord, for example, find that when one gender far outnumbers the other, it tends to result in more power for the majority gender on the structural level. However, it tends to have the opposite effect on the micro level, where the gender in the minority tends to hold greater exchange value precisely because, as we saw in the section on exchange theory, they are in a position of relative scarcity.

Do Women and Men Have Different Ways of Perceiving the Social World?

According to **standpoint theory**, the structure of our society and culture provides a lens through which virtually all of our perceptions and knowledge is formulated (e.g., Harding 2004 & 2006; Hartsock 1998). Because gender is such a strong and ubiquitous concept, it is virtually impossible for a person, male or female, *not* to be affected by their gender. For this reason, gender standpoint theorists emphasize the ways in which males and females uniquely (or at least primarily) perceive the world.

Similarly, Smith (1987, 1990) argues that because men have been the dominant figures throughout history, what is often perceived as objective truth in a society is itself the result of a male-dominated viewpoint. This view has at least partial support from the work of Nancy Chodorow.

Chodorow (1989) approaches this question from the basis of Freudian theory, but with certain major qualifications, particularly in terms of gender. Chodorow argues that while Freud's work is helpful in calling attention to the psychodynamic aspects of human development, it fails to address certain important issues in its perception of gender. First, Freud sees the development of girls through male eyes. The development of girls actually follows a somewhat different trajectory, Chodorow points out, and therefore is not entirely analogous to the more male-centered theories that Freud originally developed.

For Chodorow, girls tend to develop a stronger sense of empathy and social bonding, whereas boys tend to be more competitive and individualistic. There is some empirical research that appears to validate Chodorow's position. Beutel and Marini (1995), for example, in a sample of adolescents in the United States, reported that girls were more likely to show a concern for the well being of others and to have a higher level of interest in finding meaning in life than were boys. Boys in their sample tended to express a greater interest in competition and "materialism."

Gender in the Workplace

One of the ways that gender stratification reveals itself the most blatantly is in the wage disparity that exists between men and women. Although this gap has closed slightly since the 1960s, it continues to persist with women earning 78 percent of what men earn on average. By examining the **labor force participation rate**, which gives official rates of full or part-time employment, we can see that the number of women in the labor force has increased steadily since World War II. With so many women as part of the work force, how has this gap in earning persisted? Even with legislation such as the Equal Pay Act of 1963 in effect, which requires equal pay for men and women who perform equal work, why do women still earn considerably less on average than men? Furthermore, why are men and women concentrated in certain sectors of the job market? Occupational segregation is evident in the perception of many types of employment. When you think of an elementary school teacher, for example, you probably think of a woman. In fact, 81 percent of elementary school teachers are women. Interestingly enough, elementary school teachers are paid less on average than most male-dominated career fields.

Women often face discrimination in the workplace as a result of motherhood. Sociologists Stephen Benard and Shelley Cornell (2010) call this phenomenon the "motherhood penalty." They point out that, across a range of samples, survey data shows a wage penalty for mothers. They attribute this discrimination to perceptions on the part of employers that mothers are less able to commit to their job. In a similar article, Budig and England (2001) discuss a wage penalty for motherhood, and cite data from the National Longitudinal Survey of Youth showing a wage penalty of 7 percent per child. Additionally, the wage gap between mothers and non-mothers was found to remain even after controlling for things like work experience. (Budig and England 2001). Studies have also shown that women managers who are visibly pregnant are viewed as less authoritative and less committed to their job (Halpert, Wilson, and Hickman, 1993).

Women who have children experience disadvantages during employment, but also when it comes to finding employment. In one study, researchers conducted an experiment to test how employers perceive and react to motherhood when it comes to hiring, promoting, and recommending starting salaries. The following excerpt is taken from the conclusion of the study:

> By experimentally holding constant the qualifications and background experiences of a pair of fictitious job applicants and varying only their parental status, we found that evaluators rated mothers as less competent and committed to paid work than non-mothers, and consequently, discriminated against mothers when making hiring and salary decisions. Consistent with our predictions, fathers experienced no such discrimination. In fact, fathers were advantaged over childless men in several ways, being seen as more committed to paid work and being offered higher starting salaries. (Correll 2007)

This study by Correll is somewhat unique in that it uses an experiment to observe employer reaction to motherhood rather than using secondary data. An interesting note here is that having children actually provided an advantage for men, while the opposite was true for women. The question that arises, then, is why are women seen as *less* committed to their job if they have children, when men are seen as *more* committed to their job if they have children? The answer probably has something to do with ideals regarding traditional gender roles. Men with children have traditionally been regarded as the primary breadwinners who are supposed to work outside the home, while women with children have traditionally been viewed as caretakers for children. While these views are becoming less prevalent, they do still undoubtedly play a role in the experience of women in the job market.

There is some weight given to the idea that women earn less, on average, simply because they are more likely to be employed in lower-paying positions, such as schoolteacher or administrative worker. There is some truth to this. Career fields that are typically dominated by women do pay less, on average, than many male-dominated career fields. This explanation does not paint the full picture, however. In one study, sociologist Michelle Budig investigated the pay gap between men and women in all types of jobs: male-dominated jobs, female-dominated jobs, and gender-balanced jobs. Using longitudinal data from the Bureau of Labor Statistics, Budig found that when it comes to pay and wage growth, men are advantaged in all job types, regardless of gender composition (Budig, 2002). That is to say, even in career fields wherein men are the minority, such as schoolteacher, men are advantaged in terms of pay and wage growth, compared to women.

Gender and Family

Just as traditional gender roles shape the experience of women in the workplace, they also continue to shape the division of labor that occurs in marriage. Women tend to shoulder a disproportionate share of household labor and childcare. Even women who are employed outside the home, which is increasingly common, are responsible for the majority of domestic duties. In her classic work *The Second Shift: Working Parents and the Revolution at Home*, Arlie Hochschild describes the *second shift* as the additional work that is performed by women in the home after working all day outside the home. The "double burden" as it is called, falls disproportionately on women.

The growth of women in the workforce has been quite substantial in the last several decades. In 1950, 28 percent of married women with children between the ages of six and seventeen worked outside the home. By 1986, this figure had risen to 68 percent (Hocschild 1989) and continued to rise slowly, evening out at about 71 percent in the first decade of the twenty-first century.

Though the growing number of women in the workforce can be viewed as an indicator of increasing egalitarianism in marriage, the fact is that many women now simply perform work outside the home in addition to the traditional domestic duties in the home. In recent years, it has become more common for men to perform domestic duties, and even be stay-at-home dads. This scenario is still relatively rare, though. Many studies have been undertaken since *The Second Shift* was published, and virtually all of them have found that, by nearly every measure, women spend more time than men performing housework and childcare duties. This is the case even when the man and the woman have full-time jobs.

The changing role of women in the workplace and the rising number of women in full-time jobs has led many to question the long-term effect of the increased burden on women. As professional work and families are both institutions that require undivided commitment, women are often forced to make difficult choices regarding how many children to have, how many hours to work, or whether or not to have children at all (Coser, 1974; Percheski, 2008). These are challenges that are not typically experienced by men, as men are generally expected to have full-time jobs regardless of whether or not they have children. Many scholars and media outlets have speculated about the long-term effects of this increasing burden faced by women. Some predict that it will result in women opting out of professional careers. A well known example of this is a *New York Times* article published in 2003, which describes an "opt-out" revolution wherein there was an exodus of professional women leaving the workforce for motherhood (Percheski, 2008). One study regarding employment rates of professional women between 1960 and 2005, however, finds that professional women's employment rates have held steady over the last two cohorts (Percheski, 2008). This implies that women are not "opting out" of professional careers in order to have children. Rather, it implies that women choose to remain in professional careers while shouldering the double burden. If there seems to be an increasing occurrence of professional women leaving the workforce, it is likely due to the fact that because there are more women in professional careers today, there are simply "more women available to exit" (Whittington 2000). As such, the average person is more likely to know a professional woman who has left the workforce (Percheski 2008).

The Second Shift

The double burden of participation in the work force coupled with domestic labor at home falls disproportionately on women.

Perceptions of differences in workload between mothers and fathers vary. In one study of contemporary families with preschool children, sociologists found that mothers' workloads were greater than fathers' by a week and a half per year, rather than one month per year as previously suggested (Milkie, Raley, Bianchi 2009). The study also found that mothers experience greater time pressures and have less leisure time than fathers.

Gender and Crime

When it comes to gender and crime, the first and perhaps most obvious observation is the higher crime rates among males. Secondly, we observe differences in types of crime generally committed by males and females. Some argue that the reason crime is more prevalent among men is because women are socialized into less risk-taking roles. Crimes committed by women tend to be non-violent offenses, such as fraud and embezzlement. The most common of these offenses are shoplifting, credit card fraud, writing bad checks, and drug offenses. Though women on average commit less crime than men, crime among women has increased in recent years. One possible explanation is that women are being employed in positions that present the opportunity for things like embezzlement and fraud.

General strain theory (GST) is a prevalent theory of crime that seeks to explain the reasons that people engage in crime. It focuses on strain as the cause of delinquency, and identifies three types of strain that people experience that might lead to criminal behavior: **1)** the) failure to achieve positively valued goals, **2)** the removal of positively valued stimuli, **3)** the presentation of negative stimuli.

Broidy and Agnew (1997) applied general strain theory to the study of gender and crime to answer important questions: How can we explain the higher rate of crime among males? How can we explain why females engage in crime? Using GST to explain the higher crime rate among males might lead us to one of the following conclusions:

- Males experience more strain than women.
- Males are subject to different types of strain that are more conducive to crime.
- Males have a different emotional response to strain that is more conducive to crime.
- Males are more likely to respond to anger/strain with crime.

(Broidy and Agnew, 1997)

According to Broidy and Agnew, who developed GST, the literature shows that females experience as much strain as males, if not more, but that the strain experienced by females is less conducive to crime. Females are more likely to report the experience of low prestige in work and family roles, excessive demands from family members and restrictions on their behavior. These types of strains are generally less conducive to crime. Several feminist theorists have argued that males are more concerned with material success and extrinsic achievements, while females place higher value on the establishment and maintenance of close relationships (Broidy and Agnew, 1997). This helps to explain the differences in perceived strain between genders. Additionally, males and females often respond differently to strain. Females are more likely to experience depression, guilt, and anxiety as a result of strain, while men are more likely to experience moral outrage. These differences stem largely from gender socialization (Sharp 2002).

The types of strain that are generally experienced by males, such as criminal victimization and the inability to achieve goals that males are socialized to desire (monetary success, attainment of positions of authority etc.) are more conducive to crime. Overall, differences in types of strain and the emotional response to them help us to understand gender differences in crime.

Just as males carry out the majority of crime, the majority of those who study crime are males as well. One could say that, in nearly every respect, crime is a male phenomenon. Because gender is clearly a factor of crime, it seems that a gender-based approach could undoubtedly be helpful in understanding crime. Feminism can help provide such an approach. For the most part, feminist perspectives have not been a central focus in criminology. This is due, in part, to perceptions that criminology is about men and feminism is about women (Naffine 1996). But because feminist perspectives emphasize gender, and gender is so clearly a factor in crime, feminist perspectives can contribute to our understanding of this topic. There are a few notable exceptions in this regard. Recent work by women on crime includes that of Susan Sharp (2002, 2014). Sharp was also founding editor of *Feminist Criminology*, a journal recently established to focus on these questions.

From a feminist perspective we are able to see that crime is not only a male problem. It is women, for example, who must shoulder the economic and emotional responsibility of childcare when male parents are incarcerated (Flavin 2001). There are also certain types of crime that are, by and large, a problem experienced by women. In the vast majority of domestic violence and rape cases, the victims are women. A gender-based approach, which is offered by feminist perspectives, can help us understand how gender socialization contributes to huge differences in crime and victimization between men and women.

Gender and Sexuality

Scientific research into human sexuality is still somewhat lacking compared to other sociological phenomena. This is especially true of women's sexuality. Many models of sexual orientation that have been used in the past have proven to be unsupported by evidence. In this section we will address some of those models and discuss some of the factors related to gender and sexuality.

The Illness Model

For much of the twentieth century, homosexuality was considered a mental illness. In fact, until 1974, the American Psychiatric Association officially listed it as such. The illness model has informed many theories about sexuality, which have included the notion that lesbians have arrested psychosexual development (Peplau and Garnets 2000). Such ideas have led to the development of stereotypes that gays and lesbians are unable to adjust to normal life and form satisfying relationships. A growing body of research has, of course, refuted this. Many standardized measures have shown that the psychological well being of homosexuals is not adversely affected by their sexual orientation. Additionally, research has shown that homosexuals are comparable to their heterosexual counterparts when it comes to personal adjustment (Peplau and Garnets 2000).

The Inversion Model

In the early nineteenth century, experts on sexuality developed an inversion model of homosexuality. The model proposed that normal, heterosexual women are feminine in their physiology and personality, while lesbians are the inverse. That is, they are masculine in their physiology and personality (Peplau and Garnets 2000). This model has been discredited as the link between heterosexuality and femininity is not demonstrable.

Biological Models

Research has shown that biological factors, such as levels of atypical prenatal hormones, do not significantly influence the development of women's sexuality. Nor is there any causal relationship between adult hormone levels and sexual orientation (Peplau and Garnets 2000). Some studies have been conducted to determine whether or not atypical levels of prenatal sex hormones play a role in developing homosexual orientation. In the majority of such cases, however, the women turn out to be heterosexual. These findings suggest that there is little evidence that biological factors play a significant role in the development of women's sexuality (Peplau and Garnets 2000).

Other research has placed more emphasis on social and psychological factors that might affect sexuality. Some scholars have suggested that women's sexuality tends to be fluid and malleable compared to men, and more likely to be affected by things like religious ideology and educational background. The emerging view in the study of sexuality, however, is that no single factor, biological or social, reliably predicts a woman's sexual orientation.

CHAPTER SUMMARY

- **Gender** refers to how we develop ideas, roles and norms, behaviors and expectations relative to our sex in a social and cultural context. **Gender socialization** can be described as the process by which individuals learn about the norms, behaviors and expectations associated with each gender. Through this process, individuals learn to conform to such norms and expectations.
- The **second shift** refers to the additional work that is performed by women in the home after working all day outside the home. It includes domestic labor and childcare.
- Crime, particularly violent crime, is much more prevalent among males. Crimes committed by women tend to be non-violent offenses, such as fraud and embezzlement. Differences in crime rates and types of crime between men and women have much to do with the way boys and girls are socialized.
- Old ideals regarding sexuality, such as the illness model, the inversion model, and biological models, have become outdated. Research shows that there is no single factor, social or biological, that can predict sexuality.

11 Historical and Comparative Development and Global Inequality

In this chapter, we will examine several theories that address the questions: how do societies evolve, and how do some come to be advantaged relative to others? The natural environment plays a key role, as do technology and economics. Some societies develop earlier than others. It is these societies that are able to control and use resources to their advantage, often at the expense of those societies developing later. Thus, in examining the trajectory of societal evolution and change, we'll ask the important question of *how* societies reach more developed levels relatively *early* in the evolutionary trajectory.

Social function, social conflict, and social exchange approaches are some key elements of these theories. Each receives more or less attention relative to the element of society under discussion. Because theories of the more microscopic focus of the social interaction perspective do not apply very well to the large-scale or macro-sociological issues, we will not consider them in this chapter.

Generally speaking, the first three theories we examine can be considered as having primarily a *social function* (and, to a lesser extent, a *social exchange*) focus, because they emphasize how societies came to develop the way they did in the first place, with labor divided among the population and how they now "function" in light of that development. The fourth theory, world-system theory, focuses primarily upon social exchange and social conflict in general. It emphasizes the relative power and exploitative capacities of early developers compared to the late developers with whom they trade.

Lenski's Eco-Technological Theory of Societal Evolution

In the model proposed by Gerhard Lenski and his various collaborators, technology and the natural environment are two major factors that play a key role in societal development and inequality. Of those two, Lenski views technology as having the most critical importance. More specifically, it is the type of societal production, or **subsistence technology**, which Lenski sees as the chief factor constraining society's ability to extract and use natural resources. We use the term technology to refer not only to physical implements such as tools, but also to the ideas needed to use them and to apply the resources from the surrounding environment.

The type of subsistence technology used within a society has a number of profound implications for the human social arrangements of that society. For example, the size of the population a society can sustain increases dramatically with better technology. It is not surprising that there are also profound ideological differences between more-evolved and less-evolved societies. With greater population and social complexity (the "division of labor"), inequality in terms of power, prestige, and the distribution of other scarce economic and social resources changes significantly. In this way, subsistence technology functions to improve societal conditions by altering the potential for social conflict vis-à-vis the exchanges people make.

Lenski classifies societies by the subsistence technology available to the most advanced portion of that society. While he identifies ten different types of societies (as well as hybrids among some of these ten types), the most important, in the order they evolve, are: hunting and gathering societies (the most primitive, or least evolved), horticultural societies, agrarian societies, and industrial societies (the most evolved). Let's now turn to examining each of these, emphasizing the functions, exchanges, conflicts, and stratifications involved in their classification.

The smallest and most primitive of the societal types are **hunting and gathering societies.** Utilizing historical evidence, Lenski concludes that the average size of hunting and gathering societies has been about forty people, the members of which are typically comprised of extended families or clans. As a rule, the people are nomadic, and use of technology is extremely limited, with only a few exceptions such as the use of rocks or sticks. Due to these factors, the hunting and gathering society typically does not amass food or vital necessities beyond immediate needs. That is, it does not generate a **surplus**. Technology functions to fulfill only basic necessities. There is little division of labor in these societies, only rudimentary exchanges, and the division of labor and exchanges that do exist typically stem from physical differences, such as sex and age. With these conditions, **stratification** in the society tends to be minimal, as does social conflict over the distribution of excess resources.

Lenski points out that use of **natural resources**, such as the land and minerals, at this stage of evolution is very primitive. *Any* given society has some potential to overuse its resources to the point of depletion. In the case of hunting and gathering societies this overuse can come in the form of hunting animals in a given area virtually to the point of extinction. When this has occurred, it has resulted in movement of the hunting and gathering peoples to a new location. In fact, this scenario was a key motivating factor in many of the human migrations of primitive times. However, the lack of technology, the inability to extract natural resources, and the relatively small size of such societies reduce their environmental impact.

The next society type Lenski identifies is the **horticultural society**, which evolves alongside the advent of simple implements such as a digging stick or hoe. This technology functions so as to permit the society to *settle* in one place. Now, with the advent of simple tools to till the soil, a society has the capacity to plant and harvest crops. In so doing, members of a horticultural society can develop more permanent shelter and protection from the environment.

As it begins to develop techniques of land usage, a horticultural society is able to generate more food than a hunting and gathering society can. The use of this simple technology serves to sustain a larger population, ranging in size from about 1,500 to over 5,000 persons. The labor-intensive work required to constitute a horticultural society is often more time-consuming than hunting and gathering. However, the fruits of such labor can be more consistently depended upon, allowing for the potential of a *surplus* of food. While a dry spell of a week or even a few days was life threatening to a hunting and gathering society, the occasional surplus in a horticultural society could help it to ride out a time of lower productivity.

In one way or another, in a horticultural society, nearly everyone is involved in said horticulture. However, as the population size increases, individual members begin to fall into unique roles in order to produce more specialized goods for exchange. In this way **social differentiations** emerge in the form of rudimentary distinctions based on the kinds of labor engaged in and commodities produced. Some people, for example, spend as much or more time making pottery and exchanging it as they do tilling the soil. With surplus food and other items to exchange comes an increasing incentive for individuals to accumulate resources for themselves. During this phase we witness the genesis of human stratification systems, as people are differentially successful at garnering resources and exchanging them for the benefit of themselves and their next of kin.

Also during this phase, we witness the possibility of social conflicts over control of surplus goods. In fact, as a society accumulates a surplus, it sets the stage for *other* societies to have a potential interest in invading it and plundering its resources as well. As such, the society must defend itself from potential invaders. This scenario necessitates the rise of a warrior class. Warriors devote a significant portion of their adult lives either to defending their society's resources or attacking another society for their resources. Desired goods in principle could be secured through exchanges. However, in every exchange some resources are "given up" in the trade for desired goods. Victory in a social conflict may cost less than an exchange, and warriors may serve a vital function in this regard.

Further, there is a need to provide the leadership function for society, and here we see the rise of a political class. However, it is important to note that the "class" of which we speak here is not fully developed, as warriors and political leaders are typically still involved in horticulture as well. Much of society is still based on patterns of extended kinship, such as clans.

The next phase in the evolution of a society is the **agrarian** stage. This stage arises with the advent of more sophisticated tools for the tilling of soil, such as the plow, along with the domestication of beasts of burden. In so doing, it can use the natural environment more effectively than ever before. Technology functions to produce more food, greater levels of surplus, and increased production. These advances allow the size of an agrarian society to increase to over 100,000 members, sometimes numbering even in the millions.

It is this population increase that may function to permit greater societal *complexity*. While most people in agrarian societies are still involved with agriculture in some way, we also see a significant proportion of the population engaging in some occupation other than agriculture, such as metalworking, building, or weaving. This expansion in the types of occupations in which people are involved gives rise to the formation of cities. Here as well, we witness the rise of classes of priests, politicians, warriors, and nobles, in which people are devoted to this as a *full-time* occupation.

Lenski shows the potential for such stratification is greater in this technological stage than in any other. As desired resources are traded among more and more specialized producers, it results in greater levels of social exchanges. However, it also leads to greater potential for differentiation in terms of the degree of stratification, or levels of inequality. With even greater surplus and exchanges than before, greater disparity is possible between the "haves" and "have-nots." Disparities, of course, act as a powerful catalyst for social conflicts.

As a society becomes more complex, there is an increasing need to have some over-arching belief system ("ideology") that serves the function of social integration. People must be tied back to the larger collective, to prevent their self-interests from leading to social conflicts that threaten to destroy the society. As Durkheim tells us, the existence of an overarching belief system, and people believing in it and internalizing its values, has an integrative function for the society. An integrated society can be defined as a society in which deviance and other social pathology is low (but *not* nonexistent), and where there is a cooperative and productive division of labor in which individuals feel they and the roles they fill are an integral part of the larger collective. Traditionally, religion has helped to serve that function. In agrarian societies, there is an increasing emphasis on religion, and especially as a society advances, to believe in a *monotheistic* (one God, as opposed to a number of gods) religion. The function of these overarching belief systems is to provide a means of social integration, allowing individual members of a society to feel tied to something bigger than themselves.

After the agrarian subsistence technology phase, the next phase in the evolution of societies, Lenski notes, is the **industrial** phase. Here society develops and becomes heavily dependent on *complex machinery* and "inanimate" energy sources, such as that provided by coal, natural gas, oil, and nuclear fission. Industrial societies are able to sustain a population of millions more people than agrarian societies. This is due to the use of heavy machinery as the basis of *subsistence technology*, which allows for the productive capacity of a society to increase exponentially.

This increasing population size, in turn, paves the way for even more complexity in the division of labor, which can be observed as an increase in occupational differentiation, or specialization. In this phase, resources are being produced and exchanged at an historically unprecedented rate. Industrial society is able to sustain production such that it often is able to generate a tremendous surplus of material goods. This surplus functions to even out crisis times; famine, for example, does not present such an immediate danger as it does in more primitive societies where production is more closely tied with immediate consumption.

The surplus generated in industrial societies has a number of other functions. For example, the surplus of goods allows for the welfare state to arise, for instance. Lenski posits that there is actually *less* social inequality in advanced industrial societies than in agrarian societies. In other words, with increasing technology and surplus comes increasing societal inequality until the industrial phase, during which time inequality declines. Because of the tremendous abundance, even the poorest people have some of the advantages that the industrial society has to offer, such as access to schools and health care, public assistance and other welfare programs.

This thesis of decreasing inequality in the industrial phase is, of course, at odds with the emphases of a number of social conflict theorists, most notably Karl Marx and his followers. Marx and Engels focused on the increasing inequality attendant to industrial society, and the misery for the masses associated with that inequality. However, this view can be at least partially reconciled with Lenski's theories of "declining inequality" by emphasizing the fact that while in agrarian societies, a very small number of elites may control virtually all the wealth, modern industrial societies are different in that the wealth is shared among a greater number of elites, causing a middle class to form between the very wealthy and the poor. It is in these respects that social stratification may decrease, while remaining as a key axis for social conflicts in industrial society.

Alongside the utilization of technologically advanced machinery, we witness the ability to extract and recombine natural resources much more rapidly than ever before. While this, of

Lenski's Eco-Technological Theory of Societal Evolution

Lenski identifies four major phases of societal evolution: (clockwise from top left) hunting/gathering, horticultural, agrarian and industrial.

course, is associated with tremendous productivity and escalating social exchanges, it is in the industrial phase that we see the greatest potential for environmental degradation. The technology to plunder the environment is most accessible, at the same time that resources from the environment are viewed as most essential.

Rostow's Theory of Economic Growth

Economist Walter W. Rostow offers another important model of development, theorizing five stages of societal economic growth. In Rostow's model, as societies move through five stages of evolution, each succeeding stage is characterized by a greater impact on its natural environment. This evolution finally culminates in a stage in which the implications of such impact are felt beyond the confines of the society itself, as it greatly influences all the other societies involved in social exchange or trade relationships with it. While Rostow as an economist does not always draw out the implications of his schema for social conflicts and social inequalities, it is a significant perspective nonetheless.

The first phase according to Rostow, the **traditional society**, is characterized as having very minimal capacity for social exchange and production. This capacity is based on what Rostow and others refer to as *pre-Newtonian attitudes*, especially as they pertain to the natural environment. This phrase, of course, refers to the work of Isaac Newton, whose life work had a profound effect on the scientific revolution. One major outcome of this revolution was a rising *faith* in the scientific method, which included *methodical* observation and testing of the environment, and the *systematic* application of the technology developed.

How is the production capacity of a traditional society affected by pre-Newtonian attitudes? According to Rostow, the lack of systematic implementation of science and technology in these traditional societies had the effect of constraining the ability of the society to surpass some limited level of output and trade. Thus, the surplus in traditional societies was not of appreciable magnitude. Here we can more clearly appreciate Lenski's theory describing the relatively lower levels of social inequality in such societies. Because of this relatively low productivity (combined with the ever-present need to produce enough food for people to get proper sustenance), traditional societies devoted much of their energy and resources to agriculture. As an aside, you may note here that each of Lenski's phases, through the agrarian phase, would be considered by Rostow to be in the first phase of development ("traditional society").

The second phase, which Rostow calls the **preconditions for take-off**, involves a number of factors stemming from the society's natural ecology. The "preconditions" describe the social and political conditions made possible by a combination of geography, natural resources, as well as the opportunities for trade that these factors provide.

In Rostow's theory, England serves as the prototypical case, as England is considered the first nation-state to industrialize. The fact that the Industrial Revolution saw its genesis there was no accident—the precise combination of several circumstances found in England gave it an advantage over other geographical areas. As an island with warm-water ports available for exploration, England was able to colonize other, resource-rich environs such as India and the

New World. Social exchanges or trade with its colonies was very functional to England, as they provided much of the raw material needed for its burgeoning textile industry. The wealth generated from its industrial production in textiles and other goods allowed England to amass sufficient wealth to transition to the next phase of economic growth. Based on Rostow's reasoning, it could be argued that when England used its colonies this way it pushed them down the same path to development that England had taken.

The third phase in Rostow's model is the **take-off phase**. In this phase, investment rises to ten percent or more of the national income as the surplus that is generated in small amounts in the prior phase reaches a level sufficient to form the basis of entrepreneurial investment capital.

While some of these entrepreneurial ventures fail, others succeed, and some emphatically so. There is an increasing synergy between technology and growth that occurs during this stage, such that leading-edge technology is largely spurring the growth, which generates profits, much of which are then invested in the development of further technology.

In this stage, technology has an effect on agricultural production as well. Farming becomes more machine-intensive, for example, and requires fewer people for a successful yield. At the same time, industrial production, much of which is centered in cities, is expanding dramatically, requiring an ever-increasing number of workers. Thus, the cities serve as magnets for people being displaced by intensifying agriculture in rural areas. The effect of these factors is the rapid urbanization of society.

In fact, one of the key differences between traditional and modern societies is the tremendous urbanization in the latter. The social dislocation stemming from industrialization and urbanization, and its associated problems such as crime, suicide, delinquency, social malaise, etc., is what inspired the early sociologists to theorize about society in the first place, and to conjecture about how such problems may be addressed.

If the industrial and economic growth of the take-off phase can be sustained, the society enters the fourth phase, or the **drive to maturity**. This stage is characterized by the production and exchange of a broader array of goods and services. In other words, during the take-off phase, economic growth centers around a relatively narrow range of highly profitable industries, while in the drive to maturity, the economy and the technology underpinning it diversify. This diversification is, often in no small measure, a function of the society finding its way into the international economy. In so doing, goods that are produced more efficiently elsewhere may be exchanged for, rather than produced at home. What is manufactured at home may have components from a number of different places.

This economic diversification leads to diversification of the labor force as well. A number of new occupations emerge, many of which are in skilled jobs or in management, professions, or clerical sectors.

This sets the stage for the fifth phase, the age of **mass consumption**. In this phase, we see a large portion of the population earning a level of income beyond what is required for the basic necessities of food, clothing and shelter. Stark inequalities exist, leading of course to the potential for social conflicts over them. Yet, a significant proportion of the societal surplus is accessible by an increasing segment of the population. Many people, rather than reinvesting surplus income, will simply spend it. The management of consumption spawns an entirely new economic sector, as businesses related to commissioned retail sales and advertising begin to form.

As the society itself responds to its surplus of wealth, we see the rise of the welfare state in the form of social programs such as unemployment insurance and old age or retirement programs, and in some cases national health insurance or public assistance. While the function of these safety nets is to prevent a large segment of the population from succumbing to the gravest of circumstances, they certainly do not eradicate sharp social inequalities.

As implied by its name, it is in this phase that the society consumes tremendous resources. This stage also witnesses a heretofore-unsurpassed demand on the natural environment as the technological capability, combined with high demand that accompanies surplus wealth, requires. The consequences of this personal and societal demand can be seen both in terms of depletion of the natural resources necessary to sustain it, as well as in terms of garbage dumps or "sinks" needed for the refuse and pollution associated with it.

Talcott Parsons and Social Change

Building upon Durkheim's ideas about moral and material density, Talcott Parsons (1966) developed a model of societal change. Like Durkheim, Parsons adopted an evolutionary model of society, in which a society moves from primitiveness to modernity. Also like Durkheim, Parsons utilized notions of volume (numbers of people), material density (physical interaction), and moral density (social interaction), considering them to be essential factors that cause a society to move toward modernity.

As a society moves toward modernity, four major aspects of social change occur. These are, respectively:

1. **Differentiation.** This is analogous to Durkheim's theory of the division of labor in society. There are two main types of differentiation: a) *horizontal*, and b) *vertical*. Horizontal differentiation is characterized by specialization. Vertical differentiation is characterized by the advent of structural inequality, or stratification. For Parsons, stratification was not a bad thing. Instead, he viewed it as an inevitable occurrence in an expanding and therefore differentiating society.

2. **Adaptive Upgrading.** As a society gets bigger and has more interaction, it is more likely to improve the ways in which it allows its members to adapt to the environment. To explain this, Parsons adopts Weber's ideas about *formal rationality*, arguing that social institutions begin adopting standardized procedures and formal rules in order to function more efficiently. This modernization process includes the adoption of a money and market economy through which a wider variety of goals can be attained by the society, as well as its members, based on a general medium of exchange.

3. **Inclusion.** Furthermore, Parsons adapted Weber's idea that as a society modernizes, its authority system moves from a *traditional* one characterized by ascription, to a rational-legal one, characterized by a meritocracy. In this way, opportunities become available to more people, especially those who traditionally have been excluded.

4. **Value Generalization.** Ideas are cast in a less specific and more universal way. Members of society come to see phenomena in terms of underlying general forms rather than specific content. In terms of religion, for example, people increasingly perceive the similarities in religions rather than dwelling on differences.

Parsons' model has been criticized for its assumption that *all* societies will respond to demographic change and modernization in a similar manner, and also for failing to address rapid change, such as what occurs during revolutions, in his model.

Dependency in the Modern World-System

A number of social theorists have developed the implications of social exchanges and social inequalities for society in its global context in response to more functionally oriented approaches such as Rostow's. In doing so, they have addressed the tendency for more developed countries, primarily those developing *early* relative to others, to exploit and even further impoverish less-developed countries. This tendency began long before the development of the modern geoculture, which refers to the values that are widely shared throughout the world-system (Wallerstein 2011). These theorists argue that due to this process, the prospects for the less developed countries *ever* developing to the extent of some of the richer countries, are bleak indeed. This perspective is often referred to as **world-system theory**. World-system theory stands out in that its unit of analysis is the entire world and its networks of exchange, exploitation, conflict, and dependency, rather than a single given society. World-system theorists focus on the development of the capitalist world-economy, which is a global system of markets (e.g., Wallerstein 1979; Chirot 1986). The logic of the system is, of course, based on the maximization of profits. A truly capitalist and *world* economy probably emerged at least as early as the fifteenth century with the global military and mercantilist reach of Spain and Portugal. This era of increasing global exploration and trade was catalyzed by declining profits among the European states, coupled with the fall of Constantinople to the Turks and the resultant loss of easy access to Eastern markets. Spain and Portugal were the first among many later nations to turn their technological prowess to the development of national economic infrastructures and navigational capabilities (including command of the compass), which allowed for the accumulation of capital from plunder and trade, far-reaching commodity exchanges, and distant shipping.

Spain and Portugal's positions of supremacy in the world system were promptly challenged. By the close of the sixteenth century, the Netherlands, England, and France had entered the global market. A turning point came when England dealt Spain a debilitating naval defeat with Sir Francis Drake's victory over the technologically inferior Spanish Armada. There is some debate on the matter, but coupled with ecological and economic advantages, it was the better technology of the Netherlands, England, and France that catapulted them over Spain and Portugal as the dominant global economic and military powers of the time (Wallerstein 1974, 1980, 1989; Chirot 1986).

In the first centuries of the world economy, Spain and Portugal, and then England, France, and the Netherlands occupied what world-system theorists refer to as "core" positions in the global system (Wallerstein 1974, 1979). Wallerstein refers to these countries as the **core** or center of an increasingly global economy based on both local and distant markets. The key of the early core nations' success depended upon their technological reach and resultant ability to harness inexpensive raw materials and labor, including enslaved labor, in order to produce goods that were profitably exchanged in a growing world system. This concomitant expansion of human capital, coupled with technological prowess proved mutually beneficial as the core countries became ever more adept at using cheap labor to convert raw materials (such as wool), often obtained from peripheral areas of the system (i.e., the **periphery**, or areas with little natural wealth or resources), to finished products (e.g., clothing). Core economic actors and their allied states enjoyed mounting profits and power, while gaining a continuing economic advantage over the poorer peripheral societies of the "New World" and the other more middle-income countries of Europe, the **semiperiphery** (Wallerstein 1974).

Core Country

Core nations, such as the United States, are characterized by well-developed infrastructure, resource abundance, wealth, and power.

Peripheral Country

Peripheral nations, such as Ethiopia, Burma and Bangladesh, are characterized by poverty, poor infrastructure, and resource shortage.

In the long run, England outdistanced France and the Netherlands due to her superior technology and mobilization of human talent, coupled with resultant economic and military advantages. But the expansion of the core to include other nations as well was set into motion by the diffusion of technology, innovation and parallel access to resources, labor and markets. Technical powers such as Germany, Switzerland, Belgium, and the United States emerged to enter the core of the world system in the late 1800s and early 1900s (Chirot 1986).

By the turn of the twentieth century, mainly through the formal establishment of African and Asian colonies or spheres of influence in Latin America, core nations had established pervasive control over non-core nations. Likely, it was the fear of unlimited contention over these globally spread resources that so gripped core and challenging semiperipheral powers that military contention among major world-system actors was inevitable. At stake was the plausible redistribution of world-system spoils (Chirot 1986).

Despite the historical importance of technological prowess and military might, these factors did not provide a conclusive resolution to such contests. Indeed, the overall logic of the world system remained substantially intact after World War I, and in roughly one generation, competition supported by even more lethal technical firepower ensued. It was technology that brought World War II to a close and ushered in the United States as the **hegemon** or dominant power of the world system during the middle of the twentieth century. This overall logic of the world system remains effectively unaltered today, in spite of shifts in global leadership, including some successful and modern challenges mounted against the United States by capitalist core powers and the rising semiperiphery—the so-called "BRIC" countries (Brazil, Russia, India and China) among the most notable in this regard.

Snyder and Kick (1979), in examining networks of trade and dependence, explore this logic. In doing so, they find that for a variety of economic, political and military exchanges, core societies tended to be central to those exchanges, peripheral societies tended to be relatively isolated, and semi-peripheral societies tended to be somewhere in between. The names of the types of societies, in fact is descriptive of, and stems from, their relative positions in these global exchange networks.

While there are exceptions to this, the ideal-typical trade relation in the modern world-system tends to conform to the following trajectory: First, raw materials are extracted from peripheral countries. It is important to keep in mind that these peripheral countries tend *not* to have diversified economies. Rather, they are likely to possess only a handful of raw materials with any value on the world market. What little wealth a country is able to accumulate from its position in the world economy, however, is largely associated with the extraction of said raw materials. Typically, peripheral countries are not in a position to dispute this extractive mode of production, either economically or militarily. Because of its position, it is more dependent on the country with which it is trading (typically a relatively more powerful semi-peripheral country) than vice-versa. Thus, its global social exchanges, or trade, tend to be exploitative, with the peripheral country receiving little for its resources, while simultaneously being forced to incur most or all the costs (e.g., resource depletion and the pollution from mine tailings, etc.).

Semi-peripheral countries tend to have economies centered on a few industries. They take raw materials from their own and other (typically peripheral) countries and do *value-added labor*, such as the assembly of electronic equipment, computer chips, shoes and other types of clothing. This type of work is often dangerous or unhealthy. For example, many of the worst sweatshops are found in the semi-peripheral areas of the world. This is because many of the regulations in place to protect workers found in the more developed countries of the world (such as regulations enforced by the Occupational Safety and Health Administration in the United States) are absent in semi-peripheral areas.

It is in the core countries where capital is most heavily concentrated, and thus where we typically find the headquarters of Multinational corporations (MNCs). As the investments of these MNCs and the banks associated with them earn profits, the effect is to concentrate capital even more in core countries. This concentration of capital leads to the relatively high rates of disposable income we discussed above, and thus extremely high rates of consumption. This does not imply that there are not sizeable populations of poor people in core countries—indeed there are. However, a significant proportion of the population in core countries is quite affluent. Social inequalities *between* countries in the world system interact with stratification processes *within* the country.

World-system theorists do acknowledge that a country's position is not necessarily static, but may change over time—in other words, the possibility for *mobility* within the world-system. While *any* country is potentially mobile in the world-system, the greatest chance for this is found in the semi-periphery. Typically, core countries are firmly ensconced at the top of the hierarchy and are able to use their advantageous position to further ensure their dominance. Peripheral countries are barely above subsistence, and have little economic and social capital (such as education) with which to build. These countries are so marginalized, in other words, that they typically stay "beneath the wheel" indefinitely.

Although the number of wealthy people in semi-peripheral countries does not approach the proportions found in core countries, semi-peripheral countries tend to have a small class of elites who are extremely wealthy, along with a correspondingly high level of social inequalities. However, the elites in semi-peripheral countries often have an interest in developing their economies in order to successfully compete with core countries. To this end, elites in semi-peripheral countries, often in conjunction with venture capitalists from the core, are able to concentrate financing in what they may see as key industries. Such investments can at times give a semi-peripheral country the chance of propelling itself into the core. Japan is one example of a semi-peripheral country that achieved this successfully.

On the other hand, with enough investment capital to finance modern technology in the extraction and use of resources, combined with a relative absence of sufficient government regulation sometimes found in developed countries (e.g., the Environmental Protection Agency in the United States), semi-peripheral countries are in a position to decimate the environment more efficiently and easily than the periphery, and with more abandon than the core. Thus, it is also in the semi-periphery that some of the worst environmental degradation takes place. This is another example of how the world system even produces global inequalities in the distribution of pollution.

That is not to say that environmental degradation is not a worldwide problem, for indeed it is. However, the proximal causes of environmental degradation often vary across countries as a function of development. In peripheral countries, for example, deforestation is largely a function of landless or otherwise extremely poor people using wood for heating fuel; while in semi-peripheral countries, a more salient cause of deforestation would be the international exchanges related to the wood trade (Burns et al. 2003).

On the same note, another major cause of deforestation in the semi-periphery is the clearing of forests for ranching. For example, it has been estimated that about 85 percent of the deforestation that has occurred in Costa Rica was caused by clear-cutting so that the land could be used for ranching (in many such cases the wood is not even used—rather, it is burned or wasted in some other way). Much of the ranching in semi-peripheral countries is to raise beef for trade with developed countries, who use the beef in fast-food restaurants. In this way, the practice is inextricably connected to the functioning of the world-system. Thus, it is reasonable to conclude that the mass consumption of the core is at least partially responsible for a significant portion of the resource depletion and social inequalities in the Third World (Jorgenson 2003; Jorgenson and Burns 2007). There is literature on the "ecological footprint," which we will discuss in a later chapter.

Conclusion

In this chapter, we have discussed several major theoretical approaches to how societies evolve. Approaches taken by Lenski, Rostow, and Parsons tend to follow the social functions approach, insofar as they emphasize social wholes, functionality, and societal evolution. They also focus on exchanges, as does the other macrosociological theory discussed—world-system theory. However, unlike the others, world-system theory essentially falls under the social conflict paradigm. Each of the approaches fit well within the sociological imagination, as they explore different aspects of the social in macrosociological domains.

CHAPTER SUMMARY

- Each of the four key theories we have considered in this chapter approach the evolution of societies from a macro-level perspective.
- Each of these four theories discusses societal development and its relationship to social stratification.
- Lenski, Rostow and Parsons essentially utilize a social functions approach, whereas Wallerstein and other world-system theorists tend to take a social conflict approach.
- The modern world system can be described as having three sectors or tiers—a wealthy and powerful *core*, a poor *periphery*, and a *semi-periphery* that exists within an intermediate position between the core and the periphery.
- Social inequalities *between* countries in the world system interact with stratification processes *within* the country.
- Stratification arises with changes in societal technology, economy, and structural position in a world system.

12 | Family and Kinship Institutions

An examination of family structure across cultures and across history shows that **families** are a cultural universal. That is, all known societies have had some form of family. This does not mean, however, that there is just one family structure across space and time, or that there is perfect agreement among social scientists on what constitutes a family. A recent survey carried out by sociologists in the United States found that virtually everyone felt that a man and a woman who are married with children constitute a family. (Powell 2012) The survey also found that 93 percent of people considered a man and a woman who are married but have no children to be a family as well. Additionally, about 94 percent of people believe that an unmarried man or woman living with their children make up a family. It is also noteworthy that 53 percent of Americans feel that two gay men living together with children constitute a family, and 55 percent believe that a lesbian couple living together with children makes up a family. These figures regarding families headed by same-sex couples have increased significantly from recent decades.

We will approach the family as a social organization and social group comprised of interdependent roles and interactions among individuals who occupy those roles. Moreover, the family is characterized by kinship and often involves co-habitation within a residency. Families also serve to carry out specialized functions, especially the bearing and rearing of children. **Kinship** is a social bond that is based on blood relationships, relationships as a result of marriage, or by adoption.

Throughout the world, families typically are based on **marriage**. Marriage is the legally sanctioned relationship that prescribes an enduring commitment to the relationship, and the fulfillment of roles and responsibilities. Sociologists refer to a structure in which two adults live together in a household with their own or with adopted children as a **nuclear family**. The structure of an **extended** family may include sisters and their husbands, brothers and their wives, grandparents, aunts and uncles, and nephews and nieces all sharing the same household. Sociologists also refer to **families of origin** and **families of procreation**. Our family of origin is the family into which we are born. As we build our own families as adults, we are part of the family of procreation. Of course, our family of procreation is our children's family of origin.

Virtually all societies across time and space trace their kinship over generations, a process referred to as **descent**. Industrial societies generally trace descent through both men and women. That is, people on both sides of the family are viewed as relatives. This is not universal, however. Many pre-industrial societies, for example, traced kinship only through either the mother or the father. A system that traces kinship through women is known as **matrilineal descent**. In this instance, mothers pass their property on to their daughters. Matrilineal descent is typically found in horticultural societies in which women are the main food producers. More prevalent, however, is the system that traces kinship through men, which is referred to as **patrilineal descent**. Children in patrilineal societies are related to others through their fathers and not their mothers, and fathers typically pass on their property to their sons. This system is generally encountered in pastoral and agrarian societies.

Nuclear Family
Families are a cultural universal, although their structures differ throughout societies.

Just as they regulate descent, societies also regulate a family's area of residence. In preindustrial societies, a newly married couple may maintain an economic advantage as well as security for their livelihood by remaining near their parents. In this way, preindustrial societies are either **patrilocal**, meaning that couples live near the family of the father, or **matrilocal**, living with or near the wife's family. In industrial societies, on the other hand, married couples often travel to distant locales seeking economic opportunities. When couples leave home in this way, the pattern is referred to as **neolocality**. Under neolocality a married couple lives apart from the parents of the husband as well as the parents of the wife.

Societal norms also tend to prescribe desirable or undesirable characteristics in a marriage partner, in what is referred to as **endogamy**. This is marriage between people who may share a number of critical characteristics. While these characteristics change from society to society, some common elements of endogamy include mates who are about the same age, the same social standing, the same race, and the same religion, among other things.

On the other hand, members of some societies marry according to the rules of **exogamy**. Under conditions of exogamy, an individual attempts to select a marriage partner with different characteristics within a range of categories. With endogamy, or the marriage of like by likes, traditional patterns are upheld for future generations. However, under the system of exogamy, there is cultural melding as different groups meet, marry, and produce offspring with distinct cultural heritages. Envision, if you will, a fully exogamous world, where no significant distinctions are drawn between people anywhere. Is such a world possible?

Virtually all industrial countries today prescribe **monogamy**, which limits marriage to only two partners. However, while monogamy is the rule throughout the Americas and Europe, in many developing countries marriages may be based on **polygamy**, or the unity of three or even more individuals. Polygamy, which is permitted or condoned in many societies in the developing world, comes in two types: the first is **polygyny**, a type of marriage that unites one male with two or more females as his wives. Some Islamic societies in southern Asia and Africa, for example, allow men to have up to four wives. In fact, while polygamy is technically illegal in the United States, communities who still practice it can be found in the western part of the country. The second form of polygamy is called **polyandry**, in which one female is joined with two or more males. Polyandry is rarer, but nevertheless still occurs, particularly in developing countries.

The many different types of kinship structures forming a family tend to maximize the possibility for individual and group survival and establish the requisites for optimizing quality of life. For this reason, the family structure has persisted across time and geography. Families are vital to reproduction and sustenance. That is, all species are driven to reproduce themselves. This, of course, requires mating behaviors, which are facilitated through the coupling of individuals. Furthermore, in addition to mating, family structure norms have also emerged out of the necessity for biological protection. Newborns cannot feed, protect, shelter, or clothe themselves. While different societies have different kinship norms regarding how the infant is protected, the biological father and biological mother have historically been designated as the primary caretaker of infants.

One interesting aspect of this process can be understood from a sociobiological perspective. Consider the fact that a woman only produces from 350 to 400 sex cells, or ova, throughout the course of her entire life. Men, on the other hand, can produce more than one billion sex cells or spermatozoa in a single day. This difference is pertinent to what is termed the law of **anisogamy**. According to the law of anisogamy, the behaviors of the two sexes are a reflection of their very different reproductive strategies. This can be illustrated in a study by Buss (1989), which focused on the differences in mate preferences between the sexes. This study, encompassing 37 samples amounting to over 10,000 individuals in 33 countries across 6 continents, found that the two sexes agreed on dependability as one of the basic requirements of a good mate. However, some of Buss's other findings reflected different reproductive strategies that are indicative of anisogamy. Females were a great deal more likely than males to value mates who were ambitious and industrious, representing a good financial prospect. On the other hand, males tended to value the characteristics in mates who were physically attractive, younger than themselves, and at the peak of their reproductive value, more so than females.

Family Functions and Structure

A family unit also serves to fulfill the important function of productivity and the **division of labor**. While the economic roles of both males and females were largely dictated by biological necessity in hunting and gathering societies, family arrangements in the early Middle Ages and later were also conditioned by economic needs. In the early Middle Ages, marriages were arranged and children began work well before they were ten years old. Furthermore, households very rarely had distinct rooms, with sleeping arrangements and family business taking place in the main room.

The family became somewhat more private in the later Middle Ages as the husband's dominance over the family, and family life in general, grew. A decline in arranged marriages was visible, leading to an increase in the concept of **romantic love**. Nevertheless, historians have asserted that parents in the Middle Ages, as a whole, had very little awareness of the distinctiveness of children. Children were viewed as tiny adults, even being portrayed as such in their portraits, and had no special status. Because childhood was not viewed as a distinct developmental stage, parents did not adopt the same sort of strategies for rearing children as they do today.

Changes in the family were evident in early colonial America. As early European immigrants arrived in America, they brought with them the norms of the European lower classes. These norms included a preference for a marriage that was not arranged but rather chosen by the individuals to be married. Families were once again the basic unit of production and the nuclear family was well established. With the genesis of the Industrial Revolution in the early nineteenth century, American families still remained as a unit of production, but they were no longer the primary unit. Instead of working or producing goods in the home, families, often including their children, were increasingly likely to work in the factories that began to spring up alongside industrialization.

As people became more and more removed from the home for a greater part of the day to fill the growing need of factory-based economic activities, households correspondingly became smaller and a great deal more private. Affection also became a characteristic of the relationship between husbands and wives. Furthermore, separate spheres of activities developed between husbands and wives—women became guardians and family nurturers, whereas men more typically became primary wage earners. With the onset of the early 1900s, childhood was now viewed as a distinct stage of life, a stage that was worth recognizing and protecting. It is noteworthy that in the early 1900s only 1 in 10 marriages in America ended as a result of a divorce.

After the Great Depression, as the United States was entering World War II, a significant event which would affect the family structure occurred. As men were shipped off into battle, women entered the labor force in record numbers in order to fill the necessity for workers. Many of these women remained on the job even after the war ended. To be sure, the 1950s represented what is often thought of as the golden age of the American family, as couples began to get married at the youngest age on average in the entire twentieth century. The baby boom, which began right after WWII, peaked in the 1950s. Traditional gender roles were the hallmark of the family of the 1950s, with fathers viewed as breadwinners and mothers viewed as responsible for nurturing and child care. While reliable information is somewhat limited, it appears that most women and many men at that time had their first sexual intercourse experience with their spouses, and then, only after their marriage had begun. In that period only 5 percent or less of babies were born out of wedlock. By the end of the decade, and then again at the end of the 1960s, these circumstances shifted dramatically, with the trends established in that time carrying over to today. For example, consider that in 1970, 40 percent of all households were comprised of a husband, wife, and children under eighteen, while today this configuration exists in only about 20 percent of all American households. Additionally, in 2012, approximately 21 million children—or about 28 percent of children in the United States—lived with only one parent. Of those, the majority lived with their mother (U.S. Bureau of the Census 2012).

Also consider the fact that in 2012, about 20 percent of adults age twenty-five and over had never been married, compared to only 10 percent in 1960. Further illustrating this shift is a comparison of census data on divorces, age at marriage, and premarital births. Between 1960 and 2012, the median age at first marriage increased from 22.8 to 28.2 for males, and from 20.3 to 26.1 for females. The number of unmarried U.S residents over the age of eighteen has increased significantly as well, reaching 44 percent in 2013. The birth rate for unmarried women in 2007 was 80 percent higher than it was in 1980 and increased 20 percent between 2002 and 2007.

Marriage and Family in the Modern Era

For some, the future of marriage and family in the United States is a matter of deep concern. While some sociologists see these changes as normal when viewed in relation to other societal trends, some view them as indicative of the very demise of the Western family. To be sure, there is less stability in the modern marriage than has been true for prior generations. Yet, marriage remains as one of the most important events in an adult's life, as is the having of children.

It is a legal commitment, in fact a contract ratified by the state, which can only be dissolved with the permission of the state.

What are some significant trends in modern marriages? First of all, in the past, divorce carried much more of what social interactionists refer to as a "stigma" (Goffman 1963), whereas today it does not. Divorce simply does not attach the type of negative labels to individuals that it used to. In fact, nearly half of all marriages today involve at least one partner who was previously married. In other words, today divorce does not create nearly as many "identity" problems as it did earlier in U.S. history. Today, many people may find it surprising that divorce could become a deeply negative **master status**, or primary identity, for the individual, only a few decades ago.

Another significant shift in American marriage patterns, interracial marriages, have nearly tripled over the last thirty years. Even taking this increase into consideration, however, fewer than 2 percent of all marriages involve a husband and wife of different races. Racial endogamy remains a very strong feature, and is a noteworthy indication in its own right about the nature of race relations in contemporary America. Imagine, if you will, a society based on racial exogamy. In this society marriages would bring together the different races, resulting ultimately in the elimination of the specific racial distinctions made today. Is this possible in America?

What other factors do people consider important when making the decision to marry? Almost 50 percent of Americans who are aged 18-24 believe that having enough money is critical in the marital decision. So too, is having a job. In fact it is even more important for women that their partner has an established employment status. Thus, even among 18-24 year olds there is a tendency to rate the man's job as important. Women are also a great deal more likely to marry an older man than vice versa. Likewise, they are far less willing to marry someone who is five years younger than they are. Finally, and perhaps not surprisingly, people in general, women especially, are quite willing to marry someone who makes more money than they do (Chadwick & Heaton 1992).

Why is it that young Americans place such a high value on earning good money and maintaining steady employment in their considerations of a worthy marriage partner? Do you think it frivolous or humorous that, in principle, characteristics other than money and stability could be the central axes for social exchanges in marriage? What about love, trust, affection, maturity, companionship, common values, or the mutual desire for children? Perhaps these notions are perceived as romantic and old-fashioned relics. If this is the case, then what sort of cultural statement can be made about American society? Do social norms now require a cost-benefit analysis on a prospective partner, just as we would do if we were purchasing an automobile? Perhaps we follow the expectations of social exchange theorists in our rational, trade-based analysis of marriage. Most surely, the search for dependable, employed, and well-paid marriage partners reinforces endogamy with respect to those with money and, quite possibly, singlehood for many who are poor.

Marital expectations, of course, differ somewhat by social class. Rurly and Rubin (1976) found a generation ago that lower-class wives felt a good husband would refrain from being violent, would not drink too much, and would hold a steady job. By contrast, her middle-class respondents never mentioned these items—they just assumed a husband would provide a safe and secure home. Their ideal husband, instead, would be a man they could communicate with easily and with whom they could share their feelings and experiences. Note again the differences between these most important characteristics and the ones chosen today.

Issues of race, as well as class, make a difference in both decisions and opportunities to marry. Twenty-five percent of African-American women over the age of thirty-five have never married, whereas that figure for white women is only about 8 percent by comparison. Certainly, this indicates that African-American women are more likely to be single heads of households. In fact, in the mid-1990s, women served as the heads of household in nearly 50 percent of all African-American families compared to 14 percent of white families, 25 percent of Hispanic families, and 13 percent of Asian or Pacific-Islander families.

The implications of this are profound. While the data may be viewed as somewhat suspect, census figures suggest that nearly 70 percent of African-American children are born to single women, and about half of all African-American boys and girls grow up in poverty. It was these troubling figures indicating the growing number of single mothers and absent fathers that led U.S. Senator Patrick Moynihan to argue that the African-American family was in crisis. He argued then that these circumstances tended to compromise the level of supervision and care provided for children. In his view, a cycle of poverty that had been established in the African-American community would perpetuate disadvantages across generations. Certainly, it is important to understand the initial role of poverty in generating this scenario, as initial poverty may be a crucial cause of illegitimacy in the first place. The most vital intervention strategy may be coping with economic hardship, an agenda prescribed by social conflict interpretations.

While social conflict theorists provide a relatively cogent interpretation of this dynamic, social functions interpretations would adopt a different view. Could it be possible that female-headed households are a highly reasonable evolutionary adaptation to circumstances, and thus, in a sense, very functional in modern America? Could it be a natural working out of relationships that follows the law of anisogamy? If so, we might expect this pattern to evolve comparably to animals. In fact, it does parallel the sorts of patterns found among wild elephants and lions—where male behavior is dangerous to offspring, and males are not nearly as crucial to family life as females.

It is true for all racial groupings in the United States that rates of illegitimacy are high or increasing. This parallels patterns of **cohabitation**, another trend on the rise in America. Cohabitation describes a situation in which unmarried couples live together in a sexual relationship, which is an increasingly widespread dynamic in the United States as well as in Western Europe. Statistics show that about 60 percent of cohabitating couples end up marrying, but a large proportion of the rest simply just break up. These patterns indicate that **serial monogamy** is an apt description by which to characterize this and (given the divorce rate) later marriage in America.

Considering the fact that only 10 percent of cohabitating couples remain that way for more than five years, cohabiting can be viewed as an experimental period with one future track leading to marriage and other tracks leading to singlehood or other cohabiting experiences. Cohabitation, then, appears to be an increasingly important alternative to extended "dating" or a marriage where there is concern or doubt about the prospective partner's ability to provide desired resources in a long-term social exchange relationship. This is not to say, however, that marriage and the American family are an outmoded institution that serves no social function. Quite the contrary is true.

Social Functions and Social Conflicts

One of the most important social functions of the family and of marriage is the regulation of sexual activities. One of the most important themes comes in the form of **incest taboo**, a near cultural universal, forbidding marriage or sexual relationships between certain kinds of kin. Different cultures, however, sanction different configurations of marriage and sexual relations that are permissible. In some societies, for instance, it is forbidden to marry a relative of one's mother. Others, such as our own society, apply the incest taboo to both sides of the family, although we limit the taboo to very close relatives such as parents, grandparents, brothers, sisters, uncles, and aunts. Families, additionally, serve the function of monitoring younger children to ensure that they do not prematurely engage in sexual behaviors. With teenage illegitimacy rates in America as high as they are, we might question the functionality of the family in regard to this particular role. To be sure, the age at which young children *can* physically conceive and bear children is a great deal earlier than the age that they typically do so.

While parents and adults, in general, may serve these regulatory functions, it is also the case that social conflicts and abuses may emerge from such relationships. **Sexual abuse** is defined as the carrying out of sexual acts by adults with children below the age of consent, which is usually sixteen years old. Incest, again, refers to sexual relationships between close kin. Because incest and sexual abuse are universally forbidden and thus generally secretive, it is not possible to obtain exact or close to reliable figures on the occurrence of these types of behavior.

Another important social function of the family is the provision of **emotional support**. Families serve as primary groups for their members, meaning that they are close-knit groups based on emotional ties. They give people a sense of emotional security and a sense of belonging, in what can be a harsh world. It is said that when Mayor Richard Daley, Sr. of Chicago was asked why he hired family members for the city payroll, he replied, "If you can't trust your family, who can you trust?" In this light, it is understandable why nearly half of all people in the United States feel that their mother and father were very close to one another in their marriage. Of course, this figure is lower than in some other countries, such as South Africa, where the percentage is nearly 70. However, it is significantly higher than it is in other nations. In Germany and Japan, for example, only 30 percent of the population reports feeling that their father and mother were very close to each other. It is also worth mentioning that well over half of Americans report feeling satisfied with their current home life. In Mexico, the figure is just a little higher than 1 in 2, while in Japan only 1 in 10 individuals are very satisfied with their home life.

This expected function of emotional support to be provided by families has a dark side as well, which can be seen in the prevalence of **domestic violence** and related social conflicts that are so apparent in modern American life. It is commonplace to observe that individuals are more likely to be physically assaulted, sexually victimized, beaten, slapped, or spanked inside their own homes than in any other sphere in their life. The National Center on Child Abuse and Neglect (1981) has conducted surveys to measure the incidence of child maltreatment in the United States, finding that over one million children are maltreated in the United States every year. We do not refer here to the fact that only about 10 percent of all parents report they *never* spank their children, but rather to the fact that nearly well over 500,000 children are abused, physically, sexually, or emotionally, and 500,000 children are neglected. Each year well over a thousand children are injured to the point of death and well over 150,000 suffer serious injury. Nearly one million suffer some sort of more moderate injury.

To what degree are parents aware of the abuse of their children? Chadwick and Heaton's (1992) study on the extent of awareness indicates that in regards to physical abuse, only about 2 percent of fathers in the United States feel that their child has been abused and only 6 percent of mothers. With respect to emotional abuse, 13 percent of fathers and only 15 percent of mothers feel that any of their children have been abused. Respectively, 4 percent of mothers and 3 percent of fathers report that sexual abuse has occurred to at least one of their children. Interestingly, however, when parents report memories of their own childhood, they tend to recall a great deal more physical, emotional, and sexual abuse. Thirteen percent of both mothers and fathers believe that they were physically abused as children. Nearly 1 in 3 mothers and 1 in 4 fathers feel that they were emotionally abused. Sixteen percent of mothers and 17 percent of fathers feel that they were sexually abused. What we see here, in other words, is that the percentage of parents who believe that they were abused as children is much greater than the percentage that feels their own children are abused. Are parents intentionally covering up the extent of such abuse, do they use different criteria to refer to their receipt of abuse as a child, or have all forms of abuse become less prevalent with widespread public campaigns against them? There are no adequate data to answer these questions definitely.

When Americans think of domestic violence, they often think of child abuse or marital violence. However, the most common form of family violence, hands down, is physical fighting between siblings. The first National Family Violence Survey (see Strauss & Gelles 1990: 3-16) found that 42 percent of children had punched, kicked, or bitten a brother or sister; that 40 percent had hit their brother or sister with an object; and that 16 percent of all children had "beat up" a sibling. In the United States, guns or knives are used in 100,000 incidents each year in fights between siblings.

Certainly the violence of parents to their children is a matter of great public attention. By contrast, far less frequently mentioned in public discussions is violence *from* children to their parents. Yet, the First National Family Violence Survey shows that every year, between three-fourths of a million and one million parents have violent acts committed against them by children in their teens, most of which is perpetrated by a teenage male and directed towards the mother.

The mass media frequently portrays men as the violent member in incidents of domestic violence. To be sure, men account for a disproportionately high number of physical assaults in American criminal statistics. But, when we observe the home, a slightly different pattern emerges. National survey data presented by Strauss and Gelles (1991) show that women are frequently as or more violent than men. For instance, mothers are slightly more likely than fathers to abuse their children. One explanation for this, of course, is that mothers simply spend more time with their children than fathers do, and they, therefore, have more *opportunity* to be violent and abusive.

If we use the amount of damage done and who initiates family violence as measures, women seem to be the clear and disproportionate victim of family violence. However, in other contexts, there is a close parallel between violence perpetrated by women and violence perpetrated by men. Gelles and Strauss demonstrate that husbands and wives are nearly equally likely to push, grab or shove their spouse; to throw something at their spouse; to slap their spouse; to try to hit the spouse with another object; to kick, bite or hit their spouse with a fist; to beat their spouse up, or to choke their spouse. In other words, Strauss and Gelles show that incidences of wife and husband beating are about equal. As in all such statistics, which use individual reports on sensitive items, caution must be exercised to make sure the Strauss and Gelles data are not over interpreted. Yet, these data should at least be viewed as enlightening, if alarming, for many who view domestic violence solely as a matter of violence against women. As in social interactions, generally, there is reciprocity in emotional and physical actions that suggest a sociological analysis of the family grouping as a totality. The most fruitful sociological analysis of the family examines the two-way social exchanges and interactions that characterize family life.

Division of Labor and Social Exchanges

Social functions interpretations see the **division of labor** among family members as a necessity for the optimal functioning of the family. In this context, division of labor refers not only to such obvious and traditional roles as doing household chores and making a living, but also to the family members' well being as well as decision-making. Based on these latter axes of interest, observed differences between the family roles of husbands and wives have led some researchers to identify the concepts of **instrumental** and **expressive roles**. Instrumental leaders in any organization or group are **task oriented**, whereas expressive leaders are often responsible for group agreement and solidarity. Based on this distinction, it seems almost natural that in the United States as well as other industrialized countries, childcare, which requires affection and interpersonal social interactions, is assumed more by the wife than the husband. So, too, does the husband's traditional role in providing the outside resources that are necessary in family life seem natural to many—this is part of the so-called **"provider role."**

Yet, these distinctions have become a great deal more blurred in modern America, as over half of all married women are now employed in the workforce. At one time, domestic relationships could be more accurately stereotyped as social exchanges of household services for money earned in the market place. However, it is increasingly true, that the resources exchanged by husband and wife are essentially the same. They are based on money as well as household work. Sometimes, when the wife is employed or earns a large income, or both, the husband takes on a greater share of household work responsibilities. Nonetheless, many have concluded that the husband's contribution to household work is not as large as the wife's is, even if they provide roughly the same income.

The different social perceptions of male and female parents are quite interesting, as Chadwick and Heaton (1992) reveal. When asked, "How are the childcare tasks divided in your family," only 29 percent of the mothers answered that both parents were equally responsible while 61 percent of them felt that the wife was responsible for the majority of tasks. In contrast, when fathers were asked, only 44 percent felt that both parents were equally responsible, while 51 percent felt that the wife was most responsible for childcare tasks. It is certainly evident that differences of opinion regarding tasks and responsibilities exist between mothers and fathers. We see similar responses in national surveys when people are asked, "Which parent in your house is the disciplinarian?" Forty-two percent of the mothers felt that they were the primary disciplinarians, and 49 percent felt that it was both parents. Yet, for the fathers, only 18 percent felt that it was the mother, 53 percent felt it was both parents, and 28 percent felt it was primarily the father! Here again, we see major perceptual differences between genders.

Jessie Bernard (1972) maintains that perceptions, as well as expectations for marriage differ between wives and husbands. For instance, a number of studies indicate that men appear to be less apt in terms of relating to emotional issues as well as verbal communication. Since husbands and wives have different responses to perceptions of marital problems, divorce, perceived marital quality, and equity in their relationship, it is unsurprising that family conflicts emerge in interactions about exchanges and expectations.

As a counterbalance to this observation, however, it is important to recognize that overall, marital satisfaction is high in America and has not varied much over the years. Almost two-thirds of men and women surveyed reported that they are "very happy" with their marriage, with an additional 30-35 percent indicating that they are "pretty happy." Meanwhile, those who reported feeling that their marriages were "not too happy" accounted for less than 5 percent.

Furthermore, it is also quite likely that the level of communication between husbands and wives has increased over the last half century. Married couples in America are interacting with each other more frequently, and are engaging in more activities with one another than they did in the past. This is true despite the fact that married couples still report that they disagree about how much time they should spend together, as well as things such as children, family economics, and sex.

Sadly, however, Martin and Bumpass (1989) have projected that about two-thirds of all first marriages in the United States will ultimately end in divorce. Marriages that do end in divorce tend to last about seven years on average, while the average age at divorce is usually in the mid-thirties. Interestingly, individuals whose parents were divorced during their childhood are more likely to divorce themselves. Further, divorced or separated couples generally agree that it was the women who wanted the marriage to end. Social exchange theorists would argue that this is because resources traded in marriage hold less value for women, today, and alternatives to marriage often appear to be more rational. Though this may be true, over 80 percent of the American population feels that marriage is a life-long relationship and it should not be ended except under extreme circumstances.

Functions and Conflicts: Parents and Children

Now that we know what husbands and wives disagree about, what are some of the issues that cause disputes between children and their parents in modern America? The number one response for both mothers and fathers is that of division of labor. This issue sparks social conflicts between parents and their children more than any other. Many parents view their children as an unwilling part of the household division of labor; as a functional unit with respect to the home's overall workload. It seems as though children often do not share this perspective of the division of labor, or if they do share it, such work is seen as onerous and to be avoided at all costs. This contrast between the nature of functionality for American children between two centuries ago and today is stark in the extreme.

There are other important issues that result in family conflicts as well, such as matters relating to schooling and money, the way children dress, and getting along with the family. Certainly it is not only husbands and wives with conflicting perceptions over roles and exchanges in the family, but their children as well.

On the topic of relationships between parents and children, it is relevant to discuss the feelings of parents towards their aging parents. A national sample of parents was asked to rate their agreement with the statement that "Aging parents should live with you when the parents can no longer live by themselves." Results showed that African-American and Hispanic families were a great deal more likely to agree with this sentiment, with nearly 2 out of 3 African-American and Hispanic families responding in this fashion. Meanwhile, only 4 in 10 whites shared this agreement. Still, only a fractional percentage of all groups reported that they strongly disagreed with the statement. What we are seeing here is that parents from the "baby-boom" generation must increasingly cope with responsibilities for both their children and their parents, precisely when issues of their own parental division of labor are in most crisis. This phenomenon has led some to refer to these aging baby boomers in such a situation as the "sandwiched generation." This scenario also presents a partial contrast to neolocality trends in the United States, which for many years have pulled children away from their family of origin.

The World System and Family Structure

Up to this point, we have examined several approaches to the American family, and the data accompanied by them. It is important to examine family structure, exchanges, conflicts, and functions in other social settings as well. Using the perspective of **modernization** that we have discussed in previous chapters, for example, Goode (1963) argues that the institution of the family is especially critical to national advancement the world over. In his modernization approach, he argues that in the global march towards urbanization and industrialization, traditional family structures are shifting towards the **conjugal or nuclear family system** that characterizes families in the United States. The independence of nuclear families from traditional extended kinship ties simultaneously parallels the valuation of egalitarianism and the triumph of the individual over lineage. Goode thus views the conjugal family system as tied with the ideologies of economic and technological production, which when taken together, stimulate societal development.

Of course, the family further serves to play a crucial role in the process of socialization. It is the social interactions of the family that serve as a socialization vehicle, inculcating values favorable to **universalism** and **achievement orientation**, in lieu of **particularism** and **ascription**. Universalism and achievement orientation refer, respectively, to evaluation of others on an equal footing and with merit as the primary concern, quite apart from personal relationships and characteristics (i.e., particularism and ascription; Parsons 1951). Further, the well-socialized citizen exhibits characteristics such as political participation, religious tolerance, command of information, consumption orientation, and ambition. Social functionalists view these characteristics as a prerequisite for societal modernization, while to a large degree acting as a function of modern family structure and family socialization.

Macrosocial conflict theorists emphasize a slightly different perspective. They argue that in poorer, peripheral countries outside the core of the world system, families are more likely to be characterized by lower marriage rates, larger household size, higher illegitimacy rates, and children's early involvement in work rather than educational activities. These forms suit domestic production needs in the periphery, and the adoption of Western institutions such as the "conjugal family" may result in few, if any, tangible economic benefits for periphery countries. As an illustration, consider that small nuclear family units, such as those in the United States, are poorly suited to peripheral modes of production in agricultural spheres. In many parts of the world, agriculture is requisite for daily subsistence, and is essential for international trade for many peripheral societies.

The mobility of labor across geographic boundaries in peripheral societies is another mechanism for subsistence and production, even though it contributes to lower marriage rates and higher rates of illegitimacy as fathers work in distant locales. This may be a far-from-preferred dynamic in Western countries, but a near-necessity in the poorer areas of the world system, such as Africa. What's also important to keep in mind is that in peripheral areas outside the core of the world system, the benefits of receiving an education beyond a basic level are often relatively marginal in comparison to the benefits of workforce participation by children. In other words, as harsh as this dynamic may seem from a Western perspective, the early involvement of children in domestic and industrial labor contributes to national economic growth and family well being in heavily agricultural or industrializing peripheral nations.

World-system adherents see semiperipheral nations, which hold an intermediate structural position in the global system, as a rapidly changing admixture of the core and the periphery. As we discussed in previous chapters, the semiperiphery's intermediate position in the world system is an indication of its ability to maintain economic domination over the periphery through the exchange of relatively more finished goods for raw materials. This dynamic also results from its economic dependence upon the core, and the international exchanges that accompany it. As semiperipheral countries industrialize, they also undergo corresponding shifts in their traditional institutions—for example, semiperipheral countries have marriage rates similar to those of the core, but an average family size that resembles that of the periphery. Further, illegitimate birth rates are much higher than the core's, while the participation of children in education rather than the workforce fall right between the core and periphery.

Should the semiperiphery family follow the modernists' advice and move closer to the characteristics of the Western conjugal family? Would the adoption of Western nuclear family structures increase the potential for economic growth in the semiperiphery? In certain cases, the grafting of Western values on traditional ways may do more harm than good. Competing values may generate the very sort of internal conflicts that can compromise nations just as they are ready to rise in the world system. Furthermore, it could be argued that traditional values, such as those contained in Confucianism, have fostered the ethos of hard work, loyalty, frugality and dedication that likely lead to favorable economic results for many nations.

The Western family model praised by Goode (1963), has worked well for the core countries even if the wholesale transfer of Western practices (nuclear family, neolocality, monogamy, endogamy) may not be advisable for much of the world system. However, many of the *trends* relating to the family that we see in nations such as the United States, including divorce and illegitimacy, appear to stand in contrast to those that will enhance national well being. Here we can make good use of the sociological imagination to project the future of America and the world if such trends continue.

Same-Sex Marriage and Families

According to the most recent surveys, the majority of Americans now consider a gay couple with children to be a family. As views regarding homosexuality have evolved in recent years and a number of states have legalized same-sex marriage, we have seen an increase in families headed by same-sex couples.

As recently as the 1990s, fewer than one third of Americans supported same-sex marriage. This has changed dramatically in recent years. A Gallup poll conducted in 2013, for example, found that the slight majority of Americans (52 percent) say they would support a law that legalizes same-sex marriage, while 43 percent stated that they would vote against it. As a result of these evolving views, gay and lesbian couples are able to pursue things like marriage and raising a family, much more so than in the past.

Gathering data regarding the number of same-sex marriages that have been performed in the United States is somewhat difficult. This is due, in part, to that fact that marriage is regulated by the states and each state decides how it collects and publishes data on marriage. Some of the states wherein same-sex marriage is legal have yet to com-

Same-Sex Families

The definition of what constitutes a family is changing. An increasing number of Americans believe that a same-sex headed household constitutes a family.

pile data on how many there have been, and estimates vary.

Since Massachusetts became the first state to legalize gay marriage in 2004, it has been estimated that at least 71,000 gay marriages have been performed in the United States. In 2010, there were approximately 594,000 same-sex households in the United States, making up about 1 percent of all couple-headed households. About 20 percent of those reported having children (Pew Research Center 2013).

CHAPTER SUMMARY

- Although conceptualizations of what constitutes a family may structurally differ, the family itself is a cultural universal.
- Family types differ the world over, but may evolve in tandem with other social organization needs.
- Sociological foundations, such as anisogamy, influence the processes of partner seeking, marriage, and divorce.
- Family patterns in the United States have drastically shifted over the past decades, with key increases in women who work outside the home, later age of marriage, higher rates of illegitimacy, single parenthood, cohabitation, divorce, and changes in the family division of labor.
- A significant number of American families experience violence, and when they do, it can sometimes involve the entire family unit.

13 Education and Society

The study of educational systems is an important area of inquiry for sociologists. This is because so many people, particularly young people in their formative years, spend so much of their lives in school, but also because educational institutions are closely tied to many other social institutions, and particularly to the stratification system.

Much of the sociology of education is organized around functional and conflict theoretical perspectives. While we have covered those perspectives in previous chapters, we will now examine how the education system and related institutions can be viewed from these perspectives. In so doing, we seek to gain insight into the role education plays in the overall society.

Education serves several functions in a society. Two primary such functions are promoting societal integration and providing people in society with the necessary skills to be productive members of the economy. This first function can be thought of as a crucial aspect of secondary **socialization**. The second function, often referred to as **human capital** (Becker 1975), refers to acquiring the educational background needed to perform work efficiently.

Why does a society have schools? While there are at least as many answers to that question as there are societies, cultural and economic purposes generally make the top of the list. The very earliest schools tended to have a **charter** from the state, which explicitly spelled out the school's purpose. The idea of a charter was similar to today's "mission statement" of a school—but unlike many of the mission statements of today, the charter was taken very seriously.

The concept of a charter stems from a time in which organized assembly was forbidden unless an official proclamation (charter) was granted, stating the social purpose of the assembly (Meyer 1970, 1972, 1977). Initially, a school's charter was its legal justification for existence. Today, although the specific purpose of the school is rarely stated explicitly as it was in the first days of the charters, sociologists of education find it useful to view education in these terms. This is because many of the effects of the school can be attributed to the society's externally institutionalized definition of what the school is.

Researchers (e.g., Meyer 1972: 109) have found that if schools are similar in their charters, they are likely to exercise similar effects upon their students. The charter is important because schools are embedded in a network of institutional linkages, and changes in a school system are likely to be intimately connected with changes in a broader array of social institutions, such as the political system, the economy and the family.

Culture and Education

In examining some of the original charters, one finds that the purposes that schools are meant to serve, and entire educational systems for that matter, are concepts such as "character building" and "citizenship." Viewing these goals in functional terms, it can be said that the values being promoted include such things as students learning and internalizing a common system of norms, values, and beliefs, thereby allowing them to become integrated into society. Many functional theorists, including Talcott Parsons and John Meyer, have built their ideas about the sociology of education from these insights.

The education system serves as an institutional means of socializing citizens (Durkheim 1961; Parsons 1951; Meyer 1992, 1977; Meyer et al. 1979; Ramirez and Boli 1987). There is a two-way interaction between the individual and society that is mediated in the school system. As students are integrated into society through education, they learn and internalize social norms from an early age, thus strengthening the society in turn.

As we saw earlier, as societies modernize, there tends to be a gradual shift from traditional to rational-legal authority systems. Corresponding to that shift is a rise in a meritocratic system, and an accompanying decline in ascription. As this occurs, someone's family background becomes less important in terms of his eventual position in the stratification system. Instead, a person's position in the stratification system becomes associated with the level and quality of formal education they have received.

While conflict theorists stress the *ascriptive* aspects of the stratification system (and, by extension, tend to focus on how education systems even "reproduce" the stratification system by directing children toward an occupational status close to that of their parents), Meyer and other functional theorists tend to emphasize different aspects of the educational system. For functional theorists, the role of educational institutions is much more than simply "reproducing" the class system. Education, they emphasize, functions as a primary entry point into the process of stratification *independent of* family background. Educational institutions do this by conferring statuses, and training individuals to perform roles commensurate with those statuses for the rest of their lives.

Another function of education systems in modern society is to create and legitimate entirely new occupations. Let's take the profession of nursing as an illustration. Historically, the way to become a nurse was through on the job experience. Before 1970, very few nurses had a college degree. In 1960, for example, only about 7.7 percent of nurses in the United States aged 25 and over had completed four years of college (Hammack 1982). Yet today, most jobs in nursing require some type of higher education—at least two years, and increasingly four years in many instances. Through this process we have witnessed a "professionalization" of nursing, during which nurses have gained a higher professional status in the sphere of health care. Naturally, this has resulted in an increasing emphasis on standardized curriculum and training in nursing schools. Viewing nurses as a status group in Weberian terms, the status of nurses has increased over time, and has done so roughly in parallel with its association with formal schooling, a standardized curriculum and set of examinations (Hammack 1982). Thus, education itself can confer status, either alone, or in combination with the professionalization of some occupation.

Francisco Ramirez and John Boli (1987) propose the idea that expansion of mass schooling is best understood as a social movement stemming from concerns with nation-building and the ideology associated with it. They see an increase in educational enrollments as a response to certain key "legitimating myths" which come to be diffused throughout the society (viz.):

- the individual is the primary "unit of action";
- the nation is an aggregate of individuals;

- childhood socialization is the foundation of adult character;
- there is increasing individual and national progress toward a better future;
- the state is the guardian of the nation and the leader in the march of progress.

These concepts lead to a belief that schooling is an institutional prerequisite for nation building. Schools do more than legitimate the society of which they are part, however. Expansion in the educational system can be viewed as stemming from an evolution in value systems in which education is held as increasingly important.

As these institutionalized values come to be generally accepted throughout a society, education becomes increasingly viewed as advantageous, providing an avenue of participation in both individual and national improvement. Accordingly, increases in communication, transportation and urbanization lead to rises in education because of their roles in spreading attitudes about the value of education (Burns 1991).

Further, enrollment in prior cohorts will increase the likelihood of enrollment in the current cohort (c.f. Archer 1982); schooling itself becomes a self-reinforcing process through its role of not merely educating, but of simultaneously promulgating a belief in the value of said education as well.

As we saw earlier, because schools are enmeshed within a broader network of institutional linkages, the importance of the charter is that the expansion or contraction of a school system is likely to be intimately connected with changes in a wider array of social values and beliefs. Correspondingly, there tends also to be a growing emphasis on education in a society as these social values and beliefs spread. For example, Meyer et al. (1979) found evidence that the primary motivator for school expansion in the United States was a commonly held "ideology of nation-building" incorporating elements of evangelical Protestantism, entrepreneurship and individualism.

Education Systems and the Economy

Why are you in school? While you are likely here for several cultural and personal reasons, an important reason may also well be to prepare yourself for a career. In fact, one of the key functions of the education system is to prepare people for their upcoming roles in the society, a large part of which specifically involves preparing individuals for their position within the labor market.

At least since the industrial revolution, we have seen an increasing link between the education system and the economy. Since the beginning of the twentieth century in particular, a person's income, as well as occupational status, have increasingly corresponded with the level and quality of formal education one receives.

Over time, the nature of work, as well as its associated labor market, changes. As the nature of work changes, so too does the nature of education, and both the nature of work and of education have changed dramatically since the industrial revolution. With regards to the economy, there has been a massive shift in what social scientists have termed the **labor market**, or the types of jobs that are available for people to hold. Prior to the Industrial Revolution, the vast majority of working adults (over 95 percent) worked in agriculture either directly (as farmers) or indirectly (as blacksmiths, for example). Today however, in most developed societies, such as the United States, fewer than 5 percent of adults are employed in the agricultural sector—the preponderance of people are now employed in marketing, information systems, management, industry, and other service jobs in sectors of the economy that barely even existed in past centuries.

Since the Industrial Revolution, and since World War II in particular, the types of occupations in which people can be expected to participate have changed dramatically. As agricultural employment has declined, the industrial and service sector employment has correspondingly risen, resulting in great changes to the nature of human capital. Whereas stamina and physical strength were major characteristics of human capital in agrarian economies requiring long bouts of strenuous physical labor, the majority of today's jobs require more specific skills, the attainment of which requires some formal education.

Starting shortly after the industrial revolution, countries started to see an increase in education levels, and those levels have continued to increase even to today. The most dramatic increases have occurred since World War II. Within industrialized countries in particular, more people today are receiving education at all levels than in the past.

During this time, education in itself has become more differentiated, meaning that many more specialized options can now be found within the education system. Further, as the number of levels of hierarchy have increased in the labor market, so too has there been an increase of people pursuing advanced degrees.

As we saw in the chapter on stratification, there has been a general decline in the level of ascription across generations in modern societies, meaning that people do not simply inherit their parents' occupations as much as they did in the past. As a result, the labor market has increasingly rewarded skills acquired outside of the family context, typically through the education system.

Economic Functions and Expansion in Education Systems

Why has educational enrollment increased so steadily since the Industrial Revolution? As we discussed, large macro-level technological changes and the changing labor market have been prime motivators for the expansion in educational enrollments over that time. Let's now turn our focus towards more specific aspects of this larger trend.

Industrialization Theory. Recall that in our consideration of stratification and mobility earlier in the book, we discussed the Bendix and Lipset hypothesis, which posits that a country's level of industrialization is a very good predictor of overall social mobility. Much of this mobility is mediated by the education system. Through what specific social dynamics does this occur?

Industrialization theory emphasizes the idea that capital becomes increasingly concentrated as capitalism matures (Averitt 1968), resulting in a differentiation of the labor force (Blau & Meyer 1987; Blau & Schoenherr 1971), a separation of manual and mental labor (Braverman

1974), and a concomitant rise in the number of relatively well-educated managers and professionals (Blau & Schoenherr 1971; Ehrenreich & Ehrenreich 1979; Poulantzas 1975, 1977).

As a country develops technologically, there is an increasing need for workers with sophisticated skills, such as higher mathematics and engineering. This is a key reason why the expansion of a country's education systems parallels its level of technological development (Rubinson & Ralph 1984). The growing education system in turn feeds the technological expansion even more, as people bring their academic skills to bear on production.

Industrialization Theory

According to industrialization theory, the structure of a nation's education system reflects its need for workers with more sophisticated skills as it develops technologically.

As organizations expand, the need for service sector employees, such as managerial and clerical workers, likewise expands. The labor force differentiation correspondent to this expansion tends to increase opportunities to enter positions carrying higher status, even if these positions do not provide higher wages. Such increases are likely to raise the demand for education.

This effect could also be expected to vary by gender. As an increase in capital concentration leads to a differentiation of labor and a rise in the relative number of white-collar positions, a new set of skills becomes the arbiter of mobility (Tilly & Scott 1987; also see Pareto 1935). These skills are independent of physical prowess and are, in many cases, new and unknown, and thus do not yet have an exclusive cultural mystique with which they are associated. For these reasons, such a change could be expected to provide women with new career opportunities, for which a higher education would help prepare them. Since World War II, as we've discussed, an important factor attracting women into the labor force has been the changing nature of the labor market, in which a large number of service sector occupations has been created.

Research examining secondary and post-secondary educational expansion in the United States over most of the twentieth century indicates that educational expansion can be predicted by changes in the occupational structure. Research by Pamela Walters (1984), for example, demonstrates that a model in which students are preparing for future occupations can explain the ongoing expansion of education. Walters finds a strong parallel between professional and technical employment on the one hand, and school expansion on the other. The most probable explanation for this parallel relationship is the upgrading of certification requirements and an intensifying competition for credentials required for the most attractive jobs.

Human Capital Theory. The idea of human capital theory, which we introduced briefly earlier, is that employers notice skilled employees performing more efficiently, rewarding skills with material incentives such as wages (Becker 1975; Mincer 1962, 1979), which entices individuals to acquire skills through education. Underpinning human capital theory is the assumption that there exists a free market, which is subject to the laws of supply and demand. As merit-based rational-legal systems have come to supplant the more traditional ascription based systems, there has been a corresponding rise in the emphasis on individual human capital and thus, by default, a rise in educational enrollments.

On the macro level, societies with large populations of more highly educated people tend to exhibit both higher standards of living and higher levels of productivity per capita than those with lower overall levels of education. Human capital theorists argue that this is because the human capital of the workers makes them more productive and efficient. Thus, the society as a whole tends to be more productive.

However, the correlation between educational expansion and economic growth is far from perfect. In some societies, these correspond to a great extent, while in others they do not. Why might this be the case? Research by Maurice Garnier and Jerald Hage (1990) indicates the answer may lie in the relationship *between* the education system and the labor market, a phenomenon known as **institutional coupling**. In an environment of **tight institutional coupling**, students typically find jobs in the field they studied in school, and for which they are well qualified (but not over- or under-qualified). In contrast, a situation in which students do not work in the field in which they were trained, or where they do work in that field but in situations where they are under- or over-qualified, is referred to as **loose institutional coupling**. In the United States, for example, the majority of recent college graduates do not work in the field of their major, making it an example of a society with loose institutional coupling between the educational and economic systems.

Jerald Hage
Jerald Hage studies social complexity and innovation, formal organizations and institutions. Much of his work has focused on education systems in a comparative and historical context.

In countries like Germany where there is tight coupling between the education system and the labor market, there tends to be a very high correlation between educational expansion and subsequent economic growth (Garnier & Hage 1990). Conversely, in situations where the coupling is loose, no strong correlation between these two variables can be discerned.

Conflict Theories and Education

Credential Inflation Theory. Like human capital theory, credential inflation theory connects education with material incentives—but for very different reasons. Credential theory is most closely associated with Randall Collins (1971, 1979; also see Berg 1970), who argues that educational requirements serve as a function of the interest employers have in locating well-socialized and respectable employees. In this system, concern for technical skills is of lesser importance. From the perspective of credential inflation theory, the more elite the status of the employing organization, and the greater the need for normative control over its employees, the higher its educational requirements.

In other words, a diploma becomes a quick screening device for employers. Students respond by staying in school longer and attaining more degrees. In turn, requirements for a given occupation become stricter over time, due to the pool of increasingly well-educated people from whom employers are able to choose. Over time, this system takes on a life of its own, and drives educational expansion even further, as more and more education becomes necessary simply to remain competitive in the market.

Collins holds that with the advent of mass secondary and higher education systems in the United States, the ideal of possessing technical skills became part of the predominant culture upon which status judgments were based. The increasingly specialized educational requirements of jobs, coupled with the concomitant higher level of education among people holding those jobs, tends to increase the demand for education. This interaction between formal job requirements and the advent of informal status spawned by the mystique of education sets the stage for status struggles which further fuel the demand for education and result in a spiral of increasing educational requirements and attainment. The result of this interplay is a preoccupation with the attainment of credentials rather than the informal, on-the-job skill acquisition of the past.

The field of law is a prime example. Believe it or not, a few generations ago it was not necessary to attend law school to become a lawyer. People typically prepared to be lawyers by serving as a clerk to someone practicing law for a time, and then taking the bar exam. An example of a lawyer who trained in this model is Abraham Lincoln, who, like most lawyers of his generation, never went to law school.

When the law school requirement was instituted as a prerequisite to being admitted to the bar, a college degree was not a prerequisite for law school. It was not until the twentieth century that the current requisites of four years of college, followed by three years of law school, become virtually the only way to enter the legal field in the United States. Today, by comparison, four more years of formal education are required than was the case two or three generations ago, and seven more years are required than was the case a century-and-a-half ago.

Thus, while both human capital theory and credentialing theory connect education and labor market position, the two theories differ on the precise nature of that connection. Basically, while human capital theory focuses on the connection between skills learned and productivity, credentialing theory places that focus on the attainment of higher education as an effective way of screening potential applicants. In this way, both theoretical positions recognize education as an effective way of enhancing one's position in relation to the labor market, and both view material incentives as predictive of educational enrollments.

Warehousing Theory. It has long been the case, particularly in the United States, that an economic downturn tends to lead to increases in enrollments. This particular scenario is addressed by warehousing theory, which states that educational institutions are places in which to keep—in the words of Karl Marx—"reserve armies of unemployed." O'Connor (1973:11) asserts that the education system can be used, at least temporarily, to move surplus labor away from the labor market. In a related vein, Grubb & Lazerson (1982) develop the argument that education can be used as an alternative to direct participation in the labor market. In other words, young people can simply go to school during economic downturns or other periods of low demand for labor. Grubb and Lazerson cite the explosion in the number of community colleges in the 1960s as an example of public policy designed to temporarily "warehouse" unskilled or marginally skilled members of the labor force.

Research in this area lends support to the general idea of warehousing theory. In essence, it argues that during the early part of the twentieth century in the United States, an influx of unskilled labor, coupled with advancing technology, effectively led to an erosion in the labor market position of school-age workers. The result of this combination of circumstances was to drive expansion in secondary and post-secondary educational enrollments in the United States during that period (Ralph & Rubinson 1980; Osterman 1979).

A Strong Labor Market: The Flip Side of Warehousing. Just as "warehousing" leads to higher levels of enrollment during times of high unemployment, booming economies with low levels of unemployment tend to have the opposite effect of making education a less attractive short-term prospect. For example, Fuller (1983) finds that an increase in blue-collar jobs in the United States was accompanied by a decrease in school enrollments for both males and females, especially in urban areas where the growth of the manufacturing sector was most dramatic. Thus, an economic boom could, for certain social groups—specifically those least likely to be the beneficiaries of the rewards of an education—lead to decreases in enrollments.

Because of the central or peripheral labor market position of various classes or status groups, warehousing and its flip side could be expected to have differential effects in a society. Also, while warehousing theory is conceptualized primarily in terms of class, the principle is applicable to gender as well. This can be observed during periods of high demand for labor, such as in times of war, when women enter the labor force in greater numbers than usual. This was dramatized in the movie *Swing Shift*, in which Goldie Hawn stars as a worker in a military airplane factory in Los Angeles during World War II. In the movie, the women work heroically to keep up production to bolster the war effort. When the war ends, conflict occurs as the men return from the battlefields, expecting their jobs back. In actuality, once many of the women came into the labor force, they did not go back out.

Contrarily, during times of peace and when labor is in oversupply, women become less crucial to the labor force, and thus may be more subject to warehousing than men (especially men in elite or even in middle class occupations), whose position in the labor market economy is often more stable. In this way, while warehousing theory emphasizes issues of class-differentiated stratification systems more so than it addresses issues of gender, it has important implications for gender as well. One of the profound and lasting social changes that came out of World War II was the unprecedented number of women who came into either the labor force or higher education, or both.

Conflict Theory, Education and Culture. As we know, conflict theorists such as Marx focus their analyses on the exploitation of the lower classes by the upper classes. It follows, then, that conflict theorists in the sociology of education focus on how this exploitation is promulgated through the education system. In particular, conflict theorists emphasize the theory that the primary function of education systems is **social class reproduction**, in which students are socialized into roles that perpetuate the class relations of previous generations (e.g., Bourdieu 1977; Bourdieu & Passeron 1977; Bowles & Gintis 1976).

Katz (1975:108 ff.) concludes, in an historical study of educational change in the United States, that values driving the expansion of public education—particularly those emphasizing uniformity, efficiency and order—have strong class overtones. According to Katz, even educational reform was brought into fruition by motives of "inculcating the poor with acceptable social attitudes" (p. 116). Given these class considerations in the American educational system, their implications are perhaps even more dramatic in the more class-differentiated education systems in the nation-states of Western Europe.

In fact, research indicates that a child's performance in school is often tied to his or her parents' ability to understand the relevant school charters and to help position the child accordingly. In a study by Baker and Stevenson (1986) focusing on the United States, a correlation was observed between the socio-economic status and education of parents on the one hand, and their ability to understand and therefore to manage their children's school careers on the other.

In a similar study in Germany, Oswald, Baker, and Stevenson (1988) found parents' interventive actions in their children's school careers to bear a strong relationship to the type of school charter. Class reproduction theorists believe that whether a child goes to a mass or elite institution depends largely upon recommendations of the child's teachers and principal. These recommendations, however, are based on the perception of the parents' social background and their aspirations for the child's education as much as they are based on the student's performance itself.

Researchers have also found that certain aspects of the success or failure of a student in school is attributable to the way the child has learned to organize knowledge and to speak about it—in terms they learn in the family context, before ever beginning school. Bernstein (1971; also see Bernstein & Bernstein 1979) found that students tend to display what he termed **elaborated codes** of speech about things with which they were very familiar. An elaborated code is a heightened sense of perception, accompanied by a specialized vocabulary, about some aspect of the person's social reality. For example, a child spending a great deal of time and attention playing a certain musical instrument would tend to have heightened perceptions and an elaborate vocabulary to describe various aspects of that instrument.

These elaborated codes of middle class children, Bernstein found, tended to be closer to those of the teachers' (who themselves tended to be drawn heavily from the middle class) than were the elaborated codes of lower class students. We note here that Bernstein found children of all classes to have roughly equal vocabularies—but the vocabularies were about very different things. Middle class students tended to have the kinds of vocabularies that more closely matched those of the teachers and the people making up the tests. Because of this, Bernstein reasoned that it was not surprising that middle and upper-middle class students tended to do better in school, on average, than lower class students. In other words, because the type of education one receives is so intimately linked to the class to which one will eventually belong as an adult, this phenomenon tends to "reproduce" the class structure.

Toward a Unifying Model of Educational Growth

Of course, educational growth cannot be entirely explained by either material or cultural models alone. Thus, the optimal way to explain the dramatic growth in educational systems over the last few centuries appears to be a combination of both conflict and functional approaches. Several studies conducted within the last two decades shed light on how educational expansion is attributable to a wide array of causes, sometimes interacting in complex ways.

To illustrate, Fuller (1983) found that in the United States, industrialization led to growing numbers of white-collar jobs which in turn resulted in an increase in enrollments, an effect that was especially marked among females. This effect can be largely attributed to an industrializing *economy* creating new kinds of jobs along with increased incentives for performing them, combined with a strong *cultural* belief in the value of education. Fuller attributes his findings to two major forces shaping secondary school enrollments in the United States at the turn of the century: changes in the structure of the labor market brought about by urbanization and industrialization; as well as rural Protestant beliefs in the value of education itself.

Walters and Rubinson (1983) find a relationship between secondary educational expansion and economic output in recent years in the United States, although such has not uniformly been the case when going back as far as the last century, or even the early part of the current century. They argue that the economic contributions made by the school system is not so much a result of the training provided by education, but rather more so a result of its socializing effects (c.f. Collins 1971, 1979; Berg 1970). Walters and Rubinson suggest that legitimation effects work "through the level of schooling that is becoming a mass institution." They suggest that the institutionalization of mass education, at least in the United States, can be viewed as a means of legitimating the economic structure in general—albeit a structure in which material incentives play an integral role.

Taken together, there appears to be an increasing body of evidence that material and cultural forces considered *in conjunction with* each other are more effective in accounting for educational expansion than are either in isolation. Thus, we note here that functional and conflict models actually have a good deal in common, despite initially appearing irreconcilable. For example, both functional and conflict models place an emphasis on the socializing influences of education. The point of departure comes in the values by which educational socialization is judged. For functional theorists, socialization is a crucial process for the optimal functioning of society, while conflict theorists would view socialization primarily as a vehicle of oppression. While either position could be argued plausibly, the important point for students of society to take from it is that a primary function of schooling is socialization, and to understand some of

School Success and Failure

Studies have found that parental involvement in children's learning can override the effects of poor schooling to a significant degree.

the socializing mechanisms. We have now considered a number of studies that examine just how the socialization process operates in the educational system.

Some Causes for School Success or Failure

There are a number of social factors associated with students' academic success or failure. These include such factors as the cultural milieu in which one is raised, individual motivation, as well as individual intellectual ability—both inherited from one's parents and developed on one's own (e.g., Dougherty & Hammack 1990:333 ff.). Ultimately, a student's failure or success stems from interactions among these factors rather than being solely a result of any one of them alone.

In examining such interactions, we note a strong relationship between socioeconomic status of the parents and school achievement of the child. While the reasons for this association are often rather complex, it appears that one cause for this association is simply that resources available for educating children tend to be related to a family's position in the stratification hierarchy, with wealthy families having access to more than poor families. For instance, in much of the United States local public schools are funded primarily by property taxes. Since the property tax base is appreciably higher in wealthier areas where high SES families tend to live, there are typically greater resources available to those local school systems.

However, while there is a correlation between spending and school achievement, that correlation is surprisingly *low*, which indicates that there are clearly other variables at play in terms of school achievement. In a series of large-scale studies of social factors associated with school success commissioned by the U.S. federal government, James Coleman and colleagues (Coleman et al. 1966; Coleman, Hoffer, & Kilgore 1982) found a much higher degree of variability of student achievement *within* schools than they did *between* schools—meaning that a range of both high and low academic performance by students can be found in both affluent and poor schools. Further, much of the differences between schools (in terms of the overall achievement levels of their students) that Coleman and his colleagues did find, had to do with factors other than spending.

In their studies, which involved both public and private, parochial (e.g., Catholic) schools, Coleman and his colleagues found that the most important factors associated with school success had to do with the link between school and home life, and the resulting promulgation of a strong sense of values. Specifically, the Coleman studies found that children tended to be more academically successful when parents were involved in their learning. To a significant degree, this involvement could even override the effects of a poor school. This type of involvement is typically associated with the child doing regular homework that is followed-up at home by the parent(s). Further, when there is a strong value system and discipline that is promoted in school, and that value system and discipline are reinforced at home, students often tended to be high achievers academically.

Further, differences in upper and lower class children in school performance tend to *diminish* over the course of the school year. This effect seems to occur independently of the financial resources of the school itself. Yet it is often the case that those differences persist over time. How can this be? In an interesting and incisive study, Barbara Heyns found that during summer vacations from school, higher SES children are much more likely to spend significant time reading than are lower SES children. Time spent reading is strongly associated with school success, regardless of the financial state of the school—even though what is being read may be for pleasure, and be virtually unrelated to schoolwork. In other words, the "SES effect," in which the SES of the parents is associated with a child's performance in school, is (ironically) greatest during the summer—largely because higher SES children are more likely to read then (Heyns 1978).

There are some important lessons here. On the macro level, there is certainly a correlation between SES and academic performance. Yet much of the correlation stems from high SES parents being, *on average*, more involved with *their* children's education than are low SES parents with their children's education. But the term "on average" should be taken advisedly, and there are many exceptions. There is no shortage of people who have succeeded academically despite attending resource-limited schools, as well as those who have fared poorly despite having access to the best educational resources in affluent schools.

Education in a Comparative Perspective

Some striking patterns emerge when comparing education in the United States with that of other countries. For example, the United States has a far higher percentage of college-educated adults than any other country in the world. This fact would come as no surprise if we were making this comparison with only Third World countries. However, this remains true in comparison to other highly developed countries as well. Consider that American adults have between two and *three* years more formal education than British adults on average, for instance.

Why might this be? One empirical study comparing the U.S. and British systems provides an illustration. While in the United States, the type of secondary school curriculum tends not to have much of an effect on subsequent occupational prestige (where school charters tend to be broad but without much variance between schools); the opposite is true in Britain, where the type of charter associated with the secondary school attended *does* have an effect on subsequent occupational prestige. This differential effect by type of charter can be found independently of number of years of schooling (Kerckhoff & Everett 1986).

The education system in the United States is one in which students are on a roughly equal footing with others in their same grade level. Thus, students tend to compete with one another throughout school. Based on this observation, Ralph Turner (1960) coined the phrase **contest mobility** to describe the type of mobility gained in this circumstance. Conversely, in British society, a smaller number of students are picked (or "sponsored") at a fairly early age, and given elite prep school educations which in turn lead to highly rewarding occupations. Turner refers to this system as **sponsored mobility**.

In essence, in the British system, as well as most education systems in the world *other than* the United States, there is a much clearer distinction between elite education and mass education. **Elite education** refers to a separate school system in which a few privileged students receive educations meant to prepare them for prestigious universities and eventually for high posts in the government, academe or industry. **Mass education** is a much larger system of schools intended to train children for lower middle and working class occupations.

Unlike much of the rest of the world, the preponderance of high schools in the United States (commonly referred to by students of education systems as **comprehensive high schools**) is characterized by being far less stratified than the average British school. To be sure, comprehensive high schools tend to have both academic ("college prep") and commercial tracks, yet the tracking is much more flexible than a system with separate schools for the elites and masses. The comprehensive schools themselves usually allow for students to change tracks, and the different tracks that do exist tend to be *within* a school, rather than having a completely different set of schools for elites and the masses, complete with a different set of school charters.

Raymond Boudon (1982) ties the existence of separate systems for elites and the masses together with a number of theoretical perspectives discussed earlier, including rational choice theory and the "class reproduction" thesis. Boudon points out that members of different classes make rational choices about educational enrollments based on a calculus of cost and reward associated with the respective systems. Because the rewards for educational attainment in the mass system are fewer, enrollment in this system is less attractive and thus carries an inherent *disincentive* for students to enroll in it.

While Boudon's analysis focuses on class, his work holds implications for the effects of gender as well, especially in an educational system with separate tracks for *both* gender and social class. It is plausible to assume that the decision making process of potential students and their families in selecting a school is greatly influenced by the differentiation between these educational systems, and by different expectations for what types of employment are possible upon leaving. In sum, because of the differential effects of these material incentives, the calculations regarding school enrollment decisions are likely to vary both by class (Boudon 1974) and by gender (c.f. Garnier & Hage 1991).

In addition to the cultural and economic factors influencing demand for education, it is also important to consider the political questions of both the length and type of education available. Craig (1981) demonstrates that as different systems were instituted in Europe, educational expansion was effectively checked. The effect of such a stratified system was to render the number of years of education less important. In other words, the *type* of education received became more important than the *length* of education received—an education from an elite institution became necessary for admission into the university and/or into an elite career track, while a diploma from a non-elite institution did not allow university admission (although it many times signified preparation for work in a trade or non-elite occupation).

In a historical study of the French system, Hage, Garnier, and Fuller (1988) give evidence that the connection between mass education and state economic expansion is facilitated by a "strong and active" state limiting access to, and exercising standardization and quality-control over, the educational system. This establishes a tight coupling between the education system and the labor market, imposed by the state, which limits the numbers of certain kinds of schools, or numbers of available places in those schools, in the first place. To support their thesis, Hage, Garnier, and Fuller highlight divisions of secondary school enrollments into middle and working class specific educational streams. In this way, the state is better able to ensure quality of output by means of establishing exclusive systems of education, and in doing so, maintaining control of the status competition and credential inflation predicted by credentialing theory. In sum, the promulgation of state policy had the potential to affect school enrollments, especially as it alters the availability or supply of schooling.

The closest analogies to such a system in the United States would be the service academies (such as the Naval Academy or West Point), or medical schools. In those cases, because the places are severely limited, only a small percentage of actual applicants can be accepted. Those few who make the cut can be considered as being "sponsored" by the society. They are chosen from among many, and the educations they receive are typically subsidized by the society. Furthermore, students completing one of these curricula are in a very strong position to have an elite career (military officer, physician). Yet educational opportunities with severely limited admissions are common for *many* fields in European systems.

Richard Rubinson (1986) finds two salient characteristics of the U.S. educational system when compared to the European: **1)** higher educational levels, and **2)** lower degrees of stratification within the education system itself. The stratification Rubinson refers to is the existence of separate mass and elite tracks—since these are rarer in the United States, he characterizes the U.S. system as being less *stratified* than most European systems. These two attributes Rubinson identifies are related. Because there is less emphasis on the *type* of education in the United States than in most European countries, American students are more likely to distinguish themselves by the *amount* of education they receive (Rubinson 1986). Over time, this tends to lead to a spiral of educational credential inflation. The educational spiral lowers the value of education on every level, resulting in the necessity for everyone involved to increase educational attainment in order to maintain the status quo.

In Europe, the economic and social costs of this spiral were dealt with by developing separate schooling systems with their own defining curricula, charters, entrance requirements and leaving credentials (Armstrong 1973; Suleiman 1978). European students, in contrast to their U.S. counterparts, tend to choose a specialty much earlier in their education, where the distinction between academic and technical tracks is much more clearly differentiated.

Of course, these two very distinct systems each have their respective advantages and drawbacks. Students in the United States have greater opportunity to pursue different educational agendas. However, credential inflation is much greater in the United States than in Britain. The British system tends to keep credential inflation down because the type of educational institution one attends (such as an elite prep school) tends to be a more important determining factor concerning one's place in the labor market than does the number of years of education. However, British students tend to have less opportunity to change educational paths than do their American counterparts.

Education and Third World Development

It has been long recognized by researchers that the role of education is a crucial one in national development. Modernization theorists commonly acknowledge the intimate connection between a nation's modernity, and the emphasis that nation and its citizens place on education (Inkeles and Smith 1974).

More recent work in the sociology of education has refined original statements about the generic positive effects of education. There is now evidence that the societal benefits of education is most pronounced when an institutional linkage between the education system and the economy exists; or in other words, when the education received prepares individual members of society for the specific positions in the labor market they eventually occupy.

One reason education is important in a Third World context is the role it plays in economic differentiation. An educated labor force is better able to perform in an economy specializing in service and industrial sectors, according to human capital theory. On the other hand, when a country specializes in the export of raw materials, its overall development will suffer because the value of raw materials is declining *relative to* manufactured goods produced in other countries (Chase-Dunn 1979:135). This results in an unequal exchange between the core and the periphery characterized by a disproportionate transfer of value from the undeveloped countries to the developed countries.

Education in Developing Nations
Expanding educational opportunities, especially for young women and girls, is instrumental in reducing poverty in developing nations.

Over time, however, such unequal exchanges can be offset by the development of human capital within a country. Education in many Third World countries, particularly secondary education, is slowly coming to emulate the kind of education found in developed countries, allowing countries to build their human capital.

Morgan and Armer (1988), for example, in their study of education systems in Nigeria, identify two key functions of education at the primary level: equalizing the effects of inequality connected with the nation's former colonial status, and transmitting the unique traditions of the country. Here, education in fact still retains some of the vestiges of traditional practices at the elementary level. At the secondary level, on the other hand, education systems are much more similar to those found in modern Western society. This is true of both the curriculum itself, and in the emphasis on modern educational credentials important for labor market entry and economic well-being (Morgan & Armer 1988).

In other words, "Western" education is likely to be one in which one acquires a standard set of skills amenable to the workplace, or human capital. As this system is increasingly adopted, it is reasonable to expect a slow but steady increase in both the country's productivity as well as its standard of living.

The theories we have considered in this chapter, both in isolation and in conjunction with one another, help us to navigate the many intricacies of educational systems. As we have seen, the study of educational systems is an important branch of sociology in that it influences, and is influenced by, many aspects of social life. Let us now turn our attention to current trends in education.

Current Trends in Education

Educational attainment in the United States has been on the rise in recent decades. Between 1990 and 2013, the percentage of 25 to 29 year olds who had completed at least a high school diploma increased from 86 percent to 90 percent. More statistically significant is the increase in the percentage of 25 to 29 year olds who had completed a bachelor's degree or higher, which increased from 23 percent to 34 percent in that same time period (U.S. Department of Education 2014). Consider the fact that as recently as 1950, only about a third of the population age 25 and older had completed high school.

Differences in educational attainment by gender have shifted in recent years as well. In 1990, the percentage of males and females who had completed a bachelor's degree was about the same. In 2013, it was about 7 percent higher among females (37 percent) than for males (30 percent). This trend only began around 2000, however. Prior to that, educational attainment had been higher among males since data has been recorded.

Educational attainment also varies by race. In 2013, 94 percent of whites ages 25 and 29 had received at least a high school diploma or its equivalent, compared to 90 percent for blacks and 76 percent for Hispanics. This figure was highest among Asians (95 percent). These differences are even more pronounced when it comes to higher education. In 2013, 40 percent of whites had completed a bachelor's degree, compared to only 20 percent of blacks and 16 percent of Hispanics. Asians had the highest bachelor's degree completion rate at 58 percent.

For many people in developed nations, basic education is practically universal. For others, opportunities for education are dismal. In India, for example, the second most populous nation in the world, educational attainment is far below average. In the 2007-2008 school year, only about 13.6 percent of college-aged people enrolled in higher education (Organization for Economic Cooperation and Development 2011). Even fewer than that actually completed a degree.

The majority of the world's school-aged children who are not in school reside in Sub-Saharan Africa. There, 36 percent of school-aged children are not enrolled in primary school. The majority of those are female (UNICEF 2001). Educational expansion in Third World countries has been of primary importance in recent decades, as education is a powerful instrument in reducing poverty.

In discussing the lack of educational opportunities that exists in certain parts of the world, it is necessary to examine the factors that drive educational expansion. Many studies have been devoted to understanding what factors drive educational expansion, and what factors inhibit it. One such study examined Britain's education system and found that an important determinant of educational expansion was state supply. State supply refers to things such as availability of seats, creation of school systems, and improvement in quality (as measured, for example, by student-teacher ratio). The study found that state supply has a remarkably strong effect on educational expansion (Burns, Hage, and Garnier 2004). Drawing such correlations is useful in developing governmental policies related to education.

With students continuing to come to college in the United States from all over the world, it is no exaggeration to say that one of the great exports of the United States is higher education. Higher education in the United States continues to rank among the very highest of nations.

The story is a bit different at the primary and secondary levels, however. Over the last several decades, a number of countries have surpassed the United States in standardized measures, particularly in mathematics and some of the sciences. By 2009, for example, tenth graders in the United States ranked twenty-third (out of 65 nations in the sample) in mathematics worldwide. By 2012, the United States had fallen to thirtieth. In that same period, U.S. students fell from eighteenth to twenty-third in science (OECD 2013).

Conclusion

In sum, education continues to be intimately connected with other institutions throughout society, particularly the labor market. There are a number of theories that are useful in understanding educational dynamics. Over time, educational outcomes change, but the theories we use to make sense of them apply across a wide array of societies and circumstances.

CHAPTER SUMMARY

- One crucial function of education systems is socialization, or the integration of students into the society.
- A second key function of education is cultivating human capital in students to prepare them for entering into the labor market.
- School charters often give a sense of how a particular school system is connected with other social institutions.
- Conflict theorists emphasize that educational socialization tends to "reproduce" the class system.
- As societies have modernized, educational systems have expanded. There are multiple reasons for this, and a number of theories attempt to explain why. Some of these include:
  - cultural integration
  - industrialization
  - human capital
  - credential inflation
  - warehousing and labor markets
  - cultural reproduction
- There are many reasons for success or failure in school, independent of the school system. Some notable findings are that parental involvement in learning, as well as a learning environment stressing a healthy discipline and strong value system, tends to be factors optimizing chances of student success.
- Formal education levels in the United States are higher than anywhere else in the world, even when comparing them to other developed countries. This is partly attributable to credential inflation.
- As societies increase levels of education, the standard of living also tends to increase, but the correlation between these two is only moderate.
- The correlation between education and economic growth increases dramatically when a tight coupling between the education and economic systems can be found in a country.

14 Religion and Society

Sociologists of religion tend to focus on the many **social** functions of religion. The functions of religion as a social institution are far-reaching. Religion serves as an institution that is larger than the individual—to which the individual "belongs." In fact, the word religion derives from the Latin *religare*, which means, "to bind together." In many contexts, religion serves to bind an individual to the larger society.

Religion as a Social Institution

Religion can be defined as an interrelated set of beliefs and practices about the sacred, which address questions of ultimate meaning. Religion, along with family, is one of society's oldest institutions, predating education, politics, and most other institutional practices.

Virtually every human society, both primitive and modern, has religion(s). The advent of "atheistic" societies (such as Maoist China or Stalinist Russia) came only in modern times. However, while these atheistic societies officially banned religious practices, they still attempted to address questions of ultimate meaning, thereby endeavoring to supplant traditional religion with some totalitarian ideology.

Primitive societies tend to have precisely one religion, to which each of the members of the society adheres. As societies modernize and differentiate, they tend to move towards **religious pluralism**, a situation in which there are many religions practiced in a given society.

It has often been the case throughout history that religions have served as a primary vehicle through which "right and wrong" are judged. And as a broad overarching institution that ties many diverse sectors of the society together, religion serves to legitimate broad societal ideals. In other words, religions have historically propagated the norms of a society. Religions that tend to place an emphasis on the individual (e.g., "I have a personal relationship with Jesus Christ") are found primarily in modern societies.

In societies that experience general breakdown of strong religions, a number of social problems typically follow. Without a religious system to which people feel tied, and which does not promulgate a normative system, many people feel "cast adrift" often resulting in a state of normlessness, a breakdown of order, and a number of ensuing social pathologies.

Since the dawn of sociological science, researchers and theorists have been fascinated by the role religions play in society. Auguste Comte (remember him?—he's the one who coined the word "sociology") theorized that society progressed through three stages of development. According to Comte, the most primitive stage was the "theological" stage, in which answers to life's most perplexing questions (e.g., "Where do we come from?" "What should we do?") were resolved by seeking guidance through religious experience filtered through a priestly class.

Many of the early pioneers of sociology had complex and detailed ideas about religion's role in society. At the risk of oversimplification, we may say that Émile Durkheim viewed religion as a source of social solidarity, and Max Weber saw it primarily as a source of social change. These Durkheimian and Weberian frameworks for analyzing religion are still useful, nearly a century later. Let's look more closely at their theories.

Religion and Society · 201

Religions
Religion has been a part of virtually every human society throughout history. (clockwise from top left: Buddhist monks, Hindu sadhus, traditional African faith healing, Muslims at the Kaaba in Mecca, Saudi Arabia, Jews and Torah scrolls, Catholics celebrate Easter Mass.

Émile Durkheim on the Central Role of Religion

Much of the early definitive work in the sociology of religion was written by Émile Durkheim, whose other work we discussed in a previous chapter. Throughout the course of his life studies, Durkheim took special note of the religious beliefs and practices of many societies. Eventually, Durkheim developed a theory about the central role of religion in society, drawing from his lifelong research.

The culmination of this research was the book *The Elementary Forms of Religious Life* (1912/1965), but we also see his ideas about religion interwoven throughout his other works. For example, we see religion playing a prominent role in his book *Suicide* (1897/1951).

In *The Elementary Forms of Religious Life*, Durkheim concludes that while there are great *substantive* differences among the various religions of the world, virtually all religions had certain similarities to one another in *form*. Further, he observes that religions in general tended to have the following characteristics in common:

- Religion provides a discipline for its adherents, promulgating a common normative system in the process.
- In providing this discipline, all religions divide our experience in the world into the *sacred* and the *profane*. **Sacred** objects or people are set apart in some way, and given a privileged status. Everything not given a privileged status is **profane**. In Durkheim's view, the profane status does not necessarily imply that something is bad. Rather, it is simply something ordinary, as opposed to special.
- Relative to sacred objects and people, a society performs **ritual**. For Durkheim, ritual has the following characteristics:
  - There tends to be some repeated or scripted action.
  - A grouping of people is physically present in the same location.
  - There is a commonality of focus and perceptions.
  - Ritual serves to reaffirm social bonds, which in turn strengthens society.

An example of ritual could be found when members of a primitive society have a totem pole ceremony. A group of people gathers to perform repetitious activity, in which there is a common focal point. This serves to strengthen the bonds of the society. There are many examples of ritual in our own society as well, such as weddings, funerals, and Sunday church services, for instance.

Durkheim also allowed for ritual in secular activity. In such situations, the same characteristics as religious ritual are found, but without the sacredness. Cheering for the home team at a ball game would exemplify a secular ritual (Goffman 1963).

In Durkheim's view, societies needed the discipline and common normative system that religions could provide. A breakdown of norms, he theorized, would lead to egregious social problems.

As we discussed earlier, the two major causes of social pathologies, of all sorts (e.g., crime, delinquency, addiction, abuse, etc.), and particularly of suicide, are **egoism** (a lack of ties binding individuals to anything larger than themselves), and **anomie** (a lack of norms that function to govern people's behavior in the society).

Religion, according to Durkheim, counteracts these problems by providing a discipline that strikes a *balance* between being commanding and lovable. The commanding aspect of the religion (e.g., the Ten Commandments in the Judeo-Christian tradition, or *Sharia* Law in the Islamic tradition) helps to promote a common system of norms. Once people have **internalized these norms** (organized their own thinking and behavior so that the norms are part of themselves), the society itself becomes more orderly as a result. Likewise, the lovable aspect of the religion is necessary (consider, for example, the larger theme contained in the parable: "As my Father in Heaven loves me, so I love you") in order for people to feel connected to something larger than themselves. This would provide a social fabric to the society that transcends individuality and its own selfish interests.

The fact that society has been able to function as smoothly as it has is largely due to religion, in Durkheim's outlook. It has served the social purpose of preventing the anarchy of a war of all against all.

Religion as a Source of Social Change: Max Weber's Protestant Ethic and the Spirit of Capitalism

In the late nineteenth century, at the time Max Weber was composing his works of social theory, Karl Marx's writings were also popular. Specifically, the Marxian belief that ideology was a function of one's economic class position was increasingly met with widespread acceptance. Weber's work, while acknowledging the importance of economics, argued that a belief system, rather than being caused by an economic system could, in fact, indirectly be the cause of an economic system. Weber (1904-5) set out to demonstrate this in his landmark work, *The Protestant Ethic and the Spirit of Capitalism*. (It should also be mentioned here that Weber focuses primarily, though not exclusively, on **Calvinism**, a specific type of Protestantism prevalent in Western Europe at the time of capitalism's ascendancy).

Weber viewed the Protestant ethic as an interwoven set of ideas, or values (as Weber used the word **ethic**, it literally means an interrelated system of values), which can be characterized thusly:

- An emphasis on individual, rather than communal, salvation.
- A belief in predestination.
- A tendency to work hard to succeed in worldly affairs, as a vehicle of assurance that an individual is one of God's chosen.
- An asceticism (extreme self-denial), which rejected vice and dissipation, such as alcohol and tobacco, dancing, and extramarital sex.
- A belief that pursuing individual economic interests is not merely selfishness but is, in fact, an ethical duty.

Weber did not argue that Protestantism directly results in capitalism, or vice versa. Rather, the Protestant **ethic** leads to a public *spirit* in which hard work and **reinvestment** of one's earnings make it *possible* for capitalism to flourish. He did not imply that greed is the beginning of capitalism. He even goes so far to point out that Calvinism did not have the creation of capitalism as a goal. Rather, he considers the arrival of capitalism as an *unintended consequence* of the Protestant ethic.

Weber makes a distinction between **traditional capitalism** and **rational capitalism**. By traditional capitalism, Weber meant a relatively undisciplined short-term plan for turning a profit. In such a case, the profit was typically spent rather than reinvested in the business. The behavior of rational capitalism, on the other hand, implies a much more systematic process. Typically, rational capitalism involved a great deal more discipline, a trait that the early Calvinists were likely to exhibit due to their asceticism. Hence, profits were typically reinvested in businesses, helping them to grow over time—sometimes spectacularly. Over time, this rational capitalism in the economic arena, and rational-legal authority systems in the social and political arenas grew more and more compatible, and thus would contribute to the growth of one another.

However, the Protestant ethic alone, Weber argued, was insufficient in order for capitalism to arise. There should be other structural considerations in addition. The greatest structural barrier to capitalism was a system dominated by traditional authority (kings, lords, etc., who come to their position by way of inheritance), rather than a rational-legal system in which people are allowed to rise according to a system of merit. Other structural considerations Weber mentions were the process of industrialization, as well as the rise of a free market.

Without rational-legal authority, industrialization, and a free market, it would be difficult, if not impossible, for capitalism to flourish. However, these are not enough; Weber points out places where these conditions *were* present, yet did not breed capitalism. These characteristics *in combination with* the Protestant ethic were what led to a spirit in which capitalism could, and often did, flourish.

In this regard, Weber's theory takes into account both micro and macro level explanations, as well as objective and subjective ones. Of course, Protestantism itself is a macro level phenomenon. Weber's theory involves a connection from the macro to the micro level when he discusses the effect Protestantism (most notably, but not exclusively, the Calvinist variety) has on its individual adherents.

To illustrate, an individual Protestant may hold the belief that work, rather than merely a means of subsistence, is a noble end in itself. This belief, being held by the individual, is subjective in nature. To the extent such a belief is widely held by a number of Protestants, it can be said to be an "ethic" (comparable to Durkheim's idea of collective beliefs).

Weber notes that once capitalism has begun to flourish, the Protestant ethic is no longer necessary to *maintain* it. Thus, capitalism as we know it today has become its own self-sustaining social force.

Of course, there were other religions as well that emphasized religious aspects other than those favored by Protestants. For example, an aspect of Catholic theology contains the scriptural caveat that "It is easier for a camel to pass through the eye of a needle than for a rich man to enter the Kingdom of Heaven." Weber notes that this ethic is much more compatible with participation in the working class than it is for an elite class of business owners in a capitalist setting. In support of his theory, Weber found that Protestant (particularly Calvinist) areas have historically been significantly more economically prosperous than Catholic areas. He attributes these differences to the collective ideas held by people in these faiths.

Using Weber's theories as a foundation, many sociologists have noted the connections between religion and the stratification system in a society. We turn our attention next to work focusing on those connections.

Theorizing about Social Stratification and Religion

H. Richard Niebuhr's (1929) *Social Sources of Denominationalism* is considered one of the most thorough and insightful studies of the link between religion and stratification. As we discuss this work, we will also introduce a number of concepts (such as the distinction between church and sect) that sociologists have utilized when considering the social functions of religion.

A **sect** tends to place an emphasis on emotional experiences. The image of God is very near. People tend to pray informally and extemporaneously. Borrowing Weber's terminology, Neibuhr posits that sects tend to exhibit an **other-worldly orientation**. A **church**, on the other hand, is a more stable institution, which tends to intellectualize religious dogma and restrain emotion. The image of God is remote, and people tend to pray formally. Again, borrowing Weber's terminology, churches tend to have a **this-world orientation**.

According to Neibuhr, churches tend to place a greater emphasis on success in this world; whereas sects tend to help render otherwise miserable lives bearable. For this reason, churches tend to appeal to the upper classes, while sects tend to appeal to the lower classes. In both cases, the orientation dovetails with class interests. To bolster his case, Neibuhr points out that on average, members of churches with a this-world orientation (e.g., Episcopalianism) tend to be of higher SES than sects with an other-worldly orientation (e.g., Holy Rollers).

Trajectories of Religious Institutionalization

One interesting and noteworthy trend has been studied in depth by Rodney Stark and William Bainbridge (1980, 1987); namely, as religious organizations (and their members) become more successful, the emphasis increasingly shifts from the other-world to this world.

Stark and Bainbridge make the observation that virtually *all* religions begin as *cult movements*, or innovative religious movements, typically formed around a charismatic leader to which followers are drawn and feel a sense of attachment. While this has been true historically, Stark and Bainbridge focus most of their studies on modern societies.

They find that in modern societies, people who are most likely to join cults often come from *higher SES*, but *religiously inactive*, families. Further building upon the Weberian model, Stark and Bainbridge argue that as cults become successful, they tend to routinize into a set of systematic rules and practices.

As a cult grows bigger, more successful, and more routinized over time, it slowly evolves first into a sect, and then into a church. As a church becomes increasingly oriented to this world, it ironically becomes "secularized," meaning that its conception of God becomes more abstract.

This combination of routinization and secularization sets the stage for a *revival*, or a movement, often within the religion itself, back toward a sect, rather than church, model. This sect formation revives the conventional religious tradition and moves back towards its original other-worldly direction.

The existence of many different sects and churches in a society fills a number of niches, and potentially offers something for a great number of people. As a matter of fact, church attendance is highest in places with a high degree of religious pluralism (e.g., United States). This religious pluralism, as well as the cult/sect/church model, is most common in modern societies.

Religious Trends and Trajectories of Social Change

As we have seen, as societies modernize, their religious practices correspondingly change as well. In this grand trajectory of history, there have been some milestones. The Protestant Reformation, in both Weber and Durkheim's view, along with the social changes that occurred because of it, was one such milestone. As Peter Berger (1967) notes:

> At the risk of some simplification, it can be said that Protestantism divested itself as much as possible from the three most ancient and most powerful concomitants of the sacred—mystery, miracle, and magic. The process has been aptly caught in [Weber's] phrase 'disenchantment of the world.' (P. 111)

From a Durkheimian perspective, the Protestant Reformation itself could be considered as a milestone on the road to modernization, in which there is an increasingly greater emphasis on the individual, relative to the society as a whole.

In any case, there have been major shifts in religious practices corresponding to the modernization of society. Some of those shifts have been toward a greater similarity of religious form. Again, Berger (1967) notes that:

> [M]odernization is today a worldwide phenomenon and...structures of modern industrial society, despite great modifications in different areas and national cultures, produce remarkably similar situations for the religious traditions and the institutions that embody these. (P. 170)

In sum, there have been religions in virtually every society throughout history. Religions serve a number of key social functions, particularly those articulated by Durkheim, including binding individuals to a larger collective and promoting a normative system necessary for an orderly society. While religions have changed somewhat as society has modernized, they continue to perform these crucial functions, and are likely to continue to do so for the foreseeable future.

Current Trends in Religiosity

By some measures, religiosity has been on the decline around the world in recent decades. The majority of U.S. adults, however, still identify as religious. In the United States, 78 percent of adults practice some form of Christianity. Of all Christians, 51.3 percent are Protestant, 23.9 percent are Catholics, 1.7 percent are Mormons, and the rest are comprised of Orthodox Christians, Jehovah's Witnesses, and other lesser-practiced forms of Christianity (Pew Research U.S. Religious Landscape Survey 2013). Historically, the preponderance of religious adherents in the United States has been some form of Protestant, but significant declines in the number of Protestants has occurred in recent years.

Current Trends in Religiosity
African Americans are more likely to be religious than any other ethnic group in the United States.

About 25 percent of adults between the ages of eighteen to twenty-nine say they are not affiliated with any religion. The number of adults who identified as atheist, agnostic, or of no religion grew from about fourteen million in 1990, to about 29 million in 2001, and 34 million in 2008 (U.S. Census Bureau Statistical Abstract of the United States 2012). Many of those who claim no particular religion, however, identify as spiritual, but not religious, indicating that they may prefer the personal nature of spirituality to the institution of organized religion. The number of people who claim no religion is significantly lower among older Americans, who tend to hold more traditional views regarding religion. Only about 10 percent of adults aged sixty-five and over say they have no religious affiliation (Pew Research U.S. Religious Landscape Survey 2013).

Of all races and ethnicities in the United States, African Americans are the most likely to report a formal religious affiliation. In fact, African Americans are more religious overall than the rest of the population, with 87 percent describing themselves as belonging to a religious group. Of those, 78 percent are Protestant, compared to only 53 percent of whites, 27 percent of Asians, and 23 percent of Latinos (Pew Research U.S. Religious Landscape Survey 2013).

Historically, the majority of Hispanics in the United States have identified as Catholic. This remains true today as about 60 percent of Hispanics identify as Catholic. That figure is slightly lower than in recent years, however. This decline may correspond with the increase in the general population of people who are religiously unaffiliated. Another possible explanation for the decrease in Hispanics who identify as Catholic is the increase in the number of Hispanics who identify as Protestant (Pew Research U.S. Religious Landscape Survey 2013).

Asian Americans are the most likely to be unaffiliated with any religion with 23 percent claiming no religion. Among Asians who are affiliated with a religion, 17 percent are Catholic, 17 percent belong to an evangelical church, and 23 percent practice a historically Asian religion, particularly Hinduism or Buddhism (Pew Research U.S. Religious Landscape Survey 2013).

Patterns of church attendance in the United States have modified significantly throughout the twentieth century, a trend that continues today. The percentage of people who say they seldom or never attend church increased from 25 percent to 29 percent between 2003 and 2013. During that period, the number of people who attend church weekly declined slightly as well (Pew Research Center 2013).

Amidst the decline in church attendance, one notable phenomenon is the increase in megachurches across the United States. A megachurch is a Protestant church that has 2,000 or more weekly attendees. Many such churches often have attendance of 20,000 or more. The ideology among such congregations tends to be conservative, corresponding to the surge in conservatism that has occurred over the last decades of the twentieth and the beginning of the twenty-first century.

The growth of conservative denominations has, in some ways, contributed to a so-called "culture war" in which "a struggle over the meaning of America" is taking place (Hunter 1992). In his book *Culture Wars: The Struggle to Define America*, sociologist James Davison Hunter described a widening gap between traditionalists and progressives. Religious belief and political ideology are often inextricably linked, and in this seminal work, Hunter offers a nuanced examination of that link and its role in public sentiment. Hunter argues that public opinion polls can mask subtle differences among religious and political groups. Catholics, for example, are generally thought to be relatively conservative. Variations among Catholics do exist, however. As a small example, consider current Vice President Joe Biden and Congressman Paul Ryan, the 2012 vice presidential candidate. Both are Catholic, but their political ideologies are, in many ways, vastly different, a fact that was illustrated in front of the American public during the 2012 campaign. So while religious belief and political ideology are generally correlated, predicting a person's political ideology based on their religious affiliation should be done advisedly.

CHAPTER SUMMARY

- Religions serve crucial social functions, including binding individuals to a collective larger than themselves while functioning as a means through which people internalize norms that allow for the orderly functioning of the society.
- Many large social changes, including the advent of capitalism, have come about largely because of religious belief systems.
- Regardless of the society (including those officially promoting atheism), there is evidence of a common tendency to seek answers to ultimate questions. Religion functions as a social vehicle for this tendency.
- Religions typically divide experience in the world into the sacred and the profane, and tend to perform ritual around the sacred.
- There is a correlation between socio-economic status and religious practices, with lower SES individuals more likely to join sects, and higher SES members to join churches.
- Institutionally, religions tend to follow a trajectory, typically beginning as cults. As they grow, they tend to become sects, and then finally churches. As they grow, they tend to become routinized, and move from an other-worldly orientation to a this-world orientation.

15 | Politics and Society

One of the most central of society's institutions is the **polity**, or the political system, which distributes **power** across societies. A central component of politics is power. Max Weber, as you'll recall, defined power as the ability to achieve desired ends despite resistance from others. The distribution of power intimately affects the decision-making that sets the course for society's distribution of wealth and resources, as well as the services we take for granted. In one way or another, political decisions at all levels of government impact almost every aspect of our lives. As illustrations, consider the city's weekly garbage pickup, your state's provision of funding for state colleges and universities, and the federal government's grave decisions about the making of war on other nations.

Power is not the same thing as **force**, which is physical might, nor is it the same thing as **authority**, which Max Weber defined as the power people perceive as legitimate rather than coercive. In this chapter, we'll review and expand upon the issues of power and types of authority we introduced in Chapter 7. Recall the three critical forms of authority identified by Weber: 1) **traditional authority**, 2) **charismatic authority** and 3) **rational-legal authority**. Let us revisit these forms of authority in turn.

Traditional Authority
King Louis XIV of France is an example of a traditional authority figure who claimed a divine right to rule.

Traditional Authority. Under conditions of traditional authority, social power is legitimated by a widespread respect for long-held patterns of governance. One example is the rule of the nobility in Medieval Europe, where the supreme authority of leaders was based on a hereditary family rule and the commonly held perception that leaders were divinely ordained. In other words, to challenge traditional authority in this society was to challenge the authority of God.

Few, if any, leaders of the Western world today would claim a divine right to rule. This situation is far from universal, however—traditional authority typically declines only as societies industrialize. Thus, for some non-Western societies today, just like Western societies at early points in their history, rule is still based on traditional authority. This is most commonly encountered in those poorer peripheral and semiperipheral countries where the citizenry shares approximately the same heritage, where there is widespread agreement or *homogeneity in worldview*, and where the highly *rationalized* worldview of the West has not yet found a foothold. Some scholars see the rapidly encompassing world economy as a battering ram poised to strike down tradition within our lifetimes, and extinguish traditional authority the world over.

Charismatic Authority. With charismatic authority, a different type of circumstance emerges. Max Weber recognized that charismatic authority, in addition to traditional authority, has also been critically important throughout human history. Under charismatic authority, power is gained through the extraordinary personal abilities of leaders, which may appear superhuman, even divine.

Charismatic personalities inspire devotion. History is filled with charismatic leaders such as Jesus of Nazareth, and in other parts of the world, prophets such as Buddha, Confucius, and Muhammad. In more recent times, Mahatma Gandhi in India, Winston Churchill and Margaret Thatcher in Britain, and John F. Kennedy and Martin Luther King in the United States exhibited precisely this type of charismatic ability that imbued them with leadership and authority.

Rational-Legal Authority. A third type of authority Weber identified, he referred to as rational-legal. This type of authority springs from power legitimized by rules and regulations rather than tradition or individual charisma. This can be seen in the development of bureaucracy, which is a common element in the daily conduct of life in industrial and postindustrial societies. Weber emphasized that bureaucracies are highly rationalized; indeed, he feared someday that bureaucracies would become so rationalized, so dependent on rules, regulations, and technological pursuits, that life would become increasingly oppressive for all.

Modern bureaucracies are imbued with rational-legal authority as the central organizing principle of their existence. Rules of the organization, which are **codified** (written) and rules that are handed down by word of mouth, now guide virtually every aspect of daily organizational life. Organizational leaders are followed not because they are particularly charismatic or hold traditional authority, but rather due to the authority of their position.

It is not only in the organization of bureaucracy that rational-legal authority is pervasive among Western societies, and increasingly, the rest of the world. This form of authority governs most of our lives, outside the home. Rules and laws regulate virtually all of our daily activities, ranging from our drive from home to school or work, to our experiences in the classroom, our sexual behaviors, and even the disposal of our bodies when we die.

To be sure, we take rational-legal authority for granted. The rational and legalistic view of our world, which largely has replaced traditional customs, lives with us quietly, except for those occasions when we are jolted from our complacency. Next time you stand in a long line at your university, for instance, consider your attention to the dynamics of rational-legal authority!

Some final words on types of authority are needed. It should be understood that traditional authority, charismatic authority, and rational-legal authority are **ideal types**. Max Weber is associated with this conceptualization through his usage of ideal-type characteristics. Remember that these are not characteristics that are ideal in the sense that they are "good." Rather, they are characteristics that best exemplify a specific type of dynamic. That is to say, they are simply ideal representations of a phenomenon of interest. Some Middle-Eastern countries are "ideal" illustrations of traditional authority, but traditional authority by no means characterizes *all* of daily life in them.

Certainly, today's rational-legal authority is worldwide, even if it is mainly characteristic of the Western industrial and postindustrial societies. Charismatic leadership is evident the world over, as well, even if it is less important, in many ways, to the authority structure of the developed countries. Many societies undoubtedly exhibit some combination of these three ideal types of authority, even if only one of them is predominant.

Types of Political Systems

Macrocomparative sociologists often examine the overall types of political systems that characterize societies, typically focusing on four of the most critical types: democracy, monarchy, authoritarian, and totalitarian systems. Let's now examine each of these in turn, beginning with democracy, the system most familiar to Americans.

Democracy. Democracy is the political system in which the citizenry exercises power broadly. That is, governmental decision-making, whether it is at the federal or local level, depends on the participation of citizens at least to some extent. This participation can be direct participation in principle, or it can be indirect through the use of representatives. In the latter case, the **representative democracy** is indirect and places authority in the hands of elected leaders instead of directly in the hands of citizens. Democracies are rational-legal in character.

Does the United States engage in **direct democracy** or **indirect democracy**? Only rarely do we vote directly on the social issues that affect us most intimately. Instead, we far more typically select leaders who make those determinations for us, engaging in representative democracy. Direct democracy, as sociologist Robert Michels observed, requires the participation of all or most members in a society in making decisions, thus making it feasible only in very small societies, and essentially impossible in large societies. In larger societies, it is not plausible to bring the people together in a sufficiently timely fashion to meet the necessity for prompt and efficient voting actions. To be sure, we could anticipate a time when electronic voting permits every citizen, even in huge nations, to instantaneously register opinions on a myriad of issues. But for now, in the democratic societies of the world, including the United States, the delegation of authority becomes necessary.

In addressing this, Michels points out an appropriate concern: once power is delegated, it is possible that democracy can give way to rule by elites. An unfortunate consequence of the coupling of large societies with indirect, or participatory democracy is the increasing tendency for **voter apathy**. Apathy creates an increasing distance between voter will and the actual actions of their elected officials. A large portion of the population in the United States reports feeling alienated from the political process. Important decisions, they feel, are made in distant places by individuals who do not share their interests. But should we be alarmed? How pervasive is voter apathy in the United States?

In the 2012 elections, only about 58 percent of eligible citizens voted, down from about 62 percent in 2008. Voters and nonvoters alike list a number of reasons for their decision whether or not to participate in voting. Generally, people vote because they feel it is their obligation as a citizen, or because they feel that their vote makes a difference. People fail to vote, again, because they feel apathetic, and because they believe their vote doesn't matter within such a large population. Also, in many places, especially pockets of extreme poverty, information essential to voters does not reach a substantial number of people, and the effort needed to physically get to voting booths is viewed as overwhelming.

Beyond the voting behaviors of the population, let's take a look at the political process in general. The Constitution of the United States requires that states apportion their representatives according to their population. To determine this, a population census must be taken every ten years as a basis for these appointments. Each state must have at least one representative in the House of Representatives and the total number of representatives from the 50 states is 435, with each representative being elected for two-year terms. Did you know that the United States Senate is composed of 100 members? Two from each state are elected to serve for a term of six years. One-third of the senate is elected every two years.

It is noteworthy that **political action committees** have assumed a position of prominence in American government processes. Political action committees or PACS officially are independent of political parties. Their purpose is to achieve political goals by raising money from citizens and spending it to promote specific interests. They are, in fact, what are referred to as **special interest groups**, which are alliances of individuals who share an interest in some economic, political, or social issue and work together to pursue outcomes associated with those issues. Most frequently, they hire lobbyists to become their advocates to governmental decision makers.

In 1980, there were a little over 2,500 political action committees in the United States. This figure had increased to 4,600 in 2009. In 2014, those committees raised about $1.6 billion for political parties and candidates.

Some political leaders have questioned the political commitments of the younger generations of Americans. Among other things, their concerns probably are based on an understanding of the distribution of age in the members of the U.S. Congress itself. In the last twenty years, for example, the average age of members has become higher in both the House of Representatives and in the United States Senate. Compared to the 1980s, there are fewer members who are under the age 40, either in the house or senate. Correspondingly, there has been a dramatic increase in the numbers of individuals in the House and Senate who are aged 60 or over.

While interest in the democratic political process in the United States may be declining, the opposite is true in many other parts of the world. The last two decades have seen sweeping changes in Eastern Europe and many other countries in the developing world, as a result of a global procession towards more democratic forms of government. To a large extent, this movement is a result of international organizations, such as the United Nations and the World Bank. Many poorer countries desperately need lower-interest loans, and the World Bank often ties the provision of such resources to democratizing movements in the nation. It is important to understand the forms of government that these countries held before their switch to democracy, and it is equally important that we understand the types of political system that still are pervasive in developing countries.

Monarchy

In a **constitutional monarchy** such as Great Britain's, the royal family are merely symbolic heads of state. Actual governing authority is left in the hands of elected leaders.

Monarchy. One type of political system that is associated with traditional authority is monarchy, in which power is transferred through a single family from generation to generation. Monarchy is supported by tradition, as seen in the case of the British monarchy. It should be recognized, however, that Britain has a **constitutional monarchy**, as do other countries in Western Europe. In a constitutional monarchy, monarchs are **symbolic heads** of state. Elected officials are responsible for the actual governance of societies, and these countries are guided by a formal constitution that prescribes government organization, in most cases. In essence, governmental operations differ little from the representative democracy of the United States. It is the elected officials that make the critical decisions for the society.

This is in sharp contrast to **absolute monarchs**, who monopolize power and frequently claim a divine right to rule. Several Middle Eastern countries are still ruled by absolute monarchs who have complete control over their societies.

Authoritarianism. In a democracy citizens may choose **not** to participate in the activities of government, whereas in authoritarian systems citizens are barred from any popular participation in government whatsoever. Essentially, an authoritarian government completely restricts the political freedoms of the citizenry. Authoritarian governments appear frequently in the developing world, especially in Africa, the Middle East, and Asia. Often these authoritarian governments are supported by, or are in fact themselves, military regimes founded by **coups-d'état**, which are takeovers of normal government processes. It is important to emphasize that the authoritative government form may or may not involve itself directly in the lives of citizens. That is, in principle, it is possible for an authoritarian regime to exercise total control over government processes without carefully monitoring the lives of citizens. Such is not the case for the final governmental type we consider, totalitarianism.

Totalitarianism. In a **totalitarian** system, the individual behaviors and everyday lives of citizens are extensively regulated. This regulation occurs whether or not the citizens recognize the regulation. In totalitarian governments, the concentration of power is totally in the hands of a few decision makers. The right to assemble, the right to political action, and the right to meaningful voting are denied in totalitarian governments. The state demands total allegiance.

A key characteristic of the totalitarian political system is the extensive monitoring of all citizens. Monitoring is used as a tool to keep careful control of both the thoughts and behaviors of the citizens. Advanced technology such as sophisticated surveillance systems has made totalitarian rule a distinct possibility for governments the world over to listen to, watch, and record the daily activities of citizens.

Another important tool utilized in totalitarian societies is propaganda, a means by which governments control all forms of the media and use it to enforce compliance from citizens on all aspects of daily life. Family members may even reveal to authorities those other members of the family who are acting in ways, or thinking in ways, which stand in opposition to the totalitarian government. The pervasive reporting about one another by family members, especially children, in Nazi Germany is an illustration, as are the political climates in Cambodia and North Korea in more modern times.

Totalitarian systems attempt to ensure that all institutions of society, including the family, the military, educational systems, and religion, demonstrate complete loyalty to the state. This typically includes harsh punishment for opposition to the regime. These themes are explored in several popular twentieth century dystopian novels such as George Orwell's *1984* and Aldous Huxley's *Brave New World*.

Is it possible that countries such as the United States could ever be subject to a totalitarian form of political control? Certainly, in many industrial and postindustrial societies today, the technology allowing for nearly complete governmental control based on the surveillance of citizens is both plausible and available. Our day-to-day activities, including doctor's visits, school attendance, and payment by use of checks or debit cards for a wide range of goods and services, are accounted for in the form of computerized records. The potential for control increases as information on these daily activities is physically coupled with our recorded behaviors in front of surveillance (video) cameras. Consider the video cameras that are now pervasive in department stores, on many sidewalks, streets, and even on interstate highways. When taken together, a substantial segment of our daily activities are now "recorded," computerized, and ready for use.

One of your authors vividly remembers his introduction to such possibilities when he bought his first car in the early 1970s, and the car's title was erroneously made to a "David" (not Edward) Kick by the state of Illinois. Within three weeks, junk mail started arriving, all addressed to "David." Apparently, the state had sold the name and other information to businesses around the country.

While the potential for totalitarian states exists broadly in the world, it is limited by the active participation of citizens in the formation of government. An alienated, poorly informed, or apathetic populace is precisely the most susceptible to totalitarian rule.

The Distribution of Power

To what extent is power disbursed in a representative democracy such as the United States? Do political decisions reflect the interests of the majority or simply small, but powerful, interest groups? Alternative forms of political systems and types of authority suggest the need for inquiry regarding the nature of power distribution in the United States and elsewhere.

These questions are addressed in social function and social conflict interpretations. Social function interpretations utilize a model that emphasizes **pluralism** and analyzes politics with an emphasis on the dispersion of power among a broad range of competing interest groups, while conflict interpretations argue that the wealthy class (**power elite**) controls the political process. As you will see, when these two types of interpretations are taken together, they provide a relatively thorough understanding of political dynamics in the United States.

Robert Dahl (1982) is a well-known proponent of pluralist argument. He has written that power is diffused across all of American society, which means rarely does only one small group control the power and set in motion all the critical decisions for a society such as the United States. Instead, building on Weber's theories, Dahl and other pluralists suggest that power has many dimensions. In other words, the population, including elites, is likely to be divided on any given issue.

Power can be based on wealth, personal charisma, the favorable evaluation of others, or **prestige**, and it can be based on special access to society's resources or **privilege**. Pluralist arguments emphasize that these bases of power rarely converge to the point that only a very small group of individuals controls the entire political arena in a representative democracy. Rather, the political process should be understood as a system of negotiations where no individual party can ever expect to gain victory in the pursuit of all of their goals. The constantly shifting compromises and alliances bring different interest groups together, resulting in political decisions that enjoy a broad support base. In essence, from a pluralist perspective, when the decision-making process is taken as a whole in the representative democracy, the outcomes represent the greatest good for the greatest number of people.

Social conflict interpretations argue the opposite. The conflict theorist C. Wright Mills argued that there are three main sectors of society in the United States: the economy, the government, and the military. According to Mills, there exists a **power elite** that traverses all three of these sectors. This power elite, comprising the very wealthiest families, exerts a highly disproportionate influence in determining the course of politics and socio-economic outcomes in the United States. While pluralists emphasize that each American has the right to have their voice heard, social conflict theorists like Mills argue that in actuality, only the voices of a slim minority of wealthy individuals (the power elite) really count. Social-conflict theorists are not the only ones who have seriously questioned the political and distributional dynamics of America. Even our former president, Dwight David Eisenhower, a World War II general, warned the country to beware of what he referred to as the **military-industrial complex.**

Certainly, these two interpretations could be treated as contending views of the American political arena. Our preference, however, is to emphasize that when these two interpretations are taken together, they provide a reasonably realistic and thorough understanding of American politics. Comparatively speaking, the representative democracy of the United States permits citizens to exercise individual voting rights and a broad range of political and economic freedoms. That being said, it is also true that a small group of people with disproportionate access to wealth and power do indeed exert far greater influence over the political process than do the average citizen or groups of citizens.

Types and Causes of Collective Behavior

The possibility of **dissent** as a result of the functioning of the political system has led sociologists to distinguish between the sorts of dissent-related **collective behaviors** that have little enduring significance, and those that have an enduring impact on society. Sociologists often point to protest movements, crowds, mobs, and riots as types of collective behavior that often have little enduring significance.

At one time or another, we've all been a part of a **crowd**. The crowd is temporary, as people come together to share a common focus of attention. Social interactionists would emphasize that members of a crowd influence one another as they interact and define social situations. There are many types of crowds, some of which involve collections of individuals who simply wish to enjoy the excitement of an event. Other crowds are a great deal more deliberate. The purpose of **protest crowds**, for example, is to exert influence on political processes.

Throughout the history of the United States, as well as other industrial and postindustrial societies, protests have occurred, in which small or sometimes very large groups of individuals gather to collectively voice their concerns over social issues. Protest behaviors are often episodic. While there are rarely highly visible protest movements today, protest movements were common in the 1960s and the 1970s as people collectively displayed their concerns about such issues as civil rights and the participation of the United States in the Vietnam War.

An important distinction to understand is that both crowds and protest movements are different than **mobs**, which are characterized by their high level of emotionality as well as the probability they will engage in some otherwise violent or destructive activity. The media often depicts mobs, frequently showcasing mob hysteria, as in the case of lynching mobs in the early Southern or Western United States. Regardless of venue, mobs are sad reminders of the hysteria that can bring people together, and motivate them to act in grossly irrational and destructive ways.

Another form of collective behavior of interest to sociologists is the **riot**. Like mobs, riots are highly emotional and violent. Unlike a mob or protest demonstration, however, the riot has no central focus and, thus, is undirected. Riots tend to express a bitter rage and often they are very loosely based on identity or labor issues. The spontaneous and chaotic nature of riots, however, makes them more difficult to explain and predict in contrast to mob behaviors, and especially protest demonstrations, which are directed events.

Riots

The aftermath of the Tulsa race riot of 1921, during which hostilities between blacks and whites erupted into several days of violence.

Riots, mobs, crowds, and protest demonstrations are often isolated events. They are generally short-lived, and tend to embrace a relatively small group of people compared to the total population. There are, however, other forms of collective behavior that are more enduring, which involve large numbers of individuals across an entire society, and have lasting significance for the nation. This was certainly true for the Revolutionary War and the Civil War in the United States. Globally, **revolutions**, **rebellions** and **civil wars**, have often changed the character of entire nations in a permanent way. These typically stem from longer-standing social movements. It is to these forms of collective behavior that we now turn.

Social Movements and Their Causes

There is a great deal of debate among scholars about what constitutes civil wars, rebellions, and revolutions. Some have argued, for example, that revolutions are rebellions where dissenters have won in their struggle with the state. For our purposes, what is most significant is that each of these represents a violent social movement that creates a lasting impact on the polity, the economy, and, indeed, the entire structure of the society. In these aspects, social movements differ significantly from the other forms of collective behavior discussed earlier.

The fundamental importance of these social movements underlies the attention that sociologists have given them, in order to explain why people collectively challenge governments and change entire social systems. When considering the interpretations, we can again divide their analysis into either a social function or a social conflict orientation.

Social Functions in Social Movements. From a social function perspective, social movements differ greatly from everyday political activities. Rather, they are viewed as large-scale cathartic experiences for the participants, resulting from a venting of pent up emotions. Social functions arguments place a premium on the equilibrium of societies. Social movements are viewed as a challenge to that equilibrium, typically made by individuals as attempts to alleviate their personal frustrations.

Gustav LeBon was an early theorist adopting this perspective. LeBon, a French aristocrat who viewed the French revolution and the overthrow of the old French order disfavorably, was a social critic who argued that when individuals gather together for social movements, they exhibit new psychological characteristics. Indeed, the conscious personality of individuals seems to disappear in crowds and a collective mentality takes over. People are caught up in the frenzy of the gathering and they quickly become irrational.

American sociologists Park and Burgess (1924) further elucidated the stages of social movements in the 1920s, although some of their understandings run in parallel with those offered by LeBon. They felt social movements begin with a crowd milling about, after gathering for dissent due to their uncertainties and stress. On the heels of their "milling about," crowds develop a leadership structure. They form an organization based on ideological dogmatism. Following these initial organizational steps, a broad-based acceptance and institutionalization of the organization and its doctrines appear.

This is not far from the ideas of Émile Durkheim (1897/1951) and Talcott Parsons (1951), who presented the themes of what may loosely be referred to as "social disorganization." Their work suggests that rapid structural or demographic changes in societies produce widespread social disorganization, which in turn, gives rise to individual strain, ultimately leading to collective action. Rapid transformations disrupt prior equilibrium in a social system and thereby adversely affect the integrative functions of social groupings (Durkheim 1951). Such disruptions create strain in individuals who then engage in irrational collective behavior in the absence of group restraint as they seek release for their tension. Disorganization themes thus consider the effects of large-scale or macrophenomena on individual psychological states and the influence of the latter on social movements.

William Kornhauser (1959) offered a similar interpretation of social movements. Social movements, he argued, attract individuals who feel insignificant and isolated from society, and therefore have more of a personal than a political complexion. It is alienated and unconnected individuals who are drawn to them.

Relative Deprivation Theory. Another important orientation to the causes of social movements, **relative deprivation** analyses rely on varying conceptualizations of the discrepancy between what people have and what they expect. An overriding assumption of this framework is that a social system remains in equilibrium and free from collective movements when peoples' expectations match their achievements. However, when expectations and achievements become decoupled, expectation/achievement gaps result in individual frustration and anger, which often collectively translate into politically directed aggression.

Among the most important works in this perspective are those of Davies (1970). Davies has argued that collective violence is most likely to occur when a long period of rising expectations and rising gratifications is followed by a short period of sudden reversal, during which the gap between expectations and gratifications quickly widens and becomes intolerable. Davies uses evidence from social movements as diverse as Door's Rebellion of 1842, the French and Russian Revolutions, and black and student unrest in the United States during the 1960s to substantiate his claims.

Gurr (1970) offered another relative deprivation approach, arguing that the fundamental cause of **civil strife** is deprivation-induced discontent. As the discrepancy between what people believe they deserve and what they think they are capable of attaining increases, so too does their discontent, Gurr explained. The more intense and widespread discontents are in a society, the more intense and widespread social movements are likely to be. For this reason, the *scope* and *intensity* of the expectations/achievements gap is vitally important in Gurr's theory.

A condensed version of Gurr's argument is that social and psychological factors lead to perceptions of relative deprivation, which spawn discontent ("potential for political violence"), causing political violence (of various forms). Although objective conditions may be important to Gurr's causal scheme, it is important to remember that primacy is placed on subjective interpretations. In other words, the basic, catalyzing condition for social movements is discontent stemming from the *perceptions* of relative deprivation. Gurr successfully brings together basic themes from social interaction interpretations and macrosocial forces, such as social movements.

Although perceptions, aspirations, and societal conditions are focal points in relative deprivation treatments, other social forces are important as well. Society's institutions play a crucial role in absorbing, deflecting, or channeling discontent rather than allowing it to manifest as violent collective action, for example. Gurr's (1970) relative deprivation paradigm further suggests that cultural proscriptions against overt aggression, the degree of success of past political violence, and regime legitimacy play conditioning roles in the translation of deprivation into collective political strife. Thus, legitimate authority, whether due to traditional, charismatic, or rational-legal leadership, is a foundational source of societal stability.

Social Conflicts and Social Movements

Whereas social function approaches emphasize the normality of social equilibrium and the irrationality that generates social movements, social conflict theories offer a counterpoint—namely, that much of social movement behavior is indeed rational. Social conflict interpretations view social movements as normal consequences of the social structure. A particularly significant contribution to the social conflict approach to movement causation is offered by resource mobilization studies.

Resource Mobilization. The resource mobilization approach to collective violence has stressed changing power balances among contending collectivities in a society (for a discussion see Smelser 1962). Moving a causal step closer to the phenomenon of interest than do relative deprivation theorists, resource mobilization theorists, rather than focusing on gaps between expectation and achievement, argue that there is always a potential pool of discontents in society. Thus, they focus on the organizational capacities of collectivities (and the outside restraints), which facilitate or inhibit the achievement of group objectives.

Resource mobilization theorists have proposed that an emphasis on the accumulation of power resources, the mobilization of these resources, and subsequent resource-based power struggles among contending collectivities provides a fruitful approach to understanding social movements and collective violence. For instance, Tilly (1975) makes the case that within any specified population there always exists basic groups of political actors: the **government**, or state, the organization which controls the principal concentrated means of force; and **contenders** for power, or groups within a certain population which collectively apply resources to affect government from time to time. These contenders are of two basic types: (a) **polity** members (i.e., those who have gained a "legitimate" influence position within the polity); and (b) **challengers** or non-members. Within every polity there is ongoing power struggle among challengers, polity members, and for government. From this perspective, grievances and deprivations are an inevitable factor in society, and what is necessary for political action is the mobilization of necessary resources. Consequently, the organization of discontent is crucial to action. At the same time, successful organization is not an inevitable factor, since constraints on mobilization emerge due to member commitment, group structure, the larger societal structure, and the group's current stock of resources.

Within this paradigm of constant power struggle, collective violence and social movements are most likely to occur when one group lays claim to a set of resources, and at least one other group challenges that claim. Mobilization capabilities largely determine the outcome of such conflicts. In other words, groups are most likely to be victorious when they have better resources such as leadership, size, organization, and supplies, and when their opposition has less access to these things.

There is a natural affinity between resource mobilization theory, and Ralf Dahrendorf's work from an earlier chapter. In both, conflict flows from unequal power and the recognition of that, typically as articulated and mobilized by competent or charismatic leadership.

Attempting a Theoretical Synthesis

The strengths of the resource mobilization perspective are in its attention to the importance of power balance among contenders. However, it has been criticized for, failing to identify the critical antecedents to social movements. A synthetic approach which addresses this issue, as well as mobilization dynamics, is offered by Smelser (1962). Smelser posits a structural strain theory, which identifies critical factors to social movements.

Structural conduciveness is one of these factors. It explains that while all societies experience certain social problems, some of those problems, such as poverty, are more critical, thus making them especially conducive to producing social movements. When a society is unable to meet the routine expectations of its people, such as in the delivery of basic resources, structural strain ensues. With the advent of structural strain, social interactions serve to spread interpretations of the strain. Clear understanding and articulation of the strain then lead to a fruition of organized dissatisfaction by the masses. Smelser recognizes that this sort of discontent can happen over a long period of time, but sometimes with the spark provided by a specific event, **precipitating factors** provide a catalyst for the social movement to erupt. It is at this point that a mobilization for action occurs. That is, the resources discussed by resource mobilization theorists are put into action. At this stage, the behavior of authority becomes critical—whether traditional, charismatic or rational-legal. Agents of authority, such as the police, the military, and more generally, public officials, can fail to stifle a social movement by insufficient power, by their ineptitude, or by their seeming lack of concern with the grievances held by members of the movement.

World Market Forces

The social function and social conflict models discussed thus far appear especially apt at explaining past and present social movements in the core, or Western countries. However, it overlooks the vital dynamic of social conflicts in *peripheral* countries that have occurred in the last century. This is the role of international forces in producing social movements outside the core of the world system.

Although not as common, several relevant analyses have considered international economic factors in their descriptions of mass political violence. For instance, Hobsbawm (1959) examined the introduction of capitalist legal and social relationships into southern rural Spain during the first half of the nineteenth century. This infiltration of capitalist market forces, he argued, led to destabilization of the traditional authority of the church and the feudal land-holding system, resulting in "cataclysmic consequences," including widespread rebellion against the new economic paradigm.

Wolf's (1969) comparative case study similarly maintained that the penetration of Western capitalism into peasant economics created fertile conditions for revolution in a number of countries, including Cuba, Mexico, and Algeria. He argued that because capitalism is impersonal, **market forces** led to major social dislocations such as the breakdown of traditional authority and its protective structures, which in turn instigated insecurity and rebellion among peasant populations. It is interesting to note that traditional authority and "power elites" are essentially perceived by the peasants as providing more protection than the new capitalist alternatives, which, as we discussed earlier, introduced many components of rational-legal authority to the society. Although commercial forces affected both poor and "middle-class" peasants, as resource mobilization themes would suggest, only the latter stratum was able to initiate widespread social movements, due to its organizational and tactical capabilities.

The rapid intrusion of commercial market forces is also considered in Tilly's (1964) analysis of the Vendee revolution in post-1789 France. He emphasized that the Vendee revolt against Jacobin reforms originated in a region that was relatively unaccustomed to commercial agriculture and that neighboring towns, which were already commercialized, had no interest in rebelling against the Republican government. It is worth noting that the peasant movements in Tilly's treatment occurred over two centuries ago, so it stands in sharp contrast to others that emphasize more contemporary social movements in peripheral countries. When considered alongside other studies, nevertheless, his social conflicts model suggests that international forces, national forces, and mobilizations jointly determine social movements. The evidence suggests, too, that the combinations of causes for collective behaviors may be quite different around the world. Let's consider this possibility.

A Global Approach to Social Movements

Taking as a whole many of the arguments made thus far, it would appear that the direction of social movements is heavily influenced by groups' **organizational capacity** for collective action, their **beliefs** especially about the effectiveness of political contention, the structure of **incentives** to pursue political action, and the current and past **behaviors of authorities**. *Organizational capacity* refers to a group's control of a wide range of resources, either generated internally (e.g., numbers of loyal members or organization dues), or provided by external sources (e.g., supportive groups). *Beliefs* refer to individual and collective perceptions of the likely risks and rewards of a social movement, and incentives are the probability of achieving political and economic advantages. The behavior of authorities includes the prior and anticipated future actions on the part of elites and their delegated agents of social control, such as the police or military.

The likelihood a group will engage in a social movement tends to increase when their capabilities are high, the structural incentives are high, there are favorable risk/reward ratios, and when the state does not interfere with their resource accumulation and mobilization. For example, in a wealthy democracy characterized by rational-legal authority, power groups are likely to engage in limited conflict, though seriously violent conflict with the state would be both unwise and unnecessary.

Keep in mind that while these sets of variables may be helpful in explaining conflict from a global perspective, they may operate in fundamentally different ways depending upon variations in national political systems and authority types. Commonly, the frameworks reviewed earlier are based on Western democratic systems only, and assume: 1) the prevalence of monetary resources; 2) an increasingly wealthy society with wider distribution of discretionary funds; 3) a sympathetic elite, or democratic processes that will respectively generate and distribute resources; 4) reasonable risk/reward ratios; and 5) a general lack of state interference with effective mechanisms (e.g., media advertising) for accumulating resources.

These conditions, of course, are not present throughout the world. Thus, there are *cross-national* variations in domestic conflict profiles: core nations tend to experience increased protest activity, but very little intense political contention such as social movements; whereas peripheral nations tend to experience minimal protest, but are more likely to see violent social movements. Because of their relative position, semiperipheral locations tend to inhibit power struggles. Nonetheless, they are sometimes the site of violent conflict and social movements.

World System Position, Political Economy, Mobilization for Collective Action

World-system themes and the conclusions discussed earlier suggest several primary correlates of structural position in the international system. First, the dynamics of world capitalism have resulted in an accumulative wealth advantage and disproportionate rates of *economic growth* for core countries relative to the periphery and, to a lesser extent, the semiperiphery (Chirot 1977). Second, core countries exert greater legitimate state authority than peripheral and semiperipheral nations, due in part to their economic status and growth.

In the core, several factors combine to reduce the frequency and intensity of conflict. Strong and legitimate states more effectively institutionalize conflicts among internal parties (e.g., labor and management) by developing and enforcing rules of the game. The state itself is unlikely to become embroiled in mass social movements of intense conflict because its very strength and capacity for social control, when necessary, discourage efforts to seize the government. Moreover, that capacity rarely needs to be fully exerted since politics in the core is not a "one-winner and one-loser" or **zero-sum game**. The democratic political system of the core, coupled with an increasing pool of economic resources, results in a high probability that groups seeking recognition and/or material benefits will actually acquire some of them. Further, the characteristic rational-legal authority structures of the core bureaucratize and legitimate bounded political conflicts. This type of opportunity, or cost structure does encourage the formation of sporadic conflicts such as riots, or conflict groups with limited goals, such as protests or strikes.

Furthermore, it is even more likely from the perspective of the population at risk for recruitment into such groups—there is a relatively large pool of people in the democracies of the core who are unwilling to risk involvement in unlimited political conflict or in governmental changes that such conflict may initiate.

In the periphery, on the other hand, these structural conditions fundamentally differ, as do the corresponding forms and magnitudes of political struggle. Several factors taken together tend to ensure that the typically weaker peripheral states are neither able to effectively institutionalize conflicts among conflicting parties as democracies do, nor are they easily able to deter attempts at government overthrow. Some of these factors include world historical conditions, internal political and economic attributes, and direct foreign (e.g., CIA) interference with governmental control. Incentives to seize the state are further heightened by the difficulty of acquiring political influence in circumstances where authority rests on the inheritance of traditional power structures such as monarchies. Because these alternatives are inaccessible, in other words, politics more closely resembles a zero-sum game. Indeed, the conventional model of political challenges developed for Western political arenas may be largely inapplicable under these conditions.

In such settings, there is a large pool of individuals with relatively less to risk and more to gain from violent social movements. This revolutionary potential is further heightened by direct foreign interference into the internal affairs of peripheral countries. In the not too distant past, for example, competing global **power blocs** that were mainly capitalist (NATO) or "communist" (Warsaw PACT) have propped up contending factions in the periphery. This can be seen in foreign arms sales to insurgents, often accompanied by corresponding provision of arms, troops, advisors, economic aid, etc., to beleaguered governments (e.g., in the 1950s, 1960s, and 1970s, Vietnam, Congo, Somalia/Ethiopia).

Consequently, although there have been some recent changes, the periphery has been characterized more by conflicts of unlimited means, mass social movements, and unlimited ends (revolutions) and less by the types of conflict that are typically found in core settings. In a way, international political and economic domination of the periphery by the core has become a mechanism whereby conflicts with revolutionary potential are "transferred" from one position to another in the world system. In other words, the international division of labor perpetuates differences in the political authority structures between developed and developing nations. These differences, in turn, may ultimately serve to deflect revolutionary social movements from the core into the periphery.

The most recent example of this type of conflict in non-core countries is seen in the Middle East, particularly Iraq, Syria, and Afghanistan. The militant group known as ISIS (Islamic State of Iraq and Syria), which has been designated as a terrorist organization by the United Nations, has sought to seize control of Iraq, Syria, and other parts of the Middle East through violent means. The militant group known as Al-Qaeda is a global organization, but it operates primarily in Middle Eastern peripheral countries. Like ISIS, Al-Qaeda engages in violent conflict to achieve its goals. The conditions often found in non-core nations, such as political instability and poverty, make it more likely that such types of conflict will arise.

It is possible that democratization movements can initiate substantial changes in the political systems of peripheral and semiperipheral nation. However, at this point, it is simply too early in the process to know whether democracy can be institutionalized in countries saddled with poverty and thus less able to provide substantial resources to domestic contenders before they initiate social movements.

It is instructive to take note of the experiences of some semiperipheral countries since the end of the Second World War. During this period, semiperipheral (or semicore) countries in Eastern Europe came as close to totalitarian regimes as any countries in the modern era. Many of the conditions that motivated violent social movements in the periphery (e.g., difficulty of acquiring political influences, zero-sum political circumstances) were present as well in Eastern Europe. However, the strength of the state, especially as they were supported by the Soviets, as well as the totality of the rule, successfully inhibited the sort of political challenges throughout Eastern Europe that have characterized the periphery of the world system. When conflict finally erupted, much of the state itself became party to revolutionary change, and thus zero-sum circumstances, along with violent social movements, were largely avoided. The lasting impact of such changes, however, is open for debate in Eastern Europe and elsewhere.

We encounter a number of lessons arising from a cross-national analysis of polity, authority and social movements, irrespective of the outcomes of the global movement towards democratic political systems. One important understanding is that political systems and authority structures interact with a number of other domestic forces in producing collective behavior, including social movements. Another point worth emphasizing is that, despite obvious contrasts in emphases, most of the political interactions reviewed in this chapter, rather than standing in stark opposition to one another, are in fact complementary. A final observation is that the multifaceted experiences of different nations around the world system suggest that theories of polity and society must be broadly nuanced to sufficiently explain a wide range of diverse political experiences the world over.

Current Trends in American Politics

In the 2014 midterm elections, the Republican Party took control of the Congress with sweeping victories in both the House of Representatives and the Senate. In the 2008 and 2012 presidential elections, the Democratic Party took control of the executive branch with Barack Obama winning both elections. Prior to that, the Republican Party controlled the executive branch for two consecutive terms. As predicted by the Neo-Machiavellian theorist, Vilfredo Pareto, earlier in the twentieth century, public preference in political parties tends to be cyclical, oscillating back-and-forth, as is demonstrated by election results over time. What seems to be rather steady as of late, however, is the overall decline in confidence that Americans have in government.

In a 2013 survey of U.S. citizens, it was found that only 10 percent of Americans had "a great deal" or "quite a lot" of confidence in the Congress. This figure stood at 37 percent for the presidency and 34 percent for the Supreme Court (Gallup 2013). This is in contrast to the confidence they felt regarding other types of institutions, such as organized religion (47 percent) and the public school system (32 percent). This may help to explain lower voter participation in recent elections. In fact, by 2013, of all the institutions, respect for the polity had dipped the lowest. At the other end of the spectrum, the military ranked highest in public confidence (76 percent).

Despite the fact that voting-age population increased by about 8 million between 2008 and 2012, the number of actual voters fell from about 131 million to 126 million. In the 2012 election, voter turnout was down in every state except for Iowa and Louisiana (Bipartisan Policy Center 2013).

Between 1960 and 1996, voter turnout in presidential elections declined steadily with the exception of the 1984 and 1992 presidential elections. Then, beginning in 1996, there was an increase in voter turnout for three elections in a row. The 2008 presidential election saw the highest voter participation rate in 40 years with 56.8 percent of U.S. adults voting.

Public opinion tends to shift over time when it comes to important political issues, such as gun control, gay marriage, and abortion. Support for the protection of gun rights is at its highest in more than two decades. As of 2014, 52 percent of U.S. adults say it is more important to protect gun ownership rights, while 46 percent say it is more important to control gun ownership. In 1995, these figures were reversed, with 57 percent saying that it was more important to control gun ownership, and 34 percent saying that it was more important to protect gun rights (Pew Research Center 2014).

When it comes to abortion, public opinion has not shifted quite as dramatically as gun control. Overall, the percentage of Americans who believe abortion should be legal in all or most situations has declined from 60 percent in 1996 to 54 percent in 2013. In that timeframe, the percent of Americans who believed abortion should be illegal in all or most cases remained fairly steady at 38 percent in 1996 and 40 percent in 2013 (Pew Research Center 2013).

Between 1996 and 2014, support for gay marriage increased dramatically. In 1996, only 27 percent of Americans supported same sex marriage, compared to 54 percent in 2014. The percentage of U.S. adults who oppose same-sex marriage fell from 65 percent in 1996 to 39 percent in 2014 (Pew Research Center 2014).

CHAPTER SUMMARY

- Power is not the same thing as force or authority.
- Max Weber delineates three major types of authority—traditional, charismatic, and rational-legal.
- There are four major types of political system—democracy, monarchy, authoritarian, and totalitarian. The system of the United States is a representative and indirect democracy, characterized by a high level of voter apathy and the operation of special interest groups.
- Pluralist and power-elite interpretations of the distribution of power in the United States should be considered in conjunction, in order to shed light on the American polity and society.
- There are many types of explanations of collective behaviors. Social function and social conflict interpretations respectively emphasize system equilibrium and individual pathology, or conflicts between people or groups seeking resources.
- A synthesis of interpretations appears necessary, as does theorization based on the very different polities and societies characteristic of core, semiperiphery (semicore), and periphery nations.

16 Population and Modernity

In 2011, the world reached a major milestone—human population reached 7 billion, and today that number is rising. The United Nations predicts that if current population trends are maintained, the world population will reach 8 billion by 2025, 9 billion, by 2050, and 11 billion by 2100.

Let us put this growth into perspective. It took all of human history until 1900 for the world population to reach 1 billion people. Then, it grew to seven times that in only about 111 years. This exponential growth has a myriad of sociological implications involving crime, poverty, health, the environment, and sustainability, to name a few. These are the issues that we will address in this chapter.

Demographic Transition Theory

There are many sociological frameworks that are utilized to examine the characteristics of human populations. The **demographic transition theory** is a model used to explain population trends within societies as they transition from undeveloped societies to developed modern societies. Essentially, the theory emphasizes the connection between fertility rates, mortality rates, and modernization. Using this model, we observe four stages of demographic transition. **1)** The first stage characterizes undeveloped societies, which exhibit high fertility rates and high mortality rates. High mortality rates are due, in part, to the relative absence of quality healthcare and medical advancements. In such societies, families tend to have more children, which increases the likelihood that at least some of their children will survive into adulthood. **2)** During the second stage, as modernization occurs, mortality rates decline. This occurs because modernization is generally coupled with medical advancements, better healthcare, and improved food supply. Naturally, life expectancy increases and more people survive into old age. During this stage, fertility rates remain high. Because fertility rates remain high and mortality rates decline, the population increases dramatically. **3)** As modernization continues to occur, fertility rates drop significantly during the third stage. **4)** A stable population characterizes the final stage, as people live longer lives, on average, and people have fewer children. In other words, fertility rates and mortality rates are low and steady. During this stage, some societies experience a decline in population because birth rates have become so low.

Demographic Transition Theory

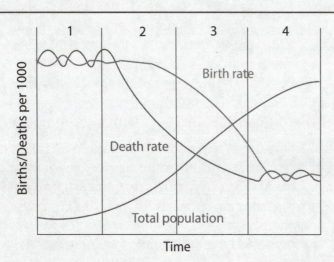

The demographic transition theory helps to explain why the fastest growing cities in the world are in semiperipheral countries. As you will recall from Chapter 10, semiperipheral countries are the middle-income countries of the world. They are more developed than peripheral countries, but less developed than the core countries. The fertility and mortality rates in semiperipheral nations, such as India and China, resemble the second stage of demographic transition. These nations experience high fertility rates and declining mortality rates, compared to the most developed nations in the word, which results in fast-growing populations.

Population and Environmental Impact

In our ever-growing world, there is an increasing concern about the level of environmental degradation that is occurring. After all, the everyday practices of the world's 7 billion people are not without implications. As such, scientists have developed a number of ways to measure environmental impact. One model, developed by biologists Barry Commoner, Paul Ehrlich and environmental scientist John Holdren (now senior advisor to Barack Obama on science and technology issues) emphasizes the relationship among three major factors: population, affluence, and technology. The formula used to illustrate this model is quite simple—(Environmental) **Impact = Population x Affluence x Technology**. This formula is well known today as simply **IPAT**. **Population** undoubtedly plays a role in the environmental impact of a society. More people simply require and use more resources. **Technology** also plays a role. In developed societies, advanced technology allows people to easily exploit the earth's resources. Think, for example, about the ease with which people in the United States can obtain clean drinking water, compared to people in many African nations. This is largely a result of sophisticated water processing facilities and plumbing systems that distribute water to homes. The technology and infrastructure used for such a process is virtually non-existent in some parts of the world. The other element, **Affluence**, refers to the means of a society to obtain and use resources. This is different than the technological aspect of the IPAT model. There is a relatively high level of affluence in highly developed societies, which means many people within those societies possess the means to obtain environmental resources. Water usage is high in the United States compared to Africa, for example, simply because many families can afford to use as much water as they wish. We will delve into this in greater depth in the next chapter.

Population Pyramids

The study of populations involves much more than simply measuring the number of people in a society and predicting resource usage. There are many nuances that must be taken into account. The work of demographers involves examining and, to some degree, predicting age and gender ratios within a society. The implications of these ratios are great and we will discuss them throughout this chapter. The data used by demographers are often quite complex and sometimes more easily interpreted through a visual illustration. One such type of illustration is called a **population pyramid**. The population pyramid is an important tool because it allows demographers to present the internal distribution of a population in a manner that is easy to comprehend.

A population pyramid illustrates the number of males and females within each age group. The age groups are typically represented in intervals of five. In the pyramid for Central African Republic, one can see a large number of males and females in the younger age groups, and fewer

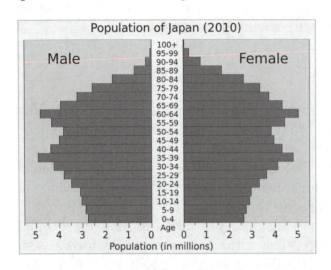
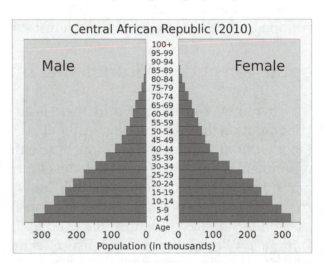

people in the older age groups. This indicates a high fertility rate. The first and most obvious conclusion to be drawn from this distribution is that the population of Central African Republic, like other peripheral countries, will grow rapidly in the coming years. With the majority of the population being at the bottom of the pyramid (younger age groups) the population will increase as these age groups move into reproductive age.

Contrast this with the population pyramid for the developed country of Japan, where the pyramid is smaller at the bottom, indicating a relatively low number of young people. Looking at the top half of the pyramid, one can see that the majority of the population is age 40 and up (a large proportion of which is in post-reproductive age). Because there are fewer people who will reach reproductive age in the coming years, there is likely to be a decline in population.

Comparing the population pyramid of Central African Republic and Japan side by side, highlights two different stages of demographic transition: Central African Republic in the undeveloped stage, and Japan in the modern, postindustrial stage.

Issues in Current Population Trends

The age distribution in Central African Republic is similar to many of the world's undeveloped nations. This has the potential to present many problems for poor, undeveloped nations. If populations increase in societies where poverty is prevalent and resources are already scarce, more strain is added to the people and government of those societies. In many undeveloped countries, particularly in Africa, there is a shortage of clean drinking water, medicine, healthcare, and food supply. These problems will undoubtedly be compounded when populations increase.

As you can probably guess, the age distribution in Japan is similar in other developed nations. In countries like Japan, Canada, United States, and Switzerland, birth rates are relatively low, and people are living longer. The average life expectancy in Switzerland, for example, is 83, compared to only 49 in Central African Republic. There are important issues to consider in societies with declining populations. One such issue that has received a fair amount of media coverage in the United States is Social Security. Millions of retired people in the United States rely on Social Security in order to meet their basic needs. As people live longer lives, they rely on Social Security for a longer period of time. The average life expectancy for Americans in the 1930s when Social Security was enacted was about 60 years. Today, life expectancy for Americans is 79. This means that people are drawing from Social Security for much longer than in past decades. Additionally, there are *more* people drawing from Social Security as the number of retired people increases. Following WWII, between 1946 and 1964, a generation known as **baby boomers** began. During this time, there was a boom in the birth rate in the United States. Those baby boomers are now either approaching retirement, or are already in retirement. As a result of the decreased fertility rate, there are fewer people of working age contributing to Social Security. Those people who are in retirement stand to suffer if there are inadequate funds for Social Security.

As you can see, the practical uses of demography and population pyramids are important. The data upon which population pyramids are based are extremely useful for policymakers around the world. There is serious debate in government about how to deal with the potential Social Security crisis as well as other issues that may arise from a declining population. Governments around the world are working to deal with lack of resources, poverty, and growing populations. The economic and social implications of such issues are great. Through the use of demography, we get a glimpse of a country's potential future issues that must be addressed.

Sex Ratios

In demography, it is important to consider, not only overall human population, but also sex ratios within societies. Sex ratio refers to the proportion of males to females in a given population. If there were 105 males per 100 females in a population, the sex ratio would be 1.05. If there were 100 males per every 100 females, the sex ratio would be 1.00. Similarly, the sex ratio at birth (SRB) refers the proportion of males to females being born in a given population. The sex ratio at birth in the United States is 1.05, meaning that there are more males being born than females. The overall sex ratio, however, is 1.00. This reflects the higher mortality rate among males. This trend has been observed in most countries of the world throughout history. Some suggest that the higher number of males being born is nature's way of counteracting the disproportionate mortality rates among males and females throughout history.

In a society with normal population distribution, there is roughly an equal amount of males and females. This would seem to be the ideal scenario wherein marital and reproductive norms are maintained. In some countries, however, we see an increasing gap in the sex distribution. In the world's most populous country, China, the sex ratio among 0 to 14 year olds is 1.16. In 1979, the Chinese government instituted a one-child policy in an effort to slow the growing population, which stands at nearly 1.4 billion today. When the law was enacted, the population of China was roughly 975 million; over three times the current population of the United States. The government cited potential overcrowding, as well as economic and environmental strain, which can result from overpopulation, as the reason for enacting the law.

Though it was lifted in 2013, the effects of the 35-year policy are still being experienced, and will continue to be in the coming decades. Estimates of the number of births prevented as a result of the law range from 250 million to 400 million. The law also gave rise to sex-selective abortions. Many families in China preferred their one child to be male. This was due, in part, to culturally imposed ideals. Sons are preferred because of their higher wage-earning capacity and because they can carry on the family name. Additionally, sons are responsible for taking care of their parents in old age. With the advent of ultrasound technology, many parents began to terminate their pregnancy if the sex of the child was female. In a country with over a billion people, the unequal sex at birth ratio results in a significant excess of males in the population. Sex-selective abortion and the problems associated with it are also seen in India, the world's second most populous country. Estimates of the sex ratio at birth are as high as 1.25 in some Indian states. In the next 20 years, there is expected to be a 10-20 percent excess of young men in China and India (Hesketh et al. 2011).

The millions of excess males in those Asian countries, many who are poor and uneducated, see diminished marriage prospects and social opportunity. In those countries, as in the United States, young, unmarried males carry out the majority of violent crime. The more obvious result is that many males will be unable to marry and have children. In China, 94 percent of unmarried people between the ages of 28 and 49 are male. Of those, 97 percent have not completed high school (Hesketh et al. 2011).

Life Expectancy

The differences between undeveloped and developed nations around the world are undoubtedly reflected in average life expectancy. As you can probably guess, the least developed nations in the world, the majority of which are in Africa, have the lowest average life expectancy. The average life expectancy in Sierra Leone is 45 years. In Botswana, it is 47 years. Those averages are extremely low when compared to the developed, Western nations of the world. In Switzerland, the average life expectancy is 83 years. In nearby Sweden, it is 81 years. Such disparities are observed throughout the world. With little access to quality healthcare and advanced medicine, those in poor, undeveloped countries simply die much younger, on average, than those in developed nations.

In the aforementioned impoverished African nations, as in other undeveloped nations, high fertility rates cause the population to increase at a rate much greater than the supply of food and resources. Thomas Malthus was one of the first to write about this problem. During the early part of the Industrial Revolution he warned that, while the production of resources, such as food, increases arithmetically (linearly), population increases geometrically (exponentially). In essence, human populations grow faster than resources are produced. This, of course, leads to a shortage of food and resources in societies with fast growing populations. Additionally, the governments of impoverished nations often do not have adequate funds to tackle large-scale deficiencies in food and healthcare.

Discrepancies in life expectancy are also seen between males and females around the world. Female life expectancy has long exceeded male life expectancy in virtually every country in the world. In the United States, females are expected to live an average of 81 years, while males are expected to live only 76 years. This discrepancy has a number of implications. The first of which is that women significantly outnumber men in older age groups. In 2010, two thirds of those over the age of 85 were women. This goes a long way in explaining why the majority of those in nursing homes are women.

Over the next few decades, the United States is projected to see major growth in its older population. In 2050, the number of Americans over the age of 65 is projected to be 88.5 million (Current Population Reports, U.S. Census Bureau 2010). To put that figure into perspective, consider that in 2010, the number of Americans over 65 was only about 17 million. This projected increase in older Americans is likely to impact the organization and delivery of healthcare as the industry experiences a shift towards the treatment of a greater number of chronic diseases, such as Alzheimer's, heart disease, and osteoporosis (Wiener and Tilly 2002).

Population and Resources

Over the last century, we have seen exponential population growth in the world. As we have discussed, much of that growth continues today in the world's poorest nations. As populations grow, so too does the concern over resources and sustainability. At the current growth rate, how many people can be supported?

Mathematical biologist Joel Cohen stands at the forefront of this subject. In his book, Cohen (1995) addresses the issue of population growth and sustainability. Central questions raised in the book are, not only "How many people can the earth support?" but "How many at what level of material well-being?" and "How many with what technology?" Put another way, what will the quality of life be like for those in the world's impoverished nations where populations are growing the fastest? Cohen says the answer to the question "How many people can the earth support?" is "It depends." In elaborating on this answer, Cohen puts forth the following questions:

1. How will environmental goals be balanced against economic goals? For example, if reducing poverty requires increased industrial and agricultural production in developing countries, can the increases in production be achieved at acceptable environmental costs?

2. How will national sovereignty be reconciled with world or regional environmen-

tal and demographic goals? This question arises in the control of migration, reproduction and all economic activities that involve the global commons of atmosphere, oceans, and international bodies of water, and the management of the plant and animal populations that inhabit them.

3. How will the desire and moral obligation to alleviate poverty and suffering as rapidly as possible be reconciled with the use of local scarcities as an efficient market signal?

4. In efforts to protect the physical, chemical, and biological environments provided by this finite sphere, how will rapid population growth and economic development in poor countries be balanced against high consumption per person in the rich countries? (Cohen 1995)

Cohen concludes that an end to long-term population growth is inevitable, probably within the twenty-first century. The question is, by what means and at whose expense?

Urbanization and Population Density

In 2008, for the first time in human history, the majority of people in the world lived in urban areas. Today, rapid population growth in urban areas is a trend that continues. The trend originated during the Industrial Revolution, during which time production and employment increased in urban areas, resulting in population shifts. For most of human history, however, people have been spread out in rural areas.

Urbanization/Urban Sociology

Many sociologists, including Georg Simmel and Stanley Milgram, were interested in the effects of urban living on individuals. This research has given rise to a branch of study known as urban sociology.

In the early nineteenth century, London became the first modern city to reach a population of 1 million. According to the United Nations Department of Economic and Social Affairs, there are now 28 megacities (cities with a population of 10 million or more) in the world. A subfield of sociology known as *urban sociology* focuses on the urban and rural areas, and compares the social structure and cultural aspects of each. Urban sociologists examine the social and cultural differences that exist as a result of differing degrees of urbanization. **Urbanization** refers to a process marked by population growth and development in which communities become cities.

German sociologist Georg Simmel (1858-1918) was an early theorist who posited that individuals are significantly impacted by social structure. He argued that urban living had significant psychological effects on the individual. In particular, Simmel argued that the fast pace and intensity of urban living results in insensitivity to others and a lower emotional connection between individuals than is seen in rural areas. In urban areas, according to Simmel, the basis of interaction between people is economic rather than social. Close, personal interaction among people in urban areas occurs much less than in rural communities, as urban dwellers tend to avoid emotional involvement.

The sociological implications of urban living are many. Emile Durkheim noted the importance of "social facts" as external, yet coercive elements of society. Population distribution is an example of a material social fact that is of particular importance here. Durkheim observed the high suicide rate in areas of rapid advancement and increased population, and attributed it to the feeling of disconnection from others that individuals experienced as urbanization occurs. Egoistic suicide occurs when an individual feels little connection with others in their society. As a population grows and differentiation occurs, social bonds can become weakened as personal, emotional involvement with others declines.

Thomas Malthus (1766 - 1834)

Thomas Malthus was the first person to address the problem of diminishing resources and increasing population.

Reflecting earlier work by Emile Durkheim, social psychologist Stanley Milgram wrote that there are three important factors that must be considered when examining urban living and its effect on the individual: the number of people, population density, and homogeneity of the population. Observing these three factors, Milgram noted that when confronted with a large number of strangers on a daily basis, people tend to withdraw from the community and that, in city life, "moral and social involvement with individuals is necessarily restricted" (Milgram 1970). This urban withdrawal that accompanies high population density does, to a degree, help explain higher crime rates in urban areas. In 2010, the violent crime rate known to law enforcement in metropolitan areas was 409.4 per 100,000 people, compared to 177 per 100,000 people in non-metropolitan counties (Uniform Crime Reports 2012).

A central task of demographers is to analyze the ways in which population growth and urbanization affect people's lives. The material well-being of individuals in fast-growing areas is one such consideration. Typically, infrastructure does not develop at the same rate as a population grows. Utilities like water and electrical systems, as well as transportation, housing, communications, sewage, waste disposal, and government services, such as education and law enforcement, are all necessary in modern society. The development of such features, however, tends to lag behind population growth. Essentially, there is a mismatch between growth and society's ability to adapt. As a result, there are many deficiencies in areas of urban growth. This phenomenon is not unlike the aforementioned problems described by Malthus, who warned about the problems associated with population growth and resource lag.

This lag is evident in parts of India where poverty and a skyrocketing population have led to the formation of tent cities. With a lack of housing and sufficient infrastructure, many of the poor live in tents and have virtually no access to the types of services provided in more affluent areas. In the United States, the problem of insufficient infrastructure is seen in areas that have historically or recently experienced significant population growth. Bad roads and bridges, public schools that lack resources, and local governments' inability to address social problems are all signs of lagging infrastructure. Sound infrastructure plays a vital role in a productive and efficient society wherein people thrive and social problems are reduced.

The Functionalist Perspective on Urbanization

As you will recall from Chapter 1, **functionalism** holds that society is made up of interrelated parts that are dependent upon each other for the stability of the whole. Durkheim, upon whose work functionalism is based, was largely devoted to explaining the social phenomena that occur as societies grow. Durkheim wrote that an important feature of urbanization is division of labor. As a population grows, diversity increases, and different groups become dependent on one another to fulfill their tasks. From this perspective, as population density increases, so too does division of labor. This is necessary, according to Durkheim, because division of labor increases productive capacity and creates a feeling of solidarity among people.

From the functionalist perspective, Durkheim viewed crime as a social fact. That is, crime is a feature of society, not necessarily of the individual. Essentially, crime is not necessarily abnormal. Rather, it is an inevitable part of complex societies. A society without crime is impossible because people will naturally deviate somewhat from any established rules or norms. Additionally, Durkheim posited that crime serves a social function because it helps to establish and maintain a consensus about what behavior is acceptable.

Population Density – Attitudes and Culture in the United States

The implications of population density are manifested in the attitudes and beliefs of people and groups across the country. A general trend is that people in rural areas tend to be more conservative, and people in urban areas tend to be liberal. This might seem like a bit of oversimplification, but there is sufficient data showing this to be true. In virtually every presidential election of the last few decades, those who live in the most populous areas of the country have been more likely to vote for democratic candidates, while those who reside in rural areas have, on average, voted for the republican candidate.

To be sure, presidential election results are not the most telling indicator of attitudes and beliefs around the country. A more accurate method would be to examine the views of rural residents compared to urban residents when it comes to the major polarizing social and political issues in the United States: gay marriage, abortion, religion etc.

For quite some time, residents of urban areas have been more likely to support gay marriage than those in rural areas. In fact, the percentage of residents who say they have a "very unfavorable" opinion of gay men is twice as high in rural areas than urban areas (Pew 2003). One explanation for this is that people in urban areas are more likely to be exposed to diverse lifestyles (Rimmerman and Wilcox 2008).

Religiosity is also a factor. Many people who oppose gay marriage cite religion as the basis for their opposition. Generally speaking, intolerance of homosexuality is positively correlated with conservative religious belief (recall from the chapter on religion, however, that there is a great deal of diversity within religion, and so these differences are by no means absolute). Christianity is, of course, the dominant religion in the United States. In rural areas we observe higher religiosity and greater religious homogeneity. This means that the percentage of people who identify as religious and attend church on a regular basis is higher in rural areas, and that there is less diversity in religious beliefs.

Religion is also strongly correlated with views on abortion. Among adults polled in 2013, 80 percent of people who claimed no religious affiliation were pro-choice, while only about 39 percent of Christians, including Catholics, were pro-choice (Gallup 2014). Lower religiosity in urban areas partially explains the fact that residents of urban areas are more likely to believe that abortion is morally acceptable under certain circumstances, such as when childbirth puts the health of the mother at risk.

When discussing the social and political views of those in urban and rural areas, it is important to note that the tendencies mentioned here are just that—tendencies—not absolutes. To be sure, attitudes and beliefs are developed as a result of many factors other than residing in an urban or rural area. So, while there is a correlation between beliefs and population density, there are other factors at play. As you will recall, we touched on this idea in Chapter 2. In science there is a concept known as *ceteris paribus*, a Latin phrase meaning "all other things being equal" or "all other things held constant." This concept definitely applies here. If we were to control for other variables that affect belief, such as religious affiliation, age, and level of education, we would likely see that these variables play a role in the correlation between belief and population density. With the concept of *ceteris paribus* in mind, we are able to see general correlations, but also understand other relevant variables that affect correlations.

Rural and Urban Poverty

Poverty is observed in every region of the country. There are, however, important differences in the way that poverty is manifested in rural areas compared to urban areas. While it is true that a larger percentage of those in poverty live in urban areas, poverty rates are actually higher in rural areas. Poverty is also more persistent in rural areas. This means that those who experience poverty in rural areas often do so for extended periods of time, whereas those in urban areas are more likely to cycle in and out of poverty. In other words, people in urban areas are more likely to experience poverty for a period of time before climbing out of poverty. That is not to say, however, that those in urban areas do not also experience persistent poverty.

In 2012, the overall poverty rate in the United States was 18 percent in non-metro areas, compared to 15.5 percent in metro areas (U.S. Census Bureau 2013). This difference does not tell the whole story, however, because the difference in metro and non-metro poverty rates depends largely on region. The gap between metro and non-metro poverty rates is highest in the South. In 2012, the poverty rate in non-metro areas of the South was 22.1 percent—almost 7 percent higher than the metro poverty rate. Additionally, 84 percent of persistent-poverty counties in the United States (counties wherein 20 percent or more of the population were living in poverty over the last 30 years) are in the South (USDA Economic Research Service 2013).

Mississippi has consistently had one of the highest poverty rates in the United States. It is also one of the most rural states, with the majority of the population living in rural areas. Many of the states in that part of the country wherein a relatively large portion of the population live in rural areas, have among the highest poverty rates in the nation: Louisiana, Mississippi, Georgia, Alabama, Arkansas, Tennessee, Kentucky, and West Virginia, among others. To illustrate the persistence of poverty in rural areas, consider the following: of the nearly 400 counties with poverty rates of 20 percent or higher in every decade since 1959, 95 percent of them are rural (Miller and Weber 2002).

As previously mentioned, the majority of the world's population lives in urban areas. Unsurprisingly, most of the world's poor are in cities, where poverty tends to be concentrated in certain areas. In virtually every large city in the United States, for example, there are specific areas or neighborhoods where poverty is particularly prevalent. In such areas, crime rates are high, employment opportunities are scarce, and education is subpar. Urban minorities are disproportionately affected by poverty. In America's 100 largest metro areas between 2005 and 2009, 71 percent of residents in neighborhoods where poverty rates were over 20 percent were minorities (Kingsley and Pitingolo 2013).

The most prominent sociological theories regarding inner-city poverty, center on social stratification. Social stratification theories seek to explain how social institutions and socioeconomic trends perpetuate poverty. Education, for example, is often discussed as the pathway from poverty to the middle class. Inner-city public schools are often lacking in funds and resources, resulting in insufficient education for poor, urban children. Insufficient primary education, of course, decreases opportunity for higher education, which, in turn, lessens the opportunity for well-paying jobs later in life.

Around the world, just as in the United States, the poorest areas have been poor for quite some time. In the United States, there are areas where poverty is concentrated and persistent. This phenomenon is seen across the globe. Many of the poorest nations in the world are in Sub-Saharan Africa, Central America, and parts of Asia. In these parts of the world, poverty has persisted for much of recent history.

CHAPTER SUMMARY

- Demography is the study of populations, including the distribution and dynamics within populations, and the social factors related to population.
- It is important to examine not only overall population, but also age and gender ratios within populations and the impact of such factors such as health, poverty, resources, attitudes, and growth. Weber delineates three major types of authority—traditional, charismatic, and rational-legal.
- The demographic transition theory is a model used to explain population trends within societies as they transition from undeveloped societies, to developed, modern societies. Essentially, the theory emphasizes the connection between fertility and mortality rates, and modernization.
- Population pyramids are important tools used by demographers, and are used to represent, and make predictions about internal distributions of a population. Using population pyramids, demographers are able to observe and predict age and gender ratios, as well as make predictions about future growth.
- Population density has a number of implications regarding poverty, attitudes, and beliefs. Poverty rates are higher in rural areas, but more concentrated in urban areas. The majority of persistently poor counties are in the South. In metropolitan areas, minorities experience poverty at a higher rate than whites.
- People in urban areas tend to be more liberal, while those in rural areas tend to be more conservative. This is reflected in beliefs about abortion, gay marriage, and religion. It is important to note here that these are merely tendencies rather than absolutes, and that there are variations in beliefs and attitudes.

17 Environmental Sociology

Level of Development, Population, Technology and Carrying Capacity

As we discussed previously, the level of development in a given society is deeply affected by its production capabilities, which in turn are a function of the level of subsistence technology in the society. Use of that subsistence level technology is primarily responsible for a society's capacity to use and recombine natural resources, and to provide sustenance for its population. As technology becomes increasingly sophisticated, that process becomes even more efficient, dramatically increasing production capacity. Thus, the society is able to support a greater number of people. Industrial societies, as we now know, number in the millions. But can that level be sustained indefinitely? This question remains a matter of much research, theory, and debate.

Amos Hawley and Otis Duncan, among other early human ecologists, developed a general framework for human environmental interactions, and devised what they called the **POET model**. In this model, *Population*, (Human Social) *Organization*, *Environment* and *Technology* were the four crucial variables to be considered. That model served as a framework to orient general discussions about human-environmental interactions. This model, however, was unsuccessful at generating much empirical research in the way of assessing the impact that humans have on the environment, and thus to move in the direction of addressing the question of how many people the planet can support.

In the 1970s, a number of researchers (e.g., Commoner 1971, Ehrlich 1968) who were interested in developing more precise ways in which to assess environmental impact modified the POET model. They presented the **IPAT** model, in which (Environmental) **Impact = Population x Affluence x Technology**. This model emphasizes the *interaction* effect of three major factors. Population is an important factor, of course, and as we saw, is very closely linked to the level of technology. Thus, in advanced industrial societies, the combination of large numbers of people with advanced technology and the ability it gives those people to exploit the natural resources has a potentially devastating effect on the surrounding environment.

The third element of **affluence** is important to consider as well. In this model, more affluent societies such as the United States consume resources at a much faster rate than their less developed counterparts. Societies with low levels of affluence are not able to use resources as quickly, and thus have less of an environmental impact than an affluent society using resources at a tremendous rate.

However, this model can be criticized on several grounds. First, as we have now seen, a society's level of population and technology tends to be highly correlated. Further, as population and technology levels profoundly affect the level of affluence, *all three* are highly correlated, and can be thought of as largely coterminous with level of development.

Because of this correlation, one might be tempted simply to posit that level of development is the proximal cause of environmental impact, however manifested. Yet in many cases, the level of development in *not* linearly related to environmental impact. While it is true that the most developed countries tend to use more resources (primarily energy) than less developed countries, the correlation between development and other types of environmental degradation (such as deforestation, greenhouse gas emissions, and toxic waste) is far from linear.

A society that uses its resources sparingly, and which practices either some form of reduction/reuse/recycling of resources, or low-impact industry and farming (such as manufacturing with biodegradable materials, or organic farming), is at least potentially less likely to have a devastating environmental impact than is a society that is perhaps less affluent, but that utilizes its affluence in high-impact ways.

"Human impact on the natural environment..."

Societies that use their resources sparingly, and that practice some form of recycling or reduction of resource use, are less likely to have a damaging impact on the surrounding environment. Societies that do not may, in the near future, find themselves overrun by environmental problems.

In less wealthy countries, resources are often used for subsistence needs, such as wood for heating. In this scenario, there is seldom an interest in efficient resource usage or stewardship of the environment, which leads to the depletion of non-renewable resources, or renewable resources at a rate faster than they can regenerate. Clearly, population is a factor here—increasing numbers of people using these resources tend to have a cumulative impact. But even in this case, it makes a profound difference *where* the population is. The usage of resources in cities is quite different from resource usage in rural areas (Burns et al. 1994). Both, of course, have an impact, but the strain is felt in different ways. City dwellers tend to put a relatively greater strain on energy resources, while those in rural areas tend to put a strain on land usage and forests.

To the extent that environmental consciousness exists, it tends to be among either affluent people in developed countries, or among indigenous tribes, many who live in very underdeveloped societies. As we have noted, the greatest strain on the environment is often seen in rapidly *developing* countries, rather than in very under-developed countries or in developed countries (Burns et al. 1994, 1997, 1998; Kick et al. 1996). This distinction is often overlooked due to a tendency for environmental sociologists, in their considerations of development, to simply dichotomize countries into "more developed countries" (MDCs or "the North"), and "less developed countries" (LDCs or "the South"). Clearly, this is a taxonomic oversimplification that leads to a misconceptualization of the problem.

An important lesson here as elsewhere is to specify concepts with a level of precision that fully utilizes their explanatory power (Jorgenson and Kick 2006). In the social sciences especially, there is a tendency to conceptualize things linearly. Yet some relationships (such as the linkages between development and environmental impact) are neither linear, nor are they necessarily dichotomous. To force the conceptualization into that mode fails to truly address the nature of the relationships, and thus does not serve the cause of understanding the problem as well as it might.

Thus, the question of carrying capacity is an important one, although its models and explanations are still in the process of development. In any case, the roles of population, technology, and social organization and its related aspects, such as relative levels of affluence, are crucial elements that must be considered in any analysis of carrying capacity.

International Development, Inequality, and Resource Depletion

There are many relationships between a country's level of development on the one hand, and a number of other factors related to the environment on the other. Using the *IPAT* model as a starting point, let us now examine a number of factors that have implications in terms of *environmental impact*, and also on the differential carrying capacities of different societies.

As we have seen, *population* growth tends to be inversely related to level of development. While the mortality rate is slightly higher in less developed countries than in more developed countries, the opposite is true of the birth rate. Thus, while the world's population is now over seven billion people and increasing, the greatest population increases are seen in the least developed countries. Unless resources can be increased (through technological advance, for instance), the proportion of resources allocated for any given person, especially in the poorest countries of the world, will *decrease* over time.

While no one knows the exact carrying capacity of the planet for sure, there are a number of tradeoffs that eventually must be made. For example, one of quantity for quality, in which the planet may support a population of upwards of ten billion people, but at a lifestyle greatly diminished from the current one, especially in the core, mass-consumption societies (Cohen 1995).

Historically, the more developed a society, the greater the *urbanization* of that society. A century ago, virtually all of the major cities of the world were in developed countries. Over time, however, the rapidly developing countries, especially those in the semiperiphery, also came to rapidly urbanize. The United Nations (1992) projects that sometime within the twenty-first century, nine of the ten largest cities in the world will be in what world-system theorists would classify as semiperipheral countries.

With urbanization comes the concentration of human-created waste that is produced much faster than the time it takes to biodegrade. Hence, the Third World will likely be even more plagued by a number of environmental problems associated with urbanization in the years to come. However, rural population growth also brings its unique problems. It is often the case that deforestation is precipitated by encroachment into rural areas, for example, and that in turn is related to population growth.

Population growth is related to environmental impact in a number of complex ways (Burns et al. 1998). Ultimately, every individual requires a certain amount of energy to survive. However, the level of *affluence* must be very carefully considered as well. In terms of the level of affluence, there is a great deal of inequality, both within and between countries.

One society's affluence can sometimes have a profound impact on the environment of another society in ways that may not be obvious at first glance. For instance, in Costa Rica, it is estimated that about 85 percent of deforestation has occurred in order to raise cattle for export (Guess 1979). While Costa Rica is considered a semiperipheral country, much of the beef it raises on that land will ultimately be exported to core countries, such as the United States, for consumption in fast food restaurants.

Furthermore, the lifestyles to which people have become accustomed in mass-consumption societies require a great deal more energy consumption. Energy consumption is very highly correlated with a number of *environmental impacts*, most notably greenhouse gas emissions (Burns et al. 1997).

Technology as well is becoming increasingly widespread throughout the semiperipheral societies of the world, although it remains most readily available in core societies. It is true, however, that if environmental regulation is promulgated at all; it tends to be done so primarily in core societies. Thus, the semiperipheral societies often have a combination of technology with little control or *regulation*. This is the reason that semiperipheral societies often see the worst levels of ecological degradation.

Gore (1993), for example, gives a tragic illustration of the Aral Sea drying up, and some of the socioeconomic dynamics leading to it. The Aral Sea had once been the fourth largest landlocked body of water in the world, and had provided the livelihood for thousands of people. Many factors contributed to this, namely an irrigation system that had been used to grow cotton in an otherwise desert climate. The cotton was grown originally for economic reasons—it could draw a better price on the world market than virtually anything else that could be grown there, but only in the short run. In the long run, the diversion of water effectively changed the hydrological cycle in that area. Once the hydrological cycle is changed, it is often changed permanently.

This is a case of technology being sophisticated enough to drastically alter the natural ecology. This occurred as a short-term response to economic pressures for survival in an increasingly competitive world. There was another component to the problem as well—with the dissolution of the Soviet Union, the Aral Sea was no longer entirely in one state (it was in part of two contiguous newly created states, thus rendering environmental regulations insufficient to

Energy Use and Environmental Degradation

In core and semiperipheral nations, energy consumption is positively correlated with greenhouse gas emissions, among other environmental impacts.

address the impact of technological sophistication.

Individual and Group Priorities and Their Implications for the Environment

As a number of theorists have pointed out, individual and group priorities often conflict. For *rational choice theorists* (e.g., Olson 1965; Boudon 1982; Coleman 1986; Hechter 1989), individuals make choices based on **utility maximization** (maximizing their benefits and minimizing their costs).

When an actor such as in individual or a nation-state utilizes the benefits of a resource without taking responsibility for the costs, it is known as a **commons problem** or **the tragedy of the commons** (Hardin 1968). In our last example, with the creation of two independent states, both with access to a common resource of the Aral Sea, there developed an incentive for each to use the resource, with neither taking full responsibility for its stewardship.

People tend to maximize utility based on their own *individual interests*, as Hardin (1968) points out. Both benefit and cost calculations, then, tend to be in terms of how they affect the individual, rather than the collective. Moving up a level of analysis, we have seen how this commons problem can occur between political entities.

In an increasingly competitive world, the commons problem is increasingly likely to occur. As populations continue to increase, and resources are depleted, competition over scarce resources is likely to become more intense.

In situations where the technology is sophisticated but the regulation is primitive or nonexistent, use of technology can lead to ecological catastrophe. Such situations can potentially occur anywhere, but are most likely to occur in places that have experienced political upheaval. Such political instability is most closely associated with semiperipheral countries.

In sum, the theoretical ideas we have discussed, including rational choice theory and the IPAT model, can be applied not only within societies, but on a global scale as well. Societies vary in their environmental impacts, and those are often largely a function of population, affluence, and technology. Increasing population puts strains on the world's resources, and population increases are greatest in the poorest countries. Affluence in one society often can lead to environmental degradation in another society. Technology can sometimes be used to temporarily increase affluence. However, use of technology in this manner, without the **common good** in mind, can lead to ecological catastrophe in the long run.

Environmental damage can have serious and even catastrophic repercussions, the gravest of which often come in the form of threats to health and well-being. A plethora of recent research points out a number of these health problems that can occur as a result of environmental irresponsibility.

Environmental Factors and Public Health

As we now know, environmental degradation has a number of pernicious consequences. While some linkages between the environment and health have been established for a long time, others we are just beginning to understand.

To examine the connection between environmental factors and health, we'll first discuss the question of health and sickness from the perspective of human ecology, or through the lens of adaptation and natural selection. We'll then turn our attention to how selection factors and environmental degradation interact, and how that interaction has consequences for human health.

Why We Get Sick: A Darwinian Approach to Health

Although Darwin proposed his theory of selection over a century ago, and medicine has been around for much longer, there has only very recently been serious theorization in what has come to be called "Darwinian medicine." While it can be quite complex, the book *Why We Get Sick* by Neese and Williams (1994) summarizes this basic theory. The premise is that virtually everything our bodies do is the result of adaptation and natural selection, which takes place over the course of millennia.

Every organism is selected for adaptation to its environment, but we must keep in mind that environments are quite variable, and so "fitness" for one environment may imply lack of fitness for another. That is to say, adaptation to one set of circumstances can be quite maladaptive in another set of circumstances, when taken to extremes. In fact, given a relatively stable environment (when it is not stable, other selective pressures come into play, which we will discuss in turn), there is a natural tendency to avoid extremes or, to put it another way, to strike an optimal *balance point* between extremes.

A wonderful example of the balance principle in practice is height selection. While there are tall and short people, height tends to be a normally distributed trait, with the majority of people tending toward medium height. Tallness was a desirable trait for optimizing the chances of getting enough food, for example, for people to be able to pick fruit as high as possible. On the other hand, smaller people need less food, so would tend to survive times of food shortages better than larger people, all else being equal. The balance principle comes into play as well in explaining a wide array of diseases. Two otherwise disparate examples serve to illustrate this point: sickle cell anemia and allergies.

Sickle cell anemia, so named because of the tendency for blood cells to fold in such a way that they resemble sickles when examined under a microscope, is a debilitating and sometimes deadly disease found among people of African extraction. When a person inherits a recessive trait for sickle cell anemia from one parent, the trait is useful in producing an immune response to malaria. In fact, in areas in which prevalence of malaria has historically been the highest, the trait is most common. For millennia, this trait was selected by virtue of the fact that while many people were dying of malaria, those who inherited this trait were more likely to survive to reproductive age. The problem occurs only when this relatively rare trait is inherited from both the mother and the father. In this case, some of a good thing is adaptive, while too much of a good thing is maladaptive.

In the case of allergies, we find the balance principle in operation as well. Over the course of millennia, our immune systems and other defensive reactions (e.g., sneezing, coughing, vomiting) have adapted to expel foreign substances and disease causing agents ("germs"). In fact, these responses are highly sensitive, and a foreign agent (e.g., a disease causing bacterium) is often combatted by some combination of antibodies and other defensive reactions. An allergic response occurs when this highly sensitive response is heightened to the point of over-sensitivity.

Allergies are most proximally connected to an imbalance of certain parts of the immune system (especially Immunoglobulin-E, or "IgE"). If this balance is disrupted during certain critical periods, the chances of developing allergies go up. Infants who are not breastfed are at higher risk for allergies later in life, probably because they never establish a proper balance in their immune systems. Continued exposure to certain elements, especially during critical periods, disrupts the immune system balance, and thus increases the likelihood of allergy.

The prevalence rate for respiratory allergies is ten times higher now than 150 years ago, Neese and Williams (1994:170) point out. While no one can say for certain why this is, one likely explanation would involve the imbalances in the immune system which are set in motion by lack of exposure to needed elements, or by too much exposure to toxic elements, during critical periods. Immune system imbalances, combined with chronic exposure to toxic elements anytime thereafter, would be likely to set off a hyper-immune, or allergic response.

Thus, the body is a delicate organism, which has adapted to external circumstances over many millennia. The organism requires balance. When the body goes out of balance in some way, the result is typically disease. An imbalance can occur from within the body (as in the example of sickle cell anemia), or can occur when the external environment no longer conforms to what the body and its responses have been selected for.

Natural selection takes place over long periods of time, and works gradually. Thus, while a people can adapt to changes in external circumstances over a number of generations, they can only do so in response to gradual changes. When change occurs more rapidly than a people can adapt to it, a crisis state eventually will occur. What concerns us here are not gradual (in terms of evolutionary time) changes, such as the slow changes from the ice age to warmer temperatures on the earth. Rather, we refer to changes that occur rapidly enough to render adaptation impossible, or at best problematic. When these rapid changes occur, such as the introduction into the environment of toxic chemicals, the environment can be said to be out of balance.

Sickness as a Function of an Environment Out of Balance

In the course of the adaptation and natural selection process, people (and other organisms) tend to develop immune responses to the diseases and other threats to their well-being that are indigenous to the place in which they develop. In malaria-prone regions, for example, people developed defenses against malaria over the course of many generations for the reason that those who did not have such defense mechanisms were far less likely to reproduce. Thus, the genes that survived and were passed on were those that carried the adaptive trait.

In another example, over the millennia, people have adapted to breathing air that is a mixture of oxygen and other substances, such as nitrogen. Selection has ensured that this mixture, or something very close to it, is optimal for human health. When the balance of that mixture is disturbed, such as in the case of elevated levels of methane or carbon dioxide (both of which are naturally occurring—the problem is when they occur in higher concentrations than they otherwise would), the natural environment does not conform to the one adapted to over the course of millennia. When that is the case, a common response is to get sick or, when the imbalances get extreme, to die.

In some limited cases, the immune system can temporarily adapt to minor imbalances (**pollution**) in the natural substances that sustain life (e.g., by coughing on a polluted day, or being lethargic in order to place a somewhat reduced demand on the body for heavy breathing). In more serious cases, the immune system breaks down, and results in more serious maladies, such as cancer of the lymph nodes or other glands.

The vast extent of human evolution took place prior to the mass urbanization that characterizes much of the developed world. Human beings have never fully adapted to life in city environments, being exposed to greater varieties of toxins in greater densities than ever before. Because of the increased probabilities of exposure to toxins, in combination with greater concentrations of waste, areas with very high population density (which would, of course, include cities, but also places such as crowded hospitals, prisons, etc.), tend to be "microbe heavens" (Garrett 1994:235). In fact, until recent times (when the widespread use of pesticides, herbicides and other toxins in agriculture has allowed rural areas to "catch up"), urban areas exhibited higher disease rates and lower life expectancies than did rural areas.

Yet, people often develop immunities after exposure to some toxins over time. Measles, mumps, and chicken pox, for example, tend to promote antibodies to prevent subsequent exposure to the disease. When someone with an immune system that has developed antibodies comes into contact with someone whose immune system has not developed those antibodies, the tendency is for the person without the antibodies to become sick. Because highly urban peoples tend to have developed tremendous numbers of antibodies due to their repeated exposures to toxins, when they come into contact with less urban peoples, the tendency is for the less urban to catch the diseases of the urban peoples more than vice versa. One theory (Crosby 1986; also see McNeill 1976) of how Europeans were able time and again to subdue indigenous peoples

Pesticides

Only about 0.1 percent of pesticides actually are ingested by insects; the other 99.9 percent becomes part of the ecosystem. The increase in pesticide use since WWII has been paralleled by increases in birth defects, many kinds of cancers, and other diseases.

in the new world, is that the diseases Europeans brought incapacitated (and in some cases decimated) indigenous populations.

It is not only humans to whom these principles apply. When living organisms, which have not previously been in contact come into contact, they often exchange their diseases. This is because immune responses have not yet adapted to the "foreign" allergens they encounter. As humans moved from hunting and gathering societies to territorial forms of social organization such as horticultural societies, the domestication of animals came about. Subsequently, a wide variety of theretofore-unknown diseases were introduced to humans (Crosby 1986:31).

As humans and animals come into contact in ways that were previously unlikely or impossible (and the chances for contact increase exponentially with the rise of technology), the balance resulting from millennia of co-evolution can be thrown off. With these imbalances, the advent and spread of new diseases becomes increasingly likely.

One popular theory about the introduction of the AIDS virus to human populations involves the virus "jumping" between species. In this case, there was a simian immunodeficiency virus (SIV) carried in the blood of monkeys that at some point came into contact with human blood. In combination with other elements, the SIV was transformed into the deadly human immunodeficiency virus (HIV). This jumping of species of course is made more likely with increases in human incursions into natural habitats of animals (such as tropical rainforests).

After the jump to humans, the HIV virus spread only with increasing contact among human beings. The spread of the virus is associated with the building of transportation routes, such as the Kinshassa highway through central Africa, because people once in remote villages were now able to come into contact with the world at large.

The use of synthetic pesticides, fertilizers and herbicides has increased tremendously since World War II, as has been pointed out by a number of authors (e.g., Carson 1962; Steingraber 1997). This increase has been paralleled by dramatic increases in a number of diseases, most notably certain types of cancers.

Steingraber (1997) points out that only about 0.1 percent of pesticides actually are ingested by insects; the other 99.9 percent becomes part of the general ecosystem where they are likely to travel far and wide. Colborn et al. (1997), for example, found that particles of toxic chemicals manufactured in Alabama have been traced over thousands of miles—north from Alabama through the Great Lakes and carried from there by eels to the Sargasso Sea in the Atlantic Ocean, back north by other fish eating the eels, all the way to the Arctic where they are ingested by polar bears.

There are important broader questions concerning who is at risk for diseases and other maladies resulting from environmental calamities and other consequences stemming from the imbalances of the natural environment. Certain risks inversely correspond with social class. For instance, poor people, many of whom are minorities, are more likely to live in less desirable areas, such as those near waste dumps, polluting factories, etc. The wealthy are often able to "buy their way out" of such situations, by living in safer, cleaner, environments.

Another factor of concern is that nobody (including EPA "experts") really knows what the true risks are (e.g., Beck 1992). For example, DDT was banned after many of the environmental and health risks associated with it were revealed. Today, however, there are literally thousands of chemicals in use, the associated risks of which are largely unknown for the majority of them.

Ultimately, in a world out of balance, everyone on the planet is at risk. Air and water pollution, global warming, and other environmental problems affect everyone on some level. The effects are not confined to the external environment. Many of the effects are on the health, and sometimes the very life, of human beings and other living creatures.

Culture and the Sociology of Knowledge

As crucial as the work covered thus far is in helping us come to an understanding of humankind's relationship to the natural environment, it is limited in its tendency to focus on the more material causes of environmental degradation. In this section, we consider the harder to measure, but no less important, cultural factors that influence how we interact with the natural environment.

As we saw in our discussion of the IPAT model, for example, the key material variables causing (environmental) Impact, are Population, Affluence, and Technology. The POET model looks at Population, (Human Social) Organization, Environment, and Technology. An array of studies has pointed out a number of qualifications and limitations of this approach, however (e.g., Dietz and Rosa 1994; Kick and McKinney 2014; Burns et al. 1994, 1997, 1998). For example, in his book *Environment, Scarcity and Violence*, Thomas Homer-Dixon (1999) points to a number of times in history when sex ratio differences, particularly when there have been significantly larger numbers of men than women, have had macro level violent outcomes, such as war. In other work (Burns et al. 1994, 1997, 1998), we see that population growth in rural areas tends to be associated with certain kinds of environmental degradation (e.g., deforestation), while urban growth and the related changes in consumption patterns tends to lead to increases in greenhouse gas emissions.

The variants on this theme are nearly endless. The overall point is that to come to a deeper understanding of humankind's effect on the planet more generally, it is important to step back and see a larger picture—(If you can forgive the metaphor, particularly given our discussion of deforestation, it is important not to lose sight of the forest for the trees!).

There is a growing body of work that situates our current condition amidst a rising tide of a culture of modernity going back to the Industrial Revolution, and gaining momentum since then. Ways in which people see the environment, and act toward it, are embedded in the cultural milieu in which they participate. To a large degree, culture arises in the first place out of people reacting to the natural environment of which they are part (Burns 2009).

But over time, particularly with the rise of industrialization, the linkage between the natural environment and the culture tends to get lost. As technology becomes more efficient, and able to extract and recombine the earth's resources more profoundly, people come to see the source of their livelihood arising from technological innovation and the economy (Borgmann 1984; Cobb 1991). These changes take place as part of the large, interconnected processes of modernity.

This culture of modernity largely ignores humankind's primary dependence upon, and embeddedness in, the natural environment (Burns 2009; Primavesi 2003). This is leading to slow and inexorable changes in the earth, in which the cumulative degradation will be so profound as to make the earth virtually uninhabitable unless drastic improvements occur soon (Lovelock 2007).

In the late modern period, there has, to a large degree, developed a culture in which profligate use of resources, and the expectation for even greater consumption in the future, has come to outstrip the planet's natural ability to keep pace (Burns 2009). This has led to a **treadmill of production** (Schnaiberg 1980; Gould et al. 2008), in which continual economic growth is seen as a positive and, in fact, comes to be taken for granted. This growth eventually places such a burden on the resources of the planet, that it will not be able to sustain this indefinitely. Absent of cultural changes that stem the tide, this will lead to overshoot and ecosystem collapse.

In a related vein, this treadmill of production is intimately tied to unequal ecological exchange. The **ecological footprint**, or strain that people put on the planet by their patterns of consumption, is uneven. Affluent countries tend to have a much higher ecological footprint than do poor countries (Jorgenson 2003), and that gap is not closing, but appears to be widening over time (Jorgenson and Burns 2007).

The twentieth century has seen unprecedented levels of humanly created environmental change (McNeill 2000; Ponting 1992). A number of researchers and ecologically minded intellectuals have pointed to the culture of late modernity as taking for granted the very kinds of growth that modernity has made possible (Burns 2009), and in so doing speed toward ever greater levels of degradation of the natural environment (York 2010).

Addressing Problems: Moving Toward Solutions

Ethicist Mary Evelyn Tucker (2007) makes the case that, particularly in the current age of globalization, the best way to address such problems is to have a "dialogue of civilizations," in which the shared and pressing nature of these problems are acknowledged, with an eye of working toward building a global culture that is equipped to confront the type of global environmental problems modernity has created.

Environmental sociologist, Beth Schaefer Caniglia (2010) makes a case that there are important leverage points that societies and people of good will can bring to bear to address runaway environmental problems. She sees the role of a rising environmental consciousness that employs networks of social actors in non-government organizations as well as environmental social movement organizations, working in concert with various levels of government, as the best way to address environmental problems.

Environmental sociologist Riley Dunlap sees humankind facing a fundamental choice between an older way of seeing the world (what Dunlap calls a **Human Exemptionalism Paradigm**) that continues to drain the planet of its resources, and a **New Environmental Paradigm** that values planetary resources and emphasizes humankind's role in stewarding the planet responsibly.

In a similar vein, Philosopher John Cobb (1991) sees a cultural ethic arising out of a growing planetary awareness, and moving beyond older ways of conceptualizing problems primarily in economic terms. In fact, for Cobb, there is a crucial choice we will necessarily make (either consciously or by default) in the twenty-first century and beyond. If the planet is to survive, Cobb holds, there must be a significant cultural change from older ways of seeing the world as resources there for the taking (**economism**) without replacement or stewardship, and a more enlightened **planetism** that holds the environment as precious and irreplaceable.

Conclusions: Toward a Comprehensive Model of Humankind's Interaction with the Natural Environment

The human ecological models have proven worthwhile in orienting theorization and understanding about the dynamics of humankind's interaction with the environment. The POET and IPAT models have been helpful in this regard. However, they do tend to largely ignore aspects of culture, particularly the culture of late modernity that tends to take for granted the pattern of ever widening and deepening incursions into the natural environment.

The sociology of illness and health around environmental imbalances is a historically under-researched phenomenon that is now coming more clearly into the awareness of sociologists. The science of Darwinian medicine looks at the mismatches between how humankind has evolved and adapted over the course of millennia, and the challenges and affronts to our immune and adaptive systems in environments that are out of ecological balance.

Historically, sociologists have been excellent at finding and pointing out problems, but less adept at helping devise workable alternatives that can point in the direction of long term solutions, sustainable balance in the natural environment, and more harmony between humankind and the planet on which we all depend.

In summary then, we can use the models devised by the early human ecologists, and update them with aspects that are crucial to coming to a fuller understanding of human-environmental interactions. We can characterize this with a **POETICAA model**:

o **(P)opulation**

It bears noting that while overall population is a crucial variable, other important factors in predicting types of environmental degradation include urban/rural, age and gender distributions.

o **(O)rganization**

This includes the various institutions through which people act, and which in turn have an effect on how humankind impacts the environment. Such institutions include the economy, the political and education systems.

o **(E)nvironment**

This refers to all aspects of the environment, including forests, water sources, and air, as well as to the degradation of those systems. Note that a given factor, such as population, may impact the environment differently, depending upon how it is operationalized and measured.

Rural population growth, for example, is a strong predictor of deforestation, while urban population growth, particularly in combination with heavy consumption patterns, is highly correlated with the generation of greenhouse gas emissions.

It also should be noted that environmental degradation is typically operationalized as a dependent variable (e.g., deforestation or greenhouse gas emissions). However, there is a small but growing body of work that looks at social outcomes (such as violence, illness, and economic decline) resulting from environmental degradation.

- **(T)echnology**

Technological innovation has a complex relationship with the natural environment. On one hand, certain aspects of technology can have deleterious effects on the environment. On the other hand, the advent of clean technologies can help the environment, particularly when used wisely. Here, understanding the interaction of technology with other of these variables, particularly culture, is of vital importance.

- **(I)llness and Health**

Particularly since the landmark work of Rachel Carson in the early 1960s, there has been a rising awareness of how ecological imbalances can cause serious health issues, including but not limited to, a rise in cancers, asthma, emphysema and other breathing problems, birth defects and loss of fertility. Darwinian medicine looks particularly at the mismatches between how humankind and other species have evolved, and the shock and challenges to our immune and adaptive systems caused by environmental pollution.

- **(C)ulture**

With the rise of modernity and industrialization, there was also an increasing alienation, or distancing of humankind from the natural environment. This distance became part of the culture itself, particularly in late modernity. As students of culture, it will be important for sociologists to look at aspects of culture that are sustainable into the third millennium and beyond.

- **(A)ffluence**

As societies and the people that compose them become more affluent, consumption patterns tend to increase, sometimes more exponentially than linearly. People in developed countries in particular, and people with disproportionate amounts of wealth, tend to consume huge amounts of resources, particularly energy. In general, unequal distributions of resources, both at the micro and macro levels, have profound environmental implications.

- **(A)ddressing Problems**

Historically, sociology as a discipline has been far better at finding problems, than it has been at positing viable solutions—and in this regard, environmental sociology has, at least thus far, not been an exception. Moving forward, it will be important for sociologists to think more in terms of praxis, and to use the sociological imagination to envision creative and workable ways to address the daunting ecological problems societies face.

While the classical sociologists shed a great deal of light on many of the problems of modernity (such as alienation, anomie and egoism, the iron cage of rationality), they did not fully appreciate the human social causes of environmental degradation, nor did they engage how societies might come to live more in concert with the natural environment on which we all depend. As sociology moves forward, it is crucial to address this lack (Burns and Caniglia 2015). Environmental sociologists are engaged in this, and take the human-environmental interface seriously—as it is perhaps the most important social problem of all, if humankind is to survive and thrive from this point forward.

CHAPTER SUMMARY

- Particularly in the third millennium, any study of sociology needs to consider seriously the linkages between humankind and the natural environment.
- As articulated by rational choice theorists, the tragedy of the commons (or commons problem) is an important way of conceptualizing the cause of a number of environmental problems.
- While environmental degradation is a worldwide problem, its effects appear to be most pronounced in developing countries, such as the semiperiphery of the world system.
- A common model for conceptualizing social causes of environmental impact is the IPAT model, in which environmental (I)mpact is a function of (P)opulation, (A)ffluence and (T)echnology.
- Another, older model for making sense of the human-environmental interface, is the POET model, where it is important to consider (P)opulation, (O)rganization, (E)nvironment, and (T)echnology.
- Recent research has identified probable causal links between environmental degradation and a number of health outcomes, including cancer.
- It is important to consider culture, particularly the culture of consumption inherent in late modernity, as a crucial factor in leading to environmental imbalances.
- The POETICAA model synthesizes earlier work with recent emerging important considerations. It holds that a sociological view of the human interface with the natural environment should consider (P)opulation, (O)rganization, (E)nvironment, (T)echnology, (I)llness and Health, (C)ulture, (A)ffluence, and (A)lternatives to harmful ways of relating to the environment.
- While the classical sociologists shed a great deal of light on many of the problems of modernity they did not fully appreciate the human social causes of environmental degradation.
- Environmental sociologists now seek to use the sociological imagination and insights of the sociological method to understand this most crucial of social problems—the interaction between humankind and the natural environment.

18 | Crime and Deviance

In the United States, very few issues occupy as much popular attention as does that of **crime**. Crime is a special sort of conduct that violates the law. Crime is frequently listed as one of the top concerns in life, and statistics suggest those concerns probably are well founded. For example, in the year 2009, there were almost 10,639,000 crimes in the United States alone that were known to the police. Taken together 7,225,800 people were in jail, prison, or on probation or parole. It is equally disconcerting that for many crimes, only a portion are reported to police—by some estimates, 55 percent of rapes and sex assaults, 50 percent of assaults, 68 percent of robberies, 31 percent of personal thefts, and 57 percent of household burglaries (Statistical Abstract of the United States 2012).

Non-Sociological Causes

Throughout human history people have been attempting to explain the causes of crime. This longstanding concern with crime is reflected in the works of the ancient Greeks. They postulated that climate conditions affect the four bodily humors—blood, phlegm, yellow bile, and black bile—and that disease and crime are the result when these humors are thrown out of organization due to changes in the climate. Their approach may appear primitive, but it is, in fact, noteworthy that the Greeks were able to see a synthesis between the state of the individual and the surrounding environment as the potential cause of abnormal behavior.

This interpretation changed radically during the Middle Ages, when an entirely different mode of causation was emphasized. In Medieval Europe, for example, deviance and crime were seen as a result of possession by demons. Exorcisms were a prescribed methodology for addressing this possession. Today, many would scoff at these conservative religious interpretations, but certainly our culture in modern times reflects very similar concerns. It is not uncommon today to hear such phrases as "the devil in him" is at work. Nor is it uncommon to see films that emphasize such themes, perhaps the most famous example being *The Exorcist*.

In more modern times, such as the mid- to late-1800s, a more scientific approach to criminal causation was advocated in the work of Cesare Lombroso (1911), a pivotal member of what is called the Italian School of Criminology. Lombroso, a medical doctor who was trained in both psy-

Cesare Lombroso (1835 - 1909)
Italian criminologist Cesare Lombroso attempted to link crime with inherent individual characteristics rather than environmental factors. Criminals, he believed, could be identified by physical attributes.

chology and biology, was very much aware of the work of Charles Darwin, who by that time had connected modern human beings with their nonhuman past through his theory of evolution. Deeply occupied in his study of the physical differences between normal people and criminals, Lombroso sought the causal factor of **atavism** or "throwback to primitive times." Indeed, Lombroso thought that individuals were "born criminal."

Criminals, Lombroso believed, were specific types who possessed particular physical traits that distinguished them from normal individuals. The traits were not the cause of criminal behavior, but their appearance did permit the scientific observer to identify people who were atavistic beings, or throwbacks to earlier stages of evolution. On an evolutionary scale, criminals were considered to be closer to apes or early primitive humans than they were to modern individuals. Lombroso found the problem of the nature of the criminal during an autopsy on a famous robber. He saw this atavistic tendency being reproduced in his person of study, causing the ferocious instincts of criminal humanity, as well as the inferiority of the animal kingdom. He noted enormous jaws, high cheekbones, solitary lines in the palm, extreme size of the orbits, the nature of the ears, an insensibility to pain, very acute eye site, tattooing, love of idleness, and what he termed as an irresistible craving of evil for its own sake. The atavistic being had the desire not only to extinguish the life in the victim, but also, in his own words, to "mutilate its corpse, tear its flesh, and drink its blood" (Lombroso 1911).

Lombroso's strange and almost frightening account of criminal causation seems exaggerated by modern standards, but again it should not be forgotten that a number of other more modern theorists have advocated rather comparable models of individual pathologies and crime. Individual biotype, in a more modern interpretation, has been linked with **juvenile delinquency**. There are three human body types of interest according to this approach (Sheldon 1949). The **endomorphic** body type is soft, round, and pudgy and enjoys comfort. Perhaps we should be reminded of the Pillsbury Doughboy! The **ectomorphic** body type is thin, tall, fragile, and possesses weak bones and muscular structure. These individuals have overly fast reactions, and are inhibited, apprehensive, and chronically fatigued. Neither the ectomorph nor the endomorph is a likely candidate for criminal behavior. A far more likely candidate is the **mesomorph**. The mesomorph has a large bone structure, well developed musculature, and is very strong. They are energetic and love to dominate, which, according to Sheldon's theory, make them far more likely than the other body types to engage in delinquent behavior. Certainly, sociologists would find this approach far more compelling if the three body types were linked to more *sociological* interpretations of the causes of crime. For example, perhaps the mesomorphs are more likely not only to engage in crime, but also to be able to successfully enact crimes with some ease, due to their muscular build!

Alternative individual-level theories also come from psychology and biochemistry. For example, in the domain of psychology many authors have asserted that one can detect innate tendencies towards **antisocial behavior** during childhood. Antisocial behavior is not necessarily criminal behavior. Often it is best classified in the more encompassing category of **deviant behavior**, which is behavior that does not conform to social expectations. Later in life, **psychopathic** individuals are relatively unemotional, impulsive, immature, thrill seeking and unconditionable, psychologists note. The fact that such traits are detectable early in life suggests the probability that their origin was in childhood rather than later developmental stages of adulthood. Further, delinquent and criminal lifestyles have also been attributed to intellectual deficits, and these deficits can arguably be inherited. Also, biochemical dynamics, such as male and female hormones have been linked to aggressive and criminal behaviors.

What appears certain, however, is that an enormous number of individuals engage in criminal and deviant behavior, even though they do not display "atavism," mesomorphic body type, or the biochemical or genetic factors identified as important causes of criminal behavior. Moreover, many individuals who do, in fact, exhibit one or more of these traits identified in biochemical or genetic studies, are not criminals. This has led sociologists to search for other *social* factors that are the most critical dynamics in producing deviance and crime. Generally, these factors are represented in two primary theoretical approaches: the social function approach and the social conflict approach. Social interactions and exchanges, to be sure, are also important in the **etiology** or study of the causes of crime and deviance.

Social Functions

In previous chapters, we noted that the social functions approach takes the seminal works of Emile Durkheim (1933, 1951) as its foundation. Recall that Durkheim employed an organic treatment of society, arguing that the basis of society is a moral order and that moral consensus is the foundation for human social organization. Rational agreement and social exchanges between people cannot, initially, hold a society together, he argued. We must have established a **precontractual solidarity** before we can ever engage in rational contracts. In other words, we must trust one another before we can exchange and evolve to a well-established social division of labor.

What creates a fundamental solidarity? Durkheim argued that it was a sense of belonging to a community, shared emotional feeling, and a moral obligation to live up to their expectations—a **collective conscience**, in other words. These moral feelings come from our social interactions with others. In particular, they spring from the ritualistic interactions we engage in that focus on the collective, and that make us see ourselves as part of the larger whole. For example, churches have rituals that they use so that the parishioners feel they are part of something much larger than them-

Collective Conscience

Durkheim described a shared sense of community that arises out of ritualistic interactions among members of a society, such as collectively reciting the "Pledge of Allegiance."

Boundaries of Toleration

Timothy McVeigh being led out of a courthouse two days after the Oklahoma City bombing. When the media depicts crime and deviant behavior, it allows society to establish "**boundaries of toleration**."

selves. This is also why the national anthem is played *first* to indicate the symbolic unity of the crowd during an athletic event. Many of you probably recited the pledge of allegiance to the United States flag as one of the first rituals of each day in elementary school.

These rituals were fundamental in early human history. Durkheim argued that primitive society was held together by ritual and by harsh laws, which created a moral consensus and **mechanical solidarity**. Over time, the establishment of solidarity and trust led to productivity and specialization, thus facilitating the division of labor, or social exchange. With trust established, people could be bound more by need due to their exchanges with one another, and this interdependency led to **organic solidarity**. In this way, Durkeim was very interested in the relationship between social functions, interactions and exchanges, and in those circumstances in which the established solidarity was violated. He referred to violations of expectations or trust as **deviance**.

Durkheim's work on trust and deviance led him to two central conclusions. The first of these is that deviance is endemic in society—it will always exist. Second, and similarly, deviance is *functional* for society. There are two important social functions of deviance. One is to show us what is right and what is wrong. The other is to unite the social group in their collective moral outrage against the deviant behavior. Each time society expresses its outrage at a crime, it establishes **boundaries of toleration**, identifying what is acceptable or unacceptable behavior for all of society to see.

When this collective alarm is sounded, it brings people into unity against the deviance itself. Every time a criminal event is sensationalized in the media, you can see Durkheim's interpretation in action. The media's attention leads individuals to collectively express their shock and outrage. Our feelings in this regard are sometimes so significant that our expressions of shock and outrage may become a point of conversation that lasts for weeks, or months, and on some occasions, even for years, as people give voice to their ongoing sensitivity to the criminal event.

Modern social functions theories of crime emphasize the whole social system as a social order, while seeing society as comprised of integrated parts. They additionally emphasize the functions the parts play in the adaptation and continuance of the system. In this way, twentieth century social functions theories of crime owe a great deal to Durkheim's work.

Parsons's Functionalism

We now turn to the theory of deviance propounded by Talcott Parsons (1951), a preeminent social functionalist of the mid-twentieth century. Parsons was well aware that in any social system, even in systems comprised of just two individuals, there are roles and expectations of roles that flow from individual-to-individual in both directions. This small system, he believed, was in equilibrium if the mutual expectations each had were not violated. If expectations are broken, that is, if the equilibrium is disrupted, we have the condition of deviance. Deviance, in other words, is behavior on the part of one or more actors that disturbs the equilibrium or "give and take" of expectations.

As a simple illustration, consider your own behavior at the supermarket. After you select your items and place them on the register, the cashier will ring them up and bag them. Next, you will pay for them and exit the store with your purchase. This is a simple example of equilibrium in the social system of a supermarket. However, consider violating the cashier's expectations, producing a clear case of deviance. For instance, ask the cashier if she or he will pay for *your* groceries. The response you will receive will most likely be one of discomfort, if not anger. In this specific example, expectations have been violated, normal roles have been broken, and the equilibrium of the system has been disturbed by your deviance.

What makes people fail to perform their roles? Why do people break other's expectations? Parsons (1951) argued that strain was critical to understanding in the breaking of expectations in the social system. **Strain**, he explained, is the introduction of disturbance into the interactive system, which causes the frustration of the expectations of one or more of the actors. Strain could be caused by a physical condition, for example, an earthquake that makes it impossible for one of the two participants to perform the role expected by the other participant. However, Parsons was far more concerned with other sociological causes of strain. In particular, he focused upon **role ambiguity and role conflict**.

You are familiar with role ambiguity. Role ambiguity occurs when we simply do not know what our role is vis-à-vis another individual. It occurs when we are uncertain about another's expectations and what our appropriate behavior toward them should be. In today's world, we often have mixed definitions about what it means to be a man and what it means to be a woman. Who should mow the lawn or fold the laundry? Who should work outside the home? Who should take care of the baby? No wonder we suffer gender-related role ambiguity.

It is also true that we are members of many small social systems, which place us in situations with potential role conflict. We have roles and expectations vis-à-vis parents, brothers and sisters, friends, teachers, and so on. Often in life, it is impossible for us to satisfy the expectations of a role member in one social system as our role partner in another system expects us to perform in a particular way. Many of you, who may be mothers or fathers, may find it necessary to simultaneously attend school while working a full-time job. The expectations of your professors may not match the expectations of your employer, which may also be at odds with the expectations of your spouse, which may differ from the expectations of your children. This puts you into multiple situations of role conflict, with the only resolution sometimes being your deviant behavior to one or more of your role partners.

According to Parsons, this role ambiguity and role conflict are intimately related to strain and deviant behavior. If strain is not relieved by some other mechanism, deviant behavior will result. Parsons identified four possible directions for that deviance—the individual can become an **actively alienated deviant**, a **passively alienated deviant**, an **actively conforming deviant**, or a **passively conforming deviant**.

The actively alienated deviant is hostile to his or her role partners. They can be said to essentially be in rebellion against that partner. Their primary concern is to leave their small social system. We've all seen real life or media portrayals of this type of situation, especially involving married couples that are on the verge of divorce.

The passive alienated deviant is not hostile. He or she simply wants to leave the system. The "hobo" or the "vagrant," or in more polite terms, the street person, are examples of this type that come to mind. These are individuals who have decided that they simply do not want to be part of the larger social system with its expectations and obligations.

The actively conforming deviant overly conforms to expectations. Yes, it is possible to conform too much to that which is expected by role partners, to do more, even, than is expected of you. Have you ever thought that one of your classmates worked too hard—so hard, that everyone looked bad? This person, according to Parsons, is occupying the role of actively conforming deviant.

Passively Alienated Deviant

Henry David Thoreau can be considered a **passively alienated deviant** in Talcott Parsons's analysis of deviance. In 1845, he renounced what he believed to be a corrupt society to live alone in the woods and refused to pay taxes.

The passively conforming deviant, on the other hand, conforms, but never takes chances. The passively conforming deviant does what he or she thinks is their social responsibility as part of the system in which they operate, but they never take the chances that are expected in our culture. Certainly, you have known people who are, in other words, **ritualists**. Ritualists seem to go only so far as to meet expectations of the performance of their job, but no further, as they mechanically follow their assigned functions.

Apart from these adaptations to deviance, Parsons suggested processes by which deviant tendencies can be counteracted when they emerge, and the social system can be brought back to a state of equilibrium. Parsons listed four processes of social control to counteract deviancy. The first of these processes involves **acting out** the **deviant tendencies**. Parsons believed we could vent the frustration caused by strain in our social systems in ways other than those that are immediately deviant. Athletics, for example, can provide this outlet. Certainly the athletics in which we participate, or from which we gain pleasure as observers, act as a mechanism for equalizing the strain that may arise due to role conflict and role ambiguity. Put another way, we may divert our attention from the strain that is immediately affecting us and engage in other activities that prevent us from acting in deviant ways towards our social system partners.

Society has also evolved a number of other mechanisms for social control. One of these is **isolation**, in which the deviant is removed from the complex of interactions in their many social systems. An illustration of isolation is found in solitary confinement in prisons. A related possibility is called **insulation**, in which the deviant is only partially removed from their interactions in the larger social system. Incarceration in a mental hospital or jail, where it is still possible to interact with *some* members of the larger community but not all, is an example of insulation.

A final mechanism, **restorative social control**, involves actions deliberately meant to return the deviant to their normal behavioral patterns. Examples are psychotherapy and rehabilitation, each with the goal of bringing the patient back into normal functioning in their social systems.

The aim of all the aforementioned social control processes is to accomplish the restoration of the social system to its prior state of equilibrium. It is noteworthy that although Parsons's emphasis was on the preservation of system stability, social change through rebellion was also a possibility. In this respect, his theory and functionalism more generally, tend to be conservative in nature. Another approach to deviance that draws on social function themes, including an emphasis on social order and social control, is social disorganization theory, our next topic.

Social Disorganization

Not unlike the social functions approaches of Durkheim and Parsons, the social disorganization approach is concerned with societies' orderings. Social disorganization theorists argue that rapid change can undo basic social orders, creating a breakdown in the control mechanisms that normally harness deviant behavior. These concerns were apparent in the works of earlier philosophers known as the *social contract theorists*. One of them, Thomas Hobbes ([1957]) believed that humans are base and selfish by nature. We recognize this and fear the harm that others might cause us. According to Hobbes, therefore, we yield to some overarching authority, government or agents of the law, which control population members from exterminating one another. With this control, mutually advantageous social interactions and exchanges will flourish.

Social disorganization theory does not begin with such a harsh view of humanity's inherent nature. Social disorganization writers do, however, view external circumstances as being crucially important in generating deviant behavior, which challenges the normal ordering or organization of society.

The early development of social disorganization theory largely occurred at the University of Chicago in the 1920s and 1930s. All social theories result from the interplay of societal forces and disciplinary conditions, and in the early 1900s, sociology was concerned with its scientific status as well as its independence from other disciplines that shared similar subject matters. At the same time, in the geographical areas surrounding the University of Chicago, population movements, urban living, and unprecedented industrialization caused sociologists at the University of Chicago to apply distinct sociological models to explain social problems.

They linked a range of rapid social transformations to the breakdown of informal mechanisms of social control, hence, ultimately to deviant behavior. For instance, in their study of Polish peasants in America, Thomas and Znaniecki (1918) observed a correlation between rapid immigration and conflicts between the values and customs in the old home culture and new host culture. As children of the Polish immigrants adopted local customs, which were often in conflict with their parental customs, conflicts over appropriate customs and values led to a breakdown in the social organization of the Polish family. This breakdown in positive interactions and exchanges resulted in a loss of **informal control**, causing higher levels of deviant behavior among the second-generation immigrants, according to Thomas and Znaniecki.

In contrast, Park and Burgess (1925) examined the improvement of transportation and communication networks in the city. They observed that geographical mobility was a great deal easier with improved transportation, and with communication improvements, individuals were able to hear a great deal more about better places for employment and living. Improved transportation and communication fostered a spatial mobility that caused a breakdown in informal control within the family and within neighborhoods. These breakdowns, they argued, exacerbated deviant behavior.

In a related way, Faris and Dunham (1939) studied the encroachment of industry into the city, particularly its resultant population changeover. They noted that isolation was an important consequence of the encroachment of industry and population changes. Isolation led to a breakdown in routine interactions and exchanges, and thus instability in families and in neighborhoods. This instability led to the loss of organized family and community control over young people, and in the absence of social restraint, increased deviance was a likely outcome.

A wide range of empirical studies has examined the effects of social disorganization on deviant behavior. At the University of Chicago, ecological studies based on the work of Park and Burgess has correlated deviant behavior with different zones in cities. Zone 1, the **central business district** and Zone 2, a **zone in transition** with industrialization, have been found to be most prone to deviant behavior. They are also the zones where there is the greatest cultural conflict in the city. Outside of these two zones and further from the center of the city are a zone of workingmen's homes, a residential zone, and a commuter zone. Rates of "blue-collar" or violent crimes appear to decline as one moves further out from the city, leading Park and Burgess, among a number of other scholars, to link the social organization of each zone with the corresponding level of deviant behavior. The high level of disorganization in the intercity zones 1 and 2 appears to be the most highly generative of deviance. It is important to note, however, such studies of deviance are less interested in white-collar crime such as fraud and embezzlement, which are more commonly committed by those individuals who live in the residential and commuter zones.

Many sociologists have also studied rural community structures, rapid social changes, and related criminal behavior trends. Cressey's (1969) study of Harlan, Kentucky showed the impact of sudden industrialization on a self-efficient and isolated community. Originally, the Harlan community was a small, rural, kinship-oriented town. Around the turn of the century, coal was discovered, leading to the influx of miners and the growth of local industry. This led to a population boom, which caused a cessation in farming, and work in the mines as industry became the primary mode of employment. These processes led to a breakdown in community closeness, so that neighbors who had typically interacted and exchanged in the past rarely communicated with one another anymore.

Cressey emphasized the substantial increases in crime that accompanied these changes. He also noted, however, that when coal mining leveled off and population growth was attenuated, there were substantial reductions in crime. Thus, rapid social change, he concluded, results in a disruption in traditional community organization, culminating in a higher level of deviance and crime.

The sociologist George Homans (1950) observed something comparable in his analysis of the New England town which he renamed Hilltown. Until the turn of the century, Hilltown was based on subsistence farming. The relatively small number of residents who lived there knew each other very well. With improved transportation in the form of railroads, Hilltown was eventually opened to the outside world. Outside commerce led to aspirations for outside wealth. As farmers began to abandon the town to seek employment in the growing industries on the fringe of the town, the community no longer served as a gathering place for interactions and routine exchanges. The high level of individualization led to a low level of togetherness, general indifference, and a breakdown in community control. Homans emphasized that this generated escalating levels of deviant behavior never before seen in Hilltown.

Social disorganization studies have also been conducted in other nations. Clinard and Abbott (1973) examined a random sample of males over the age of eighteen in two slums in the city of Kampala, Uganda. One area had a high crime rate and the other had a low crime rate. After interviewing the residents of these communities, they found that there was a higher degree of internal integration in the low crime area. Internal integration was higher for four reasons: (1) Friendship was restricted only to local tribe members, (2) there were frequent visits with others in the tribal community, (3) there was frequent participation in local and community organizations, (4) and there was control by village elders over the youth. In contrast, Clinard and Abbott found that in the high crime area, there was little participation in local affairs, there was very little control by elders over the youth, and there was a very low frequency of community visits, one neighbor to the other. An appropriate conclusion is that, in all probability, the absence of internal integration found in routine interactions and exchanges leads to a loss of informal control and an increase in deviant behavior.

While any individual social disorganization study can be criticized on particularistic grounds, it is clear that as a whole, a wide range of empirical treatments supports social disorganization approach. Certainly rapid social changes in the surrounding environment can diminish the social functioning of any social system, as evidenced in disruptions to routine interactions and exchanges, resulting in a loss of informal control. While it may be possible to use formal mechanisms such as the police to offset the loss of informal control, more frequently its loss leads to a higher level of deviance and crime.

Anomie

Another sociological approach, anomie theory, was heavily influenced by the work of Emile Durkheim. Durkheim's theoretical and empirical work, which we covered in depth in Chapter 7, serves as a foundation for much of the later work in the sociology of crime and deviance. You may recall that Durkheim elaborated a condition of relative normlessness he termed **anomie** in his book, *The Division of Labor in Society*. He further developed the consequences of anomie in his book, *Suicide*. In *Suicide*, Durkheim was interested in accounting for variations in suicide rates between ranges of different social groupings. He collected his data from several European countries in the nineteenth century. He was interested in such questions as, "Why is the proportion of suicides for businessmen greater than that for workers? Why is the proportion of suicides for Protestants greater than that for Catholics? Why is the proportion of suicides for unmarried people greater than that for those who are married?"

Durkheim defined **suicide** as all causes of death resulting directly or indirectly from a positive or negative act of the victim himself that he knows will produce this result. He emphasized intentionality in his definition when he introduced "which he knows will produce this result." It is less clear why he used the terms "directly" or "indirectly" from a "positive" or "negative" act. Because he wanted to be as conceptually clear as possible, he used the term positive act to refer to an action taken which resulted in the person's death and a negative act as inaction that resulted in a person's death. In a direct suicide, death immediately followed the action involved, or the inaction in the case of a negative act. An indirect suicide involved death from complications well after the act.

Apart from these definitional issues, Durkheim discussed four types of social cohesion that were relevant to suicide. One of these, **fatalism**, is the least consequential and is barely developed by Durkheim. The three that are most important, and most elaborated, are social conditions called **egoism**, **altruism** and **anomie**. **Egoism**, he argued, is the social condition in which individual activities take precedence over collective allegiances and obligations. In egoistic societies, people are less integrated with one another, and more detached from collective life. In this case, neither society nor the group effectively controls the individual. Under stressful circumstances, therefore, people in egoistic societies are more likely to take their own lives. This is because, essentially, they have no one to turn to. The United States is a good example of an egoistic society.

In an **altruistic** society, on the other hand, social conditions in which humans are insufficiently individuated from the collectivity tend to prevail. What Durkheim meant is that in the altruistic society, people are so strongly integrated into the nation, into the group, and into their family, that they lose their individuality. This social condition heightens the possibility that an individual will take his or her own life under stressful circumstances. They may do so because they have very little development of their individual identity.

Durkheim maintained, in regards to the anomic society, that all individuals have biological needs that can be satisfied, but they have other social and economic needs, which appear to be infinite. That is, it seems the more we get of a particular resource, the more we want of others.

However, he emphasized that society normally controls these needs and people conform to expectations given their social position in life. Durkheim felt that this is normal for social functioning in the society. Drastic social change, however, upsets the effective social control of infinite needs and desires. Under these circumstances people are confronted by an **anomic** society and, under stress, they are more likely to take their own lives.

In principle, there are a number of different causes and consequences of those drastic social changes that culminate in anomie. Especially of interest are economic reversal and economic gain. Under conditions of economic reversal, increasing economic misfortune throws off the equilibrium of social relationships. People become disoriented since what was once expected, such as wealth, is no longer available. As their expectations are shattered, as is the case with economic depression, suicide becomes more likely. Other circumstances such as an economic boom, by contrast, lead to insatiable desires and aspirations, which simply cannot be quenched. Shattered expectations under these circumstances may lead to suicide as well.

Durkheim's emphasis on the normal functioning of the social systems is reflected in the later works of Robert K. Merton (1938), a sociologist who expanded Durkheim's concept of anomie. Anomie, of course, means normlessness and disorientation, and this is precisely the point of departure for Merton's theory of deviant behavior and crime.

Merton began his theorization with the assumption that all societies provide certain goals for their members to achieve, and society's structures provide means or mechanisms for obtaining those goals. For example, the acquisition of wealth is a pervasive cultural goal in the United States. But do the available means allow everyone to achieve this goal? Perhaps this would be true in the perfectly functioning society, but Merton recognized that this is not the case in the American social structure. In fact, for many people there is a disjuncture between the cultural goals and the means to obtain them. When means are available to reach goals, normal behavior results, but when there is a disjuncture between goals and means, the resulting feelings of anomie make deviant behavior a likely outcome. Anomic feelings lead people to search for ways of adapting, or **modes of adaptation**. There are five such modes in Merton's theory—the first, **conformity**, indicates an internalization of social goals, and of the means to achieve those goals. The other four modes represent some form of anomie.

One of these modes is **innovation**. The innovator accepts the overall goals of society, but rejects society's prescribed means to obtain them. The innovator thus creates new ways to obtain society's goals, perhaps through illegal or deviant activity. In Merton's typology, a person who steals from the local supermarket is an innovator.

It is also possible to reject both society's goals and means in order to deal with the painful situation of anomie.

Modes of Adaptation

Che Guevara sought to replace old social orders with new ones, but rejected society's established means of doing so.

Individuals who do this are known as **retreatists**, that is, he or she seeks an alternative lifestyle. Hermits are viewed as retreatists.

According to Merton's paradigm, some individuals experiencing anomie adapt by becoming a **ritualist**. Ritualists accept the means for obtaining the ends in society, but they reject the ends themselves. Ritualists can be seen each day toiling at their jobs, performing them with some degree of perfection, but caring little about the end result.

Rebellion is the final mode of deviant adaptation. The social rebel rejects current means and goals and substitutes his or her own, seeking a revolutionary situation. The rebel wants a new social order in place of the old one. In many ways, the rebel resembles Parsons's "actively alienated deviant." In fact, there are many parallels between Parsons's **directions of deviance** and Merton's **modes of adaptation**.

Merton's paradigm has been criticized for its inattention to some important details. Cloward (1959), for example, levels the criticism that while the retreatist may reject normal society, they may be unsuccessful in deviant subcultures as well. This group, Cloward points out, might be called **double-failure retreatists**, because they fail in both normal and deviant worlds.

Social Interactions

The social function, social disorganization, and anomie approaches to deviance and crime all are macrosociological in nature, and they tend to place less importance on everyday actions and interactions in the life of the deviant. It is Edwin Sutherland's (1947) sociological theory of **differential association** that more carefully takes these later processes into account. In examining this other side of deviance, Sutherland began by stating that criminal behavior is not a product of biology, strain or macrosocial conditions. Like normal behavior, he argued, it is learned. While these may be important considerations, the key factor is learning, which occurs through social interactions, principally within the context of intimate groups.

This learning, Sutherland said, includes the techniques of committing crimes, specifically, but also the definitions of such behavior as favorable or unfavorable. Can we learn definitions favorable to law violations from upright citizens? Yes. Everyone, at some point, presents some ambiguity in his or her definitions of right and wrong. Parents may teach morality, for instance, but when they cheat on their income tax, they are providing definitions favorable to law violation. It is an excess of definitions favorable to law violation, not an excess of association themselves, that lead to criminal behavior, argued Sutherland.

The strength of definitions, according to Sutherland, depends on their **frequency, duration, priority**, and **intensity**. Frequency relates to the question, how often does the interactional contact providing definitions occur? Duration is the length that each contact lasts. Priority is how early in life the association began, and intensity is how significant the definer is. Associations, thus, are important for the *strength* of the definitions that they provide. Associations that are frequent, over long duration, with priority and intensity, are the ones that provide the strongest definitions that are either favorable or unfavorable to law violation. If those definitions favor violation of the law, the likelihood is greater that law violation will ensue.

Sutherland's theory remains one of the most important in criminology today. It has, however, been refined in some noteworthy ways. For example, Glazer's (1956) approach, **differential identification**, argues that learning includes a choice of models upon which we base our behavior. The models' definition of what is good and what is not influences us to act accordingly. The models with which we identify could be determined by our economic position, our current set of frustrations in life, our moral standards, or even the nuanced characteristics of our personality. But for Glazer, the important point is that we choose models, including models in the media, and those models determine whether we are likely to engage in criminal behavior or not. Of course, Glazer's emphases would make us very concerned with the content of films and television programs. With his interpretation, we would argue that entire generations of individuals, who have been raised with heavy media exposure would likely be deeply impacted by the models presented in it.

Labeling History

Social interactions are equally important to the labeling theory of deviant behavior. Society's reaction to deviant behavior and the effects of that reaction on the identity of those who are labeled are the focus of labeling theory. Also, it deals with the impact of that identity on subsequent deviant behavior. An essential premise is that all of us engage in **primary deviance**. That is, almost on a daily basis, we do something that others might consider to be deviant. However, some individuals are caught, successfully labeled, and as a result of the label assume an identity as a deviant. Overtime, this leads them into **secondary deviance** or deviant careers (Lemert 1951).

Labeling theory begins by assuming that we all have a **typification need**, a need to type others with shorthand methods that characterize them with minimal definitional work. Accordingly, we need a small and workable set of identifications that we assign to others so that we know how to deal with them, or put another way, how to initiate and continue interactions with them. Which sort of typification work do you do when you interact with your professors? Ask yourself right now, for example, what does a typical chemistry professor look like? What formalities do you observe in your meetings with faculty members? What expectations do you have for their typical behaviors? How do you typically address them, and what is their typical reaction when you ask them for a grade change? As you consider these questions, consider also how you typify or define others throughout your day.

For labeling theorists, it is vital for us to understand that not only do we socially construct our definitions of others, but we also construct definitions of deviance. These definitions often stem from legal definitions of what is acceptable and what is unacceptable behavior. The labeling theorist asks the question, who is it that creates these legal definitions in the first place? One obvious answer is that governmental agencies, legislatures, a judiciary that interprets the law, clinicians such as psychiatric personnel, and police officers make these definitions. But aside from **formal agents** of social control, labeling theorists emphasize what we define as deviant in our own daily activities. The ability to create definitions of deviance and apply those definitions to others is not equally vested among us. Some definers are more powerful than others, and their definitions are the most likely to be adopted. For example, a label is more likely to be successful when a powerful or high status individual or group is doing the labeling. On the same note, a label is far more likely to be successful when a lower status or powerless person is the one who is being labeled.

Labeling theorists go on to suggest that a label is more likely to stick if the violation being labeled is a serious one. A deviant label for having committed a murder is more likely to stick than a deviant label for jay walking. Why is this? Well, if we return to Durkheim's paradigm again, more serious crimes tend to outrage the public a great deal more than others. In other words, it is the outrage that leads to the strength of the label.

A label is more likely to be successful if an individual or groups stands to gain from having made the label. Have you ever considered the labels that you apply to others or the labels that others apply to you? Have you had a vested interest in labeling them? That is, could you stand to gain from them being labeled? Conversely, could they stand to gain from labeling you? If so, their labeling actions as a group are more likely to be successful.

It almost goes without saying that if an act is not witnessed, it is difficult to label it. Labeling theorists argue that the greater the visibility of a deviant act, the greater the likelihood of it being labeled. Secret acts of deviance are simply not labeled by others, since they are not known about. When acts are known publicly, there is a significantly greater chance for a concerted, unified, and effective labeling effort. Of course, some people are wrongly labeled. When innocent people are labeled, according to labeling theorists, they, too, could end up adopting an identity that is commensurate with a deviant label and act accordingly.

Labeling theorists further argue that the greater perceived will or responsibility of the actor, the greater the likelihood that they will be labeled. For example, we often allow intoxicated individuals greater leniency in the punishment for some acts than we would a person behaving in full knowledge of their actions. It is clear, furthermore, that we make certain allowances for individuals when they are under circumstances of extreme stress, and we view some of their behaviors as fully understandable.

Another important principle of the labeling theory is that the likelihood of labeling increases the greater the social distance between the actor and the labeler. Social distance has to do with sociological togetherness or apartness between individuals as they interact. We know from experience that we often are reluctant to set one of our kind apart and label him or her as a deviant. We are less likely to damage individuals with a label when we have closer feelings for them. Studies of mental illness in the family often show that family members are the last individuals to formally label one of their family members as mentally ill (Yarrow 1955). Until they are forced by the actions of outsiders to attach a deviant label to the behavior, they treat it as normal. It should be emphasized that the social distance principle operates at the same time as all other principles in the labeling approach. When all of these conditions are met, the likelihood of the label being "successful" is far greater than when any one of them, or set of them, is missing.

After the successful imposition of the label, the primary deviant is on track to becoming a secondary deviant. The likelihood of this is increased if some type of official or formal processing of the primary deviation takes place. That is, sometimes the person engaged in witnessing a deviant act, is not only processed by unofficial labelers (a spouse, a friend, or a group), but also by official agents of social control. These agents not only hold a legal mandate to label, it is their official responsibility. Certainly, their interactions with the prospective labelee are quite a bit different than the social interactions that characterize friends who label one another.

In other words, official labeling is done according to routine, using established procedures. These procedures are often formalized, and written right into a job description. For instance, police have written routines for handling offenders. These include rules on making arrests, on reading rights to offenders, writing up complaints, and so on. There are also procedures that are a great deal more informal. These are items that are not codified but rather passed on by word of mouth; for example, when veteran police officers teach rookies how to deal with certain types of offenders in situations that are not anticipated in official police handbooks.

Labeling theorists assume that formal agencies such as the police, courts, and mental hospitals deal with deviance in terms of organizational requirements. These requirements are somewhat independent of their own personal feelings. Formal agencies must interpret deviance according to bureaucratic routine in order to maximize organizational efficiency. To do so, they create categories to classify deviants, and they process classified individuals according to organization rules. One purpose of these procedures is to speed up the work involved in dealing with individual offenders. If the police or the courts were to spend considerable time with each offender, they would never get around to dealing with most of the other offenders. Thus, efficiency and speed must guide the actions of formal control agents and the bureaucracies in which they work.

Perhaps an illustration is in order. A few years ago, a friend of the author appeared in Chicago traffic court for having driven the wrong way up a one-way street. The traffic court judge asked everyone whose last name began with A-K to stand up, and dismissed all of those cases on the spot. Cases L-Z had to pay a fifty-dollar fine to the bailiff. (Now *that* sounds like organizational efficiency!)

A traffic ticket in court is unlikely to make much of a difference in terms of a primary deviant turning into a secondary deviant and occupying a career of deviant behavior. Nevertheless, secondary or **career deviance** is a great deal more likely when more severe acts of deviance occur. This happens partly because as individuals are defined as deviant, they tend to pick up deviant identities. Social interaction theory says that identities cause behaviors. Thus, the assumption of a deviant identity necessarily leads to greater deviant behavior. This deviant behavior becomes more public with a greater likelihood of the subsequent impositions of labels. In this vicious cycle then, the label leads to identity, which leads to deviant behavior, which leads to further labels. In this way, acts of primary deviations turn into careers of deviance through this spiraling process.

Both the labeling approach and the differential association approach rely heavily on tenets from social interactions interpretations. The labeling approach also shares some explanatory concepts with a social conflict framework, our next subject of discussion.

Social Conflicts

The social conflicts perspective on deviance is an outgrowth of the 1960s and the 1970s, and in some forms is referred to as **new criminology**. It elaborates the role of power in determining the definition of deviance and the exposing or treatment of the deviant. With some degree of precision, it complements the labeling approach by elaborating who the powerful are, and suggesting how the powerful have, in specific cases, greatly influenced social definitions of deviance. It is different from the labeling approach in its emphasis on macrosociological dynamics; making it closer to the social functions framework in this respect. While a social functions perspective on deviance might argue that the diverse elements of the society are integrated into a comprehensive system based on common values, this is not what social conflict theorists argue. Instead, they argue that law is not a compromise of interests; it is the imposition of some groups' interests over others.

The social functions perspective might also suggest that law is a barometer that measures, as Durkheim puts it, the **moral consciousness** of the society, or a generalized sentiment over what is right and what is wrong. In contrast, social conflict theory argues that groups with power gain control of government processes and pass laws that help them maintain their own socioeconomic position.

The social functions perspective sees law as the adjustment and resolution of individual interests in society. On the other hand, the social conflicts perspective argues that rather than being characterized by consensus and stability, society is characterized by **diversity, conflict**, and **coercion**. Law is not a compromise of interests—it helps the interests of some at the expense of others.

A social functions perspective would also suggest that the law reflects the interests of society as a whole. Law is based on the principle of the greatest good for the greatest number. Again, it is a compromise of competing interests. The social conflicts approach, in comparison, emphasizes that power groups control the creation of law by virtue of their influence in government. They also control the administration of law by virtue of the police and courts, who represent the interests of the power-elite. Further, since they control taskforce reports on crime, the media, and the schools, these powerful interest groups are able to shape public attitudes toward crime. In fact, social conflict theorists contend that the powerful also control universities, as is evidenced in the previous dominance of social functions perspectives in colleges, instead of social conflict theories of deviance.

Quinney (1970) offered propositions regarding conflict and the American legal system. It is interest groups, he said, that determine public policy, including laws, as well as the social sanctions for crime. Interest groups are grossly unequal in their influence. The American ruling class, which controls economic issues, determines virtually all of public policy. The legal system only protects the ruling class and serves to maintain class divisions. For Quinney, the solution is a socialist state, in which law does not reflect the interests of any specific social group.

Social conflict theorists have made testable hypotheses out of these assertions. Their research indicates that lower-class people are more likely to be watched by formal agents of the law and therefore are far more likely to be observed in any violation of the law. They are also more likely to be arrested if they are discovered under any suspicious circumstances, more likely to spend the time between arrest and trial in jail, more likely to come to trial, and more likely to be found guilty when they are tried. Finally, lower class individuals are more likely to receive a harsh sentence when he or she is found guilty.

Not all studies agree with the evidence accumulated by social conflict authors. Nevertheless, the social conflicts approach offers some excellent augmentation that is necessary to any comprehensive understanding of deviant behavior and crime, when taken alongside insights from the social functions approach, as well as the social interactions approach. That said, we offer one final approach for consideration that puts crime into its world-system context.

Social Control, Self-Control, and General Strain Theories

Among current sociological theories of crime is **social control theory**. Developed by criminologist Travis Hirschi, this theory suggests that there is a common system of values shared by society, and social norms are internalized due to social bonds with others. In other words, social relationships, commitments, shared values, and beliefs all work to encourage adaptation to social values through conformity. Individuals will voluntarily limit deviant behavior due to their inclusion within larger groups or communities. Echoing many of the insights of earlier sociologists, particularly Durkheim, Hirschi describes four elements of the social bond: **1) Attachment** to others in the society. **2) Commitment** to obeying laws and conforming to norms. **3) Involvement** in normal, shared activity. **4) Belief** in a shared value system.

This interpretation proposes that although people may feel some propensity towards deviance, their own internal means of control, such as one's own conscience or set of values emerging from their relationships to other individuals and society, are powerful factors in decreasing the likelihood that one will deviate from social norms.

This theory stands in contrast to the emphasis on external means of control described by conflict theory, in which individuals conform because an authority figure (such as parents or the state) threatens punishment as a result of deviance.

Hirschi later developed **self-control theory**, along with criminologist Michael Gottfredson. This theory posits that the central factor in crime is the absence of self-control on the part of individuals. Individuals with high self-control tend to consider the long-term consequences of their actions, while those with low self-control do not, making them more likely to commit crime. Low self-control is attributed, in part, to ineffective parenting. According to Hirschi and Gottfredson, children develop a certain level of self-control by the age of about seven or eight, and that level remains relatively stable throughout the life course. Those with low self-control are less able to delay gratification, causing them to act impulsively, which results in risk-taking behavior (i.e., crime).

Sociologist Robert Agnew developed **general strain theory**, which we discussed briefly in Chapter 10. The theory focuses on strain as the cause of crime and delinquency, and identifies three types of strain that people experience which lead to criminal behavior:

1) The failure to achieve positively valued goals – This occurs when an individual is unable to achieve the goals that are positively valued in society, such as financial security and stable employment.

2) The removal of positively valued stimuli – This refers to things such as the end of a relationship or loss of a job.

3) The presentation of negative stimuli – Physical or emotional abuse and dangerous living conditions, such as those in high-crime areas, are examples of negative stimuli.

Individuals who experience these types of strain over a period of time are more likely to engage in criminal behavior.

The World System and Crime

Significant insights into the etiology of crime can be ascertained through the social functions, social interactions, and social conflicts perspectives. We would suggest, however, that they could be successfully complemented by an approach that is more global, and which takes *opportunities* for crime as an important factor in explaining crime (Kick and LaFree 1985). The concern with opportunities for crime and resultant crime rates is particularly useful for our efforts to explain cross-national variations in rates of murder and theft. The successful carrying out of murder or theft requires an offender, a person or object providing a suitable target for the offender, and the absence of capable guardians willing to prevent violations. These elements are directly related to levels of economic development within nations, which result from their structural position in a global system.

Murder. A striking feature of murder is the frequency with which it is committed by offenders who have known the victim with some degrees of intimacy prior to the crime. Conditions favorable to murder, as well as those favorable positive expressions of emotion, are produced by frequent and long-lasting interpersonal contacts among large numbers of social intimates and acquaintances.

Sociology has sufficiently established the idea that societal development affects the nature of intimate interpersonal contacts, as suggested by the prior review of major sociological approaches to crime and deviance. Development is a broad social force, which reduces the frequency and duration of contacts among intimates, which are so crucial to differential association and labeling interpretations. First, development lessens daily contact among intimates by pulling men, women, and often children, out of the home for work, education, and leisure. Second, precisely as suggested by social disorganization themes, development is associated with incentives for spatial relocation and vast transportation infrastructures that greatly expand geographical mobility. These forces ultimately reduce the numbers of contacts among intimates and acquaintances. Finally, development is closely related to the transition to small family size, which acts as a key demographic force that most directly and radically decreases the total number of contacts among intimates.

By pulling intimates out of the family for work, education, and leisure, development diminishes the frequency and duration of contacts among the individuals who are most apt, through opportunity (geographic closeness) and willingness (emotional bonds) to kill one another. By providing more opportunities for mobility, development further reduces the kind of intense social interactions among family, friends, and neighbors that commonly results in murder. Mobility also provides greater escape opportunities for potential victims (or perpetrators) from the ongoing feuds and recurring hostilities that often characterize developing, agrarian-based societies. Furthermore, with the reduction of family size as a result of development, the number of contacts among those who are among the most likely to kill one another is further and perhaps most dramatically attenuated. Notice that these themes stand in some contrast to social functions and social interactions explanations. Recall, however, that these perspectives tend to be based on the experiences of industrial or post-industrial (core) nations rather than periphery nations. Also, these perspectives do not focus on crimes of murder, which may be explained in different ways than other sorts of crimes.

Theft. One necessary feature of theft is, of course, the availability of valued commodities to steal. Theft, however, in sharp contrast to murder but equally important, is typically committed by offenders on the property of victims with whom they have not had prior relationships. "Professional," "serious," and "career" property offenders rarely steal from people who are well known to them. In part, this relationship is a simple function of the crime: thieves, compared to murderers, generally choose strangers as victims to reduce their chance of detection, and tend to commit their crimes more frequently. Further, to avoid detection, the thief needs to find social contexts in which not only the potential victim, but also friends, relatives, and others are not available to protect the victim's property. The social context most favorable to theft is one in which a large number of desired and portable commodities is available with infrequent and short-lasting contact among small numbers of intimates and acquaintances. These circumstances differ greatly from the social forces that foster murders.

Economic development augments opportunities for property offenses through the expansion of commodity production and distribution. That is to say, it increases the volume and variety of commodities "worth stealing." In core countries, a large number of small but expensive items are available to wide segments of the population; while in the non-core people tend to own fewer commodities that are not nearly as available to a wide variety of others, due to the more rural nature of peripheral and semiperipheral societies.

Economic development and social change also encourage theft by minimizing personal home guardianship. Nonagricultural work requirements, educational opportunities, and geographical mobility in the core of the world system cause people to be away from the home for long periods of time. In concert with development-related reductions in household size, these dynamics greatly limit personal home guardianship, and increase opportunities and incentives for theft. Similar processes in neighborhoods as a whole further decrease the effectiveness of community surveillance, while simultaneously exacerbating residential theft rates, as emphasized in social disorganization interpretations.

Economic development, and its accompanying social changes, encourages nonresidential theft by greatly expanding the marketing of merchandise in commercial settings. The widespread establishment of retailing institutions carrying expensive and portable commodities (for example, jewelry, electronic equipment) among core countries creates product availability to both consumers and thieves. This is true, as well, for rapidly developing countries in the semi-periphery (and "semicore") of the world system. The societies of the periphery are characterized by economic stagnation and limited wealth distribution, making markets smaller. In other words, shopper (and thief) anonymity is reduced as fewer items for purchase or theft are offered.

In sum, core position in the world system produces economic development, which is negatively related to murder opportunities. This is because the forces of development reduce interpersonal contacts among intimates and acquaintances. Important mechanisms are industrial and service-sector labor requirements, educational participation, and infrastructural development permitting geographical mobility. The social disorganization perspective also emphasizes these mechanisms. Across most of the world, rapes and murder are substantially greater in periphery countries than they are in core countries.

On the other hand, the world system impacts national economic development, which exacerbates social contexts favorable to theft. Countries at the top of the international hierarchy combine mass commodity production and marketing with geographical mobility and anonymity, all of which fosters theft opportunities. In the periphery, meanwhile, these conditions are opposite, resulting in lower theft rates.

This preliminary synthesis of world-system theory with social disorganization theory shows how relevant points from two perspectives may be interwoven to offer a cross-national explanation of murder and theft. One could certainly propose several ways in which the social functions, social conflicts, social interactions, and social exchange perspectives could be bridged to formulate better theories of crime. We urge you to think in such terms as you engage in your sociological imagination.

Current Trends in Crime in the United States

According to recent polls, most Americans (68 percent) believe that crime in the United States is getting worse (Gallup 2011). The overall crime rate, however, has been declining for over twenty years. Between 1992 and 2012, the violent crime rate fell 49 percent in the United States. Violent crime includes murder and non-negligent manslaughter, which fell 49 percent, forcible rape, which fell 37 percent, robbery, which fell 57 percent, and aggravated assault, which fell 45 percent (Uniform Crime Report 2013).

During that time period, the property crime rate decreased by 42 percent. Property crime includes, burglary, which decreased by 43 percent, larceny-theft, which decreased by 37 percent, and motor vehicle theft, which decreased by 64 percent (Uniform Crime Report 2013).

Declining crime rates have not always been the trend in the United States. Prior to the early 1990s, crime rates had been increasing for decades. Between 1960 and 1992, the violent crime rate increased by about 370 percent and the property crime rate increased by over 180 percent.

Crime rates vary by region, just as they do over time. In 2011, the South experienced the highest overall rate of crime, with 41.3 percent of all crime occurring there. In the West, 22.9 percent of all crime occurred, 19.5 percent occurred in the Midwest, and 16.2 percent occurred in the Northeast (U.S. Department of Justice 2011). These regional differences have remained fairly consistent in recent decades.

CHAPTER SUMMARY

- Crime is an important issue to people in the United States; this is not surprising, given the U.S.A.'s high crime rate in the third millennium.
- Throughout history crime has been explained from many perspectives (e.g., bodily conditions, devils, body types, individual psychology, biochemistry), but sociology offers a more comprehensive perspective.
- Social Control, Self-Control and General Strain Theories are efforts to make sense of the complex interactions between individuals and the larger social system that lead some people to crime.
- Crime is a violation of law, while deviance encompasses behaviors that violate normative expectations.
- The social functions approach emphasizes the functions of deviance, crime, and system equilibrium. Related themes are found in the crime causes of strain, social disorganization, and anomie.
- The social interactions approach emphasizes definitions of criminal behavior, differential association, and the importance of societal reactions or labels to identify subsequent deviant behaviors.
- The social conflicts approach specifies how law and its implementations favor powerful groups over weaker groups.
- An "opportunities" approach offers a cross-national view of the causes of murder and theft.

19 The Sociological Imagination in Late Modern Society: Postmodernity, Chaos, and Complexity

As we saw earlier, profound social changes came about in the eighteenth, nineteenth and twentieth centuries that sociologists and historians refer to broadly as **modernity**. These changes included dramatic rises in population and urbanization, higher levels of literacy and formal education, labor force differentiation, rises in individualism, technological innovation, unprecedented levels of industrial production and also of the consumption of resources, greater faith in science and a decline in religious authority.

With these changes, the world saw vast upheavals in modes of production and socio-political systems that continue even now unto the current time. Virtually all of the social changes, and particularly big ones of the sort we are considering here, are uneven and involve huge amounts of cultural lag. In broad-brush terms, the world went from largely agrarian modes of production and feudal systems of social organization, to industrial modes of production with capitalist economic systems with approximations of democratic systems (or at least those holding elections) in the political realm.

No set of social changes occurs without an underside, and those occurring with modernity are no exception. The discipline of sociology itself arose in the nineteenth century, in no small part in an effort to understand the processes of modernity and the problems that came about as a result. The foundational thinkers viewed problems attendant to the processes of modernity as central; the iron cage of rationality for Weber, alienation for Marx, anomie for Durkheim are three such exemplars.

Understanding Modernity and Its Problems

The interrelated processes of modernity such as rapidly increasing population size and density, an increasing faith in science and technology, an increasingly specialized division of labor, the rise of individualism and increases in mass literacy and education, all could be said to have a common theme of increasing technological and social complexity—complexity of social institutions on the macro level and complexity of information on the micro level.

An important aspect of the modernization process is its very *unevenness*. In a related vein, the phenomenon of "cultural lag" (Ogburn 1932) is important to consider as well. Different aspects of society change at different rates, sometimes quickly and sometimes very slowly. The economy is likely to change more quickly than the political system, which in turn is likely to change more rapidly than religious institutions and practices.

Within societies, there are of course many social institutions, all of which are profoundly affected by modernization. These include the family, the economy, religion, the polity and the military, for example. Each of these institutions has multiple interpenetrations with the others—the family with religion, the economy with the polity, etc. As societies modernize and become more complex, these interpenetrations become more complex as well. Going back far enough in pre-modern society, for example, the family and the economy were not differentiated nearly to the extent they are now (Turner 2003). Before modernity, families tended to be productive units on a family farm, for instance, and children tended to follow the vocations of their parents. In contemporary society, the "nuclear family" (and even many of the "non-traditional" variants of it, such as single-parent or gay-couple households), nonetheless tends to be an institution quite separate from the productive economy. In a sense, the economy is organized around production and the family around consumption.

The modernization process is intertwined with religious practices and beliefs. Some considerations in this regard include Weber's observation that religious practices tend to become more rationalized as societies modernize. Monotheistic beliefs tend to preponderate in more developed societies, while some combination of animism and polytheism are more common in hunter-gatherer societies. Secularism for a time appeared to be so intertwined with the modernization process that it prompted a number of theorists (most notably, Auguste Comte, the person who coined the term "sociology") to see it as an integral part of that process.

The Maturing of Modern Society and the Rise of the Postmodern Condition

As a way of making sense of the world, social explanations roughly paralleled the modernization process itself. For example, with the rise of rational-legal systems as articulated by Weber, there also arose a greater reliance on statistical studies and ever more precise measurements. Yet there are challenges to the idea of modernization as a master trend. As the twentieth century progressed, the postmodern critique took on greater significance.

At the risk of generalization, it is useful to articulate three distinct modes of organizing and interpreting social experience: traditional, modern, and postmodern. One way to view these is as successive "stages," yet it bears emphasizing that, particularly for societies that have passed from the traditional to the modern, each of these aspects tends to be present in some varying degree.

In an ideal-typical sense, we can identify these three as analytically distinct ways of making sense of social and cultural experience, and these organizing principles, operate on a number of levels of analysis, but most notably on the macro-societal level, on the level of individual consciousness, and on the level of civil interaction. They have both **synchronic** (happening at the same time), as well as **diachronic** (unfolding over a long period of time) qualities.

These do not necessarily proceed in "stages" per se, at least not in the sense that one stage must be completed for another to begin. A given society and people in it are likely to contain aspects of each of them. Social theorists sometimes refer to these ways of thinking and being as "**hermeneutic circles**" (c.f. Gadamer 1989), or communities of discourse that find and express meaning with a common symbol system. The hermeneutic circles can be thought of in terms of where they fall in the modernization process.

Characteristics of the Premodern, Modern and Postmodern

Premodern/Traditional	Modern	Postmodern
Durkheimian Mechanical Solidarity	Durkheimian Organic Solidarity	Abnormal Divisions of Labor
Tradition Based	Rise of Weberian Rational/Legal Systems	Reactions Against the Iron Cage of Rationality
Clannish and Close-Knit	Rise of Individualism	Rise of Narcissism
Religion is Typically Animistic/Polytheistic	Religion is Typically Monotheistic	Rise of Atheism/Agnosticism
Rural and Agrarian	Urban and Industrial	Global and Reemergence of the Local
Connectedness with the Natural Environment	Externalization of Environmental Problems	Overwhelming Environmental Risk
Pre-Newtonian	Newtownian/Scientific/Technological	Post-Newtonian, Suspicion of Science
Cognitive Method: Myth, Allegory	Cognitive Method: Rationality	Cognitive Method: Irony

Table 19.1 (adapted from Burns, Boyd and Dinger 2003)

We can identify these three hermeneutic circles, along with some of their salient characteristics, as:

- **Premodern/Traditional**

This is a tradition-based society, marked by pre-Newtonian views of science and religion. That is to say that typically, there is an emphasis on myth and magic, rather than scientific explanations (think, for example, of the Noah's Ark story in the book of *Genesis*, or the manifestation of Krishna as a thousand "splendid suns" in the *Bhagavad Gita*).

The dominant social form is what Durkheim has termed "mechanical solidarity." There is very little division of labor and the society is small enough that all are known to each of its members. A key distinction is made between those who are in the clan relative to those outside the clan.

As Durkheim theorized, individualism has not yet arisen in premodern society. Rather social life is characterized by the pre-contractual mechanical solidarity of small societies tied together by kinship. Information itself is processed, classified and stored relative to these clannish social arrangements (Durkheim and Mauss 1903/1963).

- **Modern**

    As societies modernize and become more urban, there is a decline in agrarian ways of living and organizing experience. Paralleling macro-level social changes, there is a rise in "Newtonian attitudes," including rationality and science as ways of seeing and organizing information.

    Modernity is also characterized by the rise of "universal truths." Religious zeal takes the form of missionaries who work largely in tandem with colonial powers. The universal truth of religion dovetails well with the expansion of mercantilism, feudalism or, particularly, capitalism.

    Durkheim's oft-quoted dictum is instructive here: *"The individual is born of society—not society of individuals."* It is in modern society that we first see a rise in individualism.

    The rises in rationality and individualism are themselves intertwined. As Durkheim and Mauss point out, it is here where individual reflective thought comes into its own. This makes possible the scientific rationality, and the technology dependent upon it, that characterizes the process of modernity.

    An integral, and perhaps even defining, characteristic of modernity is a rise in complexity (Hage and Powers 1992). Social institutions grow, become more rationalized and specialized. One way of dealing with this on the macro level is through the rise of mass education systems. On the individual level, we see the rise of "experts" in some focused aspect of the overall complex social picture. Paralleling the respective areas of expertise are increasingly variegated vocabularies. While these vocabularies potentially facilitate technological advance, modern society is at risk of technology outrunning anyone in the society's ability to handle it. A closely related risk to individuals is of becoming so specialized that they lose integration with the overall society.

    As modernity progresses toward postmodernity, the older institutions, most notably religion, tend to lose their hold over individuals. This involves what Hunter (1981:4 ff.) has characterized as a de-institutionalization. Concomitant with this is a rise, at least potentially, in Marxian alienation and Durkheimian anomie. Yet these are distributed unevenly across society (Dawson 1978).

    This very unevenness is itself a social phenomenon. Paralleling the uneven distribution of economic resources, there is a rising cultural unevenness as well. A large part of this is the urban-rural dichotomy. The Marxian "metabolic rift" between town and country widens and hardens into a different set of values. This rift takes on various complexities which, in late modernity, manifest in ways such as agribusiness supplanting the family farm, overproduction, managed consumption through saturation marketing of goods of marginal value, the overweening and widespread use of credit and the fetishism of commodities.

    A number of perceptive twentieth century social theorists began to see a serious underside of the project of modernity in general, but also with the theories that sociologists had developed to understand it. In particular, critical theorists of the "Frankfurt School" in Germany (e.g., Adorno 1966: Habermas 1973; 1975; 1984 & 1987) began to articulate several paradoxes of modernity that had been predicted in one way or another by both Marx and Weber.

Life in late industrial society had become sufficiently different from earlier, not only on the macro level, but also for the lives of individuals living in that society. Life had become more differentiated, or fractured, to the point that there were competing demands and expectations on individuals (Giddens 1991; Hage and Powers 1992).

- **Postmodern**

In postmodern society, there is a decline in the all-embracing universal narrative. This is partially a function of the increasing awareness of the limits of rationality, but also of the increasing sense among disenfranchised peoples of the connection between social power and ways of organizing knowledge. For postmodern social theorists, the universal narrative of conflict theorists such as Marx (the progression from feudalism to capitalism to socialism to communism), is just as inadequate as the universal narrative of functionalists from Durkheim (with the grand transition of primitive to modern societies as characterized by the gradual supplanting of mechanical solidarity with organic solidarity) to Parsons (with a belief that there is or will be an overall value generalization).

There is a reaction to the complexity, information overload and the hyperrationality of modernism, an outcome of which is that traditional symbols begin to outrun the things they once represented. As a result, there is a rise in cynicism and sense of irony toward traditional symbols and institutions.

A symbol that becomes alienated from its original meaning is called a **"simulacrum"** (Baudrillard 1972/1981; 1983). An example of a simulacrum might be a brand name that once stood for quality, but now is a "must" to buy, not for the inherent quality of the goods, but because it has come to be a "name brand."

Paralleling the rise of irony, there is a tendency to reject modern standards of rationality. As a reaction to the fractionation of vocabularies born largely of the rise of different areas of expertise in modernity, postmodern societies are likely to meld different symbol systems in ironic ways (Beckford 1989, 1992). We stress here our emphasis on the postmodern condition itself (Derrida 1984), more than the postmodern theory that arose to explain it.

This leads to there being numerous discourses to which individuals are exposed simultaneously, precipitating a possibility of information overload, in which people tend to shut down and become "alienated" or, alternatively, to combine discourses in ironic ways. This latter condition, sometimes referred to as **"memetic contagion,"** contributes to the ironic melding of disparate ideas, interpretable as anything from creativity to chaos (Dear and Flusty 2002:227). What alienated and desperate people in the midst of the postmodern condition come to see as "individual" style statements (e.g., wearing sneakers with formal clothing, or baseball caps with tassels to graduation) reflect this larger trend.

Paralleling the decline of modern colonialism in the wake of the World Wars of the twentieth century was the advent of a neo-colonialism, characterized by unequal exchange relationships, a worldwide division of labor and huge economies of scale. With these changes came new degrees of environmental degradation. Urban areas, particularly in Third World countries, would burgeon as never before. Yet, the cultural imperialism of modernity was supplanted in some significant degree by a rise of irony in the social reconstruction of culture in the developed world (Gurnah 2002).

Postmodern Social Theory

Postmodern social theory arose in response to these widespread social conditions that, taken together, comprise what sociologists characterize as the postmodern condition. Postmodern social theory is diverse, but tends to have certain characteristics (Rosenau 1992; Ritzer 1997). These include:

1. Postmodern theory is critical of modern society. It sees society largely in terms of its failures and excesses, rather than in terms of its positives.
2. Postmodern social theory rejects overarching theoretical statements, grand theory and "metanarratives" that see large historical trends and meaning in those trends.
3. Postmodern social theory rejects modern standards of science and rationalism, preferring emotion, feeling and intuition.
4. Postmodern social theory holds that there is no universal truth. Rather, truth is relative. What is seen as true and right in a situation typically turns out to be intertwined with power relations. Put another way, people in power often are able to define what is true for a given society and culture.
5. Postmodern social theory is skeptical of traditional boundaries, not only between disciplines, but also between fact and fiction.
6. Postmodern social theory is often "decentered." What a critical mass of people in modern society see as central, postmodernists see as no more important than that which may have been traditionally excluded or marginalized.

Postmodern Social Theorists

Jean Baudrillard was a French sociologist who many viewed as the most important representative of the postmodern approach (Ritzer 1997). Though Baudrillard did not consider himself a postmodernist, many of his ideas fit well into that philosophy. When it came to sociological theory, for example, Baudrillard stated, "the only thing you can do [with theory] is play with some kind of provocative logic" (Baudrillard 1993). This rejection of the application of some general theory to society as a whole is a cogent example of the postmodern tenet that there is no universal truth, and that overarching, grand theories are of little use. Early in his career, Baudrillard was influenced by the work of Karl Marx, only to later distance himself from, and even critique, the Marxian perspective. In his later years, Baudrillard strayed from established sociological thinking and began to focus his work as a critique of contemporary society. Baudrillard believed that society has entered a new phase of meaningless and endless proliferation, which resembles the growth of cancer, AIDS, obesity, and the like (Ritzer 1997).

French philosopher **Michel Foucault** was one of the most influential social theorists of the second half of the twentieth century. Foucault was a self-proclaimed historian of systems of thought, who argued throughout his career that power is derived from discursive networks. For Foucault (1965; 1966; 1969), the modern hermeneutic circle, in particular, conflates knowledge and power. In modern society, Foucault and others believe there is too much faith in authorities such as psychiatrists, physicians and scientists. Their specialized knowledge becomes a way of performing social closure, and maintaining power differentials. In describing the nature of discourse and its role in society Foucault states:

Jean Baudrillard (1929 - 2007)

Baudrillard's rejection of the application of general theories fits in well with post modernist thought. He is considered by many sociologists to be the most important representative of the post modernist approach.

> [I]n every society the production of discourse is at once controlled, selected, organized and redistributed according to a certain number of procedures, whose role is to avert its powers and danger, to cope with chance events, to evade its ponderous, awesome materiality." (Foucault 1969)

Jacques Derrida (1930-2004), whose work was influential in a number of disciplines, including philosophy, art, political theory, and even architectural theory, initiated a philosophical paradigm known as *deconstructionism* in the 1960s. **Deconstructionism** falls under the umbrella of postmodernism, as it questions the traditional methods by which truth, identity, and certainty are derived.

In his seminal book *Of Grammatology*, which is considered a foundational text in deconstructionism, Derrida challenges many traditional ideas in Western philosophy. In particular, Derrida puts forth the idea that one of the weaknesses of traditional Western philosophy is that writing seems to be viewed as merely a derivative form of speech. To Derrida, writing was of great importance, believing that it is more general than, and encompasses, speech (Ritzer 1997).

Another early developer of postmodernism, Polish sociologist **Zygmunt Bauman**, directed his work to modernity and postmodern consumerism. Not unlike Weber before him, Bauman posited that hierarchical bureaucracies, regulation, and control, all of which came about as a result of modernity, served to remove unknowns and uncertainties, thus removing individuals' personal insecurities.

Bauman then made a distinction between modernism and postmodernism by identifying two types of practitioners: *legislators* and *interpreters* (Ritzer 1997). Legislators engage in a modern type of intellectual work, making authoritative statements, which serve to arbitrate where differences of opinion exist. These are the modernists. Interpreters, on the other hand, are engaged in postmodern intellectual work; translating the ideas within traditions and facilitating communication among autonomous communities (Bauman 1992).

Jean-Francois Lyotard was a French sociologist, philosopher, and literary theorist. His book The *Postmodern Condition* was highly influential in the development of the postmodern approach. Consistent in his work was the idea that reality consists of many separate, singular events and therefore cannot be properly represented by any single rational theory. According to Lyotard, postmodernism should involve "war on totality" (Lyotard 1988). This meant that the grand narratives of modernism, with their statements of totality, should be eschewed.

French scholars Gilles Deleuze, Paul Virilio, and Bruno Latour (1993; also see Latour and Woolgar 1986) were also credited as important contributors to the postmodern philosophy, along with American scholars Richard Rorty (1979), David Harvey (1989), and Frederic Jameson (1991).

The convergence of feminism and postmodernism was seemingly inevitable. Both paradigms gained momentum in the second half of the twentieth century as a sort of reaction to traditional ideals. Philosophers Nancy Hartsock (1989), Judith Butler (1990), and Sandra G. Harding each offered a unique approach to postmodernism, working within a feminist framework.

The scientific method itself comes under the gaze of postmodernists. They analyze it and break it down in a way that takes away its mystique (this kind of critical and skeptical analysis is an example of the postmodern practice of "**deconstruction**"). Under such withering critique, science itself becomes one of many possible modes of discourse (Latour and Woolgar 1986; Latour 1993).

Theoretical Voices of Late Modernity

Many social theorists reject the idea that society has entered a stage of postmodernity, arguing instead that modernization continues today. That is, contemporary societies are exhibiting a continuation of institutional and cultural traditions brought about by modernity. This continuation of modernity is referred to as **late modernity**.

Drawing on Max Weber's work, particularly with rational bureaucracies, sociologist **George Ritzer** developed a concept known as **McDonaldization**, which describes a scenario in which a society adopts the characteristics of a fast-food restaurant. Mcdonaldization refers to the process of *rationalization*. Central to this process is the idea that any task can be rationalized. In practical terms, this means that tasks are broken down into smaller tasks until each task has been broken down to the most incremental level. This results in a method that can be repeated over and over with the same outcome. Efficiency, predictability, and calculability are aspects of rationalization. While this may seem beneficial on the surface, according to Ritzer, it can result in outcomes that were not anticipated. In the case of fast-food restaurants, the unanticipated consequences are long waits in line (despite being called *fast* food), unhealthy food being distributed to the masses, and millions of tons of trash produced, and alienated workers (Ritzer 1993).

Discussing modernity within the framework of agricultural sustainability, **Michael Bell** is best known for his work in environmental sociology. In his book *Farming for Us All: Practical Agriculture and the Cultivation of Sustainability*, Bell explores the topic of sustainable agriculture. Utilizing interviews and close interaction with over 60 Iowa farm families, Bell sought to explain why some farmers are converting to sustainable practices, while most other farmers are not. In the book, Bell posits that "cultivation in the agricultural sense depends upon an approach to cultivation in the social sense" calling for an embrace of the "creativity of difference" (Bell 2004).

Reflexive modernization is a topic explored by German sociologist **Ulrich Beck**. Exploring the complexities and uncertainties that accompany the transition from what he characterizes as first modernity to second modernity, Beck sought to develop a framework in which the dynamics of cosmopolitan societies can be explored. *Second modernity* refers to the stage in which an already modern society radicalizes itself. During this stage of second modernity, the key institutions and even the very principles of society are transformed. Beck wrote "…we are witnessing not the end but the beginning of modernity—that is, of a modernity beyond its classical industrial design" (Beck 1992). With reflexive modernization, Beck wished to repurpose sociology as a science of the present. Beck devoted his work to such an approach until his death in January 2015.

Another important late modernity theorist, **Anthony Giddens**, argued against his contemporaries who maintained that a postmodern era has emerged. Giddens referred to the modern world as a "juggernaut" and posited that "so long as the institutions of modernity endure, we shall never be able to control completely either the path or the pace of the journey" (Giddens 1990). Note here that Giddens mentions the endurance of institutions. Recall from earlier in the chapter that postmodernists theorize that traditional institutions will lose their hold over individuals. Giddens' view that institutions are, in fact, enduring, helps make clear his position as a late modernity theorist rather than a postmodern theorist.

Jurgen Habermas is one of the most well known contemporary defenders of modernity. While other theorists focus on the risks involved with modernity, Habermas (1987) maintains that modernity is an "unfinished project" that offers the potential for an ideal society. Habermas argues in favor of the idea, which arose during Enlightenment and modernity, that we should seek a rational, scientific understanding of the world, an idea rejected by many postmodern theorists.

In *Dialectic of Enlightenment*, **Max Horkheimer** and **Theodor Adorno** write:

> Enlightenment, understood in the widest sense as the advance of thought, has always aimed at liberating human beings from fear and installing them as masters. Yet the wholly enlightened earth radiates under the sign of disaster triumphant. (Horkheimer and Adorno 1947)

Adorno and Horkheimer sought to explain how the Enlightenment, which gave rise to the dominant philosophies associated with modernity, could be intended to liberate human beings, but actually led to irrationality and destruction. They focus particularly on the rise of Nazism in Europe, and the disasters of World War II and the Holocaust. "Humans believe themselves free of fear when there is no longer anything unknown" (Horkheimer and Adorno 1947). This desire to remove the unknowns and dispel myths that dominated premodernity was an underlying principle of Enlightenment and modernity. In reality, however, Enlightenment led to mythical fear being radicalized.

Building on earlier theoretical ideas, particularly from theories about industrialization, modernization, symbolic interactionism, and role theory, **Jerald Hage** and **Charles Powers** (1992) consider how the vast sea changes of late modernity have impacted not only how people see and act in the world about them, but in how they view themselves. They make a compelling case that life in the twenty-first century and beyond is in many ways fundamentally different from what it has been up until recently. In particular, Hage and Powers examine the transition from industrialism to post industrialism, and its impact on the everyday lives of individuals. In examining the micro-level effects of post industrialism, they conclude that this new society requires a different type of individual; one with a creative and flexible mind who is able to confront the challenges of the new society with innovation and mental astuteness.

Daniel Bell (1973; 1976) looks closely at the evolution from industrial to postindustrial society, in which the economy transitions from a manufacturing to a service basis, placing increasing emphasis on things like finance, welfare, education and research. These changes in the economy transform what aspects of the labor market are in demand, which in turn fuels the education system and draws people into careers such as science, medicine, engineering, as well as into advertising and finance. As these changes take place, the emphasis on theoretical knowledge and innovative thinking comes to be more highly valued.

As with earlier theories (e.g., Marx, Ogburn, Lenski), Bell sees the importance of technology as a driver of social change. However, it is no longer subsistence technology that is the focus, but the more exotic and leading edge technology that comes from universities and high-end research institutions that most profoundly lead the way.

Postindustrial society is characterized by Bell as following a three-fold ethic, with each of the three aspects at loggerheads with the other two. The economy, for Bell, is very much still ruled by an ethic of efficiency. As with Weber, formal rationality is very much the key organizing principle of economic activity. However, this is often at cross purposes with the political system which, for Bell, is driven by a value of equality. Even more problematic, however, is the cultural realm, where values about self-actualization and self-realization are most important. Economic activity remains, at least to an extent, rational, still dominated by what Weber characterized as the Protestant Ethic. The culture for Bell in postindustrial society has some major irrational aspects. This is the major disconnect of postindustrial society, and a cause of disequilibrium as societies move into the twenty-first century.

Chaos and Complexity Theories

Chaos and complexity theories provide important tools for thinking and communicating about the social world. Despite being utilized in the natural sciences since the 1970s, chaos and complexity theories are coming into the social sciences and humanities only more recently (Blackman 2000: 144). In this section, we will discuss a number of ideas from these theories. Key concepts from chaos and complexity theories include lawful unpredictability, fractals, entropy, nonlinearities, sensitive dependence (or the "butterfly effect"), and self-organizing systems.

The measure of a superior social theory is its ability to model and make sense of social reality, and there are a number of insights from complexity and chaos theories that help illustrate this point. The theories offer a useful approach for a variety of social issues including education (Byrne and Rogers 1996; Fitz-Gibbon 1996); household, population, and economic change (Hills 1998); illicit drug-taking (Dean 1997); social inequality (Wilkinson 1996); and health (Tarlov 1996).

These concepts are not mutually exclusive, neither is this list exhaustive. Many of these ideas can be found in a number of well-known theories. Yet much of the power of these theories is best experienced when a number of these concepts are applied in conjunction with one another.

Lawful Unpredictability

A key tenet of chaos theory is that specific events are unpredictable. As such, it is crucial to make a distinction between predictability and lawfulness. While systems will often follow some general pattern, none of the particulars in that pattern may be predictable. We examine some of these patterns below.

Chaos theory places emphasis on the dynamics of process rather than the static of structure, which implies an emphasis on systems that are in a continual state of flux. However, there is some regularity in those processes. Chaos and complexity theorists search for these regularities, which are often found in processes that appear to be chaotic. These regularities can be found in economic systems (Bass 1999; Arthur 1999) as well as other social institutions.

In one particular issue of *Science*, for example, mathematical biologists Julia Parrish and Leah Edelstein-Keshet (1999) discuss patterns of aggregation among animal populations. They identify two types of patterns: those that respond to external circumstances, such as food or predation, and those that are "self organizing." They begin with a deceptively simple question: "Why do animals aggregate?" In answering this question, they cite a number of evolution-based assumptions, such as increasing survival capability and optimizing reproductive success. On the micro level, individuals typically compete for position and fill niches within these aggregations.

There are times in nature, however, when the aggregation patterns found are not optimal. In such cases, there appears to be a different organizing principle operating—these aggregations are best explained as self-organizing systems. In such systems, it is often the case that events happening early in the process tend to influence later events, which themselves influence even later events, such that a cascading process occurs. From that cascade of events, a pattern begins to emerge.

The question of "scaling up from smaller groups" is a central problem for students of complex systems, just as the micro-macro linkage problem has occupied the attention of social theorists (Parrish and Edelstein-Keshet (1999:101). In any type of social system, be it human or otherwise, there is a perpetual tension between individual and group interests. (c.f. Fain et al. 1994).

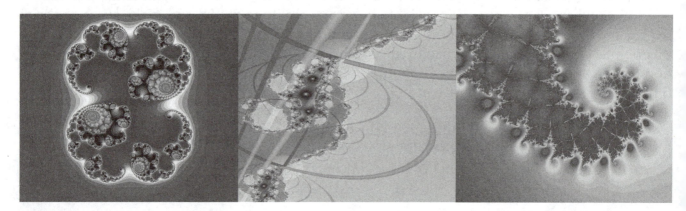

Fractals

A **fractal** is a pattern that is repeated on several different levels. Sociologists observe fractal qualities in a number of social processes. Above, are three examples of fractals.

Fractals

If we approach sociology as the study of the emergent properties of human collectives, what are the patterns that emerge? One pattern is that certain aspects of social dynamics on one level of analysis are often repeated on different levels of analysis. This characteristic is referred to in chaos theory as a "fractal" quality. Sociologists observe fractal qualities in a number of social processes.

It has been observed by researchers in a variety of disciplines, particularly chemistry, physics, geography and ecology, that patterns often repeat themselves at different levels of analysis. At each level of analysis, the pattern has different particulars, yet the universals of the pattern recur. These patterns behave similarly to a recursive function in mathematics (e.g., the factorial function where $n!=n*[n-1]!$) yet, unlike a mathematical function, the terminating condition (e.g., where $n=1$ in the factorial example) is not necessarily known, or even theoretically existent. In effect, the pattern may repeat itself infinitely. Acknowledging the recursive nature of many social processes, Bailey (1998) has recently pointed out the re-emergence of the significance of recursive theory in the social sciences.

There are interesting examples of fractals already familiar to theorists, although they are referred to by other names. One of the best known is Parsons's fourfold scheme of functional imperatives, or "AGIL" model. The four functional imperatives exist at any given level of analysis; expand on any one of the functional imperatives, and nested in it are four more functional imperatives. For example, at the level of the "unit act," *Adaptation* maps most closely with the biological organism, *Goal attainment* with the personality system, Integration with the social system, and *Latent pattern maintenance* with the cultural system. Expand on the integrative functional imperative of the social system and we observe four more functional imperatives—at the social system level, *Adaptation* maps most closely with the economy, *Goal attainment* with the polity, *Integration* with civil society, and *Latent pattern maintenance* with fiduciary institutions such as religion. Any of these four could be expanded upon, spawning its own A, G, I and L functional imperatives.

Fractals are found in group conflict as well. Conflict at one level is significanlty affected by conflict at other levels. Take, for example, two opposing political parties (e.g., Democrats and Republicans, or Labour and Conservatives, etc.), whereby battles within the Democratic party (e.g., Hillary Clinton vs. Barack Obama or John McCain vs. Mitt Romney in the 2008 primary elections) affect ways in which the Democrats then battle the Republicans. Yet again, there are likely to be disputes within the Obama camp, which affect ways in which Obama presents to McCain, etc. These conflicts are replicated within individuals as well. The determination of priorities within each level of analysis is important in tracking this conflict (Burns 1999; Burns and LeMoyne 2001, 2003).

In the religion and philosophy of Taoism, the universe (Tao) is organized into active (Yang) and passive (Yin) aspects. Each of those aspects in a sense contains the Tao, which in turn has its own yin and yang aspects. The human body is organized in yin and yang pairs (think of the sympathetic and parasympathetic branches of the autonomic nervous system). Also, every atom in the universe has the yin/yang polarities of protons and electrons. The point here is that at any level of analysis, the Tao operates. In human relationships, there is a give and take which follows principles of the yin and yang flow. The fractal nature of everything is thus inherent in the Taoist philosophical/religious tradition.

Fractals have numerous important implications. In the physical world, a fractal never has straight lines. For example, Mandelbrot (1977, 1982) asked the simple question: "How long is the coast of Britain?" Despite the seeming simplicity of the question, the answer is ultimately indeterminate because, depending upon the level of precision, the coastline is infinite. Any particular section of the perimeter being measured could be broken down to the rocks on the beach, which in turn could be broken down to the sand, etc. Each level has rough edges that become straight only when imposing linearity on them by moving up a level of analysis.

Yin and Yang Symbol

The yin and yang illustrates the fractal nature of the Taoist philophical/religious traditon.

Entropy

Entropy
Chaos theorists see the often absurd practices with some of the trappings of modernity, such as leaf blowers in terms of entropy. Creating negentropy (order) in one place necessarily creates entropy (disorder) in another.

A simple definition of entropy is energy dissipation in a system (for a detailed explanation of how entropy applies to social systems, see Bailey 1990). Energy in a system is typically manifested as order. In this sense, entropy is the opposite of order.

In chaos theoretic terms, imposing order on one part of a system will likely create disorder on another. As an example, consider the simple act of cleaning your room and throwing away unwanted items. You impose order on your room, which leads to a greater amount of disorder in another part of the system (in this case the trash can and, downstream, the waste dump).

In broader terms, there is a resonance between chaos theory and ecological theories, particularly in the case of energy flows. A number of classical theories can be examined through this lens. Consider, for example the concept of class conflict from Marxian theory. We could view class exploitation as one group (the bourgeoisie) taking energy (most notably in the form of surplus value) from another group (the proletariat). In this process, the rich accumulate wealth and the poor experience both poverty and a lack of control of their lives. Put another way, energy has been taken from the proletariat by the bourgeoisie, who in turn have increased entropy (c.f. Marx 1867/1967; Poulantzas 1975; Foster 1999; also see Straussfogel 2000).

Non-linearities

In the social sciences, the general linear model is often the default method. In this method, a change in some predictor variable(s) leads to some change in an outcome variable. This implicit model of social reality is also implemented to problems where there are no data. We see, for example, statements such as "an increase in anomie in a society will lead to increases in suicide rates." Occasionally, social scientists will model a polynomial instead of a linear function; this is still quite rare in sociology, but is more common among complexity theorists.

The ideas of thresholds, interactions, and indirect effects are also important in chaos and complexity theories. With linear regression often used in modeling and examining the social world in mainstream sociology, chaos theory acknowledges the crucial nature of thresholds. That is, there may be input to a system on many fronts, with no appreciable outcome until, at some point, there is some dramatic change in the outcome. We see an example of this in psychiatry with the **kindling hypothesis**; stressors can be added in a person's life with no discernable problems until the "straw that breaks the camel's back" is added, and the person has a crisis or breakdown. Because of this kindling effect, these thresholds, sometimes referred to as **tipping points** (Gladwell 2000) are a key focus of complexity theorists.

It is often the case that social phenomena cause outcomes only in combination with one another. Sometimes the presence of a phenomenon by itself does not lead to an outcome, causing social scientists to conclude wrongly that there is no relationship between them. As Homer-Dixon (1999) argues in *Environment, Scarcity, and Violence*, for example, environmental degradation often does lead to violence, but the linkages become clear only when that degradation occurs in combination with some other macro-social factor, such as dramatically uneven distribution of land, wealth, and/or population. This often leads to elites seizing more existing scarce resources, which in turn leads to some collective violence. Note here that a number of factors in combination with one another, none of which alone leads to discernible violence, can have catastrophic outcomes; and those outcomes themselves may be mediated by a second or third set of factors.

Equilibria and Feedback Loops

The concept of equilibrium in social systems can be traced back at least to Pareto (1935). A change in the system is presumably countered with a change in the opposite direction, driving the system back to a state of equilibrium. This state of equilibrium is referred to in chaos theory as an "attractor" state. As Goerner (1994) notes:

> In general, a dissipative system may have some initial transient behavior and then settle into a stable type of behavior. The pattern of behavior that a system moves toward over time is called an attractor. (P. 212)

In complexity theory there can be *more than one possible equilibrium state* in a given system. If the system loses equilibrium, there is a possibility that it will move into another equilibrium state.

We see this phenomenon in behavioral ecology. A given species tends to exhibit an *evolutionarily stable strategy (ESS)*, or optimal reproductive strategy. This tends to be based upon the carrying capacity of its niche, which, in turn, is largely based on food availability and the likelihood of survival based on externals such as predation. This evolutionarily stable strategy can last for a number of generations for that species. Yet when there is some shock to the system (e.g., the introduction of a parasite), the species will likely be in a state of instability for a time, but will eventually approach another ESS, which may be at an equilibrium point that is completely different from the first.

Sociologists have examined macro-level social processes for their effects on the environment (e.g., Burns et al. 1994, 1997, 2003). Given the possibility of multiple equilibria, however, pertinent questions remain unanswered. For example, at what point do small, incremental changes propel the system out of its current equilibrium? What would be the nature of the new equilibrium? While there is no clear answer, recent research (Rind 1999:106) suggests that "anthropogenic perturbations...[likely lead to]...transitions from one quasi-steady state to another."

Consequently, some attractors remain stable despite small outside disturbances; others are stable if a disturbance occurs in one direction but not the other, while others are generally unstable. Additionally, some attractors can possess different dynamics, whereby some reproduce consistent conditions in stable cycles, while others are more chaotic. These chaotic attractors are called "strange attractors" and they may generate dissimilar outcomes that are sensitive to initial conditions. Thus, we can think of attractors as being similar to social structures, but they characterize a system's long-term behavior (Blackman 2000: 146), and strange attractors can be thought of as oscillations among more than one equilibrium state.

Sensitive Dependence ("Butterfly Effect")

Drawing on his background as an engineer, Pareto made a distinction between stable and unstable equilibrium. A *stable equilibrium*, mentioned in the section above, is characterized by a *negative feedback loop*, where change in one direction is typically followed by change in a roughly opposite direction, leading to a relative stability in the system.

Pareto also allowed for *positive feedback loops*, wherein change in one direction tends to propel further change in the same direction. This tends to lead to a paradoxical state of *unstable equilibrium*. It is here that a positive feedback loop tends to self-perpetuate, even if the increment of the positive loop is in itself quite small, because even small changes become large when iterated enough times. Further, these positive feedback loops can interact with other seemingly inert phenomena, to produce some large sea change.

Therefore, an initial or prior state can be magnified and/or promulgated widely in a system. Meteorologist Edward Lorenz (1993) found that a very small difference in an initial state (e.g., in the temperature, pressure and wind velocity entered to six decimal places, versus the *same* parameters entered to three decimal places), could lead to a very different weather pattern. This led Lorenz to propose the now well-known question of whether a butterfly flapping its wings in one part of the world could cause a tornado on the other side of the world. Thereafter, a situation in which a very small change in an initial state could lead to a dramatic change in the outcome was sometimes referred to metaphorically as the "butterfly effect."

In some instances we could question whether the butterfly effect is found in social systems (e.g., would there now be an AIDS epidemic, had not the simian immunodeficiency virus made the leap to humans, through the "alpha" case of HIV?). It is also important, however, to acknowledge the doubtless larger number of cases in which the butterfly effect is not present. Indeed, not every butterfly flapping its wings causes a tornado, nor are the vast preponderance of butterflies likely to cause tornados.

The important question is *which* butterfly of the thousands flapping their wings causes the tornado? In the context of social systems, which small events lead to major social movements? Virtually all of the world's great religions, for example, began with one charismatic leader and a small group of followers. Why did some religions survive (and thrive) while countless others did not? It is plausible that some optimal level of positive feedback, where a change leads to even greater change in a similar direction, was of central importance in such cases.

An important and related idea is the law of increasing returns (Arthur 1999). In neo-classical economics, the law of diminishing returns posits that each additional increment of investment or effort produces marginally less returns than the one before it. In juxtaposition, in chaos and complexity theories, the principle of increasing returns states that certain outcomes tend to produce more of the same outcome.

We see an illustration of the law of increasing returns in Robert Merton's (1968) **Matthew effect**, in which well-known authors are more likely to be cited in the future, while less-cited authors are unlikely to be cited. Merton took the name of the effect from the Gospel of Matthew in the New Testament, which quotes Jesus as saying "...for whosoever has much, even more will be given, while he who has little will have what little he has taken away." (To engage in some momentary reflexivity, the fact that we cite Merton, rather than of one of thousands of other possible examples, increases the citation of the already oft-cited Merton).

We must emphasize two important characteristics of this phenomenon. The first is that once a phenomenon gets above a certain critical point (the precise location of which varies, but is analogous to the **tipping point** of a logistic regression curve, where the probability of any outcome below the tipping point is rounded to zero and above the point is rounded to one) there are increasing returns. Hence, the importance of initial conditions in chaos models, whereby, the initial condition may place two points in close proximity to one another, yet one happens to be above the tipping point, while the other may be below it. The second important aspect is that the law of increasing returns tends to attract more phenomena like itself, which in turn attract even more of a similar nature, which leads to the ideas of "self organizing systems."

Self-Organizing Systems

It is sometimes the case that these small changes serve as attractors for other energy, particularly when they become a repeating pattern, and that aggregation then serves as an attractor for other energy, and so forth. This may lend itself to a state where organization emerges from chaos (Prigogine and Stengers 1984).

We can often find the fractal quality here as well, where as systems expand, they tend to differentiate (e.g., Durkheim 1893/1964; Blau 1977). Yet, in many ways each aspect of that differentiation reflects the system itself.

Systems are self-organizing in several important ways. Most notably, by determining what is in the system and what is not, they organize their own boundaries; further, they organize the ways in which the parts within the system interact with one another (Ritzer 2000:323).

In sum then, chaos and complexity theories offer a number of insights for many fields that attempt to better understand the social world. As with any theory, though, it is important to speak to the question of scope conditions. These ideas are best considered, not in isolation, but in combination with a variety of social theories and disciplines.

CHAPTER SUMMARY

- Modernity refers to the profound social changes that came about in the eighteenth, nineteenth and twentieth centuries. These changes included dramatic rises in population and urbanization, higher levels of literacy and formal education, labor force differentiation, rises in individualism, technological innovation, unprecedented levels of industrial production and also of the consumption of resources, greater faith in science and a decline in religious authority.
- Premodern/traditional societies were characterized by myth and magic, rather than scientific explanations. There is very little division of labor and the society is small enough that all are known to each of its members.
- In postmodern society, there is a decline in the all-embracing universal narrative. This is partially a function of the increasing awareness of the limits of rationality, but also of the increasing sense among disenfranchised peoples of the connection between social power and ways of organizing knowledge.
- Postmodern social theory is critical of modern society, particularly in regard to its failures and excesses. In addition, postmodern social theory rejects overarching paradigms and grand theories that are meant to apply to society as a whole. Modern standards of science and rationalism are also rejected by postmodern social theory.
- Important postmodern social theorists include Jean Baudrillard, Michel Foucault, Jacques Derrida, Zygmunt Bauman, and Jean-Francois Lyotard.
- Late modernity theorists reject the ideas set forth by postmodernism, arguing that society has not entered a postmodern phase, but is instead exhibiting a continuation of modernity. That is, contemporary societies are exhibiting a continuation of institutional and cultural traditions brought about by modernity.

CHAPTER SUMMARY (cont.)

- Important late modernity theorists include, George Ritzer, Ulrich Beck, Anthony Giddens, Jurgen Habermas, Max Horkheimer, Theodor Adorno, Jerald Hage, and Daniel Bell.
- Chaos and complexity theories offer a number of insights for many fields that try to better understand the social world. Yet, as with any theory, it is important to speak to the question of scope conditions. These ideas are best considered, not in isolation, but in combination with a variety of social theories and disciplines.
- In that vein, we conclude with some of the salient points of chaos and complexity theories as they apply to the humanities and the social sciences.
- In this chapter we have highlighted several important key concepts of complexity and chaos theories. These are: lawful unpredictability, fractals, non-linearities, entropy, equilibria and feedback loops, sensitive dependence ("butterfly effect"), and self-organizing systems.
- We need to be very attentive to levels of analysis, their effects on one another, and their interactions. Order at one level may look like disorder at another. Imposing order on one part of the system may impose disorder on another. Also, we should be attentive to whether recurring processes tend to describe positive or negative feedback loops. Following the fractal nature of such processes, it is also important to note that sub-processes and sub-sub-processes may be on different types of trajectories than the process itself.

LW | The Last Word

The discipline of sociology arose in the nineteenth century in response to modernity and many of the problems that resulted, such as alienation and anomie. Sociologists have, to a large extent, remained focused on these problems and issues.

Social, demographic and technological changes have been so profound in late modernity, particularly since the end of World War II, that a case can be made that a new set of social issues and problems have arisen that were not adequately addressed by classical and mainstream sociology. These include problems with the environment, all-encompassing grand narratives that seem to have lost validity for many, globalization, and the fractured lives that have come about as a result.

In response to these differences, some distinct lines of social theorizing have arisen. Postmodern theory has made significant inroads into sociology, but no less incisive is chaos theory, and the tools of analysis and synthesis it brings to bear on the social condition. Meanwhile there is a rising recognition among sociologists that, while traditional theories still have the highest degree of relevance for late modernity, we must think innovatively to adapt them as society now moves into the third millennium.

The backbone of the discipline of sociology, and what gives it substance, is the set of powerful and incisive theories it brings to bear in understanding society and the actions of people in it. Exercising your sociological imagination will be an exhilarating and important challenge, as you continue in your education and in life. In so doing, you will see the relevance of theories in all sorts of circumstances and occasions, some expected and obvious—others not.

There is always room for good theory. Perhaps in thinking through the theories and findings in this book and in the accompanying readings, and applying them in life, you will come to develop theories of your own that will make a contribution to this dynamic and complex field. Welcome to that conversation…All the Best…TJB, ELK, and DP.

Glossary

Abnormal divisions of labor – According to Durkheim, one of three ways stratification can occur that does not align with the will of the people. This occurs when the governing power's first priority is something other than defending the common consciousness.

Absolute monarch – A ruler who monopolizes power. Absolute monarchs frequently claim a divine right to rule.

Accommodation – A cognitive process that occurs when a person reorganizes his or her conceptual categories in order to make conflicting information compatible with existing schema.

Account – When we discuss the reasons for our actions with ourselves or others in order to make sense of our behavior and to establish a context upon which a common definition that the social situation at hand can be built upon, we are giving an *account or accounting*.

Achievement – A situation in which people rise or fall in the stratification system, based on their own merit.

Actively alienated deviant – One of Talcott Parsons's four categories describing ways in which deviance may express itself in an individual. The actively alienated deviant's primary concern is to leave their small social system, and is often hostile to his or her role partners.

Actively conforming deviant – One of Talcott Parsons's four categories describing ways in which deviance may express itself in an individual. The actively conforming deviant overly conforms to expectations.

Adaptive upgrading – One of Talcott Parsons's four major aspects of social change that occurs as a society moves toward modernity. Adaptive upgrading describes how a society is more likely to improve the ways in which it allows its members to adapt to the environment as it gets bigger and has more interaction.

Age of mass consumption – The fourth stage in Walter W. Rostow's model of economic development. During the age of mass consumption, we see a surplus of wealth, yet stark inequalities still exist.

Agrarian society – In Gerhard Lenski's eco-technological theory of societal evolution, the stage that arises with the advent of more sophisticated tools for the tilling of soil, such as the plow, along with the domestication of beasts of burden.

Alienation – The feeling of estrangement from the product and process of one's labor, in Marx's paradigm.

Altruism – In Durkheim's analysis of suicide, altruism describes a situation in which the individual is so tightly integrated into the collective that there is little or no sense of the individual outside of that collective.

Anal expulsive – A tendency in which a child develops habits of sloppiness that develops during the anal stage if toilet training is overly lax, according to Freud's psychosexual stages of development.

Anal fixation – In Freud's psychosexual analysis, a type of arrested development that can occur during the anal stage if toilet training is traumatic in some way. The two types of anal fixations are anal expulsive tendency and anal retentive tendency.

Anal retentive – In Freud's psychosexual analysis, a tendency that can develop if toilet training is too harsh or takes place too early, which causes the child to want to retain his or her feces inside their body and may lead to the child becoming compulsive in a quest for neatness and order.

Anal stage – In Freud's psychosexual analysis, the stage that occurs from ages one to three in the child's life. During this time, the child derives pleasure from anal functions, such as the holding in or expulsion of feces. It is typical that the child undergoes toilet training during this time. If toilet training is successful and untraumatic, the child tends to pass through this stage successfully.

Anisogamy – The law that describes the behaviors of the two sexes as a reflection of their different reproductive strategies.

Anomic division of labor – In Durkheim's paradigm, an abnormal division of labor in which relationships among people is not properly regulated, thus resulting in a splintering of society.

Anomie – In the Durkheimian paradigm, a primary cause of social pathology characterized by a lack of norms that function to govern people's behavior in the society.

Ascription – When people acquire occupational roles as a result of inherited characteristics.

Assimilation – One of Simpson and Yinger's six types of ethnic integration that occurs when a minority group is absorbed into the larger culture.

Assimilation – According to Jean Piaget, the method by which a person adds new information onto her or his store of knowledge.

Atavism – A throwback to primitive times, in Cesare Lombroso's analysis of criminal behavior.

Audience – In Goffman's dramaturgical metaphor, the witnesses of an individual's social performance.

Authoritarianism – A political system in which citizens are barred from any popular participation in government whatsoever.

Authority – Power that people perceive as legitimate rather than coercive, according to Weber.

Baby boomer – A generation defined by an increase in the birth rate after WWII.

Back stage – In Goffman's dramaturgical metaphor, performers who are back stage are not attempting to make an impression and can "let down their hair."

Behaviorism – A predictive science of human behavior in which a given response could be predicted with accuracy from a given set of stimuli.

Biological determinism – A term that describes the argument that social behavior can be attributed to biological characteristics.

Bivariate regression – When we do regression with two variables in which one is a dependent variable and the other is independent.

Boundaries of toleration – The threshold of what is acceptable or unacceptable behavior in a society according to its members.

Bourgeoisie – The owners of production, in the Marxian paradigm.

Bracketing (Epoche) – An attempt to make sense of the world in which the perceiver attempts to isolate a phenomenon from the perceptions of it.

Breach – What occurs when some fundamental aspect of the way we construct the social world is challenged.

Breaching experiments – Social experiments undertaken by Garfinkel in which he had his students deliberately violate some social convention and therefore, the underlying social reality of which it was a reflection.

Bureaucracy – An organizational form based on relatively clear lines of authority, careful record keeping, work specializations, and rules and regulations.

Bureaucratic organization – Social organizations that are created for obtaining relatively specific, yet limited goals.

Bureaucrats – A class of salaried, non-manual specialists, in the Weberian paradigm.

Burke's dramatistic pentad – Kenneth Burke's paradigm in which five key elements—*act, scene, agent, agency and purpose*—are present in virtually every social interaction, regardless of the time, place, or culture.

Cause-and-effect – In a cause-and-effect relationship, a given independent or causal variable influences or determines a caused or dependent variable.

Centrality – In network exchange theories, the concept that describes the facilitation or constraint of the actor based on that actor's position in a network.

Challengers – The non-members of a polity who compete for power.

Character – In Goffman's dramaturgical metaphor, one of the two fundamental elements of the social individual; with the other being the performer.

Charismatic authority – Power that is gained through the extraordinary personal abilities of a leader, which may appear superhuman or divine.

Charter – A "mission statement" from the state, which explicitly spells out the school's purpose.

Church – A stable institution that tends to intellectualize religious dogma and restrain emotion relative to a sect, which tends to place emphasis on emotional experience.

Circulation of elites – A situation that describes new individuals constantly cycling into or out of elite status.

Civil – A war between different groups within the same state.

Class – A loosely ordered and unified social organization that is based on similarities in the power, the privileges, or the prestige of its members.

Class consciousness – A situation in which a class becomes aware of its class position and class interests.

Class interests – The oppositional interests that served to separate the two classes, in Marx's paradigm.

Coercive authority – Authority that has lost its legitimacy but attempts to retain the old power and reward structure.

Cognitive dissonance – The psychological phenomenon that occurs when new information does not fit well into existing conceptual categories.

Cohabitation – A situation in which unmarried couples live together in a sexual relationship.

Collective behaviors – Group behavior such as *crowds, mobs* and *riots* that have little lasting impact on society; as well as *rebellions, revolutions,* and *civil wars*, which often have long-lasting impact on society.

Collective conscience – In the Durkheimian paradigm, a sense of belonging to a community, shared emotional feeling, and a moral obligation to live up to the expectations of said community.

Community – A social organization that is territorially localized.

Compensatory groups – Large, *Gesellschaft* type collectives for which sanctions tend to be rational-legal in nature.

Conceptualization – The mental process whereby we take imprecise understandings and make them far more exact and specific; the process of giving names to the phenomena that we are most interested in.

Conditioned reflex – A response to a stimulus that is learned due to its association with another stimulus. The salivation reflex in the dogs in response to the sound of the bell in Pavlov's experiments was the conditioned reflex.

Conditioned stimulus – A stimulus that elicits a response due to its association with another stimulus. The sound of the bell in Pavlov's experiments was the conditioned stimulus.

Confederation – A loosely organized combination of societies that often cooperate in a mutual activity, but generally retain their independent power.

Conjugal (nuclear) family system – The family structure found in the United States and Europe, composed of a mother, father, and children.

Constitutional monarchy – A system of government in which a monarch is a symbolic head of state. Elected officials are responsible for the actual governance of societies, and these countries are guided by a formal constitution that prescribes government organization. This is in contrast to an absolute monarchy, in which the monarch holds complete power.

Contenders – Groups within a certain population, which collectively apply resources to affect government from time to time.

Control group – In a scientific experiment, the group containing subjects who are *not* exposed to the experimental condition.

Co-opting – In Pareto's paradigm, one way that elites attempt to hold onto power by recruiting capable individuals from the masses in order to prevent them from forming opposition groups.

Core – Powerful countries at the center of the global economy based on both local and distant markets.

Correlation – A measure of covariation. By definition, the correlation between any two variables will always fall between 1.0 and –1.0. A correlation of 0 means there is no relationship whatsoever between the variables.

Coup d'état – Takeovers of normal government processes by opposition groups.

Co-vary – When variables vary together in some way. Variables can co-vary positively, meaning they increase in value together, or they can co-vary negatively, meaning an increase in one variable accompanies a decrease in the other.

Craftsmen – Highly skilled manual workers, in Weber's paradigm.

Creating/defining problems – One way that elites attempt to hold on to power, in Pareto's paradigm.

Credential inflation theory – A theory stating that educational requirements serve as a function of the interest employers have in locating well socialized and respectable employees. In this system, concern for technical skills is of lesser importance.

Credited – In Goffman's dramaturgical metaphor, what occurs when the presentation of a character is indicative of the performer's true nature in a social setting.

Crime – A type of conduct that violates the law.

Crowd – A temporary gathering of people who come together to share a common focus of attention.

Deconstruction – A type of critical and skeptical analysis in which the object is analyzed and broken down in a way that takes away its mystique.

Deduction – The process of using a general theory to develop specific expectations or hypotheses. The opposite of induction.

Defense mechanism – Techniques used by the ego to avoid negative emotions, in Freud's psychoanalytic paradigm.

Deference – A symbolic means by which appreciation is regularly conveyed to someone, in Goffman's paradigm.

Demeanor – In Goffman's paradigm, part of a person's ceremonial behavior typically conveyed through deportment, dress, and bearing, which serves to express to those in his immediate presence that he is a person of certain desirable or undesirable qualities.

Democracy – A political system in which the citizenry exercises power broadly, either directly or indirectly.

Demographic transition theory – A model that emphasizes the connection between fertility rates, mortality rates, and modernization to explain population trends within societies as they transition from undeveloped societies, to developed, modern societies.

Dependent variable – In a scientific experiment, the variable that changes or varies depending on its relationship to the independent variable, which does not change.

Deprivation – According to George Homan's paradigm of exchange behaviorism, a term describing the increase in desirability of those rewards that have not been received in the recent past.

Derivations -- What people say about their behavior as opposed to the actual behaviors they display, in Pareto's paradigm.

Descent – The way societies trace their kinship over generations.

Descriptive statistics – The term given to the analysis of data that helps illustrate or summarize data in order to discern potential patterns in the data; for example, the mode, mean and median.

Deskilling – A degrading of the skills required of middle class work.

Deviant behavior – Behavior that does not conform to social expectations.

Diachronic – Unfolding over a long period of time.

Differential association theory – Edwin Sutherland's theory which states that criminal behavior is not a product of biology, strain or macrosocial conditions; but rather, like normal behavior, it is learned.

Differentiation – The specialization of labor that occurs as society evolves, leading to stratification systems.

Direct democracy – The direct participation of all members of a society in the decision making process.

Discreditable stigma – When the disparity between an individual's virtual and actual social identity is not known publicly, but which has the *potential* of becoming known at some point.

Discredited – In Goffman's dramaturgical metaphor, when a performance does not achieve its desired effect of being indicative of the performer's true self.

Discredited stigma – When the disparity between virtual and actual social identity is obvious to others.

Discrimination – Biased behavior toward someone based on his or her group membership.

Dissent – To hold or express opinions that are at odds with those that are commonly or officially held.

Distributive justice – In exchange relationships, a sense of the expected rewards in proportion to one's costs.

Division of labor – The differentiation or specialization of tasks that occurs as a population grows, diversity increases, and different groups become dependent on one another to fulfill their tasks.

Domestic violence – Violence that occurs within the home.

Domination – The process whereby subordinate groups become routinized in a subordinate position.

Dramatism – In Kenneth Burke's analysis, "dramatism" implies that language and thought are more than simply means of conveying information; they are "modes of action" in and of themselves, at least as important as labor or other types of physical activity.

Dramaturgy – In Erving Goffman's analysis, the use of theater as a metaphor to understand how people use symbols to communicate.

Ectomorphic – In Sheldon's analysis of criminal behavior, a body type that is thin, tall, fragile, and possesses weak bones and muscular structure. Ectomorphic individuals have overly fast reactions, and are inhibited, apprehensive, and chronically fatigued.

Ego – In Freud's psychoanalytic paradigm, the part of the self that serves as the "reality principle," mediating between the unbridled desires of the id and the cautiousness and guilt of the superego.

Egoism – In Durkheim's analysis of suicide, one of the primary causes of social pathology, which describes a lack of attachment of the individual to the larger society.

Elaborated codes – A heightened sense of perception, accompanied by a specialized vocabulary, about some aspect of the person's social reality.

Electra complex – In Freud's stages of psychosexual development, a girl's psychosexual competition with her mother for possession of her father. The Electra complex is analogous to the *Oedipus complex* in boys.

Elite education – A separate school system in which a few privileged students receive educations meant to prepare them for prestigious universities and eventually for high posts in the government, academe or industry.

Emergent properties – Aspects of the social that are not necessarily reducible by their individual parts.

Emotional support – An important social function of the family structure, which provides a sense of emotional security and a sense of belonging.

Empirical inquiry – Inquiry based on evidence through observation.

Endogamy – The prescription of marriage partners based on social norms of desirability and undesirability; marriage between individuals with similar characteristics.

Endomorphic – In Sheldon's analysis of crime, a body type that is soft, round, pudgy and enjoys comfort.

Entrepreneurs – In Weber's analysis of class, the privileged business class engaged in the actual day-to-day operation of commercial enterprises, unlike rentiers.

Episodic memory – The memory for specific experiences (or "episodes") that happen and can be remembered as such; as opposed to *semantic memory*, which describes the memory for a sense of the way things are generally.

Equilibrium – A state of balance in society, in Pareto's analysis of social systems.

Ethic – An interrelated system of values.

Ethnomethodology – The study of the body of knowledge and the range of procedures and considerations by means of which the ordinary members of society make sense of, find their way about in, and act on circumstances in which they find themselves.

Evaluation research – Methods that evaluate the impact of social interventions, as recommended by research.

Exchange – The form that interactions between and among people in many different times, places, and circumstances tend to take, in which we give something and receive something in return.

Exchange (circulation) mobility – A situation in which for everyone who goes up in the stratification system, someone else must go down.

Exchange behaviorism – George Caspar Homans' method of bridging the tenets of behavioral psychology from the individual into the social realm, by which he developed several principles to explain human behavior.

Exogamy – The conditions in which an individual attempts to select a marriage partner with different characteristics within a range of categories, as opposed to endogamy.

Experiment – A systematic procedure involving an experimental group and a control group intended to make a discovery, test a hypothesis, or demonstrate a known fact.

Experimental group – In an experiment, the group that contains subjects who are exposed to a given experimental condition, with the goal of discovering whether that experimental condition has an impact on the subjects.

Extended family – Family members such as sisters and their husbands, brothers and their wives, grandparents, aunts and uncles, and nephews and nieces all sharing the same household.

Extermination – The most extreme form of interaction between ethnic groups, in which members of one group kill another.

Extinction – In behavioral psychology, the decline and elimination of a learned response to a stimulus.

False consciousness – In Marx's paradigm, the situation in which a class is unaware of its own position and interests.

Family – A universal kinship structure consisting of blood relatives, common to all societies and cultures.

Family of origin – The family into which we are born.

Family of procreation – The family we build as adults.

Feral children – Children who have grown up without learning a language or the norms and beliefs attendant to a society.

Field research – A research method in which sociologists study social life in its natural setting, observing and interviewing people where they play, work, or live.

Force – Physical might.

Forced division of labor – A division of labor in which people are compelled to perform tasks that they find disagreeable, which tends to occur when people are not sorted into occupations based on interests and abilities.

Formal agents of social control – Governmental agencies, legislatures, a judiciary that interprets the law, clinicians such as psychiatric personnel, and police officers make these definitions.

Formal rationality – One of Weber's four major types of rationality, concerned with utilizing the most efficient means possible to achieve an end.

Four principles of self-concept formation – The method of self-formation conceptualized by Morris Rosenberg, which includes reflected appraisals, social comparisons, self-attributions, and psychological centrality.

Foxes – One of the two types of elites in Wilfredo Pareto's paradigm. Foxes are guileful and cunning, but too rational, and clever, with too many new ideas and too attentive to detail.

Frame – The way in which an experience is organized, arising from the social context in which it is perceived.

Free rider – A trading partner who pays essentially nothing in trade for the resources his or her partner has to offer.

Free rider problem – A situation in which an individual receives the benefit of an exchange, without paying the fair cost associated with it.

Front stage – In Erving Goffman's dramaturgy, what we allow other people to see when we realize an audience is present and are actively engaged in giving a performance.

Fundamental attribution bias – The psychological defense mechanism that describes how we tend to attribute positive outcomes to some inherent trait such as strength of character; while attributing negative outcomes to some external circumstance. We tend to give ourselves and those we perceive as like us the benefit of the doubt, while denying that to those we see as different from us.

Gender – The ideas, roles and norms, behaviors and expectations that develop relative to our sex in a social and cultural context.

Gender socialization – The process by which individuals learn about the norms, behaviors, and expectations associated with each gender.

Gendered division of labor – The difference between men and women in the context of jobs or tasks often found in the workplace, but even going so far as to profoundly influence personal and familial relationships.

General Strain Theory (GST) – a prevalent theory of crime that focuses on strain as the cause of delinquency, and identifies three types of strain that people experience that might lead to criminal behavior: The failure to achieve positively valued goals; the removal of positively valued stimuli; and the presentation of negative stimuli.

Generalized other – The process by which a person is able to develop a sense of how "other people" in society are likely to behave in a given set of circumstances.

Genital stage – In Freud's psychosexual analysis, the final stage of development in which the adolescent begins to take pleasure in sexuality.

Government – The state; the governing body of a community or nation; the organization that controls the principal concentrated means of force.

Groups' organizational capacity – A group's control of a wide range of resources, either generated internally (e.g., numbers' loyalties, organization dues), or provided by external sources (e.g., supportive groups).

Habitualization – The manner in which human activity tends to be repeated in set ways, allowing for an economy of effort in action and thought.

Hegemon – A powerful entity; the dominant power of the world system.

Hermeneutic circles – A concept describing that a given society and the people in it are likely to utilize aspects of many analytically distinct ways of organizing societal experience, operating on a number of levels of analysis.

High division of labor – A situation in which people and groups come to depend on one another more and more for what they produce and exchange.

Horizontal mobility – A type of occupational mobility in which people change occupations but don't move up or down in terms of occupational prestige.

Horticultural society – In Gerhard Lenski's eco-technological theory of societal evolution, the stage characterized by the advent of simple technological tools that permit the society to *settle* in one place.

Human capital theory – A theory describing how employers notice skilled employees performing more efficiently and reward skills with material incentives such as wages, which entices individuals to acquire skills through education.

Hunting and gathering society – In Gerhard Lenski's eco-technological theory of societal evolution, The smallest and most primitive of the societal types.

Hypothesis – In the scientific method, the expected outcome of each of these measured cause-and-effect relationships. A hypothesis states an expectation of the nature of a relationship between two variables, placing them into a causal ordering.

I – The subjective perceiver in the symbolic interactionist paradigm, as opposed to the "me," or the object of one's own perceptions.

Id – In Freud's analysis, one of the three components of the psyche serving as the "pleasure principle." Its interest lies in gratifying basic instincts, especially desires of libido. The id is not particularly concerned with consequences, and is intolerant of any delay in gratification.

Ideal type – An analytical construct or schema that accentuates key characteristics of structures or actions, which are found repeatedly in society; characteristics that best exemplify a specific type of dynamic.

Identification – The act of conceiving of ourselves as united with another person, because we see something of ourselves in the other.

Ideology – An interrelated system of beliefs.

Imperatively coordinated associations (ICAs) – The lines of authority in the society, in relation to which conflict develops.

Improper levels of specialization – One of the abnormal divisions of labor, in Durkheim's analysis.

Incest taboo – A near cultural universal, forbidding marriage or sexual relationships between certain kinds of kin.

Independent variable – In a scientific experiment, the variable that influences or causes the dependent variable.

Indexicality – The idea that social interactions and the language we use to talk about them take on different meanings, depending upon their contexts.

Indirect democracy – A system in which governmental decision making occurs through elected officials representing groups of people.

Induction – An approach in which we make a hypothesis by examining events in the world and make generalizations on the basis of individual events.

Industrialization theory – A theory emphasizing the idea that capital becomes increasingly concentrated as capitalism matures, resulting in a differentiation of the labor force, a separation of manual and mental labor, and a concomitant rise in the number of relatively well-educated managers and professionals.

Information control (impression management) – In Goffman's dramaturgy, the act in which the performer engages in an attempt to successfully represent his or her character.

Institutionalization – The process by which customs, norms or laws become accepted and used by many people; the process by which status differences become rigid as exchange patterns become routinized, resulting in stratification.

Instrumentality – The idea that knowledge has meaning only insofar as its potential in serving some specific purpose rather than being based on objective reality.

Insulation – A mechanism of social control in which the deviant is only partially removed from their interactions in the larger social system.

Interdependence – A term that conceptualizes society as an entity consisting of different parts that are gathered together in a system of reciprocity and reliance. The interdependent parts function to maintain the entire social organization.

Intergenerational mobility – One's occupation relative to one's parents.

Internalization – The process by which a child takes on the roles and attitudes of others and makes them his or her own during socialization.

Intersubjectivity – The process by which groups of individuals having a similar (though by no means precisely the same) subjective construction of their social worlds tend to perceive those constructions as objective.

Intragenerational mobility – Mobility within a generation, such as when a person starts out in a low status position and later comes to occupy a higher status position.

Iron cage of rationality – Weber's analogy describing the formally rational structures such as bureaucracies that eventually come to dominate us due to our increasing dependence on efficiency.

Isolation – One form of social control, in which the deviant is removed from the complex of interactions in their many social systems.

Joint acts – The concept that arises through repetitive or habitual behavior patterns whose meaning is established intersubjectively through culturally-embedded symbols and gives a framework through which to understand individual behavior.

Keys – Context clues provided by a social situation.

Kindling hypothesis – a psychiatric concept describing how stressors can be added to a person's life with no discernable problems until the "straw that breaks the camel's back" is added, and the person explodes, has a crisis or breakdown.

Kinship – A social bond that is based on blood relationships, relationships as a result of marriage, or by adoption.

Labeling theory – A theory focusing on society's reaction to deviant behavior and the effects of that reaction on the identity of those who are labeled.

Labor force participation rate – The official rates of full or part-time employment.

Labor market – The types of jobs available for people to hold.

Labor theory of value – In Marx's analysis, the idea that a person expresses his or her humanity through labor, and that the value of something is directly related to the human labor that went into it.

Late modernity – A continuation of modernity, in which contemporary societies exhibit a continuation of institutional and cultural traditions brought about by modernity.

Latency stage – In Freud's stages of psychosexual development, the stage in which the child focuses on the development of social and intellectual skills as the id becomes less strident in its demands for gratification.

Learned helplessness – In the behaviorist paradigm, a condition in which the individual begins to perceive punishment as being beyond his or her control, tends to quit trying different behaviors, becomes less active, and then simply accepts it.

Legitimacy – The state reached by the stratification system as it becomes routinized and people begin taking its routines for granted, following those routines rather than challenging them.

Legitimate authority – The authority of those whose power has been routinized via the stratification system.

Libido – In Freud's psychosexual paradigm, the unconscious sexual energy that motivates individual behavior.

Lions – One of the two types of elites in Wilfredo Pareto's paradigm. Lions are strong and daring, but inattentive to detail and not particularly clever.

Looking-glass self – Charles Horton Cooley's analogy describing how we come to perceive ourselves as we believe significant others perceive us.

Loose institutional coupling – A situation in which students do not work in the field in which they were trained, or where they do work in that field but in situations where they are under- or over-qualified.

Lumpenproletariat – The reserve armies of the unemployed, in Marx's analysis.

Macro – A term referring to large-scale social relationships, such as relations between nations.

Marriage – A legally sanctioned relationship that prescribes an enduring commitment to the relationship, and the fulfillment of roles and responsibilities.

Mass education – A much larger system of schools intended to train children for lower middle and working class occupations, as opposed to elite education.

Master status – An individual's primary identity.

Material density – The number of people per unit of space.

Matrilineal descent – A system that traces kinship through women.

Matrilocal – In preindustrial societies, living with or near the wife's family after marriage.

Matthew effect – A situation in which recognized authors are more likely to be cited in the future, while less-cited authors are unlikely to be cited.

McDonaldization – A scenario in which society undergoes a process of rationalization and takes on the characteristics of a fast food restaurant with the goal of achieving efficiency predictability and calculability.

Me – The object of one's own self-perception in the symbolic interactionist paradigm, as opposed to the "I," or the subjective perceiver.

Mean – The arithmetic average, computed by summing the values of the observations for a variable and dividing that figure by the number of total observations.

Mechanical solidarity – In Durkheim's analysis, one of two types of social solidarity in which there is little or no division of labor, individual differences are small and members of the society feel similar emotions and hold similar values to one another, leading to a strong sense of social cohesiveness.

Mechanization – A society's move towards the use of machines.

Median – A value or quantity lying at the midpoint of a frequency distribution of observed values or quantities.

Memetic contagion – A condition in which an overload of information causes an individual to shut down and become alienated, or to combine discourses in ironic ways.

Merton's modes of adaptation – In Robert K. Merton's analysis, the methods by which people adapt to the disjuncture between social goals and the accessibility of means to achieve those goals. These modes are innovation, ritual, retreat, and rebellion.

Meso – A term describing mid-size collectives or social relationships, such as a business.

Mesomorph – In Sheldon's analysis of criminal behavior, a body type characterized by a large bone structure, well developed musculature, and strength. Mesomorphs are energetic and love to dominate, which makes them far more likely than the other body types to engage in delinquent behavior.

Micro – A term referring to small-scale social relationships, such as the relationship you have with a friend.

Mob – A group of individuals characterized by their high level of emotionality as well as the probability they will engage in some otherwise violent or destructive activity.

Mode – The value or quantity that occurs the most in a frequency distribution of values or quantities.

Modernity – The social changes of the eighteenth, nineteenth and twentieth centuries, characterize by dramatic rises in population and urbanization, higher levels of literacy and formal education, labor force differentiation, rises in individualism, technological innovation, unprecedented levels of industrial production and also of the consumption of resources, greater faith in science and a decline in religious authority.

Monarchy – A type of political system in which power is transferred through a single family from generation to generation.

Monogamy – Marriage between only two partners.

Moral consciousness – A generalized sentiment over what is right and what is wrong in a society.

Moral density – The frequency of interaction among people in a society.

Moral order – In the Durkheimian perspective, the basis of society in which there is a fundamental solidarity in society, it brings people together so that they can share and exchange with one another and improve one another's well-being.

Moral outrage – A group's feelings of outrage or anger at an enemy or in response to crime.

Multivariate regression – The method used by researchers seeking to predict an outcome using a number of predictor variables.

Natural attitude (life world) – The attitude held by ordinary people under ordinary circumstances, including several component processes: People act as though an objective world exists as they perceive it; people assume that other people think and perceive things in the same way as they themselves do; over time, these perceptions and behavior become routinized, which in turn gives the impression of stability of an objective world; and, in order to maintain that stability, as new and unfamiliar information is perceived, a person attempts to fit the new information into existing categories to "make sense" of it.

Natural resources – Resources such as the land and minerals utilized by a society.

Neolocality – A system in which a married couple lives apart from the parents of the husband as well as the parents of the wife.

New criminology – An outgrowth of the social conflicts perspectives of criminology from the 1960s and '70s elaborating the role of power in determining the definition of deviance and the exposing or treatment of the deviant.

Norms – The principles of a group, which guide the behavior of its members.

Noumenon – What actually exists and is the same regardless of how it is perceived, as opposed to the phenomenon, which is the human representation of the noumenon.

Nuclear family – A structure in which two adults live together in a household with their own or with adopted children.

Obligatory groups – Small, close-knit, *Gemeinschaft* type groups for which sanctions are informal but often highly effective.

Occupational mobility – The ability to change occupations in the stratification system.

Occupational prestige – Occupations that have social, cultural or political advantages beyond simply economic value.

Oedipus complex – In Freud's analysis, the complex named after the tragic figure in Greek mythology who killed his father and married his mother, in which a boy does not adequately identify with his father and thus does not internalize the norms of society represented and conveyed by the father.

Operant conditioning – The process developed by B.F. Skinner that illustrates how a behavior that is met with positive reinforcement would be more likely to be performed in the future while a behavior that resulted in a punishment would likely be performed less frequently in the future.

Oral fixation – In Freud's analysis, a deep craving for oral stimulation of some sort throughout a person's life resulting from a lack of stimulation during the oral stage of psychosexual development.

Oral stage – In Freud's stages of psychosexual development, the first stage of life in which the child seeks stimulation through the mouth. This occurs approximately throughout the first year after birth, and explains why infants tend to put objects into their mouths.

Organic solidarity – In Durkheim's analysis the type of social solidarity characterized by the rise of an elaborate division of labor, and thus the inevitable rise of specialized labor and stratification systems.

Orienting response – The response by which a person will selectively attend to some stimuli while disregarding others.

Paradigm – A model or way of looking at the world.

Parsimony – Multiple regression models that contain a lot of information in a relatively small space.

Partial reinforcement – When a person is rewarded for a behavior only some of the time.

Partial Reinforcement Extinction Effect – In the behaviorist paradigm, the phenomenon in which behaviors that were partially reinforced take longer to reach response extinction than do behaviors that were continuously reinforced.

Participant observers – A sociological research method in which the researcher actually becomes part of the activity of the group they are studying.

Particularism – The evaluation of others based on personal relationships rather than individual merit.

Passively alienated deviant – In Talcott Parson's analysis of deviance, an individual who has decided that he or she simply does not want to be part of the larger social system with its expectations and obligations.

Passively conforming deviant – In Talcott Parson's analysis of deviance, an individual who does what he or she thinks is their social responsibility as part of the system in which they operate, but they never take the chances that are expected in our culture.

Patrilineal descent – A system that traces kinship through men.

Patrilocal – Preindustrial societies in which newly married couples live with or near the family of the husband.

Performer – In Goffman's dramaturgy, the element of the social individual who engages in information control or impression management.

Periphery – Areas of the world system with little natural wealth or resources.

Petite bourgeoisie – In Marx's analysis, self-employed persons without supervisory power over significant numbers of other people.

Phallic (Oedipal) stage – In Freud's stages of psychosexual development, the phase from age three to six when the child develops a sexual attachment to the opposite-sex parent.

Phenomenological attitude – An attitude in which the perceiver attempts to move from a *particular* way of perceiving to a more *universal* way of perceiving by suspending judgment on what is being perceived, as opposed to the "natural attitude."

Phenomenology – The philosophical method that questions how social "facts" such as class, structure, status, roles, etc. come to be viewed as real.

Phenomenon – The subjective human representation of the noumenon, which is obscured by our incomplete and faulty sense perception and limitations in our capacity to reason.

Pluralism – A type of ethnic group interaction in which different ethnic or racial groups are able to maintain their group identity with relatively little tension between groups while cohabitating within the same society.

Political action committees (PACs) – Special interest groups whose purpose is to achieve political goals by raising money from citizens and spending it to promote specific interests.

Polity members – Those who have gained a "legitimate" influence position within the polity.

Polyandry – A form of polygamy in which one female is joined in marriage with two or more males.

Polygamy – Marriage between three or more individuals.

Polygyny – A type of marriage that unites one male with two or more females as his wives.

Population pyramid – A demographic tool that illustrates the number of males and females within each age group.

Population transfer – A type of ethnic group interaction in which a minority group migrates or is forced to move.

Power – The ability to achieve desired ends despite resistance from others.

Power elite – In conflict theories, the wealthy ruling class that exerts a disproportionate influence in determining the course of politics and socio-economic outcomes in the United States.

Practical rationality – In Weber's analysis, the type of rationality we use to carry out individual pragmatic needs, and which allows us to accept the situation as it is, and attempt to discern the most expedient means of achieving a goal under the circumstances.

Precontractual solidarity – In Durkheim's analysis, the trust that must be established before individuals in a society can exchange and evolve to a well-established social division of labor.

Prejudice – An attitude or perception about a person, based on group membership.

Prestige – Favorable evaluations received from others.

Primary deviance – Individual behavior that others might consider to be deviant, but not being labeled as deviance because the individual is not caught.

Primary emotions – In Theodore Kemper's sociological theory of emotions, the four emotions (fear, anger, depression and satisfaction) associated with distinct physiological processes.

Primary groups – In Charles Horton Cooley's analysis of socialization, groups characterized by intimate face-to-face associations and cooperation such as the family in which we first learn to make sense of our world as a social place.

Primary socialization – The first type of socialization an individual encounters as a child, in which he or she internalizes the absolute norms and core values upon which later socialization experiences can be constructed.

Principle of emergence – The sociological principle, which states that with increasing size and interaction, an organization tends to become more differentiated, both vertically (in terms of levels of hierarchy), and horizontally (in terms of types of specialization).

Principle of least interest – In George Caspar Homans' analysis, the principle which states that the person with the least to lose in terminating a relationship has the most power in that relationship.

Principle of scarcity – In George Caspar Homans' analysis, the principle, which states that the person providing scarce resources or benefits to a relationship has high status in that relationship.

Privilege – Access to desired goods and services.

Profane – The opposite of sacred; anything not given a privileged status.

Projection – In Freud's analysis, a defense mechanism in which a person who fears or loathes some aspect of him-or-herself tends to see that trait in others, or project it onto them.

Prolegomena – The underpinnings of discussion and of thought; the "givens" in a person's or a group's perception of reality.

Proletariat – In Marx's analysis, the class that owns no means of production and toils for the bourgeoisie.

Protectionism – A type of ethnic group interaction in which the government may enact legislation intended to safeguard the rights of minority groups.

Protest crowd – A crowd gathered for the purpose of exerting influence on political processes.

Psychopathic – Individuals who are relatively unemotional, impulsive, immature, thrill seeking, and unconditionable.

Psychosexual stages – In Sigmund Freud's analysis, the distinct stages of growth in children in which gratification is derived primarily through different parts of the physical body.

Psychosomatic symptoms – Physical symptoms for which there does not appear to be any physical cause.

Qualitative analysis – The method by which sociologists analyze reports, events and conversations rather than offer enumerations when they conduct research.

Quantitative analysis – The numerical representation and manipulation of observations during sociological analysis.

Quasi groups – Lines of authority in a society in relation to which conflict develops. Also referred to as imperatively coordinated associations (ICAs).

Rational capitalism – A systematic and disciplined version of capitalism in which profits are typically reinvested in business, a characteristic displayed by early Calvinists.

Rational/legal authority – An authority structure based on rules and regulations, rather than past practices.

Rationalization – In Freud's analysis, a psychological defense mechanism in which a person adduces a very "reasonable" explanation for otherwise irrational behavior.

Rebellion – A type of social movement characterized by open defiance against state power.

Reciprocal typification – A social convention, in which both parties expect the other person will abide by the same social norms or rules as they themselves abide.

Reduction – When insight is gained into the nature of subjective experience itself, with regards to the phenomenological attitude.

Reflexivity – The human tendency to reflect on and to talk about our practices.

Regression analysis – A research method in which the researcher also looks for relationships between variables, but the analytical framework is one in which there is an expectation of causality.

Reification – The perception that humanly-created social arrangements are naturally occurring.

Reinforcement – In operant conditioning, some reward or benefit, such as a desired food.

Relations of production – The theory that explains how those with economic ownership of businesses were able to parlay this ownership into more general forms of domination of the non-owning working classes.

Relative deprivation theory – A theoretical conceptualization of social movements emphasizing the discrepancy between what people have and what they expect.

Reliability – A quality of measurement, which means that if different observers were to measure the same variable, they would derive exactly or close to the same results.

Religion – An interrelated set of beliefs and practices, which address questions of ultimate meaning.

Religious pluralism – A situation in which there are many religions practiced in a given society.

Rentiers – In Weber's analysis of class, a privileged class receiving income from investments in entities such as banks, factories or land.

Replication – The ability for other researchers to conduct our research again, precisely, in order to check our results, enabling us to be objective and value-free in the conduct of our sociological investigation.

Representative democracy – The participation of citizens in government decision making done through the use of representatives.

Representative sample – A demographic sample that has the same distribution of important characteristics as the population from which it was drawn.

Repression – In Freud's analysis, the defense mechanism in which thoughts and emotions are pushed out of conscious awareness.

Residues – The actual behaviors people display rather than what they say about their behaviors, in Pareto's paradigm.

Resource mobilization theory – An approach to collective violence that stresses changing power balances among contending collectivities in a society.

Restorative social control – A method of dealing with deviant behavior that involves actions deliberately meant to return the deviant to their normal behavioral patterns, such as psychotherapy and rehabilitation.

Retroduction – The weaving of induction and deduction leads scientists to derive hypotheses while reaching conclusions about social processes.

Revolution – Rebellions in which dissenters have won in their struggle with the state.

Riot – A form of collective behavior that is highly emotional and violent that has no central focus and is undirected, unlike a mob or protest demonstration.

Ritual – Ceremonial behavior by which people develop a shared or collective conscious in society.

Ritualist – In Parson's analysis of deviant behavior, an individual who mechanically follows their assigned functions in order to meet the expectations of their job and nothing further.

Role – Social behaviors that are relatively stable over time and place.

Role conflict – When a person must choose between the competing demands of two or more roles within their role set.

Role distance – In Goffman's dramaturgy, the case in which a performer will distance herself from the role she is playing by conveying the message that the role being played is not really commensurate with the true self.

Role overload – A situation in which a person cannot meet the expectations of a role due to not having enough time or energy.

Role set – The various roles a person plays (e.g., student, employee, team member, etc.)

Role strain – A term that describes competing expectations within a given role.

Routinized – The process by which patterns of power or exchange that become replicated over time, geographic space, and with large numbers of people.

Rudimentary theoretical propositions – Statements about how the world works, and that often offer prescriptions for action, which often take the form of proverbs or wise sayings.

Sacred – Objects or people that are set apart in some way, and given a privileged status.

Sample – A representative portion of the population.

Sanctions – Penalties.

Schemata – Immanuel Kant's conception describing the methods by which an individual develops abstract representational models for how the physical and social worlds are organized. Schemata provide an overall framework for what the person is likely to expect in a given situation.

Second shift – The additional work, including domestic labor and childcare, which is performed by women in the home after working all day outside the home.

Secondary data analysis – A method of research in which researchers use already existing data originally collected by others.

Secondary deviance – Deviant careers, as opposed to daily, behind-the-scenes deviance.

Secondary groups – A group that comes together to achieve a collective goal rather than for socio-emotional reasons.

Secondary socialization – Socialization that takes place at later points in life, in which an already (primarily) socialized person learns new aspects of something about the world in which he or she is living.

Sect – An institution that places an emphasis on emotional experiences as opposed to a church, which tends to intellectualize religious dogma and restrain emotion.

Semantic memory – A sense of the way things are generally, as opposed to *episodic memory*, or the memory for specific experiences.

Semantic networks – Associations that people make among bits of information that are organized into a coherent knowledge base.

Semi-periphery – Middle-income countries that exist within an intermediate position between the core and the periphery.

Semi-skilled manual workers – In Weber's definition of class, the class that has relatively less life chances than the highly skilled craftsmen, but who perform closure through what job skills it does have, as well as through unionization.

Sensorimotor stage – In Piaget's theory of cognitive development, the stage from birth to age two in which the infant develops senses and motor skills, and begins rudimentary language acquisition.

Sex – Our biological orientation at birth.

Sex ratio – The proportion of women relative to men in a society.

Sexual abuse – The carrying out of sexual acts by adults with children below the age of consent.

Simulacrum – A symbol that becomes alienated from its original meaning.

Significant symbol – A given symbol that means the same thing to both the person communicating it and to the person it is communicated to.

Social class reproduction – In conflict analyses, the socialization of students into roles that perpetuate the class relations of previous generations.

Social closure – The theory stating that people are likely to act and associate together based on their economic status, their political status, and their cultural status, and to try to exclude all others from their company.

Social cognition – The study of how people come to acquire knowledge in a social context.

Social collectives – The groups that make up society such as small groups, the family, the bureaucracies for which we work, our nation itself, and the world as a whole.

Social definition – A sociological perspective emphasizing the human use of symbols as well as the subjective meaning a person places on a situation.

Social differentiations – Rudimentary distinctions based on the kinds of labor engaged in and commodities produced.

Social disorganization theory – An approach to deviance that views external circumstances as being crucially important in generating deviant behavior, which challenges the normal ordering or organization of society.

Social distribution of knowledge – The phenomenon that describes when different people and groups in a society use different symbols and have different types of knowledge from one another.

Social dynamics – Changes in existing social patterns.

Social function – One of the major approaches to sociological research, based on the work of Emile Durkheim. In social functions approaches, society is explained in the same terms that a biological organism might be in that it consists of a number of different parts that are gathered together in a system of total interdependence.

Social interaction – Social theories emphasizing small-scale or microsociological perspectives of exchange and behavior.

Social solidarity – A cohesiveness in which the welfare of the group is more important than that of any of its individual members.

Socialization – The process through which people learn about society, its social institutions and their respective places in them.

Society – A broad and inclusive form of social organization.

Socio-economic status (SES) – A theoretical concept intended to encompass an aggregation of characteristics combining a person's education, occupational prestige, income, personal or family wealth, and the location and/or cost of one's residential neighborhood.

Sociological imagination – A paradigm enabling sociologists to see the social on a number of levels, think critically about things that others take for granted, determines what kinds of scientific problems are appropriate topics of study, how to study these problems, and the types of perspectives that are generally accepted as explanations of such problems.

Sociology – The study of social collectives.

Solidarity – Feelings of cohesiveness among the members of a society.

Special interest groups – Alliances of individuals who share an interest in some economic, political, or social issue and work together to pursue outcomes associated with those issues.

Species being – In Marx's paradigm, an ideal state in which people are connected to the product and process of their labor, to others in the society and to the human potential within.

Sponsored mobility – In British society, a process in which a small number of students are picked (or "sponsored") at a fairly early age, and given elite prep school educations which in turn lead to highly rewarding occupations.

Spuriousness – A situation in which two things are correlated, but that correlation stems from their both being correlated with some other social factor.

Stable equilibrium – In Pareto's paradigm, when change in one part of a system stimulates a reaction that reverses or minimizes that change.

Standard deviation – A measure that gives an estimate of dispersion around the mean. A large standard deviation indicates that the observations are scattered widely around the mean, while a small standard deviation indicates the observations are fairly tightly clustered around the mean.

Standpoint theory – A theory emphasizing that the structure of our society and culture provides a lens through which virtually all of our perceptions and knowledge is formulated.

Status attainment studies – Studies that measure stratification using an interval scale (typically 1 to 100), using finer distinctions than traditional mobility studies.

Status groups – Groups of people with some common social characteristic would tend to come together or coalesce and perform social closure toward those who do not possess said characteristic.

Stigma – The disparity between who the person would be under ideal circumstances (a person's "virtual social identity"), and who the person really is (the "actual social identity").

Stratification system – A system where individuals are sorted hierarchically.

Structural (stage) approach – An approach to socialization emphasizing the stages of development through which a child passes on the way to adulthood.

Structural mobility – A scenario in which many members of society move (generally up) without any downward movement, due to a shifting occupational "structure."

Structured interviews – A research method in which the same questionnaire is given to all respondents.

Subjugation – A type of ethnic group interaction in which a dominant group keeps a minority group in a subordinate position.

Sublimation – In Freud's analysis, a psychological defense mechanism in which we channel energy from unacceptable impulses into socially acceptable behavior.

Subsistence technology – Physical implements such as tools, as well as the ideas needed to use them and to apply the resources from the surrounding environment.

Substantive rationality – In Weber's paradigm, the type of rationality involved with choosing the means of achieving an end within an internally consistent set of values.

Sub-universes of meaning – Bodies of knowledge that are distinct from, yet are embedded in, the overall culture.

Suicide – All causes of death resulting directly or indirectly from a positive or negative act of the victim himself, which he knows will produce this result.

Superego – In Freud's analysis, the part of the psyche that acts as a restraint to the id; serving the function of an individual's conscience.

Surplus value – In Marx's analysis, when a price that is paid for any commodity comes from the extra hours of work over and above what the worker is actually paid for.

Survey analysis – A research method in which polls are taken by researchers to gather facts, which then determine the relationship between variables based on those facts.

Symbol – A noticeable sign that stands for something, and can be used to represent that thing in thought and language, in order for an individual or group to plan or coordinate activity.

Symbolic classification – The words that a person uses to categorize and characterize their experiences.

Symbolic heads of state – In a constitutional monarchy, heads of state not actually elected or responsible for governing.

Synchronic – Happening at the same time.

Taking the role of the other – In George Herbert Mead's analysis, the act of being both a subjective perceiver as well as the object of one's own perception; the use of a system of symbols to represent one's own behavior and the behavior of others.

Terministic screen – In Kenneth Burke's paradigm, a symbolic filter that skews and largely determines our perceptions of the world.

Theoretical rationality – In Weber's analysis, the type of rationality used when attempting to understand reality through general principles of abstraction or deduction.

This-world orientation – A characteristic of churches, including stability and the tendency to intellectualize religious dogma and restrain emotion.

Thomas's dictum – A central tenet of the social definition approach, exemplified in the following quote by W.I. Thomas: "If men define situations as real, they are real in their consequences."

Tight institutional coupling – An environment in which students typically find jobs in the field they studied in school, and for which they are well-qualified (but not over- or under-qualified).

Tipping point – A concept that describes that when a phenomenon reaches some critical point, there are increasing returns; such as in logistic regression curve, where the probability of any outcome below the tipping point is rounded to zero and above the point is rounded to one.

Total (continuous) reinforcement – In the behaviorist paradigm, when someone is given benefits or rewarded each time he or she performs a behavior.

Totalitarianism – A system of government in which the concentration of power is totally in the hands of a few decision makers and the individual behaviors and everyday lives of citizens are extensively regulated, whether or not that regulation is recognized by the citizens.

Traditional authority – An authority structure based on past practices.

Traditional capitalism – In Weber's analysis, a relatively undisciplined short-term plan for turning a profit.

Tragedy of the commons – The use of a common area, which reduces the costs to individuals while raising the costs to the collective as a whole.

Triangulation of methods – The use of multiple methodologies in any given research project in order to determine whether each methodology provides the same or different results.

Typification – Set ways of perceiving the world.

Typification need – A need to type others with shorthand methods that characterize them with minimal definitional work.

Unconditioned reflex – A response to an unconditioned stimulus, (e.g., the salivation reflex in response to the meat powder in Pavlov's dogs).

Unconditioned stimulus – A stimulus, which naturally produces a response, (e.g., the meat powder with Pavlov's dogs).

Unconscious – In Freud's paradigm, the drives of which an individual may not be fully aware, but which nonetheless motivate his or her behavior.

Universal symbol systems – Symbol systems that integrate the respective sub-universes of meaning within the overall institutional order.

Universalism – The evaluation of others on an equal footing and with merit as the primary concern.

Unskilled workers – In Weber's analysis of class, the class that tends to be the last hired and first fired, and would only be able to garner subsistence wages in dangerous and/or unpleasant work. Analogous to Marx's "reserve armies of the unemployed."

Unstable equilibrium – In Pareto's paradigm, when change in some part of the system results in even more change.

Urbanization – A process marked by population growth and development in which communities become cities.

Validity – How close a measure comes to truly reflecting what the scientist actually hopes to measure.

Vertical mobility – Refers to moving up ("upward mobility") or down ("downward mobility") along one or more dimensions (e.g., in terms of money or prestige) in the stratification system.

Volume – The number of people in a society.

Voter apathy – An increasing consequence of the coupling of large societies with indirect, or participatory democracy; a feeling of alienation from the political process.

Vulnerability – In network exchange theories, when an actor's position is threatened by its lack of centrality relative to some regional center.

Warehousing theory – A theory which states that educational institutions are places in which to keep—in the words of Karl Marx—"reserve armies of unemployed;" an increase in enrollments during times of economic downturn.

Who am I test – A twenty-question battery designed to measure empirically how a person views oneself. Manford Kuhn was the first in the symbolic interactionist tradition to develop empirical measures of subjective phenomena such as one's self-perceptions.

World system – The most macroscopic or large-scale form of social organization; all interdependent societies around the globe.

World-system theory – A theory whose unit of analysis is the entire world, and its networks of exchange, exploitation, conflict, and dependency, rather than a single given society. World-system theorists focus on the development of the capitalist world-economy, which is a global system of markets.

References

Adorno, Theodor. 1966/1973. *Negative Dialectics*. New York: Continuum.

Alba, Richard, and Victor Nee. 2003. *Remaking the American Mainstream: Assimilation and Contemporary Immigration*. Cambridge, MA: Harvard University Press.

Amsel, A. 1958. "The Role of Frustrative Nonreward in Noncontinuous Reward Situations." *Psychological Bulletin* 55:102-119.

Anderson, John R. 1983. *The Architecture of Cognition*. Cambridge, MA: Harvard University Press.

Archer, Margaret S. 1982. "Introduction: Theorizing about the Expansion of Educational Systems." Pp. 3-64 in *The Sociology of Educational Expansion*, edited by Margaret S. Archer. Beverly Hills: Sage.

Archer, Margaret S. 1988. *Culture and Agency: The Place of Culture in Social Theory*. Cambridge, UK: Cambridge University Press.

Aron, Raymond. 1965. *Main Currents in Sociological Thought*. New York: Basic Books.

Armstrong, John A. 1973. *The European Administrative Elite*. Princeton, NJ: Princeton University Press.

Arthur, W. Brian. 1999. "Complexity and the Economy." *Science* 284:107-109.

Averitt, Robert T. 1968. *The Dual Economy: The Dynamics of American Industry Structure*. New York: W.W. Norton.

Baker, David P., and David L. Stevenson. 1986. "Mothers' Strategies for Children's School Achievement: Managing the Transition to High School." *Sociology of Education* 59:156-166.

Bailey, Kenneth. 1990. *Social Entropy Theory*. Albany: State University of New York Press.

Bailey, Kenneth. 1994. *Sociology and the New Systems Theory: Toward a Theoretical Synthesis*. Albany: State University of New York Press.

Bailey, Kenneth. 1998. "Structure, Structuration and Autopoiesis: The Emerging Significance of Recursive Theory." *Current Perspectives in Social Theory* 18:131-154.

Bartlett, Frederick C. 1932. *Remembering.* Cambridge, UK: Cambridge University Press.

Bass, Thomas A. 1999. *The Predictors: How a Band of Maverick Physicists Used Chaos Theory to Trade Their Way to a Fortune on Wall Street.* New York: Henry Holt.

Baudrillard, Jean. 1972/1981. *For a Critique of the Political Economy of the Sign.* St. Louis: Telos.

Baudrillard, Jean. 1983. *Simulations.* New York: Semiotext(e).

Baudrillard *Live: Selected Interviews*, edited by Mike Gane. 1993.

Bauman, Zygmunt. 1992. *Intimations of Postmodernity.* London: Routledge.

Bauman, Zygmunt. 1993. *Postmodern Ethics.* Oxford, UK: Basil Blackwell.

Beck, Ulrich. 1992. *Risk Society: Towards a New Modernity.* London: Sage.

Beck, Ulrich, Wolfgang Bonss, and Christopher Lau. 2003. "The Theory of Reflexive Modernization." *Theory, Culture, & Society* 20:1-33.

Becker, Gary. 1975. *Human Capital: A Theoretical and Empirical Analysis, with Special Reference to Education.* 2nd ed. New York: National Bureau of Economic Research.

Beckford, James A. 1989. *Religion in Advanced Industrial Society.* London: Unwin Hyman.

Beckford, James A. 1992. "Religion, Modernity, and Post-Modernity." Pp. 11-23 in *Religion: Contemporary Issues*, edited by B. Wilson. London: Bellew Press.

Bell, Daniel. 1973. *The Coming of Post-Industrial Society.* New York: Basic.

Bell, Daniel. 1976. *The Cultural Contradictions of Capitalism.* New York: Basic.

Bell, Daniel. 1998-99. "Toward an International Human Rights (and Responsibilities) Regime: Some Obstacles." *The Responsive Community* 9(1):72-28.

Bell, Michael. 2004. *Farming for Us All: Practical Agriculture and the Cultivation of Sustainability (Rural Studies).* University Park: Penn State University Press.

Berelson, Bernard. 1978. "Prospects and Programs for Fertility Reduction." *Population and Development Review* 4:579-616.

Berg, Ivar. 1970. *Education and Jobs: The Great Training Robbery.* New York: Praeger.

Berger, Bennett M. 1986. Foreword to Erving Goffman's *Frame Analysis: An Essay on the Organization Experience,* pp. xi-xviii. Boston: Northeastern University Press.

Berger, Peter L. 1967. *The Sacred Canopy: Elements of a Sociological Theory of Religion.* Garden City, NY: Doubleday.

Berger, Peter L., and Thomas Luckmann. 1966. *The Social Construction of Reality: A Treatise on the Sociology of Knowledge.* New York: Anchor Doubleday.

Berger, Peter L., and Thomas Luckmann. 1967. *The Social Construction of Reality: A Treatise in the Sociology of Knowledge.* New York: Anchor Doubleday.

Bernard, Jessie. 1973. *The Future of Marriage.* New Haven, CT: Yale University Press.

Bernstein, Basil. 1971. "On the Classification and Framing of Educational Knowledge." In *Knowledge and Control,* edited by M.F.D. Young. London: Collier-Macmillan.

Bernstein, George, and Lottelore Bernstein. 1979. "The Curriculum for German Girls' Schools, 1870-1914." *Paedogogica Historica* 18:275-295.

Beutel, Ann M., and Margaret Mooney Marini. 1995. "Gender and Values." *American Sociological Review* 60(3):436-448.

Bipartisan Policy Center. 2013. *2012 Election Turnout Dips Below 2004 and 2008 Levels: Number of Eligible Voters Increases by 8 Million, 5 Million Fewer Votes Cast.*

Blackman, Tim. 2000. "Complexity Theory." In *Understanding Contemporary Society: Theories of the Present,* edited by Gary Browning, Abigail Halcli, and Frank Webster. London: Sage Publications.

Blau, Peter. 1964. *Exchange and Power in Social Life.* New York: Wiley.

Blau, Peter. 1977. *Inequality and Heterogeneity: A Primitive Theory of Social Structure.* New York: Free Press.

Blau, Peter. 1977. "A Macrosociological Theory of Social Structure." *American Sociological Review* 83:26-54.

Blau, Peter, and Otis Dudley Duncan. 1967. *The American Occupational Structure.* New York:

John Wiley & Sons.

Blau, Peter M., and Marshall W. Meyer. 1987. *Bureaucracy in Modern Society*, 3rd ed. New York: McGraw-Hill.

Blau, Peter M., and Richard A. Schoenherr. 1971. *The Structure of Organizations.* New York: Basic Books.

Blumberg, Rae L. 1984. "A General Theory of Gender Stratification." Pp. 23-101 in *Sociological Theory*, edited by Randall Collins. San Francisco: Jossey-Bass.

Blumer, Herbert. 1969. *Symbolic Interactionism.* Englewood Cliffs, NJ: Prentice Hall.

Boden, Deirdre. 1990. "The World As It Happens: Ethnomethodology and Conversation Analysis." Pp. 185-213 in *Frontiers of Social Theory: The New Syntheses*, edited by George Ritzer. New York: Columbia University Press.

Bonacich, Edna. 1973. "A Theory of Middleman Minorities." *American Sociological Review* 38:583-594.

Bottomore, Thomas B. 1966. *Classes in Modern Society.* New York: Vintage.

Boudon, Raymond. 1974. *Education, Opportunity, and Social Inequality: Changing Prospects in Western Society.* New York: John Wiley & Sons.

Boudon, Raymond. 1982. *The Unintended Consequences of Social Action.* London: Macmillan.

Bourdieu, Pierre. 1977. *Toward a Theory of Practice.* New York: Cambridge University Press.

Bourdieu, Pierre, and Jean-Claude Passeron. 1977. *Reproduction in Education, Society, and Culture.* London: Sage.

Bowles, S., and H. Gintis. 1976. *Schooling in Capitalist America: Educational Reform and the Contradictions of Economic Life.* New York: Basic Books.

Bransford, John D., and M. K. Johnson. 1972. "Contextual Prerequisites for Understanding: Some Investigations of Comprehension and Recall." *Journal of Verbal Learning and Verbal Behavior* 11:717-726.

Braverman, Harry. 1976. *Labor and Monopoly Capital: The Degradation of Work in the Twentieth Century.* Chapter 4. New York: Monthly Review Press.

Brewer, W. F., and G. V. Nakamura. 1984. "The Nature and Functions of Schemas." Pp. 119-160 in *Handbook of Social Cognition. Vol. 1*, edited by R. S. Wyer, Jr., and T. K. Srull. Hillsdale, NJ: Lawrence Erlbaum Associates.

Briggs, John, and F. David Peat. 1999. *Seven Life Lessons of Chaos: Spiritual Wisdom from the Science of Change.* New York: Harper Collins.

Brim, O. G., Jr. 1966. "Socialization through the Life Cycle." In *Socialization After Childhood: Two Essays*, edited by O.G. Brim, Jr., and S. Wheeler. New York: Wiley.

Brookover, W. B., S. Thomas, and A. Patterson. 1964. "Self-Concept of Ability and School Performance." *Sociology of Education*, 37:271-278.

Burke, Kenneth. 1945/1969. *A Grammar of Motives.* Berkeley: University of California Press.

Burke, Kenneth. 1950/1969. *A Rhetoric of Motives.* Berkeley: University of California Press.

Burke, Kenneth. 1966. *Language as Symbolic Action.* Berkeley: University of California Press.

Burne, D., and T. Rogers. 1996. "Divided Spaces: Divided Schools." *Sociological Research Online*, 1(2), http://www.socresonline.org.uk/socresonline/1/2/3/html.

Burns, Thomas J. 1991. *A Macro-Comparative Study of Gender- and Class-Specific Educational Expansion in Three European Nation-States.* Ann Arbor, MI: University Microfilms International.

Burns, Thomas J. 1992. "Class Dimensions, Individualism, and Political Orientation." *Sociological Spectrum* 12:349-362.

Burns, Thomas J. 1999. "Rhetoric as a Framework for Analyzing Cultural Constraint and Change." *Current Perspectives in Social Theory* 19:165-185.

Burns, Thomas J., Tom W. Boyd, and Julia R. Dinger. 2003. "Religion and Globalization in the Twenty-First Century: W(h)ither the Sacred Canopy?" Paper presented at annual conference of the Notre Dame Center for Ethics and Culture, South Bend, Indiana.

Burns, Thomas J., Byron L. Davis, and Edward L. Kick. 1997. "Position in the World-System and National Emissions of Greenhouse Gases." *Journal of World-Systems Research* 3:432-466.

Burns, Thomas J., Jerald Hage, and Maurice A. Garnier. 2004. "State Supply Policy, Employer Support, and Differential School Expansion in Britain, 1911-1975." *Humboldt Journal of Social Relations* 28(2).

Burns, Thomas J., Edward L. Kick, and Byron L. Davis. 1997. "Position in the World System and National Emissions of Greenhouse Gases." *Journal of World-Systems Research* 3:432-466.

Burns, Thomas J., Edward L. Kick, and Byron L. Davis. 1998. "Theorizing and Rethinking Linkages between Population and the Environment: Deforestation in the Late 20th Century." *Journal of World-Systems Research* 9(2):357-390.

Burns, Thomas J., Edward L. Kick, and Byron L. Davis. 2003. "Theorizing and Rethinking Linkages Between the Natural Environment and the Modern World-System: Deforestation in the Late 20th Century." *Journal of World-Systems Research* 11(2).

Burns, Thomas J., Edward L. Kick, and Byron L. Davis. 2003. "Theorizing and Rethinking Linkages between the Natural Environment and the Modern World-System: Deforestation in the Late 20th Century." *Journal of World-Systems Research* 9(2):357-390. {accessible online at http://jwsr.ucr.edu/}.

Burns, Thomas J., Edward L. Kick, David A. Murray, and Dixie A. Murray. 1994. "Demography, Development and Deforestation in a World-System Perspective." *International Journal of Comparative Sociology* 35(3-4):221-239.

Burns, Thomas J., and Terri LeMoyne. 2001. "How Environmental Movements Can Be More Effective: Prioritizing Environmental Themes in Political Discourse." *Human Ecology Review* 8(1):26-38. {accessible online at www.humanecologyreview.org}.

Burns, Thomas J., and Terri LeMoyne. 2003. "Chaos and Complexity Theories: Tools for Understanding Social Processes." *International Journal of the Humanities* 1:941-950.

Burns, Thomas J., and Terri LeMoyne. 2003. "Epistemology, Culture and Rhetoric: Some Social Implications of Human Cognition." *Current Perspectives in Social Theory* 22:71-97.

Burt, Ronald S. 1976. "Positions in Networks." *Social Forces* 55:93-122.

Buss, David M. 1989. "Sex Differences in Human Mate Preferences: Evolutionary Hypotheses Tested in 37 Cultures." *Behavioral and Brain Sciences* 12:1-49.

Butler, Judith. 1990. *Gender Trouble: Feminism and the Subversion of Identity.* London: Routledge.

Campbell, C. 1978. "The Secret Religion of the Educated Classes." *Sociological Analysis* 39:146-156.

Cannon, Walter B. 1929. *Bodily Changes in Pain, Hunger, Fear, and Rage.* New York: Norton.

Carmines, E. G. 1978. "Psychological Origins of Adolescent Political Attitudes." *American Politics Quarterly* 6:167-186.

Carson, Rachel. 1962. *Silent Spring.* Boston: Houghton Mifflin.

Catton, William R., Jr. 1980. *Overshoot.* Urbana, IL: University of Illinois Press.

Catton, William R., Jr. 1994. "What Was Malthus Really Telling Us?" *Human Ecology Review* 1(2):234-236.

Chafetz, Janet S. 2001. "Theoretical Understandings of Gender: A Third of a Century of Feminist Thought in Sociology." Pp. 613-631 in *Handbook of Sociological Theory*, edited by Jonathan H. Turner. New York: Kluwer Academic/Plenum.

Charon, Joel. 1992. *Symbolic Interactionism: An Introduction, An Interpretation, An Integration*, 4th ed. Englewood Cliffs, NJ: Prentice Hall.

Chase-Dunn, Christopher. 1979. "The Effects of International Economic Dependence on Development and Inequality." Pp. 131-152 in *National Development and the World System*, edited by John W. Meyer and Michael T. Hannan. Chicago: University of Chicago Press.

Chetty, Raj, Nathaniel Hendren, Patrick Kline, and Emmanuel Saez. 2014. *Where is the Land of Opportunity? The Geography of Intergenerational Mobility in the United States.* National Bureau of Economic Research Working Paper 19843.

Chirot, Daniel. 1977. *Social Change in the Twentieth Century.* New York: Harcourt Brace, Jovanovich.

Chirot, Daniel. 1986. *Social Change in the Modern Era.* Orlando, FL: Harcourt Brace Javanovich.

Chodorow, Nancy. 1989. *Feminism and Psychoanalytic Theory.* New Haven: Yale University Press.

Chong, Dennis. 1998-99. "Roadblocks on the Deliberative Path." *The Responsive Community* 9(1):105-112.

Clinard, Marshall B., and Daniel I. Abbott. 1973. *Crime in Developing Countries: A Comparative Perspective.* New York: Wiley.

Cloward, Richard A. 1959. "Illegitimate Means, Anomie, and Deviant Behavior." *American Sociological Review*, 24:164-176.

Cohen, Joel E. 1995. *How Many People Can the Earth Support?* New York: W.W. Norton & Co.

Colborn, Theo, Dianne Dumanoski, and John Peterson Myers. 1997. *Our Stolen Future: Are We Threatening Our Fertility, Intelligence, and Survival? — A Scientific Detective Story.* New York: Plume/Penguin.

Coleman, James S., et al. 1966. *Equality of Educational Opportunity.* Washington, D.C.: U.S. Government Printing Office.

Coleman, James S. 1986. *Individual Interests and Collective Action.* Cambridge, UK: Cambridge University Press.

Coleman, James S., Thomas Hoffer, and Sally Kilgore. 1982. *High School Achievement: Public, Catholic, and Other Private High Schools Compared.* New York: Basic Books.

Collins, Randall. 1971. "Functional and Conflict Theories of Education Stratification." *American Sociological Review* 36:1002-1019.

Collins, Randall. 1979. *The Credential Society: An Historical Sociology of Education and Stratification.* New York: Academic Press.

Cook, Karen S., Richard M. Emerson, Mary R. Gillmore, and Toshio Yamagishi. 1983. "The Distribution of Power in Exchange Networks: Theory and Experimental Results." *American Journal of Sociology* 89:275-305.

Cooley, Charles Horton. 1902. *Human Nature and the Social Order.* New York: Charles Scribner's Sons.

Cooley, Charles Horton. 1916. *Social Organization: A Study of the Larger Mind.* New York: Springer-Verlag.

Coughlin, Richard M. 2003. "Does Socio-Economic Inequality Undermine Community? Implications for Communitarian Theory." *The Responsive Community* 13(2):12-24.

Craig, John E. 1981. "The Expansion of Education." In *Review of Educational Research.* Vol. 9, edited by David Berliner. Itasca, IL: American Educational Research Association.

Crenshaw, Edward M., Matthew Christenson, and Doyle Ray Oakey. 2000. "Demographic Transition in Ecological Focus." *American Sociological Review* 65:371-391.

Cressey, Donald R. 1969. *Delinquency, Crime, and Social Process.* New York: Harper and Row.

Crocker, J., S. T. Fiske, and S. E. Taylor. 1984. "Schematic Bases of Belief Change." Pp. 197-226 in *Attitudinal Judgment*, edited by R. E. Eiser. New York: Springer-Verlag.

Crosby, Alfred W. 1986. *Ecological Imperialism: The Biological Expansion of Europe, 900-1900.* New York: Cambridge University Press.

Dahl, Robert. 1982. *Dilemmas of Pluralistic Democracy.* New Haven: Yale University Press.

Dahrendorf, Ralif. 1959. *Class and Class Conflict in Industrial Society.* Stanford, CA: Stanford University Press.

Darwin, Charles. [1872] 1965. *The Expression of Emotions in Man and Animals.* Chicago: University of Chicago Press.

Davies, James C. 1970. "The J-curve of Rising and Declining Satisfactions as a Cause of Some Great Revolutions and a Contained Rebellion." Pp. 690-730 in *Violence in America: Historical and Comparative Perspectives*, edited by Hugh Graham and Ted Gurr. New York: Praeger.

Davis, Kingsley. 1945. "The World Demographic Transition." *Annals of the American Academy of Political and Social Science* 235:1-11.

Davis, Kingsley, and Mikhail S. Bernstam, eds. 1991. *Resources, Environment, and Population: Present Knowledge, Future Options.* New York: Population Council.

Davis, Kinglsey and Wilbert Moore. 1945. "Some Principles of Stratification." *American Sociological Review* 10:242-249.

Davis, Mike. 1992. "Fortress Los Angeles: The Militarization of Urban Space." Pp. 154-180 in *Variations on a Theme Park*, edited by M. Sorkin. New York: Noonday Press.

Dawson, Lorne L. 1998. "Anti-Modernism, Modernism, and Postmodernism: Struggling with the Cultural Significance of New Religious Movements." *Sociology of Religion* 59(2):131-156.

Dean, A. 1997. *Chaos and Intoxication: Complexity and Adaptation in the Structure of Human Nature.* London: Routledge.

Dear, Michael, and Steven Flusty. 2002. "Postmodern Urbanism." Pp. 216-234 in *The Spaces of Postmodernity: Readings in Human Geography*, edited by M. J. Dear and S. Flusty. Oxford, UK: Blackwell.

Derrida, Jacques. 1984. *The Postmodern Condition.*

Dietz, Thomas, and Tom R. Burns. 1992. "Human Agency and the Evolutionary Dynamics of Culture." *Acta Sociologica* 35:187-200.

Doane, Ashley W. 1997. "Dominant Group Ethnic Identity In The United States: The Role of "Hidden" Ethnicity in Intergroup Relations." *Sociological Quarterly* 38(3):375.

Dougherty, Kevin J., and Floyd M. Hammack. 1990. *Education and Society.* Orlando, FL: Harcourt Brace Jovanovich.

Dubois. W. E. B. 1903. *The Souls of Black Folk.* Chicago: A.C. McClurg & Co.

Duncan, Otis Dudley. 1965. "The Trend of Occupational Mobility in the United States." *American Sociological Review* 30:491-498.

Duncan, Otis Dudley. 1966. "Methodological Issues in the Analysis of Social Mobility." Pp. 51-97 in *Social Structure and Mobility in Economic Development*, edited by Neil Smelser and Seymour Martin Lipset. Chicago: Aldine.

Durkheim, Emile. 1893/1964. *The Division of Labor in Society.* New York: Free Press.

Durkheim, Emile. 1895/1964. *The Rules of Sociological Method.* New York: Free Press.

Durkheim, Emile. 1897/1951. *Suicide: A Study in Sociology.* New York: Free Press.

Durkheim, Emile. 1912/1965. *The Elementary Forms of Religious Life.* New York: Free Press.

Durkheim, Emile. 1961. *Moral Education: A Study in the Theory and Application of the Sociology of Education.* New York: Free Press.

Durkheim, Emile, and Marcel Mauss. 1903/1963. *Primitive Classification.* Chicago: University of Chicago Press.

Dwyer, John M. 1988. *The Body at War: The Miracle of the Immune System.* New York: Mentor.

Easterlin, Richard A. 1980. *Birth and Fortune.* New York: Basic Books.

Ehrenreich, Barbara. 1986. "Is the Middle Class Doomed?" *New York Times Magazine* 135 (Sept. 7):44ff.

Ehrenreich, Barbara, and John Ehrenreich. 1979. "The Professional-Managerial Class." Pp. 5-48, reprinted in *Between Labor and Capital*, edited by Pat Walker. Boston: South End Press.

Ehrlich, Paul R. 1968. *The Population Bomb*. New York: Ballantine.

Ehrlich, Paul R., and Anne H. Ehrlich. 1990. *The Population Explosion*. New York: Simon and Schuster.

Ellen, Ingrid Gould. 2000. *Sharing America's Neighborhoods: The Prospects for Stable Racial Integration*. Cambridge, MA: Harvard University Press.

Emerson, Richard M. 1981. "Social Exchange Theory." Pp. 30-65 in *Social Psychology: Sociological Perspectives*, edited by Morris Rosenberg and Ralph H. Turner. New York: Basic Books.

Epstein, Seymour. 1984. "Controversial Issues in Emotion Theory." In *Review of Personality and Social Psychology* 5:64-88, edited by P. Shaver. Beverly Hills, CA: Sage.

Fain, Heidi, Thomas J. Burns, and Mindy Sartor. 1994. "Group and Individual Selection in the Human Social Environment: From Behavioral Ecology to Social Institutions." *Human Ecology Review* 1(2):335-350.

Faris, Robert E. L., and H. Warren Durham. 1939. *Mental Disorders in Urban Areas*. Chicago: University of Chicago Press.

Farley, Reynolds. 1984. *Blacks and Whites: Narrowing the Gap?* Cambridge, MA: Harvard University Press.

Featherman, David, and Robert Hauser. 1978. *Opportunity and Change*. New York: Academic Press.

Fehr, Beverley, and James A. Russell. 1984. "Concept of Emotion Viewed from a Prototype Perspective." *Journal of Experimental Psychology: General* 13:464-468.

Ferster, C. B., and B. F. Skinner. 1957. *Schedules of Reinforcement*. New York: Appleton-Century-Crofts.

Fine, Gary Alan. 1990. "Symbolic Interactionism in the Post-Blumerian Age." Pp. 117-157 in *Frontiers of Social Theory: The New Syntheses*, edited by George Ritzer. New York: Columbia University Press.

Fischer, Claude. Cultural Lag AJS article.

Fiske, Susan T., and Shelley E. Taylor. 1991. *Social Cognition.* New York: McGraw Hill.

Fitz-Gibbon, C.T. 1996. *Monitoring Education: Indicators, Quality and Effectiveness.* London: Cassell.

Flavell, John H. 1985. *Cognitive Development.* Englewood Cliffs, NJ: Prentice-Hall.

Foster, John Bellamy. 1999. "Marx's Theory of Metabolic Rift: Classical Foundations for Environmental Sociology." *American Journal of Sociology* 105(2):366-405.

Foucault, Michel. 1965. *Madness and Civilization: A History of Insanity in the Age of Reason.* New York: Vintage.

Foucault, Michel. 1966. *The Order of Things: An Archaeology of the Human Sciences.* New York: Vintage.

Foucault, Michel. 1969. *The Archaeology of Knowledge and the Discourse on Language.* New York: Harper Colophon.

Frank, Andre Gunder. 1967. *Capitalism and Underdevelopment in Latin America.* NY: Monthly Review Press.

Freeman, L. C. 1979. "Centrality in Social Networks: Concept Clarification." *Social Networks* 1:242-256.

Freud, Sigmund. 1923. *The Ego and Id.* London: Hogarth.

Freud, Sigmund. 1952 [1929]. "Civilization and Its Discontents." Pp. 767-802, reprinted in *Great Books of the Western World.* Vol. 54, edited by R. M. Hutchins. Chicago: Britannica Great Books.

Freud, Sigmund. 1952. *A General Introduction to Psychoanalysis.* New York: Washington Square Press.

Freud, Sigmund. 1959. *Collected Papers.* New York: Basic Books.

Friedman, Debra, and Michael Hecter. 1990. "The Comparative Advantage of Rational Choice Theory." Pp. 214-229 in *Frontiers of Social Theory: The New Syntheses*, edited by George Ritzer. New York: Columbia University Press.

Fuller, Bruce. 1983. "Youth Job Structure and School Enrollment, 1890-1920." *Sociology of Education* 56:145-156.

Gadamer, Hans Georg. 1989. *Truth and Method*, 2nd rev. ed. New York: Crossroad.

GALLUP. 2002. *American and Canadian Views on Abortion.*

GALLUP. 2011. *Most Americans Believe Crime in U.S. is Worsening.*

GALLUP Politics. 2013. *Americans Misjudge U.S. Abortion Views.*

Gans, Herbert J. 1979. "Symbolic Ethnicity: the Future of Ethnic Groups and Cultures in America." *Ethnic and Racial Studies* 2:1-20.

Garber, J., and M. E. P. Seligman, eds. 1980. *Learned Helplessness: Theory and Applications.* New York: Academic Press.

Garfinkel, Harold, Michael Lynch, and Eric Livingston. 1981. "The Work of a Discovering Science Constructed with Materials from the Optically Discovered Pulsar." *Philosophy of the Social Sciences* 11:131-158.

Garnier, Maurice, and Jerald Hage. 1990. "Education and Economic Growth in Germany." *Research in Sociology of Education and Socialization* 9:25-53.

Garnier, Maurice, and Jerald Hage. 1991. "Class, Gender and School Expansion in France: A Four-Systems Comparison." *Sociology of Education* 64(4):229-250.

Garnier, Maurice, Jerald Hage, and Bruce Fuller. 1989. "The Strong State, Social Class, and Controlled School Expansion in France, 1881-1975." *American Journal of Sociology* 95(2):279-306.

Garrett, Laurie. 1994. *The Coming Plague: Newly Emerging Diseases in a World Out of Balance.* New York: Penguin.

Gecas, Viktor. 1981. "Contexts of Socialization." Pp. 165-199 in *Social Psychology: Sociological Perspectives*, edited by M. Rosenberg and R. H. Turner. New York: Basic Books.

Gelles, Richard J. 1995. *Contemporary Families.* London: Sage.

Gerth, Hans, and C. Wright Mills. 1946. "Introduction: The Man and His Work." Pp. 3-74 in *From Max Weber: Essays in Sociology*, edited by Hans Gerth and C. Wright Mills. New York: Oxford University Press.

Giddens, Anthony. 1990. *The Consequences of Modernity.* Stanford: Stanford University Press.

Giddens, Anthony. 1991. *Modernity and Self-Identity: Self and Society in the Late Modern Age*. Cambridge: Polity Press.

Gladwell, Malcolm. 2000. *The Tipping Point: How Little Things Can Make a Big Difference*. New York City: Little Brown.

Glaser, Daniel. 1956. "Criminality Theories and Behavioral Images." *American Journal of Sociology* 61:433-444.

Glenn, E. N., and R. L. Feldberg. 1977. "Degraded and Deskilled: The Proletarianization of Clerical Work." *Social Problems* 25:52-64.

Goerner, Sally J. 1994. *Chaos and the Evolving Ecological Universe*. Luxembourg: Gordon and Breach.

Goffman, Erving. 1959. *Presentation of Self in Everyday Life*. Garden City, NY: Anchor.

Goffman, Erving. 1963. *Behavior in Public Places*. New York: Free Press.

Goffman, Erving. 1963. *Stigma: Notes on the Management of Spoiled Identity*. Englewood Cliffs, NJ: Prentice Hall.

Goffman, Erving. 1967. *Interaction Ritual: Essays on Face-to-Face Behavior*. Garden City, NY: Anchor.

Goffman, Erving. 1974/1986. *Frame Analysis: An Essay on the Organization of Experience*. Boston: Northeastern University Press.

Goffman, Erving. 1977. "The Arrangement between the Sexes." *Theory & Society* 4(3):301-331.

Goode, William. 1960. "A Theory of Role Strain." *American Sociological Review* 25:483-496.

Goode, William J. 1963. *World Revolution and Family Patterns*. New York: Free Press.

Gordon, Steven L. 1981. "The Sociology of Sentiments and Emotion." Pp. 562-592 in *Social Psychology: Sociological Perspectives*, edited by Morris Rosenberg and Ralph H. Turner. New York: Basic Books.

Gore, Al. 1993. *Earth in the Balance: Ecology and the Human Spirit*. New York: Plume/Penguin.

Gray, Robert Q. 1974. "The Labour Aristocracy in the Victorian Class Structure." Pp. 19-38 in

Social Analysis of Class Structure, edited by Frank Parkin. London: Tavistock.

Greenstein, Theodore N. 1990. "Marital Disruption and the Employment of Married Women." *Journal of Marriage and the Family* 52:657-676.

Greenstein, Theodore N., and Shannon N. Davis. 2006. "Cross-National Variations in Divorce: Effects of Women's Power, Prestige and Dependence." *Journal of Comparative Family Studies* 37:253-273.

Grodsky Eric, and Devah Pager. 2001. "The Structure of Disadvantage: Individual and Occupational Determinants of the Black-White Wage Gap." *American Sociological Review* 66(4):542-567.

Grubb, W. Norton, and Marvin Lazerson. 1982. "Education and the Labor Market: Recycling the Youth Problem." *In Work, Youth and Schooling*, edited by Harvey Kantor, and David Tyack. Stanford, CA: Stanford University Press.

Guess, George M. 1979. "Pasture Expansion, Forestry, and Development Contradictions: The Case of Costa Rica." *Studies in Comparative International Development* 14(1):42-55.

Gullahorn, J. 1952. "Distance and Friendship in the Gross Interaction Matrix." *Sociometry* 15:123-134.

Gurnah, Ahmed. 2002. "Elvis in Zanzibar." Pp. 347-362 in *The Spaces of Postmodernity: Readings in Human Geography*, edited by M. J. Dear and S. Flusty. Oxford, UK: Blackwell.

Gurr, Ted Robert. 1970. *Why Men Rebel*. Princeton: Princeton University Press.

Guttentag, Marcia, and Paul F. Secord. 1983. *Too Many Women?: The Sex Ratio Question*. Beverly Hills, CA: Sage.

Habermas, Jurgen. 1973. *Theory and Practice*. Boston: Beacon.

Habermas, Jurgen. 1975. *Legitimation Crisis*. Boston: Beacon.
Habermas, Jurgen. 1984 & 1987. *The Theory of Communicative Action* Vols. 1 & 2. Boston: Beacon.

Habermas, Jurgen. 1987. *The Philosophical Discourse of Modernity: Twelve Lectures*. Cambridge: MIT Press.

Hage, Jerald. 1972. *Techniques and Problems of Theory Construction in Sociology*. New York: Wiley.

Hage, Jerald, Maurice A. Garnier, and Bruce Fuller. 1988. "The Active State, Investment in Human Capital, and Economic Growth: France 1825-1975." *American Sociological Review* 53:824-837.

Hage, Jerald, and Charles Powers. 1992. *Post-Industrial Lives: Roles and Relationships in the 21st Century.* Thousand Oaks, CA: Sage.

Hammack, Floyd M. 1982. "The Changing Relationship between Education and Occupation: The Case of Nursing." *New York University Education Quarterly* :8-14.

Handel, Warren. 1982. *Ethnomethodology: How People Make Sense.* Englewood Cliffs, NJ: Prentice Hall.

Hardin, Garrett. 1968. "The Tragedy of the Commons." *Science* 162(13 Dec.):1243-1248.

Hardin, Garrett. 1993. "Second Thoughts on the Tragedy of the Commons." In *Valuing the Earth: Economics, Ecology, and Ethics*, edited by H.E. Daly, and K.N. Townsend. Cambridge, MA: MIT Press.

Harding, Sandra G., ed. 2004. *The Feminist Standpoint Theory Reader: Intellectual and Political Controversies.* New York: Routledge.

Harding, Sandra G. 2006. *Science and Social Inequality: Feminist and Postcolonial Issues.* Champaign, IL: University of Illinois Press.

Harding, Sandra G. 2008. *Sciences From Below: Feminisms, Postcolonialities, and Modernities.* Durham: Duke University Press.

Hartsock, Nancy. 1989. Postmodernism and Political Change: Issues for Feminist Theory. *Cultural Critique, Special Issue No. 14: The Construction of Gender and Modes of Social Division II* : 15-33.

Hartsock, Nancy C. M. 1998. *The Feminist Standpoint Revisited and Other Essays.* Boulder, CO: Westview.

Harvey, David. 1989. *The Condition of Postmodernity: An Inquiry into the Origins of Cultural Change.* Oxford: Blackwell.

Hawthorn, Geoffrey. 1994. *Enlightenment & Despair: A History of Social Theory.* Cambridge: Cambridge University Press.

Hechter, Michael. 1983. *Microfoundations of Macrosociology.* Philadelphia: Temple University

Press.

Hechter, Michael. 1989. "Rational Choice Foundations of Social Order." In *Theory Building in Sociology*, edited by Jonathan J. Turner. Newbury Park, CA: Sage.

Heidegger, Martin. 1967. *What is a Thing?* Chicago: Henry Regnery.

Heilbron, Johan. 1995. *The Rise of Social Theory.* Minneapolis: University of Minnesota Press.

Henry, James P., and Patricia M. Stephens. 1977. *Stress, Health, and the Social Environment: A Sociobiologic Approach to Medicine.* New York: Springer-Verlag.

Heritage, John. 1984. *Garfinkel and Ethnomethodology.* Cambridge, UK: Polity Press.

Hesketh, Therese, Li Lu, and Zhu Wei Xing. 2011. "The Consequences of Son Preference and Sex-Selective Abortion in China and Other Asian Countries." *Canadian Medical Association Journal.*

Hewitt, John P. 1997. *Self and Society: A Symbolic Interactionist Social Psychology*, 7e. Boston: Allyn and Bacon.

Heyns, Barbara. 1978. *Summer Learning and the Effects of Schooling.* New York: Academic Press.

Hilbert, Richard A. 1992. *The Classical Roots of Ethnomethodology: Durkheim, Weber, and Garfinkel.* Chapel Hill: University of North Carolina Press.

Hills, J. 1998. "ESRC Research Centre for Analysis of Social Exclusion." *SPA News* February-March: 24-26.

Hirschman, Charles, and L.M. Falcon. 1985. "The Educational Attainment of Religio-Ethnic Groups in the United States." *Research in Sociology of Education and Socialization* 5:83-120.

Hirschman, Charles, and M.G. Wong. 1984. "Socioeconomic Gains of Asian Americans, Blacks, and Hispanics: 1960-1976." *American Journal of Sociology* 90:584-607.

Hirschman, Charles, and M.G. Wong. 1986. "The Extraordinary Educational Attainment of Asian-Americans: A Search for Historical Evidence and Explanations." *Social Forces* 65:1-27.

Hobbes, Thomas. [1957]. *Leviathan.* Oxford: Basil Blackwell.

Hobsbawm, E. J. 1959. *Primitive Rebels.* New York: W. W. Norton.

Hochschild, Arlie R. 1983. *The Managed Heart.* Berkeley: University of California Press.

Hollingshead, August deB., and Fredrick C. Redlich. 1958. *Social Class and Mental Illness: A Community Study.* New York: Wiley.

Homans, George C. 1950. *The Human Group.* New York: Harcourt, Brace, & World, Inc.

Homans, George C. 1958. "Social Behavior as Exchange." *American Journal of Sociology* 63:597-606.

Homans, George C. 1974. *Social Behavior: Its Elementary Form.* Rev. ed. New York: Harcourt Brace Jovanovich.

Homer-Dixon, Thomas. 1999. *Environment, Scarcity, and Violence.* Princeton, NJ: Princeton University Press.

Horan, Patrick. 1978. "Is Status Attainment Research Atheoretical?" *American Sociological Review* 43:534-541.

Horkheimer, M., and T. W. Adorno. 1947. *Dialectic of Enlightenment: Philosophical Fragments,* edited by G. S. Noerr, translated by E. Jephcott. Stanford: Stanford University Press, 2002.

Hunter, James Davison. 1981. "The New Religions: Demodernization and the Protest against Modernity." Pp. 1-19 in *The Social Impact of the New Religious Movements,* edited by B. Wilson. New York: Rose of Sharon Press.

Hunter, James Davison. 1991. *Culture Wars.* New York: Basic Books.

Husserl, Edmund. 1965. *Phenomenology and the Crisis of Philosophy.* New York: Harper and Row.

Inkeles, Alex, and David Smith. 1974. *Becoming Modern: Individual Change in Six Developing Countries.* Cambridge, MA: Harvard University Press.

Jameson, Frederic. 1991. *Postmodernism, or the Cultural Logic of Late Capitalism.* Durham: Duke University Press.

Jenkins, W. D., and Julian C. Stanley. 1950. "Partial Reinforcement: A Review and Critique." *Psychological Bulletin* 47:193-234.

Jorgensen, Andrew K. 2003. "Degradation: A Cross-National Analysis of the Ecological Footprint." *Social Problems* 50(3):374-394.

Jorgensen, Andrew K., and Thomas Burns. "The Political-Economic Causes of Change in the Ecological Footprints of Nations, 1991-2001: A Quantitative Investigation." *Social Science Research* 36(2):834-853.

Jorgenson, Andrew K. and Edward L. Kick (editors). 2006. *Globalization and the Environment.* Leiden, the Netherlands: Brill Academic Press.

Kalberg, Stephen. 1980. "Max Weber's Types of Rationality: Cornerstones for the Analysis of Rationalization Processes in History." *American Journal of Sociology* 85:1145-1179.

Kalmijn, Matthijs. 1998. "Intermarriage and Homogamy: Causes, Patterns, Trends." *Annual Review of Sociology* 24(1):395–421.

Kant, Immanuel. 1781/1958. *Critique of Pure Reason*, translated by N. K. Smith. New York: Random House.

Kaplan, Howard B. 1976. "Self Attitudes and Deviant Response." *Social Forces* 54:788-801.

Kaplan, Howard B. 1980. *Deviant Behavior in Defense of Self.* New York: Academic Press.

Kelley, H. H., and J. W. Thibaut. 1978. *Interpersonal Relations: A Theory of Interdependence.* New York: Wiley.

Kemper, Theodore D. 1978. *A Social Interactional Theory of Emotions.* New York: John Wiley and Sons.

Kemper, Theodore D. 1981. "Social Constructionist and Positivist Approaches to the Sociology of Emotions." *American Journal of Sociology* 87:336-362.

Kerckhoff, Alan C. 1990. *Getting Started: Transition to Adulthood in Great Britain.* Boulder, CO: Westview.

Kerckhoff, Alan C., and Diane Everett. 1986. "Sponsored and Contest Educational Pathways to Jobs in Great Britain and the United States." In *Research in Sociology and Education and Socialization.* Vol. 6, edited by Alan Kerckhoff. Greenwich, CT: JAI Press.

Kick, Edward and Gary LaFree. 1985. "Development and the Social Context of Murder and Theft." *Comparative Social Research* 8: 37-58.

Kick, Edward L., Thomas J. Burns, Byron Davis, David A. Murray, and Dixie A. Murray. 1996. "Impacts of Domestic Population Dynamics and Foreign Wood Trade on Deforestation: A World-System Perspective." *Journal of Developing Societies* 12(1):68-87.

Kick, Edward L., Byron Davis, Thomas J. Burns, and Oleg I. Gubin. 1995. "International Multiple Networks in World-System Approaches." In *International Conference on Social Networks*, 3:237-248, edited by M. G. Everett and K. Rennolls. London: Greenwich University Press.

Kick, Edward L. and Laura McKinney. 2014. "Global Context, National Inter-dependencies and the Ecological Footprint: A Structural Equation Analysis." *Sociological Perspectives* 57: 256-279.

Kingsly, Thomas G., and Rob Potingolo. 2013. *Concentrated Poverty and Regional Findings from the National Neighborhood Indicators Partnership's Shared Indicator's Initiative.* The Urban Institute.

Kohn, Melvin L. 1969. *Class of Conformity: A Study in Values.* Homewood, IL: Dorsey.

Kohn, Melvin L., and Carmi Schooler. 1983. *Work and Personality: An Inquiry into the Impact of Social Stratification.* Norwood, NJ: Ablex.

Kornhauser, William. 1959. *The Politics of Mass Society.* New York: Free Press.

Krysan, Maria, and Reynolds Farley. 2002. "The Residential Preferences of Blacks: Do They Explain Persistent Segregation?" *Social Forces* 80(3): 937-980.

Kunda, Z., and R. E. Nisbett. 1988. "Predicting Individual Evaluations from Group Evaluations and Vice-Versa: Different Patterns for Self and Other?" *Personality and Social Psychology Bulletin* 14:326-334.

Landry, Bart. 1987. *The New Black Middle Class.* Berkeley and Los Angeles: University of California Press.

LaPiere, Richard T. 1934. "Attitudes versus Action." *Social Forces* 13:230-237.

Latour, Bruno. 1993. *We Have Never Been Modern.* New York: Harvester Wheatsheaf.

Latour, Bruno, and Steve Woolgar. 1986. *Laboratory Life: The Construction of Social Facts.* Princeton, NJ: Princeton University Press.

Lazarus, Richard S., A. D. Kanner, and S. Folkman. 1980. "Emotions: A Cognitive Phenomenological Analysis." In *Emotion: Theory, Research, and Experience*, 1:189-218, edited by R. Plutchnik and H. Kellerman. New York: Academic Press.

Lemert, Edwin M. 1951. *Human Deviance, Social Problems, and Social Control.* New York: McGraw-Hill.

LeMoyne, Terri, William Falk, and Alan Neustadtl. 1994. "Hyperrationality: Historical Antecedents and Contemporary Outcomes within Japanese Manufacturing." *Sociological Spectrum* 14:221-240.

Lenski, Gerhard. 1966. *Power and Privilege: A Theory of Social Stratification*, paperback edition. Chapel Hill, NC: University of North Carolina Press.

Lenski, Gerhard, Jean Lenski, and Patrick Nolan. 1991. *Human Societies*, 6e. New York: McGraw Hill.

Lepenies, Wolf. 1992. *Between Literature and Science: the Rise of Sociology.* Cambridge: Cambridge University Press.

Lewis, Valerie, Michael Emerson, and Stephen Klineberg. 2011. "Who We'll Live With: Neighborhood Racial Composition Preferences of Whites, Blacks, and Latinos." *Social Forces* 89(4): 1385-2011.

Light, Ivan. 1984. "Immigrant and Ethnic Enterprise in North America." *Ethnic and Racial Studies* 7:195-216.

Lipset, Seymour Martin, and Reinhard Bendix, eds. 1964. *Social Mobility in Industrial Society.* Berkeley, CA: University of California Press.

Lombroso, Cesare. 1911. Introduction, in *Criminal Man According to the Classification of Cesare Lombroso.* New York: Putnam.

Lorenz, Edward. 1993. *The Essence of Chaos.* London: University College London Press.

Lukacs, Gyorgy. 1922/1968. *History and Class Consciousness.* Cambridge, MA: MIT Press.

Lukes, Steven. 1972. *Emile Durkheim: His Life and Work.* New York: Harper & Row.

McNeill, William H. 1976. *Plagues and Peoples.* New York: Anchor/Doubleday.

McVeigh, Rory. 2004. "Structured Ignorance and Organized Racism in the United States." *Social Forces* 82 (3): 895-936.

Maier, Steve F., and Martin E. P. Seligman. 1976. "Learned Helplessness: Theory and Evidence." *Journal of Experimental Psychology*: General 105:3-46.

Malthus, Thomas R. 1798/1960. "An Essay on the Principle of Population, as It Affects the Future Improvement of Society." Reprinted in *On Population*, edited by Gertrude Himmelfarb. New York: Modern Library.

Maltzman, I. 1990. "The OR and Significance." *Pavlovian Journal of Biological Science* 25 (3): 111-122.

Mandelbrot, Benoit B. 1977. *Fractals: Form, Chance and Dimension*. San Francisco: Freeman.

Mandelbrot, Benoit B. 1982. *The Fractal Geometry of Nature*. New York: Freeman.

Mann, Michael. 1986. *The Sources of Social Power*. Vol. I. Cambridge, UK: Cambridge University Press.

Markus, H. 1977. "Self-Schemata and Processing Information about the Self." *Journal of Personality and Social Psychology* 35:63-78.

Martin, Theresa Castro, and Larry Bumpass. 1989. "Recent Trends in Marital Disruption." *Demography*, pp. 37-51.

Marx, Karl. 1867/1967. *Capital: A Critique of Political Economy*. Vol. 1. New York: International Publishers.

Marx, Karl. 1869/1963. *The 18th Brumaire of Louis Bonaparte*. New York: International Publishers.

Marx, Karl, and Friedrich Engels. 1845-1846/1970. *The German Ideology*, Part 1. New York: International Publishers.

Marx, Karl, and Friedrich Engels. 1848/1948. *Manifesto of the Communist Party*. New York: International Publishers.

Massey, Douglas S. and Nancy A. Denton. 1998. *American Apartheid: Segregation and the Making of the Underclass*. Cambridge, MA: Harvard University Press.

Matza, David. 1969. *Becoming Deviant*. Englewood Cliffs, NJ: Prentice-Hall.

Mead, George Herbert. 1934/1962. *Mind, Self and Society: From the Standpoint of a Social Behaviorist*. Chicago: University of Chicago Press.

Mehan, Hugh, and Houston Wood. 1975. *The Reality of Ethnomethodology*. New York: Wiley.

Mendez, Elizabeth, and Joy Wilke. *American's Confidence in Congress falls to lowest on Record*. GALLUP. 2013.

Merton, R. 1938. "Social Structure and Anomie." *American Sociological Review* (10): 672-682.

Merton, Robert K. 1957. "The Role-Set: Problems in Sociological Theory." *British Journal of Sociology* 8:106-120.

Merton, Robert K. 1968. *Social Theory and Social Structure*. Rev. and Enl. ed. New York: Free Press.

Meyer, John W. 1970. "The Charter: Conditions of Diffuse Socialization in Schools." Pp. 564-578 in *Social Processes and Social Structures*, edited by W. R. Scott. New York: Holt, Rinehart and Winston.

Meyer, John W. 1972. "The Effects of the Institutionalization of Colleges in Society." Pp. 109-126 in *College and Student: Selected Readings in the Social Psychology of Higher Education*, edited by K. A. Feldman. New York: Pergamon.

Meyer, John W. 1977. "The Effects of Education as an Institution." *American Journal of Sociology* 83:55-77.

Meyer, John W. 1992. "The Social Construction of Motives for Educational Expansion." Pp. 225-238 in *The Political Construction of Education: The State, School Expansion, and Economic Change*, edited by Bruce Fuller and Richard Rubinson. New York: Praeger.

Meyer, John W., David Tyack, Joane Nagel, and Audri Gordon. 1979. "Public Education as Nation Building in America: Enrollments and Bureaucratization in the United States, 1870-1930." *American Journal of Sociology* 85:591-613.

Michels, Robert. 1911/1949. *Political Parties*. Glencoe, IL: Free Press.

Michels, Robert. 1949/1961. "The Sociological Character of Political Parties." Pp. 603-610 in *Theories of Society: Foundations of Modern Sociological Theory*, edited by Talcott Parsons et al. New York: Free Press.

Milgram, Stanley. 1970. "The Experience of Living in Cities." *Science, New Series* 167(39):1461-1468.

Miller, Kathleen K., and Bruce A. Weber. 2002. "Persistent Poverty and Place: How Do Persistent Poverty and Poverty Demographics Vary Across the Rural Urban Continuum?" Paper prepared for the Rural Sociological Society Annual Meeting, July 2003.

Mills, C. Wright. 1959. *The Sociological Imagination.* New York: Oxford University Press.

Mincer, Jacob. 1962. "On the Job Training: Cost, Returns, and Implications." *Journal of Political Economy* 70(2):50-79.

Mincer, Jacob. 1979. "Human Capital and Earnings." In *Economic Dimensions of Education*, edited by D. M. Windham. Washington, D.C.: National Academy of Education.

Mizruchi, Mark S., and Joseph Galaskiewicz. 1994. "Networks of Interorganizational Relations." *Advances in Social Network Analysis: Research in the Social and Behavioral Sciences*, edited by S. Wasserman and J. Galaskiewicz. Thousand Oaks, CA: Sage.

Moore, Wilbert. 1978. "Functionalism." Pp. 321-361 in *A History of Sociological Analysis*, edited by T. Bottomore and R. Nisbet. New York: Basic Books.

Morgan, William R., and Michael J. Armer. 1988. "Islamic and Western Educational Accommodation in a West African Society: A Cohort-Comparison Analysis." *American Sociological Review* 53:634-639.

Mosca, Gaetano. 1939. *The Ruling Class.* Translated by H. D. Kahn, edited by A. Livingston. New York: McGraw-Hill.

Nakao, Keiko, and Judith Treas. 1994. "Updating Occupational Prestige and Socioeconomic Scales: How the New Measures Measure Up." *Sociological Methodology* 24:1-72.

National Center on Child Abuse and Neglect (NCCAN). 1981. *Study Findings: National Study of Incidence and Severity of Child Abuse and Neglect.* Washington, DC: Department of Health, Education, and Welfare.

Neely, J. H. 1989. "Experimental Dissociations and the Episodic/Semantic Memory Distinction." Pp. 229-270 in *Varieties of Memory and Consciousness: Essays in Honour of Endel Tulving*, edited by H. L. Roediger, III, and F. I. M. Craik. Hillsdale, NJ: Lawrence Erlbaum Associates.

Neese, Randolph M., and George C. Williams. 1994. *Why We Get Sick.* New York: Vintage.

Neisser, Ulric. 1976. *Cognition and Reality.* San Francisco: Freeman.

Nepstad, Daniel C., Claudia M. Stickler, Britaldo Soares-Filho, and Frank Merry. 2008. "Interactions Among Amazon Land Use, Forests, and Climate: Prospects for a Nearterm Forest Tipping Point." *Philosophical Transactions of the Royal Society B: Biological Sciences.*

Newcomb, T. M. 1956. "The Prediction of Interpersonal Attraction." *American Psychologist* 11:575-586.

Niebuhr, H. Richard. 1929. *The Social Sources of Denominationalism.* New York: Henry Holt.

O'Connor, James. 1973. *The Fiscal Crisis of the State.* New York: St. Martin's.

Ogburn, William. 1932. *The Hypothesis of Cultural Lag.*

Olson, Mancur. 1965. *The Logic of Collective Action.* Cambridge, MA: Harvard University Press.

Organization for Economic Cooperation and Development. 2011. *Economic Survey of India.*

Organization for Economic Cooperation and Development. 2013. *Programme for International Student Assessment.*

Oswald, Hans, David P. Baker, and David L. Stevenson. 1988. "School Charter and Parental Management in West Germany." *Sociology of Education* 61:255-265.

Overmier, Bruce, and Martin E. P. Seligman. 1967. "Effects of Inescapable Shock Upon Subsequent Escape and Avoidance Learning." *Journal of Comparative and Physiological Psychology* 634:23-33.

Pareto, Vilfredo. 1935. *A Treatise on General Sociology*, 4 vols. New York: Dover.

Pareto, Vilfredo. 1935/1961. "The Circulation of Elites." Pp. 551-558 in *Theories of Society: Foundations of Modern Sociological Theory*, edited by Talcott Parsons, Edward Shils, Kaspar D. Naegele, and Jesse R. Pitts. New York: The Free Press.

Park, Robert E., and Ernest W. Burgess. 1924. *Introduction to the Science of Sociology.* Chicago: University of Chicago Press.

Park, Robert E., and Ernest W. Burgess. 1925. *The City.* Chicago: University of Chicago Press.

Parkin, Frank. 1971. *Class Inequality and Political Order: Social Stratification in Capitalist and Communist Societies.* New York: Praeger.

Parkin, Frank. 1974. "Strategies of Social Closure in Class Formation." Pp. 1-18 in *The Social Analysis of Class Structure*, edited by Frank Parkin. London: Tavistock.

Parkin, Frank. 1979. *Marxism and Class Theory: A Bourgeois Critique*. London: Tavistock.

Parrish, Julia K., and Leah Edelstein-Keshet. 1999. "Complexity, Pattern, and Evolutionary Trade-Offs in Animal Aggregation." *Science* 284 (April 2):99-101.

Parsons, Talcott. 1937. *The Structure of Social Action*. New York: McGraw-Hill.

Parsons, Talcott. 1951. *The Social System*. Glencoe, IL: Free Press.

Parsons, Talcott. 1964. "Social Strains in America." Pp. 175-200 in *The Radical Right*, edited by Daniel Bell. Garden City, NY: Doubleday.

Parsons, Talcott. 1966. *Societies: Evolutionary and Comparative Perspectives*. Englewood Cliffs, NJ: Prentice Hall.

Pavlov, Ivan P. 1927. *Conditioned Reflexes*. London: Oxford University Press.

Pearlin, Leonard I., and Melvin L. Kohn. 1966. "Social Class, Occupation, and Parental Values: A Cross-National Study." *American Sociological Review* 31:466-479.

Pearlin, Leonard I., and M. Al Lieberman. 1979. "Social Sources of Emotional Distress." In *Research in Community and Mental Health*, 1:217-248, edited by R. G. Simmons. Greenwich, CT: JAI Press.

Pew Research: Religion and Public Life Project. 2003. *Religious Beliefs Underpin Opposition to Homosexuality*.

Pew Research Center. 2013. *Abortion*.

Pew Research: Religion and Public Life Project. 2013. *U.S. Religious Landscape Survey*.

Pew Research Center. 2014. *Gay Marriage*.

Pew Research Center. 2014. *Growing Public Support for Gun Rights*.

Piaget, Jean. 1951. *The Child's Conception of the World*. New York: Humanities Press.

Piaget, Jean. 1952. *The Origins of Intelligence in Children*. New York: International Universities

Press.

Piaget, Jean. 1980. *The Construction of Reality in the Child.* New York: Basic Books.

Pimentel, David, Rebecca Harman, Matthew Pacenza, Jason Pecarsky, and Marcia Pimentel. 1994. "Natural Resources and an Optimum Human Population." *Population and Environment* 15:347-369.

Plutchik, Robert. 1980. *Emotion: A Psychoevolutionary Synthesis.* New York: Harper & Row.

Portes, Alejandro, and Robert D. Manning. 1986. "The Immigrant Enclave: Theory and Empirical Examples." In *Competitive Ethnic Relations*, edited by Susan Olzak and Joane Nagel. New York: Academic Press.

Poulantzas, Nicos. 1975. *Classes in Contemporary Capitalism.* London: New Left Books.

Poulantzas, Nicos. 1977. "The New Petty Bourgeoisie." Pp. 113-124 in *Class and Class Structure*, edited by Alan Hunt. London: Lawrence and Wishart.

Powell, Brian, Catherine Bolzendahl, Claudia Geist, and Lala Carr Steelman. 2012. *Counted Out: Same-Sex Relations and Americans' Definition of Family.* New York: Russell Sage Foundation.

Price, John S. 1967. "The Dominance Hierarchy and the Evolution of Mental Illness." *Lancet* 2:243-246.

Prigogine, I., and E. Stengers. 1984. *Order Out of Chaos.* New York: Bantam.

Psathas, George. 1968. "Ethnomethods and Phenomenology." *Social Research* 35(3):500-520.

Quinney, Richard. 1970. *The Social Reality of Crime.* Boston: Little, Brown and Company.

Ralph, John H., and Richard Rubinson. 1980. "Immigration and Expansion of Schooling in the United States, 1890-1970." *American Sociological Review* 45:943-954.

Ramirez, Francisco O., and John Boli. 1987. "The Political Construction of Mass Schooling: European Origins and Worldwide Institutionalization." *Sociology of Education* 60:2-17.

Rimmerman, Craig, and Clyde Wilcox. 2008. *The Politics of Same Sex Marriage.* University of Chicago Press.

Rind, D. 1999. "Complexity and Climate." *Science* 284 (4-2):105-107.

Ritzer, George. 1993. *The McDonaldization of Society: An Investigation into the Changing Character of Social Life.* Thousand Oaks, CA: Pine Forge Press.

Ritzer, George. 1997. *Postmodern Social Theory.* New York: McGraw-Hill.

Ritzer, George. 2000. *Sociological Theory,* 5e. New York: McGraw-Hill.

Ritzer, George, and Terri LeMoyne. 1991. "Hyperrationality: An Extension of Weberian and Neo-Weberian Theory." Pp. 93-115 in *Metatheorizing in Sociology,* edited by G. Ritzer. Lexington, MA: Lexington Books.

Rockquemore, Kerry A., and David L. Brunsma. 2002. *Beyond Black: Biracial Identity in America.* Thousand Oaks, CA: Sage Publications.

Rorty, Richard. 1979. *Philosophy and the Mirror of Nature.* Princeton: Princeton University Press.

Rosenberg, M. 1954-55. "Some Determinants of Political Apathy." *Public Opinion Quarterly* 18:349-366.

Rosenberg, Morris. 1973. "Which Significant Others?" *American Behavioral Scientist* 16:829-860.

Rosenberg, Morris. 1979. *Conceiving the Self.* New York: Basic Books.

Rosenberg, Morris. 1981. "The Self-Concept: Social Product and Social Force." Pp. 593-624 in *Social Psychology: Sociological Perspectives*, edited by M. Rosenberg and R. H. Turner. New York: Basic Books.

Rosenberg, Morris, and Leonard I. Pearlin. 1978. "Social Class and Self-esteem among Children and Adults." *American Journal of Sociology* 84: 53-77.

Rostow, W. W. 1964. *The Stages of Economic Growth: A Non-Communist Manifesto.* London: Cambridge University Press.

Rubinson, Richard. 1986. "Class Formation, Politics, and Institutions: Schooling in the United States." *American Journal of Sociology* 92(3):519-548.

Rubinson, Richard, and John H. Ralph. 1984. "Technical Change and the Expansion of Schooling in the United States, 1890-1970." *Sociology of Education* 57:134-152.

Sabidussi, G. 1966. "The Centrality Index of a Graph." *Psychometrika* 31:581-603.

Sacks, Harvey. 1984. "Methodological Remarks." Pp. 21-27 *Structures of Social Action: Studies in Conversation Analysis*, edited by J. Maxwell Atkinson and John Heritage. Cambridge, UK: Cambridge University Press.

Sanders, Jimy, and Victor Nee. 1987. "Limits of Ethnic Solidarity in the Enclave Economy." *American Sociological Review* 52:745-767.

Schacter, Stanley, and Jerome Singer. 1962. "Cognitive, Social and Physiological Determinants of Emotional State." *Psychological Review* 69:379-399.

Schegloff, Emmanuel A. 1968. "Sequencing in Conversational Openings." *American Anthropologist* 70:1075-1095.

Schutz, Alfred. 1932/1967. *The Phenomenology of the Social World.* Evanston, IL: Northwestern University Press.

Schutz, Alfred. 1967. *Collected Papers I: The Problem of Social Reality.* The Hague: Martinus Nijhoff.

Scott, Marvin, and Stanford Lyman. 1968. "Accounts." *American Sociological Review* 33:46-62.

Seligman, Martin E.P., and Steven F. Maier. 1967. "Failure to Escape Traumatic Shock." *Journal of Experimental Psychology* 74:1-9.

Sharp, Susan. 2002. *The Incarcerated Woman: Rehabilitative Programming in Women's Prisons.* Upper Saddle River, NJ: Prentice Hall.

Sharp, Susan. 2014. *Mean Lives, Mean Laws: Oklahoma Women Prisoners.* New Brunswick, NJ: Rutgers University Press.

Shaver, Philip, and Judith C. Schwartz. 1984. "Prototypes and Examples of Fear, Sadness, Anger, Happiness, and Love." Paper presented at Society of Experimental Social Psychology Convention, Snowbird, UT. (cited in Kemper 1987).

Sheldon, William H. 1949. *Varieties of Delinquent Youth: An Introduction to Constitutional Psychiatry.* New York: Harper.

Shibutani, Tomatsu. 1955. "Reference Groups as Perspectives." *American Journal of Sociology* 60:562-569.

Simmel, Georg. 1907/1978. *The Philosophy of Money.* Translated and edited by T. Bottomore and D. Frisby. London: Routledge and Kegan Paul.

Simmel, Georg. 1908/1971a. "Domination." Pp. 96-120 in *Georg Simmel*, edited by D. Levine. Chicago: University of Chicago Press.

Simmel, Georg. 1908/1971b. "The Stranger." Pp. 143-149 in *Georg Simmel*, edited by D. Levine. Chicago: University of Chicago Press.

Simon, Julian L. 1983. "Life on Earth Is Getting Better, Not Worse." *The Futurist* (8):7-14.

Simon, Julian L. 1990. "Population Growth Is Not Bad for Humanity." *National Forum: The Phi Kappa Phi Journal* 70(1).

Simon, Julian L., and Herman Kahn, eds. 1984. *The Resourceful Earth: A Response to Global 2000.* Oxford, UK: Basil Blackwell.

Simpson, George E., and Milton Yinger. 1985. *Racial and Cultural Minorities: An Analysis of Prejudice and Discrimination*, 5e. New York: Plenum.

Skinner, B. F. 1938. *The Behavior of Organisms.* New York: Appleton-Century-Crofts.

Skinner, B. F. 1953. *Science and Human Behavior.* New York: Macmillan.

Smelser, Neil. 1962. *Theories of Collective Behavior.* New York: Free Press.

Smith, David, and Douglas White. 1992. "Structure and Dynamics of the Global Economy: Network Analysis of International Trade 1965-1980." *Social Forces* 70:857-893.

Smith, Dorothy E. 1987. *The Everyday World as Problematic: A Feminist Sociology.* Boston: Northeastern University Press.

Smith, Dorothy E. 1990. *The Conceptual Practices of Power: A Feminist Sociology of Knowledge.* Boston: Northeastern University Press.

Smith, E. E., E. J. Shoben, and L. J. Rips. 1974. "Structure and Process in Semantic Memory: A Feature Model for Semantic Decisions." *Psychological Review* 81:214-241.

Snipp, C. Matthew. 2003. "Racial Measurement in the American Census: Past Practices and Implications for the Future." *Annual Review of Sociology* 29: 563-588.

Snyder, David, and Edward L. Kick. 1979. "Structural Position in the World System and Economic Growth 1955-70: A Multiple Network Analysis of Transnational Interactions." *American Journal of Sociology* 84:1096-1126.

So, Alvin Y. 1990. *Social Change and Development: Modernization, Dependency, and World-System Theories.* Newbury Park, CA: Sage.

Sokolov, E. N. 1990. "The Orienting Response and Future Directions of Its Development." *Pavlovian Journal of Biological Science* 25 (3):142-150.

Sorokin, Pitirim. 1959. *Social and Cultural Mobility.* New York: Free Press.

Sowell, Thomas. 1994. *Race and Culture: A World View.* New York: Free Press.

Stark, Rodney, and William S. Bainbridge. 1980. "Secularization, Revival, and Cult Formation." *Annual Review of the Social Sciences of Religion* 4:85-119.

Stark, Rodney, and William S. Bainbridge. 1987. *A Theory of Religion.* New York: Peter Lang.

Steinberg, Stephen. 2011. "Culture Still Doesn't Explain Poverty." *Boston Review* online. http://www.bostonreview.net/BR36.1/steinberg.php
Steingraber, Sandra. 1997. *Living Downstream: A Scientist's Personal Investigation of Cancer and the Environment.* New York: Vintage/Random House.

Strauss, Murray A., and Richard J. Gelles. 1991. *Physical Violence in American Families.* New Brunswick, NJ: Transaction Books.

Straussfogel, Debra. 2000. "World-Systems Theory in the Context of Systems Theory: An Overview." In *A World-Systems Reader*, edited by Thomas D. Hall. Lanham, MD: Rowman & Littlefield.

Stryker, Sheldon. 1980. *Symbolic Interactionism: A Social Structural Version.* Menlo Park, CA: Benjamin/Cummins.

Stryker, Sheldon. 1981. "Symbolic Interactionism: Themes and Variations." Pp. 3-29 in *Social Psychology: Sociological Perspectives*, edited by Morris Rosenberg and Ralph H. Turner. New York: Basic Books.

Suleiman, Ezra N. 1978. *Elites in French Society: The Politics of Survival.* Princeton, NJ: Princeton University Press.

Sutherland, Edwin H. 1947. *Principles of Criminology.* 4th ed. Philadelphia: Lippincott.

Tarlov, A. R. 1996. "Social Determinants of Health: The Sociobiological Translation." In *Health and Social Organization*, edited by D. Blane, E. Brunner, and R. Wilkinson. London: Routledge.

Taylor, S. E., J. Crocker, and J. D'Agostino. 1978. "Schematic Bases for Social Problem-Solving." *Personality and Social Psychology Bulletin* 4:447-451.

Thibaut, J. W., and H. H. Kelley. 1959. *The Social Psychology of Groups.* New York: Wiley.

Thomas, William I. 1951/1961. "The Four Wishes and the Definition of the Situation." Pp. 741-744 in reprinted in *Theories of Society: Foundations of Modern Sociological Theory*, edited by Talcott Parsons. New York: Free Press.

Thomas, W. I., and Florian Znaniecki. 1918. *The Polish Peasant in Europe and America.* Chicago: The University of Chicago Press.

Thorndike, E. L. 1898. *Animal Intelligence.* New York: Macmillan.

Thorndike, E. L. 1913. *The Psychology of Learning.* New York: Teachers College, Columbia University.

Tilly, Charles. 1964. "Reflections on the Revolution of Paris: A Review in Historical Writing." *Social Problems* 12, 99-121.

Tilly, Charles. 1975. "Resolutions and Collective Violence." Pp. 483-555 *Handbook of Political Science.* Vol. III, edited by Fred I. Greenstein and Nelson W. Polsby. Reading, MA: Addison-Wesley.

Tilly, Louise A., and Joan W. Scott. 1987. *Women, Work, and Family.* New York: Methuen.

Trevarthen, Colwyn. 1984. "Emotions in Infancy: Regulators of Contact and Relationships with Persons." Pp. 129-157 in *Approaches to Emotion*, edited by K. R. Scherer and P. Ekman. Hillsdale, NJ: Lawrence Erlabaum.

Tulving, Endel. 1972. "Episodic and Semantic Memory." In *Organization of Memory*, edited by E. Tulvin and W. Donaldson. New York: Academic Press.

Tumin, Melvin. 1953. "Some Principles of Stratification: A Critical Analysis." *American Sociological Review* 18:387-394.

Turner, Jonathan H. 2003. *Human Institutions: A Theory of Societal Evolution.* Lanham, MD: Rowman and Littlefield.

Turner, Ralph H. 1960. "Sponsored and Contest Mobility in the School System." *American Sociological Review* 25:855-867.

Uniform Crime Report. 2012. U.S. Department of Justice, Federal Bureau of Investigation, Criminal Justice Information Services Division. Washington D.C.

United Nations. 1992. *Long-Range World Population Projections: Two Centuries of Population Growth, 1950-2150.* New York: United Nations.

United Nations Research Institute for Social Development. 1995. *States of Disarray: The Social Effects of Globalization.* New York: United Nations.

U. S. Bureau of the Census. 1970. *Statistical Abstract of the United States*, 90th ed. Washington, DC: Government Printing Office.

U. S. Bureau of the Census. 1992. *Statistical Abstract of the United States*, 112th ed. Washington, DC: Government Printing Office.

U. S. Bureau of the Census. 1998. *Statistical Abstract of the United States*, 118th ed. Washington, DC: Government Printing Office.

U. S. Bureau of the Census. 2010. *The Older Population in the United States: 2010-2050.* Washington D.C. Government Printing Office.

U. S. Bureau of the Census. *Households and Families: 2010.* Washington D.C.

U. S. Bureau of the Census, Small Area Estimates Branch. 2013. *Evaluating Metro and Non-Metro Differences in Uninsured Population.* Washington D.C.

U. S. Bureau of the Census. 2013. *Poverty Rates for Selected Detailed Race and Hispanic Groups by State and Place: 2007–2011.*

U. S. Bureau of the Census. 2013. *Statistical Abstract of the United States 2012.*

United States Department of Agriculture Economic Research Service Report. 2013. *Rural Poverty & Well-Being* from U.S. Census Bureau 2013 Annual Social and Economic Supplements.

U. S. Department of Education. 2014. National Center for Education Statistics. *The Condition of Education.*

U. S. Department of Health and Human Services. 2013. *Nursing Home Data Compendium 2013 Edition.*

U. S. Department of Justice, Federal Bureau of Investigation. *Crime in the United States, 2011.*

Vanneman, Reeve. 1977. "The Occupational Composition of American Classes." *American Journal of Sociology* 83:783-807.

Wallace, Michael, and Arne L. Kalleberg. 1982. "Industrial Transformation and the Decline of Craft: The Decomposition of Skill in the Printing Industry." *American Sociological Review* 47(3):307-324.

Wallerstein, Immanuel. 1974. *The Modern World System: Capitalist Agriculture and the Origins of the European World Economy in the 16th Century.* New York: Academic Press.

Wallerstein, Immanuel. 1979. *The Capitalist World Economy.* New York: Cambridge University Press.

Wallerstein, Immanuel. 1980. *The Modern World System II: Mercantilism and the Consolidation of the European World-Economy, 1600-1750.* New York: Academic Press.

Wallerstein, Immanuel. 1989. *The Modern World System III: The Second Era of Great Expansion of the Capitalist World Economy, 1730-1840.* New York: Academic Press.

Wallerstein, Immanuel. 2011. *The Modern World-System. Vol. IV: Centrist Liberalism Triumphant, 1789–1914.* Berkeley, CA: University of California Press.

Walters, Pamela Barnhouse. 1984. "Occupational and Labor Market Effects on Secondary and Postsecondary Expansion in the United States: 1922 to 1979." *American Sociological Review* 49:659-671.

Walters, Pamela Barnhouse, and Richard Rubinson. 1983. "Educational Expansion and Economic Output in the United States, 1890-1969: A Production Function Analysis." *American Sociological Review* 48:480-493.

Wang, Liya, Edward Kick, James Fraser, and Thomas J. Burns. 1999. "The Role of Locus of Control and Self Esteem in the Status Attainment Process." *Sociological Spectrum* 19:281-298.

Wasserman, Stanley, and Katherine Faust. 1994. *Social Network Analysis: Methods and Applications.* Cambridge, UK: Cambridge University Press.

Watson, John B. 1919. *Psychology from the Point of View of the Behaviorist.* Philadelphia: Lippincott.

Weber, Max. 1921/1978. *Economy and Society: An Outline of Interpretive Sociology*, 2 vols. Edited by G, Roth and C. Wittich. Berkeley and Los Angeles: University of California.

Weber, Max. [1946]. *From Max Weber: Essays in Sociology.* Translated and edited by Hans H. Gerth and C. Wright Mills. New York: Oxford University Press.

Weber, Max. 1958/1905-6. *The Protestant Ethic and the Spirit of Capitalism.* New York: Oxford University Press.

Weber, R., and J. Crocker, 1983. "Cognitive Processes in the Revision of Stereotypic Beliefs." *Journal of Personality and Social Psychology* 45: 961-977.

Wiener, Joshua, and Jane Tilly. 2002. *Population Ageing in the United States of America: Implications for Public Programmes.* International Journal of Epidemiology, Oxford.

Weitz, Rose. 1996. *The Sociology of Health, Illness, and Health Care: A Critical Approach.* Belmont, CA: Wadsworth.

Wilkinson, R.G. 1996. *Unhealthy Societies: The Afflictions of Inequality.* London: Routledge.

Williams, George C. 1966. *Adaptation and Natural Selection.* Princeton, NJ: Princeton University Press.

Wilson, William Julius. 1980. *The Declining Significance of Race: Blacks and Changing American Institutions*, 2e. Chicago: University of Chicago Press.

Wilson, William J. 1987. *The Truly Disadvantaged: The Inner City, the Underclass, and Public Policy.* Chicago: University of Chicago Press.

Wilson, William Julius. 1996. *When Work Disappears: The World of the New Urban Poor.* New York: Alfred A. Knopf.

Wilson, William Julius. 2009. *More Than Just Race: Being Black and Poor in the Inner City.* New York City, NY: W. W. Norton & Company.

Wolf, Eric. 1969. *Peasant Wars of the Twentieth Century.* New York: Harper and Row.

Wright, Erik Olin. 1985. *Classes.* London: Verso Press.

Yarrow, Marian Radke, Charlotte Green Schwartz, Harriet S. Murphy, and Leila Calhoun Deasy. "The Psychological Meaning of Mental Illness in the Family." *Journal of Social Issues* 11(4):12-24.

Zimmerman, Don H. 1988. "On Conversation: The Conversation Analytic Perspective." In *Communication Yearbook*, 11: 406-432, edited by J.A. Anderson. Beverly Hills, CA: Sage.

I | Illustrations

Chapter 1
p. 4, By Wazzle (Own work) [Public domain], via Wikimedia Commons
p. 4, By Bill Branson (Photographer) [Public domain or Public domain], via Wikimedia Commons
p. 8, {{PD-1923}} [Public domain], via Wikimedia Commons
p. 9, {{PD-1923}} John Jabez Edwin Mayall [Public domain], via Wikimedia Commons

Chapter 2
p. 21, Line-in Publishing
p. 23, Line-in Publishing

Chapter 3
p. 31, iStock
p. 33, iStock
p. 35, iStock
p. 37, {{PD-1923}} By Unidentified (Ensian published by University of Michigan) [Public domain], via Wikimedia Commons

Chapter 4
p. 47, {{PD-1923}} By Unidentified (published by Brittanica Online) [Public domain], via Wikimedia Commons
p. 48, {{PD-1923}} By Svelgur at en.wikipedia [Public domain], from Wikimedia Commons
p. 54, iStock

Chapter 5
p. 63, By Peter Dowley from Dubai, United Arab Emirates (Beijing 2nd Ring Road) [CC BY 2.0 (http://creativecommons.org/licenses/by/2.0)], via Wikimedia Commons
p. 67, By bpsusf (http://www.flickr.com/photos/usfbps/4607149870/) [CC BY 2.0 (http://creativecommons.org/licenses/by/2.0) or CC BY 2.0 (http://creativecommons.org/licenses/by/2.0)], via Wikimedia Commons
p. 69, iStock

Chapter 6
p. 74, iStock
p. 81, By Unknown photographer [Public domain], via Wikimedia Commons
p. 82, Line-in Publishing

Chapter 7
p. 94, By Astros4477 (http://www.flickr.com/photos/nnecapa/2865338278/)[CC BY 2.0 (http://creativecommons.org/licenses/by/2.0)], via Wikimedia Commons
p. 95, collage, Joan de Joanes [Public domain], via Wikimedia Commons; New York World-Telegram and the Sun staff photographer: DeMarsico, Dick, photographer. [Public domain], via Wikimedia Commons; By Pete Souza, The Obama-Biden Transition Project [CC BY 3.0 (http://creativecommons.org/licenses/by/3.0)], via Wikimedia Commons
p. 101, {{PD-1923}} By Unidentified [Public domain], via Wikimedia Commons

Chapter 8

p. 112, {{PD-1996}} [Public domain], via Wikimedia Commons

p. 120, By Could not be extracted automatically; most are anonymous or pseudonymous. Scanned by the Seattle Public Library. ([1] (see filename for exact location)) [Public domain], via Wikimedia Commons

p. 121, Line-in Publishing

p. 124, By David Shankbone (Own work) [CC BY 3.0 (http://creativecommons.org/licenses/by/3.0)], via Wikimedia Commons

p. 125, By Charles O'Rear, 1941-, Photographer (NARA record: 3403717) (U.S. National Archives and Records Administration) [Public domain], via Wikimedia Commons

p. 126, By Unknown (Life time: Unknown) [Public domain], via Wikimedia Commons

Chapter 9

p. 130, By Esther Bubley (Library of Congress[3]) [Public domain], via Wikimedia Commons

p. 132, iStock

p. 133, From http://www.cr.nps.gov/nr/twhp/wwwlps/lessons/118trail/118locate2.htm [Public domain], via Wikimedia Commons

p. 134, By Toffel (Own work) [Public domain], via Wikimedia Commons

p. 136, By Cornelius Marion (C.M.) Battey (1873–1927)[1] [Public domain], via Wikimedia Commons

p. 138, iStock

Chapter 10

p. 141, [[::User::en:User:Janke| [GFDL (http://www.gnu.org/copyleft/fdl.html) or CC-BY-SA-3.0 (http://creativecommons.org/licenses/by-sa/3.0/)], via Wikimedia Commons; By U.S. Navy photo by Mass Communication Specialist 1st Class Roger S. Duncan [Public domain], via Wikimedia Commons

p. 142, By Holy Trinity Lutheran Church, Thousand Oaks, California [CC BY 2.0 (http://creativecommons.org/licenses/by/2.0)], via Wikimedia Commons

p. 143, By Department of State [Public domain], via Wikimedia Commons; By Max Morse (Meg Whitman speaks at the Tech Museum in San Jose) [CC BY 2.0 (http://creativecommons.org/licenses/by/2.0)], via Wikimedia Commons

p. 147, iStock

Chapter 11

p. 156, collage, By Andreas Lederer (originally posted to Flickr as Returning from hunt) [CC BY 2.0 (http://creativecommons.org/licenses/by/2.0)], via Wikimedia Commons; By National Museum of Denmark from Denmark (Woman with a digging stick Uploaded by palnatoke) [see page for license], via Wikimedia Commons; By Yann (Own work) [GFDL (http://www.gnu.org/copyleft/fdl.html) or CC BY-SA 4.0-3.0-2.5-2.0-1.0 (http://creativecommons.org/licenses/by-sa/4.0-3.0-2.5-2.0-1.0)], via Wikimedia Commons; By Brian Davidson, U.S. Air Force [Public domain], via Wikimedia Commons

p 161, By Daniel Schwen (Own work) [CC Share Alike 2.5 Generic], via Wikimedia Commons

p. 161, By Jonathan McIntosh (Own work) [CC BY 2.0 (http://creativecommons.org/licenses/by/2.0)], via Wikimedia Commons

Chapter 12
p. 167, collage, via Wikimedia Commons

p. 179, By mydphotos (http://www.flickr.com/photos/mydphotos/4012625868/) [CC BY 2.0 (http://creativecommons.org/licenses/by/2.0)], via Wikimedia Commons

Chapter 13
p. 186, iStock

p. 187, By David Hawxhurst, The Woodrow Wilson International Center for Scholars

p. 192, By Juliana María Villa (Own work) [CC BY-SA 3.0 (http://creativecommons.org/licenses/by-sa/3.0)], via Wikimedia Commons

p. 196, Photo: POA(Phot) Sean Clee/MOD [OGL (http://www.nationalarchives.gov.uk/doc/open-government-licence/version/1/)], via Wikimedia Commons

Chapter 14
p. 201, collage, iStock; Biswarup Ganguly [GFDL (http://www.gnu.org/copyleft/fdl.html), CC BY 3.0 (http://creativecommons.org/licenses/by/3.0), GFDL (http://www.gnu.org/copyleft/fdl.html) or CC BY 3.0 (http://creativecommons.org/licenses/by/3.0)], via Wikimedia Commons;

p. 207, By John H. White, 1945-, Photographer (NARA record: 4002141) (U.S. National Archives and Records Administration) [Public domain]; Mycelium101 [GFDL (http://www.gnu.org/copyleft/fdl.html) or CC BY-SA 3.0 (http://creativecommons.org/licenses/by-sa/3.0)], via Wikimedia Commons; By Basil D Soufi (Own work) [CC BY-SA 3.0 (http://creativecommons.org/licenses/by-sa/3.0)], via Wikimedia Commons; By Tfursten (Own work) [CC BY-SA 3.0 (http://creativecommons.org/licenses/by-sa/3.0)], via Wikimedia Commons; via Wikimedia Commons; © CEphoto, Uwe Aranas / , via Wikimedia Commons

Chapter 15
p. 210, Henri Testelin [Public domain or Public domain], via Wikimedia Commons

p. 214, By Carfax2 (Own work) [CC BY-SA 3.0 (http://creativecommons.org/licenses/by-sa/3.0)], via Wikimedia Commons

p. 217, See page for author [Public domain], via Wikimedia Commons

Chapter 16
p. 228, Line-in Publishing

p. 230, By Delphi234 (Own work) [CC0], via Wikimedia Commons; By Delphi234 (Own work) [CC0], via Wikimedia Commons

p. 234, By Poppy (Photo taken by Poppy) [GFDL (http://www.gnu.org/copyleft/fdl.html), CC-BY-SA-3.0 (http://creativecommons.org/licenses/by-sa/3.0/) or CC BY-SA 2.5-2.0-1.0 (http://creativecommons.org/licenses/by-sa/2.5-2.0-1.0)], via Wikimedia Commons

p. 235, John Linnell [CC BY 4.0 (http://creativecommons.org/licenses/by/4.0)], via Wikimedia Commons

Chapter 17
p. 241, By D'Arcy Norman [CC BY 2.0 (http://creativecommons.org/licenses/by/2.0)], via Wikimedia Commons

p. 243, By High Contrast (Own work) [CC BY 2.0 de (http://creativecommons.org/licenses/by/2.0/de/deed.en)], via Wikimedia Commons

p. 247, By U.S. Navy photo by Photographer's Mate 2nd Class Michael D. Heckman [Public domain], via Wikimedia Commons

Chapter 18

p. 255, See page for author [CC BY 4.0 (http://creativecommons.org/licenses/by/4.0)], via Wikimedia Commons

p. 257, By Dorothea Lange (http://www.loc.gov/pictures/item/2001705926) [Public domain], via Wikimedia Commons

p. 258, Olaf Growald [CC BY-SA 3.0 (http://creativecommons.org/licenses/by-sa/3.0)], via Wikimedia Commons

p. 260, By villy [Public domain], via Wikimedia Commons

p. 265, By Alberto Korda (Alberto Korda (Korda)) [Public domain], via Wikimedia Commons

Chapter 19

p. 279, Line-in Publishing

p. 283, By http://en.wikipedia.org/wiki/User:Ayaleila.Pablosecca at en.wikipedia [CC BY-SA 3.0 (http://creativecommons.org/licenses/by-sa/3.0)], from Wikimedia Commons

p. 288, collage, By Solkoll (Own work) [Public domain], via Wikimedia Commons; By Avi Kedmi [Public domain], via Wikimedia Commons; By Gubbubu Creative Commons Attribution-Share Alike 3.0 Unported

p. 289, By Klem [Public domain, Public domain or Public domain], via Wikimedia Commons

p. 290, By Cbaile19 (Own work) [CC0], via Wikimedia Commons